HANDBOOK OF
EXPORT CONTROLS & ECONOMIC SANCTIONS

KAY C. GEORGI AND
PAUL M. LALONDE
EDITORS

ABA Section of
International Law
Your Gateway to International Practice

Library of Congress Cataloging-in-Publication Data

Handbook of export controls and economic Sanctions / [edited] by Paul M. Lalonde and Kay C. Georgi, American Bar Association, Section of International Law.
    pages cm
  Includes bibliographical references and index.
  ISBN 978-1-62722-050-7 (alk. paper)
  1. Export sales contracts—United States. 2. Foreign trade regulation—United States. 3. Economic sanctions. I. Georgi, Kay C., editors. II. Lalonde, Paul M., editors. III. American Bar Association. Section of International Law.
  KF1987.H39 2013
  343.7308'78--dc23

2013018488

To Magda and the kids. And to my parents, who showed me the way.

—Paul M. Lalonde

*To my parents, Jay and Marion Georgi, and my husband and son,
Paolo and Ugo Nascimbeni.*

—Kay C. Georgi

Table of Contents

PREFACE

Export controls and economic sanctions increasingly affect the day-to-day business of our clients. No company with cross-border operations or even a multinational workforce is immune from their application or can afford to ignore these laws. Though once a relatively esoteric area of legal practice, controls over the export of goods, technology, and services now represent a basic element of corporate compliance whether your client is involved in import/export activity, mergers & acquisitions, joint ventures, licensing agreements, distribution contracts, or banking and finance transactions. As even some of the largest, most sophisticated multinational corporations can attest, compliance expectations are rising and the consequences of non-compliance can include a veritable parade of horribles — multimillion dollar penalties, incarceration, investigation costs, loss of export privileges, and debarment from government contracting, much less the business and reputational harm to the company.

This book is a project of the ABA Section of International Law Export Controls and Economic Sanctions Committee, which is dedicated to developing and delivering programs, publications and advocacy in the areas of US and international export controls and economic sanctions measures. This book is intended as an overview of this complex and dynamic body of law. While it should prove a valuable resource to seasoned and novice practitioners alike, it is neither a substitute for nor should it be relied upon as legal advice in the context of specific transactions. We would like to thank and congratulate the patient and tenacious editors, Kay Georgi and Paul Lalonde, and an all-star line-up of co-authors for producing a thorough yet practical guide that will assist counsel and compliance professionals in identifying the myriad issues, navigating these rules, and managing their clients' risks in the challenging but fascinating area of export controls and economic sanctions law.

—John Boscariol & Michael Burton
Co-Chairs, ABA SIL Exports Controls &
Economic Sanctions Committee 2012–2013

ACKNOWLEDGEMENTS

The idea for this book originated at a breakfast meeting of the ABA Section of International Law Export Controls and Economic Sanctions Committee during the Section's Spring Meeting in April 2011. During the two-year journey to its publication, we were assisted by more people than we can possibly name and we are immensely grateful to everyone who lent a hand along the way. This book is the product of exemplary collaboration between members of the Section and a testament to what can be achieved by dedicated members of its committees. It is, therefore, fitting that our first thanks go to the incredibly dedicated group of chapter authors who made this book possible. They were invariably good natured about the inevitable fits and starts involved in bringing together a collective work of this kind and we could not be more grateful to each and every one of them.

We also wish to thank the staff at ABA Publishing, Richard Paszkiet, Curtis Alliaume, Monica Alejo, and Elizabeth Kulak, who guided and supported us through the drafting, editing, and production process. Our gratitude also to the then Chair of the ABA Section of International Law, Michael Burke, who supported the book from the outset and to the members of the Section's Publications Committee who believed in and gave this project the green light.

We would also be remiss if we did not single out the following individuals who often went above and beyond the call of duty in supporting our work and who are not elsewhere identified in this book: from Heenan Blaikie LLP, Christine Turcot, Susan Sims, Liane Fong, and Alex Farcas, and from Arent Fox, Corey Smith. Finally, we wish to thank the partners of Heenan Blaikie LLP and Arent Fox who patiently supported us through this time-consuming endeavor.

Editing can be a thankless task but assembling the various parts of this book into a comprehensive whole allowed us to deepen and broaden our understanding of this challenging and ever-changing area of the law. We are immensely grateful for the experience. Finally, while we are deeply indebted to all those who assisted us, we take full responsibility for any errors or omissions that may remain.

ABOUT THE AUTHORS

Paul M. Lalonde is Co-Chair of Heenan Blaikie LLP's International Trade and Competition Law Group. He has over 20 years of experience in international trade law, including import/export controls, international sanctions, anti-dumping and countervail, customs, trade and investment treaty disputes (including investor-state claims), and international anti-corruption law. Mr. Lalonde is also recognized as a leading expert in government procurement law, including as counsel in dozens of bid challenge cases. He has extensive experience in government relations and public-private partnerships and works with foreign investors to establish or expand their presence in Canada. He has been recognized as a leading practitioner in international trade and procurement law by several directories including *Lexpert*, *Chambers Global*, *Legal Post*, *World's Leading Lawyers* (Legal Media Group), *Who's Who of Public Procurement Lawyers*, *Who's Who Legal Canada*; and named 2011 Corporate INTL Magazine's 2011 Public Procurement Lawyer of the Year in Canada and 2012 Lawyer of the Year, Toronto, international trade and finance law by The Best Lawyers in Canada. He has held numerous leadership positions in the ABA Section of International Law, including Division chair and chair or vice-chair of various committees, and is currently Co-Chair of the International Bar Association North American Forum. He is called to the Bars of Québec (1990) and Ontario (1992) and is fluently bilingual in English and French.

Kay C. Georgi has more than 23 years' experience advising clients on all aspects of international trade, with particular capability in the areas of export control and sanctions, Foreign Corrupt Practices Act (FCPA), and import (customs) matters. Ranked as one of the leading International Trade: Export Controls & Economic Sanctions lawyers by *Chambers USA* and *Chambers Global*, and as a leading international trade practitioner by *Legal 500* and *Expert Guides*, Kay is known for helping large and small clients understand, comply with, and weather the investigation storms associated with the complicated set of U.S. laws and regulations governing U.S. exports and non-U.S. reexports of goods, software, services, and technology.

Kay has been a lead auditor in International Traffic in Arms Regulations (ITAR) audits conducted pursuant to the Directorate of Defense Trade Controls (DDTC) of the Department of State consent agreement/directed disclosures and served as an expert witness on the ITAR in international arbitration. She attended Cornell University for her undergraduate and law school studies, earning her BA with distinction in Classics and Archeology and her JD *summa cum laude* with a concentration in International Legal Affairs. Kay is fluent in Italian..

Thaddeus R. McBride is a partner in the Washington, D.C. office of Sheppard Mullin Richter & Hampton. Mr. McBride advises U.S. and non-U.S. companies and individuals on compliance with U.S. export controls, U.S. economic sanctions, the Foreign Corrupt Practices Act, and other U.S. trade regulations and laws.

Michael L. Burton is Managing Member of Joiner Burton PLLC with over 15 years of experience representing U.S. and foreign clients across numerous industries on compliance with and enforcement of U.S. export controls (EAR & ITAR), OFAC sanctions, antiboycott, FCPA, and anti-money laundering. Mr. Burton advises on complex trade controls issues, designs compliance systems, and obtains government licenses. He also conducts internal investigations, manages compliance audits and due diligence, and defends and resolves government enforcement actions. Mr. Burton graduated, *magna cum laude*, from Brown University (A.B., 1994) and Georgetown University Law Center (J.D., 1997). He is Co-Chair of the ABA Section of International Law, Committee on Export Controls and Economic Sanctions

Meredith Rathbone is a partner with the law firm of Steptoe & Johnson LLP in Washington, D.C., where she practices in the International Department. Ms. Rathbone focuses her practice on counseling clients on international regulatory compliance, including compliance with U.S. export controls and economic sanctions laws and regulations. She earned her undergraduate degree in International Relations from the Georgetown University School of Foreign Service, and her law degree from Georgetown University Law Center, and has been an adjunct professor teaching international law courses at both institutions.

Amy J. Lentz is an associate in the Washington office of Steptoe & Johnson LLP, where she is a member of the firm's International Department. Ms. Lentz's international trade practice involves counseling clients on U.S. export controls and economic sanctions programs, including programs administered by the U.S. Departments of Commerce, State, and Treasury. She is a 2004 graduate of Bowdoin College and received her law degree from the University of Virginia.

Anahita Thoms is a principal associate at Freshfields Bruckhaus Deringer LLP in Berlin and specializes in EU trade law, including EU sanctions and export control. Ms. Thoms completed her legal education at the University of Düsseldorf and worked several months in Brussels and London during her legal traineeship. She particularly represents clients of the manufacturing, energy and financial sector, closely collaborating with the German and EU authorities. Ms. Thoms has published numerous articles on general EU law, including trade and export control law. She is co-author of a commentary on the German Foreign Trade Act (Dorsch, Zollrecht, volume 4, Außenwirtschaftsrecht).

William E. Fork is a Senior Associate in Pillsbury's energy group. He represents electric utilities and companies on international energy transaction, export control, nuclear liability and domestic regulatory issues. He assists clients regarding the regulation of international nuclear power plants, nuclear vendor procurement, and agreements for the construction, operation, and fueling of nuclear power units.

Elina Teplinsky is a Senior Associate in Pillsbury's energy group. Her practice focuses on international nuclear energy matters, including advice to U.S. and foreign clients on a variety of regulatory and transactional issues. Mrs. Teplinsky has significant experience in nuclear export controls, including securing export authorizations and licenses on behalf of U.S. nuclear utilities and equipment manufacturers for the export of nuclear technology and equipment and developing nuclear export compliance programs for U.S. and foreign companies involved in all sectors of the nuclear industry. Mrs. Teplinsky represented an ad hoc utility group, composed of several major U.S. nuclear utilities, as well as numerous other clients, in commenting on the proposed amendments to the U.S. Department of Energy 10 C.F.R. Part 810 rules.

J. Daniel Chapman serves as the Chief Compliance Officer and Counsel for Parker Drilling Company in Houston, Texas. Since assuming this role in 2009, Mr. Chapman has coordinated the company's overall compliance efforts, with a particular focus on developing and implementing initiatives related to anti-bribery, anti-boycott, economic sanctions, and export controls compliance. Prior to joining Parker Drilling Company, Mr. Chapman served in a variety of international trade, compliance, and generalist legal counsel roles with Baker Hughes Incorporated. In addition, Mr. Chapman began his career as a securities and merger/acquisitions lawyer with the law firms of Freshfields (London) and King & Spalding (Atlanta and Houston). Mr. Chapman is a past vice chair of the American Bar Association's Committees on International Anti-Corruption and on Export Controls and Economic Sanctions. Mr. Chapman holds degrees from Emory University, the London School of Economics, and the University of Kentucky.

William B. Hoffman retired in 2012 from his position as counsel in the Washington, D.C., office of Davis Polk and Wardwell LLP after eight years handling economic sanctions and other matters. Mr. Hoffman served in the U.S. Treasury Department's General Counsel's Office from 1986 to 2003, and was Chief Counsel to the Department's Office of Foreign Assets Control (OFAC) from 1989 to 2000. He then worked on multilateral development bank and International Monetary Fund matters in the International Affairs Division and, after the terrorist attacks of 9/11/2001, was counsel to the interagency Task Force on Terrorist Financing until 2003. In 2003-2004, he worked on terrorism and other issues in the Office of Law Enforcement and Intelligence within the U.S. State Department's Legal Adviser's Office. Mr. Hoffman was in private practice in New York, Washington and Geneva from 1974-1985. He is a graduate of Harvard Law School, the Fletcher School of Law & Diplomacy, and Williams College.

Susan Klavens Hutner works in the field of economic sanctions in the Washington, D.C., office of Davis Polk and Wardwell LLP. Before joining Davis Polk in 2008,

Ms. Hutner served in the Treasury Department's Office of Foreign Assets Control (OFAC) from 2001 to 2008, where she held several positions, including Senior Sanctions Advisor and Deputy Chief of Licensing. From 1989 to 2001, she worked in the Office of the Chief Counsel to OFAC. Ms. Hutner graduated from Tufts University *magna cum laude*. She attended George Washington University Law School, where she graduated with honors and was a member of the *George Washington Law Review*. Ms. Hutner obtained an M.A. from the Johns Hopkins School of Advanced International Studies.

Jeanine P. McGuinness is counsel at Davis Polk & Wardwell LLP, practicing in the Washington D.C., office. She concentrates in U.S. trade and investment laws applicable to cross-border transactions, focusing on economic sanctions, anti-money laundering laws, anti-boycott laws, the Foreign Corrupt Practices Act, and transaction reviews by U.S. national security agencies, including the Committee on Foreign Investment in the United States (CFIUS). She began her career as a corporate lawyer with Davis Polk, advising on securities, mergers and acquisitions, and banking matters. She is a graduate of Harvard Law School and Fairfield University.

John Grayston is an English qualified solicitor and member of the Brussels Bar. He has been based and practised EU law in Brussels for more than 20 years. John has specialised in advising clients on EU trade and customs laws including both export control and sanctions issues. In 2007 he and colleagues founded the law firm Grayston & Company (www.graystoncompany.com).

Cari N. Stinebower is a member of Crowell and Moring's International Trade practice group. Cari counsels clients on compliance with U.S. economic sanctions, anti-money laundering, and anti-bribery/anti-corruption laws and regulations. She often works with multinational corporations to navigate the complex web of sanctions and anti-money laundering requirements. Cari served as counsel for the U.S. Department of the Treasury's Office of Foreign Assets Control and is a member of the American Bar Association's Gatekeepers' Task Force. Cari received her B.A. from Amherst College and her J.D. and M.A. from American University.

Wendy L. Wysong, a litigation partner with Clifford Chance, maintains offices in Washington, D.C. and Hong Kong. She offers clients advice and representation on compliance and enforcement under the Arms Export Control Act, International Traffic in Arms Regulations, Export Administration Regulations, OFAC Economic Sanctions, Antiboycott Regulations, as well as the Foreign Corrupt Practices Act. Ms. Wysong combines her experience as a former federal prosecutor with the United States Attorney for the District of Columbia for 16 years, with her regulatory background as the former Deputy Assistant Secretary for Export Enforcement at the Bureau of Industry and Security, U.S. Department of Commerce. Chambers Asia ranked her as a Key Individual for Clifford Chance's Band One Ranking for Asia Pacific Litigation and Dispute Resolution, Asia Pacific, writing "Anti-corruption practitioner Wendy Wysong brings expertise in FCPA matters and international law to the team. Her practice focuses on compliance matters, and her solid grasp of the regulations makes her a favourite for a number of U.S. and UK entities looking to invest in the region." Ms. Wysong received her law degree in 1984 from the University of Virginia School of Law, where she was a member of the *University of Virginia Law Review.*

Geoffrey M. Goodale is Special Counsel with Cooley LLP. He focuses his practice on export controls, economic sanctions, cyber-security, import compliance, intellectual property rights, international trade and investment, and the Foreign Corrupt Practices Act. The author wishes to express his thanks to Kay Georgi, for her thoughtful comments and contributions to this chapter.

Martha Harrison is a partner at Heenan Blaikie LLP. She practises international trade law, with additional focus on regulatory law, government relations and procurement, and international investor-state arbitration. In the context of her international trade and investment practice, she regularly advises on customs issues, trade remedies, import and export controls, product regulation, and foreign investment. Martha has also acted as counsel in numerous NAFTA Chapter 11 / bilateral investment disputes and investor-state arbitrations involving a variety of Foreign Investment Protection Agreements. She has been recognized as an expert in her field by a variety of legal organizations and publications, including Chambers Global, Lexpert, and Legal Media.

J. Scott Maberry is a partner in the Washington, D.C., office of Sheppard Mullin Richter & Hampton LLP. He specializes in export controls, economic sanctions, and anti-bribery. He advises U.S. and multinational companies and their directors, officers, and boards in transaction due diligence, compliance counseling, licensing, internal investigations, company-to-government advocacy, and white collar criminal defense.

John Boscariol leads McCarthy Tétrault's International Trade and Investment Group and is Co-Chair of the ABA Section of International Law Export Controls and Economic Sanctions Committee. His practice focuses on economic sanctions and export controls, anti-corruption laws and policies, rights and remedies under international trade and investment agreements, customs and tariff matters, trade remedies, and other regulations governing the cross-border movement of goods, services, technology, and investment. He is also Co-Chair of the Export Committee of the Canadian Association of Importers and Exporters.

Adam Klauder is a counsel in Clifford Chance's White Collar & Regulatory Group, based in Washington, D.C. He has particular experience counseling clients in economic sanctions, export control, and anti-corruption compliance, including the structuring of international transactions and resolution of disputes arising from governmental enforcement actions. His practice focuses on criminal, regulatory and complex civil disputes, particularly in matters involving the U.S. Treasury Department's Office of Foreign Assets Control, the U.S. Commerce Department's Bureau of Industry and Security, the U.S. Department of Justice, and other regulators. Mr. Klauder received his law degree in 2002 from Catholic University of America's Columbus School of Law, where he was a member of the Catholic University Law Review.

Katrina Reyes is an associate at Heenan Blaikie LLP practicing in the areas of international trade, regulatory, and nuclear energy law. She has degrees from the Universities of Ottawa (LL.B.) and Toronto (Hons. B.A.) and is a member of the Ontario bar. Katrina's international trade practice includes customs law, anti-dumping and countervail issues, import and export controls, and foreign investment. Katrina also works closely with the firm' s nuclear energy group on matters relating to existing nuclear facilities and the development of new nuclear programs in Canada and overseas.

Mark E. Sagrans is Corporate Counsel with E.I. DuPont de Nemours in its international trade group. Mr. Sagrans has 24 years of experience in export controls. Twenty-one of those twenty-four have been in the private sector, though he has also worked at the Office of Export Enforcement in DDTC at the Department of State and in the Chemical and Biological Controls Division in BIS at the Department of Commerce. Mr. Sagrans began his career as a consultant, but later became an attorney and along the way has represented a variety of industries including aerospace, chemicals, computers, energy, and others. In addition to working in export controls, he also worked as a lobbyist in Washington, D.C., for alternative fuels and aerospace interests (National Biodiesel Board and EADS).

U.S. Economic Sanctions Law

J. Daniel Chapman & William B. Hoffman[1]

1.1 OVERVIEW

The United States adopts and maintains economic sanctions for a variety of diplomatic, criminal enforcement, economic, humanitarian, and national security reasons. Regardless of whether U.S. economic sanctions programs originate unilaterally or from multilateral initiatives, they seek to influence and alter international behavior through various financial and commercial restrictions against targeted activities, countries, governments, individuals, and entities.

What Is Regulated? In general, U.S. economic sanctions apply to a wide variety of transactions involving targeted countries, governments, organizations, persons, and activities, and they penalize U.S. persons and, in certain cases, non-U.S. persons for engaging in or facilitating those transactions.

Where to Find the Regulations: While U.S. economic sanctions are promulgated pursuant to a number of laws, the statutory authorities for most of these programs are the 1917 Trading with the Enemy Act (TWEA),[2] the International Emergency Economic Powers Act (IEEPA),[3] and the United Nations Participation Act (UNPA).[4] Although a number of economic sanctions exist only under executive orders and do not yet have associated regulations, most U.S. economic sanctions regulations are codified in 31 C.F.R. chapter V.

Who Is the Regulator? The U.S. Department of Treasury's Office of Foreign Assets Control (OFAC) is the primary regulatory authority for U.S. economic sanctions programs.

This chapter first discusses the statutory authority behind U.S. economic sanctions, who must comply with them, how they are implemented and how they function. The chapter then analyzes list-based and country-based programs and their associated compliance risks, and it identifies certain exemptions, licenses, and compliance approaches that may mitigate these risks. The final sections of this chapter describe the consequences of violating U.S. economic sanctions and the potential for conflicts

---

1. Jeanine P. McGuinness and Susan Klavens Hutner provided substantial assistance in the preparation of this chapter and are responsible for its appendixes.
2. 50 U.S.C. app. §§ 1–44. Only sections 5(b) and 16 are currently operative.
3. 50 U.S.C. §§ 1701–1706.
4. 22 U.S.C. § 287c.

between U.S. economic sanctions and certain non-U.S. laws. In addition, this chapter and its appendices contain several "quick-reference" summaries of the various U.S. economic sanctions programs, common facilitation risks faced by companies, and significant court decisions affecting U.S. economic sanctions. Subsequent chapters 2, 3, and 4 separately cover U.S. export and reexport controls, which govern the actual or deemed transfer of regulated U.S. goods, software, and technology across international borders, and U.S. antiboycott laws, which counteract certain non-U.S. economic sanctions and non-U.S. export and reexport controls.

(a) Statutory Authority

From the time of World War I through the end of the Cold War, the primary statutory authority for U.S. economic sanctions was TWEA. During this period, this statute enabled the United States to adopt extremely broad economic sanctions programs to target unfriendly countries and their governments both in times of peace and of war. However, only sections 5(b) and 16 of TWEA, which respectively address presidential emergency authority and penalties, remained applicable after the end of World War II. In December 1977, the United States enacted IEEPA to address concerns of presidential accountability in the peacetime exercise of TWEA emergency powers. At the same time, Congress amended TWEA and limited its application to times of declared war or, subject to an annual presidential finding that a continuation is in the U.S. national interest, to TWEA-based economic sanctions programs existing at that time.[5] Of these "grandfathered" TWEA-based economic sanctions programs, only the economic sanctions against Cuba still remain effective pursuant to this annual continuation process.

IEEPA is the statutory authority for most U.S. economic sanctions adopted since 1977. IEEPA authorizes the President to impose economic sanctions to address national emergencies arising from foreign threats to the national security, foreign policy, or economy of the United States. In order to exercise this emergency authority under IEEPA, the President must submit a separate justification to Congress for each national emergency declared.

As discussed in greater detail later in this chapter, Congress amended IEEPA in 1988 and 1994 to limit restrictions on certain transactions related to travel and exchanges of information. Better known as the Berman Amendments, these changes bar the President from using IEEPA powers to prohibit or regulate, directly or indirectly, any trade between countries in most information and informational materials, as well as any transactions related to travel and its arrangement. (TWEA contains an identical exemption for trade in information. However, given TWEA's wartime applicability and the inherent need to restrict civilian travel during wartime, it provides

---

5. *See* Pub. L. No. 95-223, § 101(b).

no exemption transactions related to travel.) In the absence of certain presidential determinations, IEEPA also exempts in-kind donations to relieve human suffering.[6]

Economic sanctions based on IEEPA may be terminated at any time by the President. In addition, IEEPA-based economic sanctions automatically terminate after one year if they are not properly renewed under its "sunset" provisions or by congressional action (although Congress has never met to consider termination of an economic sanctions program as of the date of the writing of this chapter). However, the 1976 National Emergencies Act (NEA)[7] allows the President to continue to exercise certain enforcement powers related to economic sanctions even after the termination of the relevant national emergency.

Both NEA and IEEPA impose additional procedural and reporting requirements on the President in connection with declared national emergencies. These reporting requirements oblige the President to provide initial, semiannual, and termination reports to Congress on each declared national emergency. These reports describe the executive orders and regulations issued to impose or modify economic sanctions programs, the litigation involving economic sanctions, the civil penalties collected, and the expense to the federal government of administering each economic sanctions program (other than the TWEA-based economic sanctions on Cuba). The initial reports and termination reports are published in the *Weekly Compilation of Presidential Documents*. From 1979 through the mid-1990s, that publication also contained the semiannual reports. However, following the delegation in the mid-1990s by the President to the Secretary of the Treasury for the preparation and filing of the semiannual reports, neither the administration nor Congress has made these semiannual reports available to the public.

Separately, the UNPA is the statutory authority for the President's implementation of economic sanctions mandated by U.N. Security Council resolutions. Unlike IEEPA, UNPA does not include exemptions for trade in information or for travel, presidential reporting requirements to Congress, automatic "sunset" provisions, or renewal obligations. Furthermore, a number of other statutes impose particular economic sanctions on countries or on activities such as narcotics trafficking.

In addition, many economic sanctions programs imposed pursuant to the UNPA or these other statutes are implemented through executive orders that also invoke the President's IEEPA and NEA authority. Thus, these particular programs include procedural requirements associated with IEEPA and NEA. However, depending on the scope of their non-IEEPA authority, these programs may or may not include the IEEPA exemptions for trade in information or transactions related to travel.

---

6. *See* 50 U.S.C. § 1702(b)(3).
7. 50 U.S.C. § 1601–1651.

(b) Regulated Persons

All *United States persons* must comply with all U.S. economic sanctions programs. *United States persons* include (1) any individual U.S. citizen, (2) any permanent U.S. resident alien, (3) any entity of any kind organized under U.S. law (or a non-U.S. branch of such a U.S. entity), and (4) any individual or entity located in the United States (including any branch, agency, or office of a non-U.S. organization that is located in the United States).

In addition to their universal application to U.S. persons, the TWEA-based U.S. economic sanctions against Cuba and the residual IEEPA-based economic sanctions related to the 1979 takeover of the U.S. embassy in Tehran and the subsequent hostage crisis also have extraterritorial application to non-U.S. entities owned or controlled by U.S. persons. (U.S. persons and their non-U.S. subsidiaries are termed *persons subject to the jurisdiction of the United States*.) The economic sanctions program imposed to deal with the Iran hostage crisis was the first program based on IEEPA. It was also the last IEEPA-based program to require compliance by *persons subject to the jurisdiction of the United States*, although the statutory authority for this broader application of IEEPA-based economic sanctions remains.

The use of the term *person* in this chapter refers to organizations, entities, and natural persons unless indicated otherwise. The term *United States person* is abbreviated in most economic sanctions literature and will be referenced in this chapter as simply *U.S. person*. Furthermore, for ease of reference, the use of the term *U.S. person* in this chapter refers to all parties that must comply with U.S. economic sanctions (such as persons subject to the jurisdiction of the United States, except as noted in discussions of the unique extraterritorial issues implicated in the U.S. economic sanctions program for Cuba).

(c) Implementation

While there are numerous similarities between economic sanctions programs, the benefit of experience with one economic sanctions program does not necessarily transfer to other economic sanctions programs. In fact, most implementing regulations state that "[d]iffering foreign policy and national security circumstances may result in differing interpretations of similar language among [various economic sanctions regulations]."[8] These differences in each program's administration often arise from the legislation, executive orders, regulations, and regulatory guidance under which it is implemented. Moreover, each economic sanctions program has special features arising from its unique foreign policy context and history. As policy instruments of the U.S. government, the application and interpretation of U.S. economic sanctions programs must be dynamic and change with the objectives of U.S. policy.

---

8. *See, e.g.,* 31 C.F.R. § 537.101.

The implementing language of an economic sanctions program—whether in presidential executive orders or OFAC regulations or licenses—often is intentionally vague, and its literal interpretation may reach a very wide range of transactions. As a result, U.S. regulators have great latitude to "break new ground" and penalize U.S. persons, or even non-U.S. persons, for conduct that the U.S. government has not challenged historically.

Therefore, knowledge of the implementation and administration of each U.S. economic sanctions program is an essential part of understanding and interpreting these complex, dynamic, and often overlapping programs. This requires a good understanding of the statutory authority invoked and the executive orders imposing the economic sanctions program, their implementing regulations, and relevant guidance promulgated by the OFAC.

(d) Executive Orders

The vast majority of U.S. economic sanctions programs derive from executive orders. The President's authority to issue these executive orders can stem from a general statutory authority, such as IEEPA or UNPA. The President's authority may also originate from a congressional mandate that the President must implement specific economic sanctions. Examples of such congressional mandates include the 2010 Comprehensive Iran Sanctions, Accountability, and Divestment Act (CISADA);[9] the 2003 Syria Accountability and Lebanese Sovereignty Restoration Act;[10] and the Cuban Liberty and Democratic Solidarity (Libertad) Act of 1996,[11] more commonly known as the "Libertad Act" or "Helms-Burton Act."

These executive orders generally declare new, or build on existing, national emergencies; specify the threat that is posed; define the characteristics for designation of the targets of the economic sanctions; establish their effective date; and delegate authority for their implementation. In most cases, this administrative and enforcement authority is delegated to the Secretary of the Treasury, acting in consultation with the Secretary of State and other specified cabinet officials. In turn, the Secretary of the Treasury generally delegates this administrative and enforcement authority to the Director of OFAC.

(e) OFAC Regulations

As a result of this delegation of authority, OFAC is the primary regulatory authority for U.S. economic sanctions programs. It administers and enforces approximately thirty sets of economic sanctions regulations (codified at 31 C.F.R. chapter V) as well as other economic sanctions programs for which regulations have not yet been issued. In connection with these programs, OFAC may promulgate implementing regula-

---

9.   Pub. L. No. 111-195.
10.   Pub. L. No. 108-175, 22 U.S.C. § 2151.
11.   22 U.S.C. § 6021–6091.

tions, require reports relating to targeted transactions, issue licenses authorizing otherwise prohibited transactions, and take enforcement measures in connection with violations. As discussed later in this chapter, OFAC also identifies, adds new economic sanctions targets to its Specially Designated Nationals and Blocked Persons List (SDN List), and reviews requests for their removal. The SDN List is available online in various formats at http://www.treasury.gov/sdn. However, other government agencies recently have assumed increasingly important roles in the administration of economic sanctions programs, such as the U.S. State Department's involvement in U.S. economic sanctions against Iran pursuant to the Iran Sanctions Act of 1996.[12]

The regulations implemented and enforced by OFAC are available online in Title 31 of the Electronic Code of Federal Regulations website, http://www.ecfr.gov. Summaries and other guidance related to the economic sanctions programs administered by OFAC are available on its website at http://www.treasury.gov/resource-center/ sanctions/Programs/Pages/Programs.aspx. However, the frequent changes to U.S. economic sanctions necessitate that users of OFAC's website materials check their associated dates and use appropriate care to identify subsequent program changes.

1.2 COMMON TYPES OF RESTRICTIONS

The goal of economic sanctions programs is to cause an economic hardship that penalizes or influences the behavior of a targeted country, government, designated person, or any person engaged in designated activities. This section discusses how U.S. economic sanctions programs function and the tools they use to achieve their goals. The tools generally fall within one of three categories: blocking of property, vesting of property, and prohibiting certain defined types of transactions.

(a) Blocking of Property

The blocking of property is the broadest measure that the President can impose in an executive order or other directive imposing economic sanctions. Except as exempted by U.S. law or as authorized by executive order or OFAC, blocking prohibits all transfers and dealings in a target's property or interests in property within the United States or otherwise within the possession or control of a U.S. person (regardless of where the U.S. person is located). Therefore, U.S. persons have a duty to retain, or "freeze," blocked property interests within their possession or control, and they may not engage in any unauthorized disposition of a "frozen" asset.[13] Thus, U.S. persons may not perform blocked contracts, and OFAC regulations normally require that they deposit funds and liquid assets, including securities, into a blocked interest-bearing account located in the United States.[14] Blocked property must be reported to

---

12. 50 U.S.C. § 1701 note.
13. *See, e.g.,* 31 C.F.R. § 594.201.
14. *See, e.g.,* 31 C.F.R. § 594.203.

OFAC initially within ten business days of blocking and thereafter on an aggregated, annual basis.[15]

Various OFAC regulations define "property" and "interests in property" extremely broadly,[16] and they do not distinguish between real, personal, mixed, or intangible property. Examples include money, securities, debts, security rights, bills of lading, goods, accounts payable, judgments, and contracts of any nature, as well as any other present, future, or contingent interests in them. Absent authorization from OFAC, U.S. persons cannot credit or debit blocked bank accounts; sell or pledge blocked shares of stock or pay related dividends; issue, confirm, or perform under letters of credit for goods carried on a vessel that is an SDN or is owned by an SDN; or trade commodity contracts benefiting an SDN.

Blocking measures apply to all property and interests in property of any person on OFAC's SDN List; to the property and interests in property of the governments of Cuba, Iran, Sudan,[17] and Syria (including agencies, instrumentalities, or entities controlled by them, such as central banks); and to the property and interests in property of any person owned 50 percent or more by any of the foregoing. OFAC urges caution regarding dealings with entities that are less than 50 percent owned by a blocked person; these entities' assets may be subject to blocking requirements if these entities are controlled by an SDN by other means, are acting on behalf of an SDN, or are added by OFAC to the SDN List.

(b) Vesting of Property

In essence, vesting is the transfer by the U.S. government of title to blocked property from an economic sanctions target to another person or agency. For example, section 5(b) of TWEA permits assets to be vested and used by presidential directive. In peacetime, this power is rarely used. However, it was used in the 1990s to transfer blocked Cuban funds to pay compensation to the families of the "Brothers to the Rescue" pilots shot down by Cuba in 1996.

In addition, section 106 of the 2001 Uniting and Strengthening America by Providing Appropriate Tools Required to Intercept and Obstruct Terrorism (USA PATRIOT) Act[18] amended IEEPA to grant vesting authority to the President with respect to the assets of governments or persons found to have engaged in armed hostilities with, or attacks on, the United States. This authority was used to transfer blocked assets of the government of Iraq to the Development Fund for Iraq to benefit the Iraqi people in compliance with U.N. Security Council Resolution 1483.

---

15.   31 C.F.R. § 501.603.
16.   *See, e.g.,* 31 C.F.R. § 515.311.
17.   Note that the target government is that of the Republic of the Sudan, not the Republic of South Sudan.
18.   Pub. L. No. 107-56.

(c) Prohibitions on Targeted Transactions

A variety of other building blocks of economic sanctions programs may be chosen by the President to prohibit U.S. persons from engaging in, facilitating, or exporting services in support of certain defined types of transactions. These measures may target all transactions in a targeted country, with a targeted government (including entities owned or controlled by a targeted government), or involving targeted persons or activities. The definition of the targeted transaction type can range from being precise (such as the ban on all imports into the United States of goods of Burmese origin) to broad (such as the prohibition of most transactions in goods, technology, and services with Syria or its government).

Consolidated Summary of U.S. Economic Sanctions[1]

U.S. economic sanctions are complex and are subject to numerous exemptions, exceptions, and licensing programs. While a valuable tool when initiating a U.S. economic sanctions analysis, the following summary is not intended to capture all the prohibitions of U.S. economic sanctions and does not address certain associated export control regulations (such as those discussed in chapters 2 and 3, which may differ and, in some cases, be more restrictive).

Absent any proper authorization from the U.S. government (such as either a specific or general license), U.S. economic sanctions generally prohibit and/or impose blocking requirements on a U.S. person (and, in regard to the U.S. economic sanctions for Cuba, any party controlled or owned by a U.S. person) engaging in or facilitating the following transactions and activities:

Targeted countries and governments
- transactions in or with Cuba, Iran, Sudan,[2] or Syria or involving any of their governments (including companies owned or controlled by any of their governments)
- transactions involving property in which the government of Cuba, Iran, Sudan, or Syria has any interest (including companies owned or controlled by those governments)
- donations to a U.S. person by the government of Cuba, Iran, Sudan, or Syria (including companies owned or controlled by that government) other than certain educational stipends to Sudanese and Syrian nationals from their respective governments
- receipt of funds by a U.S. person from a government designated by the U.S. Secretary of State as supporting international terrorism if the U.S. person knows, or has reasonable cause to believe, that the transfer poses a risk of furthering terrorist acts in the United States, where OFAC has not issued regulations affecting that government (currently, this economic sanction applies only with respect to the government of Syria)
- unlicensed transactions involving new investment by a U.S. person in Burma (Myanmar)
- unlicensed transactions involving, directly or indirectly, the transfer of funds or the provision of financial services (other than certain personal remittances) from the United States or by a U.S. person to Burma (Myanmar)

---

1. *See* Appendix A to this chapter for descriptions of individual country-based sanctions programs.
2. Note that the target country is the Republic of the Sudan, not the Republic of South Sudan.

- owning, leasing, operating, or insuring any vessel flagged by North Korea, registering a vessel in North Korea, or otherwise obtaining authorization for a vessel to fly the flag of North Korea

Targeted persons
- transactions involving a Cuban national whose property has not been unblocked by OFAC, or involving any property in which such a Cuban national has any interest
- transactions involving any property in which a person listed on the U.S. Department of the Treasury's list of Specially Designated Nationals and Blocked Persons has any interest, or in which a person on OFAC's lists of restricted Iranian government entities or Iranian financial institutions has any interest

Exports and reexports that independently constitute a violation of U.S. economic sanctions
- direct exports of any goods, services, software, or technology from the United States to Cuba, Iran, Sudan, or Syria (other than deemed exports or deemed reexports of EAR99 items to Syria)
- unlicensed exports of financial services to Burma (Myanmar)
- reexports of any goods, software, or technology with greater than 10 percent U.S. content to Cuba or Syria (other than deemed exports or deemed reexports of EAR99 technology or source code to Syria)
- reexports of most goods, software, or technology with greater than 10 percent U.S. content (other than those designated as EAR99 or belonging to a very limited number of other export classifications) by U.S. persons to Sudan and by U.S. and non-U.S. persons to Iran

Import controls based on U.S. economic sanctions
- imports into the United States of goods, services, software, or technology from Burma (Myanmar) (except Burmese services), Cuba, Iran, North Korea, or Sudan
- imports into the United States of Iraqi cultural property or other items of archeological, historical, cultural and rare scientific or religious importance that were illegally removed from Iraq
- imports into the United States of petroleum and petroleum products of Syrian origin
- imports into the United States from certain designated persons for nonproliferation purposes

Other prohibited imports and exports
- imports to, or exports from, the United States of rough diamonds other than in accordance with the Kimberley Process Certification Scheme

1.3 COUNTRY-BASED ECONOMIC SANCTIONS PROGRAMS

Legal practitioners often categorize economic sanctions programs into one of two groups. These groups are the list-based programs covered in the next section of this chapter and the country-based programs discussed in this section. In addition, Annex A provides separate summaries for each of the country-based economic sanctions with respect to Burma (Myanmar), Cuba, Iran, North Korea, Sudan, and Syria.

Most U.S. economic sanctions adopted through the late 1990s targeted specific countries and their governments. Often called "comprehensive," "country-based," "territorial," or "traditional" economic sanctions, these programs function by imposing prohibitions on certain defined types of transactions with or within the territory of the targeted country, on most transactions with its government or involving its property, and, in rare situations, through the vesting of property.

More precisely, the country-based programs generally prohibit regulated persons from engaging in or facilitating trade in goods, services, or technology or financial transactions within a targeted country's territory or with its government (including its agencies, instrumentalities, and controlled entities). All country-based programs also incorporate some level of restriction on imports into the United States of goods, software, or technology of targeted country origin. As of March 15, 2013, these programs, except for the programs against Burma (Myanmar) and Syria, also bar the importation of services of targeted country origin. Additionally, these country-based sanctions programs often have certain list-based components for addressing SDNs associated with targeted countries and their governments.

As a general matter, the more recently adopted country-based programs tend to have a narrower range of targeted activities than their predecessors do. The oldest of the country-based programs is the U.S. economic sanctions program against Cuba. This program's TWEA-based, wartime orientation is reflected in its broad prohibition on dealings with Cuban individuals and entities—even when dealing with nongovernmental persons or when they are located in third countries outside Cuba—unless such persons' assets have been unblocked by an OFAC license. By contrast with the Cuba sanctions, the later U.S. economic sanctions programs against Burma (Myanmar), Iran, North Korea, Sudan, and Syria generally do not restrict U.S. persons from engaging in or facilitating transactions with nationals of those countries that occur entirely outside the targeted country. (However, these programs generally would prohibit a U.S. person from engaging in or facilitating a transaction outside the targeted country either with an individual acting as an agent for a targeted government or in a context that places that U.S. person on notice that the transaction—for example, a transfer of goods or technology—is intended to lead to a prohibited export or other targeted transaction or activity.) Moreover, the transactional prohibitions of the economic sanctions programs instituted against Burma (Myanmar) and reinstituted against North Korea are narrower in scope than those against Iran and Sudan.

While third countries' economic sanctions programs may mirror certain aspects of U.S. country-based economic sanctions (particularly where they are based on U.N. Security Council resolutions), the United States has often adopted country-based programs unilaterally. The unilateral nature of these economic sanctions programs makes them problematic for U.S. business. Compliance by non-U.S. branches of multinational U.S. firms with these U.S. economic sanctions programs may not be consistent with the trade and economic sanctions policies of their host countries, particularly regarding transactions involving U.S. origin goods or requiring the approval or facilitation of U.S. persons. These programs place U.S. firms at a competitive disadvantage in world markets where non-U.S. firms are not required to comply with similar restrictions.

1.4 LIST-BASED ECONOMIC SANCTIONS PROGRAMS

The United States generally followed a country-based model when implementing its earliest economic sanctions programs. These programs typically targeted the countries and governments of wartime enemies and imposed restrictions on dealing with those enemies and the territories they controlled. However, an integral part of such programs was the identification of, and imposition of economic sanctions on, "specially designated nationals" (SDNs) of the targeted country. In general, SDNs were persons acting as agents for those enemy governments and were often located in third countries. However, U.S. economic sanctions began to target persons who were not tied to specific countries or regimes, such as international terrorist organizations or narcotics traffickers; therefore, the name of this list was broadened to be the "List of Specially Designated Nationals and Blocked Persons." Nevertheless, it is still referred to as the "SDN List," and any party on the list may be loosely referenced as an "SDN."

Diverging from the mix of territorial restrictions and restricted party designations in country-based programs, economic sanctions programs that primarily rely on the designation of targeted persons and entities are called "list-based" programs. U.S. list-based programs typically target specific individuals, entities, or governments involved in activities threatening the national security, foreign policy, or economy of the United States. Among others, these targeted threats stem from terrorism, narcotics trafficking, weapons proliferation, human rights abuses, genocide, transnational organized crime, and material supporters of these targeted activities. Beginning with 1995 economic sanctions against Middle East terrorist groups and Colombian drug cartels, list-based economic sanctions programs also became the standard format for U.S. unilateral economic sanctions in the law enforcement arena. At least in part, the United States currently uses list-based economic sanctions to implement all mandatory U.N. Security Council resolutions (e.g., resolutions related to al-Qaida, the Taliban, the Democratic Republic of the Congo, Iran, Somalia, Sudan,[19] and Syria as well as related to former regime members from the Western Balkans, Côte d'Ivoire, Iraq, Liberia, and Libya), certain cooperative programs adopted with the European Union (such as programs addressing terrorism or targeting the governments of Belarus, Burma [Myanmar], and Zimbabwe), and programs targeting transnational criminal organizations and narcotics trafficking.

---

19. Note that the target country is the Republic of the Sudan, not the Republic of South Sudan.

The U.S. government's recent preference (and that of both the European Union and the U.N. Security Council) for list-based programs reflects two key traits of these programs. First, list-based programs target specific "bad actors" rather than placing the burden of economic sanctions on a country's population at large. Second, list-based programs can be implemented with relative ease through automated screening, which has become one of the most important instruments for compliance with economic sanctions. However, this recent preference for list-based economic sanctions is not without exceptions, as evidenced by the broad traits of the programs adopted in 2011 and 2012 to target the Gadhafi and Assad regimes in Libya and Syria and to tighten existing sanctions against Iran.

1.5 PROHIBITIONS ON THE EXPORTATION OF SERVICES AND FACILITATION

Many economic sanctions programs administered by OFAC have prohibitions related to the exportation or reexportation of services or facilitation. (For definitional purposes, the "exportation of services" is made directly from the United States, and the "reexportation" of services occurs from a third country if those services originated in the United States.) In general, the restrictions on the exportation or reexportation of services prohibit U.S. persons from providing services that generate a benefit that is received in a targeted country or by a targeted government. The restrictions on facilitation prohibit U.S. persons from facilitating any transaction by non-U.S. persons if U.S. economic sanctions would prohibit a U.S. person from directly participating in the same transaction. For simplicity, references in this section to an exportation of services should be deemed also to apply to a reexportation of services.

OFAC interprets these prohibitions on the exportation of services and facilitation expansively. In fact, certain activities occurring entirely outside a targeted country — but involving a transaction with or benefiting that targeted country — could equally be classified as prohibited facilitation or prohibited exportation of services to that targeted country. Examples of activities that could be classified as either a prohibited exportation of services or prohibited facilitation include approving, financing, assisting, brokering, guaranteeing, insuring, or investing in targeted transactions or other activities connected to them.

(a) Application

OFAC's longstanding interpretation of the prohibition on the exportation of services applies to the provision of any type of service (1) into or within the targeted country, (2) to a targeted government (including to its agencies, instrumentalities, or controlled entities) anywhere in the world, or (3) to any person in any location if the benefit of the service is arguably received in the targeted country or by the targeted government. (For example, see OFAC's interpretation of this restriction in section 550.422 of the former version of the Libyan Sanctions Regulations.[20]) Prohibitions on the exportation of services exist explicitly or by inference in the economic sanctions programs for Cuba, Iran, Sudan, and Syria.

Despite the breadth of the prohibition on the exportation of services, regulators introduced the prohibition on facilitation in the 1990s to address concerns that many unilateral U.S. economic sanctions programs could be undermined by U.S. persons' activities with third-country nationals, who were not subject to the jurisdiction of OFAC or these programs. During this period, the executive orders imposing economic sanctions began to include language barring the facilitation of transactions by non-U.S. persons in which a U.S. person could not engage directly due to economic sanctions. Today, the economic sanctions programs for Iran, Sudan, Syria, and Burma (Myanmar) contain explicit language about prohibited facilitation. However, many legal practitioners believe that OFAC infers that these prohibitions apply in most, if not all, U.S. economic sanctions programs—even though it may require a broader interpretation of equivalent language in other programs (such as language regarding evasion or avoidance of, or attempts or conspiracies to violate, the prohibitions in a statute or executive order).

Facilitation has an expansive definition that has a meaning similar to "enable." OFAC's broad interpretation of the facilitation prohibition covers a U.S. person's approving, financing, guaranteeing, or otherwise facilitating an offshore transaction in which U.S. economic sanctions prohibit U.S. persons from directly participating. Section 538.407 of the Sudanese Sanctions Regulations provides the most comprehensive interpretation of facilitation. That section includes the following warning to U.S. parent corporations with respect to their non-U.S. subsidiaries:

> To avoid potential liability for U.S. persons under this part, a U.S. parent corporation must ensure that its foreign subsidiaries act independently of any U.S. person with respect to all transactions and activities relating to the exportation or reexportation of goods, technology, or services between Sudan and any other location including but not limited to *business and legal planning; decision making; designing, ordering, or transporting goods; and financial, insurance, and other risks* . . . (emphasis added)[21]

Other examples of facilitation include a U.S. person making business referrals to non-U.S. persons engaged in targeted transactions, changing practices or procedures to allow non-U.S. persons to engage in targeted transactions, and providing business,

---

20.   31 C.F.R. § 550.422 (1993). The 1986 Libya emergency was terminated by Executive Order 13,357 of September 20, 2004. The revoked Libyan Sanctions Regulations were last published in the July 1, 2005, annual volume for Title 31, C.F.R.
21.   31 C.F.R. § 538.407(b).

legal, planning, or other activities in support of targeted transactions (such as advice, payroll, and information technology support). In addition, U.S. persons generally may not ship or receive goods by land or water across a targeted country because it facilitates the underlying shipping transactions within the targeted country.[22]

(b) Exceptions

Certain economic sanctions regulations specifically authorize actions that the prohibitions on facilitation and the exportation (or reexportation) of services would otherwise restrict. Absent the changes arising from a 2012 licensing program, U.S. economic sanctions have generally prohibited U.S. persons from making new investments in the economic development of resources located in Burma (Myanmar);[23] therefore, a U.S. person could not facilitate a transaction by a non-U.S. person making that type of new investment in Burma (Myanmar). However, even prior to 2012, the Burmese Sanctions Regulations contained a general license that authorized any U.S. person to divest a "pre-zero" investment in Burma (Myanmar) (i.e., an investment made prior to the imposition of economic sanctions) through a transaction with a non-U.S. person (subject to OFAC reporting requirements for transactions with a value of $10,000 or more).[24] More recently, on July 11, 2012, OFAC issued General License 17 authorizing most new investments in Burma (Myanmar), provided that new reporting requirements issued by the Department of State are met.

In addition, relevant OFAC regulations generally contain exceptions related to providing legal services and, in certain cases, performing purely clerical or administrative functions. Most programs permit U.S. persons to provide certain forms of legal advice to economic sanctions targets. However, among other limitations, this legal advice cannot facilitate targeted transactions in violation of U.S. economic sanctions, and payment cannot be received for such legal advice without a specific license from OFAC. In addition, as explicitly stated in the Sudanese economic sanctions and as often inferred into other programs since the adoption of the original 1986 Libya sanctions program, U.S. persons may engage in activities of a purely clerical or reporting nature; however, these activities cannot further trade or financial transactions with economic sanctions targets.[25] Furthermore, a U.S. person's mere receipt of information (such as receiving written reports on pending or completed transactions that are targeted by U.S. economic sanctions) does not cause a facilitation violation.[26] However, a violation would occur if a U.S. person used that information to approve or support targeted transactions or activities.

---

22.   See, e.g., OFAC's interpretations at 31 C.F.R. §§ 538.407 and 560.403.
23.   See discussion below and in Annex A of General License 17, which allows most such new investment in Burma (Myanmar) as of July 11, 2012.
24.   31 C.F.R. § 537.524.
25.   See 31 C.F.R. §§ 538.505 and 538.407(a).
26.   See 31 C.F.R. § 538.407(a).

Additionally, when a U.S. person engages in an international transaction for the sale of goods, technology, or services, he or she risks facilitating the resale and reexportation of those goods, technology or services in a subsequent transaction by the purchaser with an economic sanctions target or in an otherwise targeted transaction. In section 560.204 of the Iranian Transactions and Sanctions Regulations, OFAC mitigates this uncertainty by stating that exportation, reexportation, and sale or supply of goods, technology, or services to a third country is only prohibited when (1) the items are intended specifically to be directly or indirectly supplied, transshipped, or reexported to Iran or the government of Iran or (2) they are intended specifically for use in the production of, commingling with, or incorporation into goods, technology, or services to be directly or indirectly supplied, transshipped, or reexported *exclusively or predominantly* to Iran or the government of Iran (emphasis added). Legal practitioners often refer to this treatment as the "inventory rule" or "warehouse rule."

The inventory rule arose from a perception that, to remain globally competitive, U.S. exporters must be allowed to do business with distributors and other importers in third countries, even if a third country has a different economic sanctions or foreign trade policy toward a U.S.-targeted country. The rule was originally expressed in the former section 550.409 of the 1986 Libyan Sanctions Regulations.[27] As noted earlier, it only exists explicitly in the Iranian Transactions and Sanctions Regulations today. Nevertheless, OFAC has informally confirmed that it applies this rule with respect to exports and reexports of goods to third countries with respect to U.S. unilateral country-based programs targeting exports and reexports to Cuba, Sudan, and Syria. However, except under the Iranian program sanctions, OFAC does not generally apply this rule to exports or reexports of technology or services.[28]

The inventory rule allows U.S. persons to export or reexport to a third-country manufacturer or distributor if two conditions exist. First, the predominant business of the third-country manufacturer or distributor in the specific item to be exported or reexported, or in goods produced from that item, must not be with U.S. economic sanctions targets. Second, the U.S. exporter or reexporter must not have knowledge or notice that the specific exported or reexported shipment is directly or indirectly destined for, or for the benefit of, an economic sanctions target. Thus, the exportation or reexportation is lawful even though the U.S. exporter or reexporter may know that a minority of the items shipped could potentially come to rest in a targeted country or with its government.

---

27. 31 C.F.R. pt. 550 (1986). The 1986 Libya emergency was terminated by Executive Order 13357 of September 20, 2004. The revoked Libyan Sanctions Regulations were last published in the July 1, 2005, annual volume for Title 31, C.F.R.
28. The unwritten nature of the "warehouse" or "inventory rule" outside the Iran sanctions program leaves OFAC free to modify the rule's applicability to all, or any category of, export transactions at any time. However, the adverse trade impact of requiring an exporter to perform heightened due diligence on a customer's customers makes it likely that OFAC would provide explicit notice if such a policy change were being adopted.

(c) Considerations for Financial Institutions

Economic sanctions prohibiting the exportation of services or facilitation are of special importance for financial institutions, including organizations dealing in insurance, banking, investment brokering, securities brokering, or trading services. Regardless of the direct recipient of the services under a financial services contract, OFAC uses a test of whether any benefit is received, directly or indirectly, by a targeted government or within a targeted country to determine whether services are being exported to that country or whether an economic sanctions target's transactions are being facilitated. For example, if a U.S. citizen employed as an underwriter at an Indian insurance company arranges a casualty policy for a Norwegian company's oil drilling equipment in Iran, that individual U.S. citizen has, arguably, "exported his services to Iran" in violation of U.S. economic sanctions. The Indian insurer, which is not a U.S. person, has no direct obligation to comply with U.S. economic sanctions against Iran, and it would not be in direct violation of U.S. economic sanctions. Nevertheless, an October 2007 amendment to IEEPA made it an "unlawful act" to, inter alia, "cause a violation" of IEEPA.[29] Thus, even though it is not a U.S. person, enforcement action could be taken against the Indian company if it were subject to, or submitted to, personal jurisdiction in the United States and if it were asserted to have caused its employee to commit an "unlawful act."

The prohibitions on the exportation of services and facilitation also must be considered in connection with offerings of non-U.S. issuers' securities when they either are offered to U.S. investors or are made with the participation of U.S. underwriters, lenders, lawyers, accountants, or other advisors. In addition to the prohibition on dealing in the property of an economic sanctions target (including contracting with an economic sanctions target), a U.S. person involved in these offerings cannot purchase from, finance, or provide services to a non-U.S. person if the offering proceeds will be used for transactions in or with economic sanctions targets. Therefore, underwriting and offering agreements typically include a representation that the issuer is not, and is not owned or controlled by, a U.S. economic sanctions target. These agreements also normally include a covenant not to use the offering proceeds to finance transactions of or with U.S. economic sanctions targets.

Similarly, a U.S. person's global underwriting or reinsuring of insurance risks for a multinational group that has operations in a targeted jurisdiction or with a U.S. economic sanctions target also may constitute the prohibited facilitation of those transactions.

(d) Considerations for Multinational Companies

The prohibitions on facilitation found in U.S. economic sanctions programs also present unique compliance obstacles to multinational companies. In particular, the risk of

---

29.   *See* Pub. L. No. 110-98, § 2, *amending* 50 U.S.C. § 1705(a).

noncompliance with these prohibitions is elevated because, in many cases, persons who must comply with U.S. economic sanctions may unknowingly or unintentionally facilitate targeted activities undertaken by other persons who have no obligations under U.S. economic sanctions (such as non-U.S. agents, coworkers, customers, or vendors). If OFAC determines, after the fact, that a person required to comply with U.S. economic sanctions "should have known" of these targeted activities by others, then it may find prohibited facilitation and impose liability.

The broad interpretation of facilitation and the exportation of services may capture many corporate support functions performed by U.S. persons if they facilitate activities by non-U.S. affiliates in or with U.S. economic sanctions targets. Examples of these prohibited support activities include workflow approvals, guidance, feedback, and, if intended for use in support of targeted transactions, even certain recordkeeping or data storage functions. Among many other potential risk areas, the following chart lists circumstances in which U.S. persons working for multinational companies should exercise caution to avoid facilitating or exporting services in support of the targeted transactions and activities conducted by non-U.S. persons working for the same company.

Financial Matters
- Mandatory approval procedures that require U.S. persons to approve expenditures by non-U.S. persons
- Processing of bank transfers and payments by U.S. persons on behalf of non-U.S. persons
- Reallocations of "overhead" costs, such as management services or other support services, of U.S. persons to non-U.S. affiliates that engage in targeted activities
- Revenue allocations of customer contracts between U.S. and non-U.S. affiliates where subsequent performance could potentially involve activities with economic sanctions targets performed by non-U.S. affiliates (such as a master customer contract regulating future purchase orders)
- Financial arrangements and payments between U.S. parent companies and non-U.S. subsidiaries
- Commingling of assets and shared bank accounts by U.S. and non-U.S. affiliates
- Inadequate capitalization of non-U.S. subsidiaries creating exposure for future capital calls against U.S. affiliates
- Accounting and auditing services performed by U.S. affiliates for non-U.S. affiliates

Information Technology
Global electronic networks that are accessible by both U.S. and non-U.S. persons, including:
- Processing and enterprise software programs
- Inventory management systems
- Servers maintained by U.S. person employees or owned by entities that are U.S. persons
- Network connections routed through the United States
- Help desks staffed by U.S. persons
- E-mail and other electronic correspondence that allow non-U.S. persons to freely communicate with U.S. persons without procedures that prohibit discussion of activities prohibited by U.S. economic sanctions with U.S. persons
- International movement of cell phones, software, and laptops with U.S. content

Management Practices
- Approval by a U.S. company of its non-U.S. affiliate's activities with economic sanctions targets
- Policies developed or implemented by U.S. persons that predominantly impact non-U.S. affiliates
- Provision of general management or administrative services by U.S. persons for the benefit of non-U.S. affiliates whose activities may have shifted to predominantly targeted transactions
- Administration of the benefits of global purchases, such as individual claims under a global insurance policy, by U.S. persons on behalf of non-U.S. affiliates or employees
- Transfers of certain business activities, and the motives for doing so, from U.S. persons to non-U.S. persons
- Business referrals of potentially targeted transactions by U.S. persons to non-U.S. persons
- Changes to U.S. persons' business practices that have the effect of accommodating non-U.S. affiliates' transactions with economic sanctions targets

Human Resources and Personnel Management
- Involvement by U.S. persons in the hiring processes of non-U.S. affiliates
- Failure to terminate U.S. companies' employment contracts with employees who have been transferred to non-U.S. affiliates
- Consolidated compensation and benefits administration (payroll, life insurance, pension plans) conducted by U.S. persons on behalf of non-U.S. affiliates and their employees
- Reassignment of employees, and the motives for doing so, between U.S. and non-U.S. affiliates
- Employment of targeted country nationals by U.S. persons
- Non-U.S. persons working on, or facilitating, prohibited activities without appropriate restrictions on generic support and advice from U.S. persons (such as professional guidance on increasing revenue generation)
- U.S. person involvement in hiring decisions in regions where non-U.S. colleagues may discourage hiring U.S. persons who cannot engage in targeted transactions
- Training programs that mix U.S. person and non-U.S. person instructors and trainees

Corporate Structure and Corporate Formalities
- Divergence of functional structure from corporate legal structure
- Interlocking officers, directors, or employees among U.S. and non-U.S. affiliates
- Lack of maintenance of separate corporate formalities leading to a "piercing" of non-U.S. subsidiaries' "corporate veils" and causing their actions to be attributed to their U.S. parent companies

1.6 EXEMPTIONS, EXCEPTIONS, AND LICENSES

As mentioned at the beginning of this chapter, the United States maintains economic sanctions for a variety of diplomatic, criminal enforcement, economic, humanitarian, and national security reasons. However, there may be circumstances where the strict application of these programs would actually conflict with these goals or other important government policies. Therefore, certain exemptions, exceptions, and licensing policies and procedures apply to most economic sanctions programs in order to avoid unintended or undesired results.

The literature on U.S. economic sanctions often loosely uses the terms *exemption* and *exception* to denote any relief from the application of an economic sanctions prohibition. In this chapter, the term *exemption* either refers to a statutory provision that removes particular categories of transactions from the President's congressionally authorized powers for imposing economic sanctions or refers to a limitation in an executive order that removes stated classes of transactions from the scope of the imposed economic sanctions. As discussed later in this chapter, the term *license* is generally used when a relevant regulatory provision establishes an exception to an economic sanctions prohibition. In addition, Congress has adopted statutes that mandate certain licensing programs, such as section 906 of the Trade Sanctions Reform and Export Enhancement Act of 2000 (TSRA).[30] TSRA generally eliminated certain economic sanctions on agricultural commodities, medicine, or medical devices by directing the creation of a licensing program for exports and reexports of these items to certain targeted countries.

Statutory exemptions, regulatory exceptions, and, in most cases, general licenses are standing authorizations that apply without any further government action. They typically relate to particularly important objectives, relationships, and humanitarian or civic values of the United States.

Statements of licensing policy are placed in OFAC regulations to indicate certain frequently encountered situations in which OFAC is prepared to grant specific licenses to resolve problems created by an economic sanctions program. This regulatory language often provides guidance to applicants on what information must be submitted to OFAC to obtain a specific license. Other exceptions are made on a case-by-case basis, as ad hoc requests for specific licenses requested by an interested party may be granted by OFAC if they are found to be consistent with the goals of U.S. foreign policy and the relevant economic sanctions program. These licensing exceptions require direct interaction with OFAC and, potentially, with the U.S. Department of State. Finally, similar to a discretionary grant of a specific license, OFAC provides interpretations indicating that a specific fact pattern, as described by a license applicant or a person seeking an opinion, will or will not violate sanctions prohibitions. OFAC may request further information where a license application or request for an interpretation provides inadequate detail or specificity to allow OFAC or the U.S. Department of State to determine a matter.

OFAC often employs a mixture of general and specific licensing policies to achieve certain goals. For example, the regulatory amendments to the economic sanctions programs for Cuba, Iran, and Sudan (later adopted for Syria) use a combination of general licenses and statements of specific licensing policy to achieve the desired goal of permitting certain activities related to personal communications over the Internet.[31]

(a) The Berman Amendments

As a result of 1988 and 1994 legislation proposed by Representative Howard Berman of California to amend IEEPA and TWEA, these statutes both contain exemptions for imports from, and exports to, any country of certain information and informa-

---

30. Title IX of Pub. L. No. 106-387.
31. *See* 75 Fed. Reg. 10,997 (March 10, 2010) (*amending* 31 C.F.R. pts. 515, 538, and 560), and General License 5 to Executive Order 13582, 76 Fed. Reg. 52,209 (Aug. 17, 2011) (to be codified at 31 C.F.R. pt. 542), *see* http://www.treasury.gov/resource-center/sanctions/Programs/Documents/syria_gl5.pdf.

tional materials. IEEPA further exempts certain transactions related to travel from its grant of presidential emergency authority.

The 1988 Berman Amendment to IEEPA exempted transactions related to travel to any country from presidential control, except for travel bans then existing under U.S. economic sanctions. However, all such "grandfathered" IEEPA-based travel bans have ended with the termination of their underlying economic sanctions programs. (By contrast, the Berman Amendment to TWEA does not exempt transactions related to travel; thus, travel to Cuba remains subject to OFAC licensing under the TWEA-based economic sanctions program for Cuba.) The IEEPA travel exemption of the Berman Amendments is limited to travel and in-country maintenance transactions. However, it does not cover activities that are not purely incidental to such exempted travel (such as prohibited contracting or trade transactions), even if they occur during otherwise exempted travel.

The Berman Amendments' revised 1994 exemption in IEEPA and TWEA for trade in information and informational materials is broadly drafted, and it covers both tangible and electronic media. However, the Berman Amendments do not exempt exports of information and informational materials that are controlled under the Export Administration Act of 1979 (EAA).[32] These sections of the EAA address certain national security restrictions and certain U.S. foreign policy controls that promote antiterrorism or nonproliferation objectives. Items covered by espionage laws[33] also are not exempted by the Berman Amendments.

The Berman Amendments deny the President the "authority to regulate or prohibit, directly or indirectly," exempted travel and information. OFAC satisfies this requirement, and avoids indirect regulation, by authorizing transactions "incident" to the exempt transactions, such as certain transactions related to transportation, telephone transmissions, travel insurance, accompanied baggage, and ticket sales. Nonetheless, in determining *whether* the Berman Amendments or other statutory exemptions must be applied to a given economic sanctions program, OFAC reads exemptions narrowly to preserve its maximum flexibility for the exercise of the President's constitutional foreign affairs authority. Thus, if another applicable statutory authority is concurrently exercised in an executive order imposing sanctions and if that authority would permit broader restrictions with respect to travel or information, OFAC will normally apply the strictest measure, such as UNPA or a "free-standing" economic sanctions statute. However, if a U.N. Security Council economic sanctions program does not mandate travel restrictions or restrictions on the flow of information, the Berman Amendments' exemptions will apply with regard to economic sanctions prohibitions for which IEEPA is cited as a concurrent authority. Ironically, the congressional conference committee's report on the 1994 Berman Amendments revisions notes that

---

32.   50 U.S.C. app. §§ 2404 and 2405.
33.   18 U.S.C. ch. 37.

"[w]hile the statutory amendments made by this section do not include amendments to the [UNPA], the committee of conference has acted on the assurance of the executive branch that it intends to work to exclude limits on the free flow of information and restrictions on travel from multilateral embargoes."[34]

(b) OFAC Licensing

OFAC has very broad discretion, subject to consultation with the U.S. State Department for foreign policy guidance, to authorize transactions otherwise prohibited by economic sanctions. OFAC exercises its licensing authority through both general licenses and specific licenses. These licenses may be permissive (i.e., authorizing discretionary action) or directive (i.e., requiring action). Licenses may dictate the manner in which the licensed transactions can be performed, and they may require that certain notifications or reports be submitted to OFAC before, during, or after the licensed transactions.

A general license is a published OFAC authorization (or directive) covering any transaction that meets its stated conditions. OFAC normally publishes general licenses as provisions incorporated into the regulations of a particular economic sanctions program, although it sometimes publishes them as "free-standing" licenses in the *Federal Register*. Additionally, OFAC frequently publishes general licenses on its website in order to make them immediately available in response to an urgent natural emergency, to address a temporary condition, or to avoid the delays associated with publishing amendments to its regulations.

When general licenses or other exemptions or exceptions do not apply, a person may seek authorization for a specific license from OFAC. OFAC has discretion to issue or deny a specific license in response to a written application, which should contain the elements required by section 501.801(b) of the Reporting, Procedures and Penalties Regulations.[35] While there is no required format for most specific license applications (so long as the information required by that section is included), successful requests generally (1) provide a comprehensive explanation of the facts, parties, and proposed transactions (explaining any technical terms that are unique to the type of transaction sought to be authorized), (2) explain why OFAC has jurisdiction to issue the license, and (3) indicate why authorization of the requested transaction(s) would be consistent with U.S. economic sanctions policy, with the objectives of the relevant economic sanctions program, or, if relevant, with a compelling national interest on which the U.S. government should act. It is useful to include the precise language desired for the text of the authorization, particularly where loose or non-technical language may undermine the applicant's objectives.

---

34. *See* discussion of section 525 of the conference substitute for H.R. 2333 in H. Report 103-482 (Apr. 25, 1994), http://www.gpo.gov/fdsys/pkg/CREC-1994-04-26/html/CREC-1994-04-26-pt1-PgH59.htm.
35. 31 C.F.R. pt. 501.

OFAC generally will not issue a specific license involving novel considerations without first receiving the foreign policy advice and concurrence of the U.S. Department of State. Therefore, if a license application advocates that it be granted based on foreign policy considerations, the party requesting the license should include information that would assist in the review by the State Department and may also wish to contact the State Department separately.

Any person with an interest in the proposed transaction may apply for a specific license. Unless otherwise specified in the license, anyone participating in a licensed transaction may rely on the terms of the specific license. Persons relying on a specific license obtained by another person must ensure their own compliance with all license conditions, including any recordkeeping, reporting, or expiration provisions. Therefore, since OFAC generally will not provide copies of licenses to third parties, it is critical to obtain a copy of the relevant license directly from the named licensee and to review its text, determine its scope, and understand the conditions, expiration, and other requirements of the license. OFAC often issues specific licenses for a transaction "as described in the application"; in such cases, obtaining the application is also critical to a person's ability to reasonably rely on the OFAC license.

OFAC generally grants or denies license requests within two to three months, though some specific license requests take significantly longer. There is no deadline for OFAC to take action on a license request. OFAC's current practice is to include an expiration date in any specific license, which is typically one to two years from the date of issuance but may be much shorter. OFAC may be responsive to a request for a period required to accomplish the licensed transactions.

1.7 COMPLIANCE PROGRAM DEVELOPMENT

Compliance programs must be easy to understand, implement, and enforce. With regard to U.S. economic sanctions, effective compliance programs must look across the various economic sanctions programs, identify common principles and find synergies for efficient training and implementation. As the first step in implementing a compliance program, a company must conduct a risk assessment of its lines of business to identify their relative exposure to economic sanctions risks. A company then must develop and prioritize appropriate internal controls and determine what resources are needed for their implementation and continued operation. In general, compliance controls should seek to establish procedures or policies that will impact behavior, and the adequacy of compliance resources often dictates whether these controls will be effective.

(a) Compliance Controls

Compliance controls are tools used to regulate behavior, typically either through policies identifying behavior that is prohibited or through procedures that affirmatively define required behavior. To be effective, compliance policies must (a) prioritize compliance risks based on the business lines involved, (b) be easily understood and applied, (c) identify their scope of application, and (d) provide sufficient consequences and penalties for noncompliance.

In every case, compliance will depend on a company's ability to effectively identify and address those risks that uniquely result from its management structure, business partners, and business activities. Therefore, before a company designs and implements an economic sanctions compliance program, it should conduct a risk assessment. At present, OFAC has not issued any official guidance about the risk assessment process that nonfinancial companies should use.

However, with respect to regulated financial institutions, the Federal Financial Institutions Examination Council (FFIEC) has issued the *Bank Secrecy Act/Anti-Money Laundering Examination Manual* (last updated in April 2010).[36] This manual covers OFAC compliance programs for banks under the risk-based approach adopted by OFAC in 2006 and later affirmed in OFAC's Economic Sanctions Enforcement Guidelines.[37] OFAC worked extensively with the Council to draft these audit examination standards for the OFAC compliance programs of banks. The examination manual states:

> While not required by specific regulation, but as a matter of sound banking practice and in order to ensure compliance, banks should establish and maintain an effective, written OFAC compliance program commensurate with their OFAC risk profile (based on products, services, customers and geographic locations). The program should identify higher-risk areas, provide for appropriate internal controls for screening and reporting, establish independent testing for compliance, designate a bank employee or employees as responsible for OFAC compliance and create training programs for appropriate personnel in all relevant areas of the bank. A bank's OFAC compliance program should be commensurate with its respective OFAC risk profile. A fundamental element of a sound OFAC compliance program is the bank's assessment of its specific product lines, customer base and nature of transactions and identification of higher-risk areas for OFAC transactions.[38]

Although only applicable to financial institutions subject to FFIEC examination, the guidance contained in the manual is instructive for any company seeking to implement an effective economic sanctions compliance program.

Following a risk assessment and prioritization, a U.S. economic sanctions compliance program must establish internal policies that formally prohibit actions by

---

36. The examination manual is available online at http://www.ffiec.gov/bsa_aml_infobase/pages_manual/manual_online.htm.
37. 31 C.F.R. pt. 501, app. A.
38. *Id.* at 150–151.

its employees that may violate U.S. economic sanctions. Furthermore, it also must establish specialized procedures to address areas that present a high risk for noncompliance, such as circumstances that present an elevated risk of facilitation. In an international company, as previously discussed, areas presenting a high risk of prohibited facilitation often result from the company's corporate and management structure as well as its provision of consolidated support functions, including human resources, information technology, and financial administration. International companies should carefully evaluate their business structures and activities to avoid violations in these situations. For example, any proposed changes to the U.S. corporate or management structure that would reduce U.S. oversight over non-U.S. subsidiaries' or affiliates' activities in targeted countries must be carefully scrutinized to identify any compliance risks arising from the prohibitions on facilitation and evasion.

Externally, a company's compliance policies should attempt to encourage compliant behavior by its agents, customers, and vendors, in a manner that causes the least disruption to its business activities. For example, a company's compliance controls might include a company-wide policy requiring that vendor contracts prohibit vendors from selling or transferring products of Cuban origin to the company's facilities in the United States in violation of the U.S. prohibition on the importation of goods of Cuban origin.

(b) Resources

For a compliance program to be effective, adequate resources must be easily identifiable and available to business managers. In general, there are three types of resources that contribute to the success of a U.S. economic sanctions compliance program: automation, information, and personnel.

Most compliance programs require some form of screening, which is a function that is most efficiently undertaken by automated, electronic methods. In the context of U.S. economic sanctions, screening for persons that are included on the SDN List should be completed using one of the various commercially available interdiction software programs designed for that purpose. Often, these interdiction software programs can be effectively integrated into a company's information technology systems.

To comply with U.S. economic sanctions, a business manager must have access to compliance information. Therefore, a compliance program for U.S. economic sanctions, like all other compliance programs, must deliver this information through compliance manuals, compliance training, e-mail distributions, intranet postings, the availability of compliance advisors, and other means.

Finally and most important, adequate personnel must be dedicated to a U.S. economic sanctions compliance program for proper implementation, oversight, and enforcement. Of equal importance, at least some of these compliance personnel must be given sufficiently broad authority both over entities and personnel who must comply with U.S. economic sanctions and over entities and personnel who are not subject to U.S. jurisdiction. This broad compliance authority is required to address the risks that non-U.S. business units and personnel can create for U.S. persons, particularly with regard to the prohibitions on facilitation and the exportation or reexportation of services.

(c) Special Compliance Program Considerations for Non-U.S. Persons

For a non-U.S. person, the most cautious approach for avoiding potential liability with respect to U.S. economic sanctions is to follow procedures ensuring that (1) transactions that might violate U.S. economic sanctions are not introduced into the United States and (2) appropriate information and instructions indicating any relevant authorization or exemption accompany permissible remittance or licensed financial transactions.

Most U.S. financial institutions utilize computerized OFAC screening programs for their automated funds transfers. Therefore, non-U.S. persons initiating bank transfers authorized by OFAC through the U.S. financial system should always include the license number in the transfer instructions (i.e., the program identifier and number of a specific license, the citation of the applicable general license in the OFAC regulations, or the program and number of an uncodified general license found on OFAC's website). Thus, if a transaction is handled manually after being stopped by a computer filter, the U.S. financial institution's compliance officer can verify whether the transaction is authorized. This verification may require the compliance officer to consult with the license holder and/or staff from OFAC's Sanctions Compliance & Evaluation Division or Licensing Division.

In handling nonfinancial transactions for U.S. persons, a non-U.S. person should be alert to indications that its services are being used to intentionally violate U.S. economic sanctions. Even if a non-U.S. person is beyond the jurisdictional reach of U.S. economic sanctions, a non-U.S. company and its U.S. affiliates can suffer reputational harm in the United States if any one of them is viewed as assisting in or causing a U.S. person's violation of U.S. economic sanctions. OFAC and/or the U.S. Department of Justice could potentially assert "long-arm" jurisdiction if intentional economic sanctions violations result from a non-U.S. company's collusion with a U.S. person.

1.8 VOLUNTARY SELF-DISCLOSURES, ENFORCEMENT, AND PENALTIES

When a compliance program fails to prevent a violation of U.S. economic sanctions, a company or an individual must decide whether to disclose the violation to OFAC. While circumstances may exist where a person may choose not to self-disclose, OFAC considers voluntary self-disclosures as a strong mitigating factor. Penalties are often significantly lower in enforcement actions where voluntary self-disclosures occur.

(a) Voluntary Self-Disclosures

Potential violations of U.S. economic sanctions can be discovered independently by a person subject to U.S. economic sanctions or may be brought to attention by a third party. Upon that discovery, the potential violator may have the option to file a self-disclosure concerning the potential violation (and, if a pattern is discovered, others like or related to it) to minimize exposure to OFAC enforcement measures. Pursuant to OFAC's Economic Sanctions Enforcement Guidelines, the potential civil penalty amount from the voluntary portion of a self-disclosure will be reduced by 50 percent.[39]

OFAC's determination of the self-disclosure as "voluntary" depends largely on two factors. A self-disclosure is likely to be deemed voluntary if the disclosed information would not have otherwise been available to OFAC and if no other person had an obligation to report the information to OFAC. OFAC will not view a self-disclosure as voluntary if a mandatory report is required of, and is ultimately made by, another participant in a transaction (such as an intermediary bank in a funds transfer). Nevertheless, even in such cases, strong cooperation with OFAC may lead to very substantial (20–40 percent) mitigation of the base amount of a penalty, pursuant to OFAC's Economic Sanctions Enforcement Guidelines.[40]

Though OFAC does not prescribe the format for voluntary self-disclosures, a voluntary self-disclosure should provide OFAC the facts and context of a potential violation, including the parties and transactions involved, and the results of the transaction. When a determination is made to file a voluntary self-disclosure and an internal investigation will be required, it is generally advisable to notify OFAC of the potential violation as soon as it is discovered; this can be done through an abbreviated initial filing that identifies the potential violation and states that further information will be submitted in the future. This avoids the possibility that OFAC or a third-party participant in the transaction will become aware of the issue and report it first, which could potentially destroy the "voluntary" nature of the self-disclosure and resulting mitigation. If an abbreviated initial filing is submitted, OFAC requires that a final report containing full details required for the case's adjudication be submitted within "a reasonable time."[41] This time period depends on the circumstances; however, many practitioners apply a rule of thumb of sixty to ninety days after the initial filing, absent special circumstances (which should be discussed on a continuing basis with the OFAC case agent). If the disclosing party is engaged in business where it is required to certify to potential customers that it has had no allegations or findings of legal violations, it may be helpful to request that no pre-penalty notice be issued and that settlement negotiations commence immediately. If a settlement is reached under this approach, OFAC's settlement agreement and website publicity will indicate no

---

39. *See* Base Penalty Matrix at 31 C.F.R. pt. 501, app. A(V)(B)(2)(a).
40. 31 C.F.R. pt. 501, app. A(V)(B)(2)(b)(1).
41. *Id.* at app. A(I)(I).

allegation or finding of violations and will speak in neutral terms of "apparent violations" (meaning "actual or possible") rather than "alleged violations" (meaning "alleged by OFAC").[42]

(b) Enforcement

An enforcement case for violations of U.S. economic sanctions may be triggered by a self-disclosure by a potential violator, by a report from a third party (private, state, federal, or foreign), or by the U.S. government's own investigation. Federal criminal prosecutions for violations of U.S. economic sanctions are handled by the U.S. Department of Justice. However, OFAC's Economic Sanctions Enforcement Guidelines establish the procedures and concepts applicable to enforcement matters handled by OFAC. These guidelines provide a number of "general factors" used by OFAC to determine the gravity of a violation, including whether it is an "egregious case" deserving the maximum civil penalty available. The general factors also suggest certain mitigating or aggravating circumstances that OFAC will consider.

Where no self-disclosure has been received, an OFAC enforcement action typically starts with an administrative subpoena (also called a "602 request" from its regulatory citation, 31 C.F.R. § 501.602). A 602 request requires the recipient to provide a report with information and documents about a specific transaction or series of transactions. The subpoena specifies the scope of information that the report should contain, the documents that must be submitted, and the time period for response. Although it is very rarely exercised, OFAC also has the authority to require the recipient of the 602 request, also known as the respondent, to be present at a hearing.

If the respondent fails to answer or to cooperate in the investigation by OFAC's Sanctions Compliance & Evaluation Division (for financial institution respondents) or its Enforcement Division (for other respondents), OFAC may send a pre-penalty notice to the respondent. The pre-penalty notice states the alleged violations (which may include failure to respond to a 602 request), the relevant general factors, the maximum penalty to which the respondent could be subjected, the civil penalty proposed for the respondent (based on the information then currently known to OFAC), and the deadline for a required response. The respondent may then respond to the pre-penalty notice's elements and furnish relevant documents to support its assertions before that deadline. For potential violations of IEEPA-based economic sanctions programs, the response will be due in thirty days. For violations of the TWEA-based program against Cuba, the response will be due in sixty days. (Either period may be extended for good cause.) The respondent can also contact OFAC to request that negotiations toward settlement of the allegations in the pre-penalty notice commence and that no final penalty notice be issued while those negotiations are continuing.

---

42. *See* the definition of "apparent violation" at 31 C.F.R. pt. 501, app. A(I)(A).

If OFAC does not receive a timely response to a pre-penalty notice from the respondent, OFAC will likely issue a final penalty notice requiring payment of the penalty amount proposed in the pre-penalty notice. For cases involving a violation of an IEEPA-based economic sanctions program, this final agency action triggers the right to appeal to the appropriate federal district court to challenge OFAC's determination. A request to OFAC for reconsideration is also possible. For violations of the TWEA-based program against Cuba, a respondent has a right to appeal to an administrative law judge, but the determination of that administrative law judge can be overturned by a non-OFAC Treasury Department official. The decision of that Treasury Department official constitutes a final agency action, which may be appealed to a federal district court.

(c) Penalties and Non-Penalty Outcomes

Violations of U.S. economic sanctions are resolved through a combination of civil and criminal enforcement tools. On the civil side, OFAC's enforcement authority consists of the right to levy civil monetary penalties under the President's statutory authority to impose economic sanctions. This authority is found in IEEPA, TWEA, and special purpose economic sanctions statutes, such as the Foreign Narcotics Kingpin Designation Act (Kingpin Act).[43, 44] Maximum civil penalties vary widely. For the Cuba program under TWEA, the maximum penalty per violation is $65,000 plus inflation adjustments.[45] For IEEPA programs, the maximum penalty per violation is the greater of $250,000 or twice the value of the violative transaction plus potential inflation adjustments.[46] Under the Kingpin Act, the maximum penalty is $1,075,000 plus inflation adjustments.[47]

Additionally, the U.S. Department of Justice can initiate its own investigations and criminal prosecutions for violations of U.S. economic sanctions. Furthermore, OFAC and the other federal agencies with enforcement responsibility for violations of OFAC economic sanctions (such as the Department of Homeland Security's U.S. Customs and Border Protection, the Federal Bureau of Investigation, and the Department of Commerce's Office of Export Enforcement) can refer serious cases to the U.S. Department of Justice. As part of the adoption of the Comprehensive Iran Sanctions, Accountability, and Divestment Act (CISADA), the criminal penalties for most U.S. economic sanctions violations were made uniform and now result in fines of up

---

43. 21 U.S.C. §§ 1901–1908.
44. The UNPA provides only for criminal penalties.
45. *See* 50 U.S.C. app. § 16(b) *as modified in accordance with* Pub. L. No. 101-410 (1990), 28 U.S.C. § 2461 note; reflected in 31 C.F.R. § 501.701.
46. *See* 50 U.S.C. § 1705 *as modified in accordance with* Pub. L. No. 101-410 (1990), 28 U.S.C. § 2461 note; typically reflected in section 701 of each set of IEEPA-based sanctions regulations, *see, e.g.,* Iran penalties at 31 C.F.R. § 560.701.
47. *See* 21 U.S.C. § 1906(b) *as modified in accordance with* Pub. L. No. 101-410 (1990), 28 U.S.C. § 2461 note; reflected in 31 C.F.R. § 598.701.

to $1 million and/or twenty years of imprisonment. (Maximum Kingpin Act fines are up to $10 million and/or thirty years of imprisonment.) Moreover, criminal prosecutions may result in the forfeiture of property involved in a violation.

Frequently, however, enforcement cases are resolved through the respondent's negotiation of a settlement with OFAC. These settlements can result in the payment of a settlement amount without a finding or admission of a violation. Other possible outcomes established in OFAC's enforcement guidelines include taking no action, cautionary letters warning the respondent to be more vigilant, a formal finding of a violation, or other administrative actions (such as a cease and desist order issued by OFAC or a denial, suspension, modification, or revocation of an OFAC license).

1.9 CONFLICTS WITH NON-U.S. LAWS

As discussed in greater detail in chapters 7 and 10, compliance with U.S. economic sanctions outside the United States may violate local non-U.S. laws in certain cases. These conflicting non-U.S. laws may prohibit discrimination based on nationality or prohibit the application of extraterritorial laws if they contravene domestic public policy. They also may specifically identify and prohibit compliance with particular U.S. economic sanctions laws and regulations.

These conflicts of law issues can be particularly problematic. The fact that compliance with U.S. economic sanctions may violate an applicable non-U.S. law does not, however, excuse noncompliance under U.S. law. The preamble to OFAC's Economic Sanctions Enforcement Guidelines states:

> OFAC does not agree that the permissibility of conduct under the applicable laws of another jurisdiction should be a factor in assessing an apparent violation of U.S. laws. In cases where the applicable laws of another jurisdiction require conduct prohibited by OFAC economic sanctions (or vice versa), OFAC will consider the conflict under [a general factor], which provides for the consideration of relevant factors on a case-by-case basis. OFAC notes that Subject Persons can seek a license from OFAC to engage in otherwise prohibited transactions and that the absence of such a license request will be considered in assessing an apparent violation where conflict of laws is raised by the Subject Person.[48]

While potentially applicable to any U.S. economic sanctions program, conflicts of law issues are particularly common in connection with the Cuban Assets Control Regulations because of their explicit requirement for extraterritorial compliance by non-U.S. subsidiaries of U.S. firms. These regulations prohibit non-U.S. branches and subsidiaries of U.S. firms from trading with Cuba and, more troublesome, from providing services to or otherwise engaging in transactions with Cuban emigrants liv-

---

48. 74 Fed. Reg. 57,593, 57,599 (Nov. 9, 2009).

ing within the territory of a third country (i.e., other than Cuba or the United States) unless (1) the emigrants have obtained an OFAC-specific license unblocking their property or (2) the foreign subsidiary or branch acts under authorization from OFAC to serve such customers. Compliance with these U.S. prohibitions often violates that third country's antidiscrimination laws and trade policies. This extraterritorial assertion of jurisdiction by the United States has led members of the European Union, Canada, and Mexico to adopt measures that prohibit compliance with U.S. economic sanctions against Cuba. Through the European Union's Council Regulation (EC) No. 2271/96, Canada's Foreign Extraterritorial Measures Act (FEMA), Mexico's Law of Protection of Commerce and Investments from Foreign Policies that Contravene International Law (Antidote Law), and other related laws and implementing orders, these governments have made it unlawful for persons in their territories to comply with certain aspects of the U.S. economic sanctions against Cuba. FEMA, the Antidote Law, and, to a lesser extent, Council Regulation (EC) No. 2271/96 require domestic government notification under certain circumstances (such as requests for cooperation with U.S. government investigations or requests by a U.S. parent company that the non-U.S. subsidiary comply with U.S. economic sanctions against Cuba).

While there is no fully effective resolution of these conflicts of law issues for multinational companies, more palatable solutions are generally customized and unique to the specific circumstances under which the conflicts arise. OFAC is generally unwilling to license outright compliance with such conflicting non-U.S. laws for persons subject to U.S. jurisdiction. In the case of financial institutions, specific licenses have been issued to allow non-U.S. branches and subsidiaries of U.S. firms to provide services to individuals fitting the very broad definition of *Cuban national* upon receipt of two pieces of non-U.S. government-issued identification that demonstrate at least two years of residence in the particular country outside Cuba. In all cases, U.S. persons attempting to resolve these conflicts of law must exercise care to avoid violating the prohibition on facilitation by changing policies or practices to permit non-U.S. persons to engage in activities in which a U.S. person cannot directly participate because of the prohibitions of U.S. economic sanctions.

International Traffic in Arms Regulations

Geoffrey M. Goodale[1]

2.1 OVERVIEW

This chapter provides an overview of the defense trade controls that are enumerated under the Arms Export Control Act ("AECA")[2] and implemented pursuant to the International Traffic in Arms Regulatutions ("ITAR").[3]

What is Regulated: Temporary and permanent exports, as well as temporary imports, of defense articles identified on the U.S. Munitions List ("USML") set forth under Section 121.2 of the ITAR and defense services relating to defense articles.[4] Brokering of defense articles and services is also covered. Section 2.3 below provides additional details.

Where to Find the Regulations: Pursuant to Section 38 of the AECA, and in accordance with Executive order 11958, as amendend, the ITAR have been developed to implement the requirements of the AECA. The ITAR are contained in parts 120 through 130 of chapter 22 of the Code of Federal Regulations.

Who is the Regulator: The ITAR are administered by the U.S. Department of State, Directorate of Defense Trade Controls ("DDTC"). Section 2.3 below provides additional details.

How to Get a License: Most applications for licenses and other forms of authorization are filed electronically on DDTC's website,using the Dtrade system: http://www.pmddtc.state.gov/dtrade/index.html. The website has a handy guide called "Getting Started with DTrade."

---

1. This chapter was authored by Geoffrey M. Goodale. Mr. Goodale, Managing Member of Trade Law Advisors PLLC, focuses his practice on export controls, economic sanctions, cybersecurity, import compliance, intellectual property rights, international trade and investment, and the Foeign Corrupt Practices Act. The author wishes to express his thanks to Kay Georgi, a Partner at Arent Fox LLP, for her thoughtful comments and contributions to this chapter.
2. The Arms Export Controls Act of 1976, as amended ("AECA"), is the primary statutory authority for the ITAR. *See* 22 U.S.C. § 2778.
3. The ITAR are set forth at 22 C.F.R. Parts 120-130.
4. Defense articles include both physical items specified under the USML, including end-items, parts, components, and accessories and attachments, as well as technical data (*i.e.,* information, other than software as defined under Section 120.110(a)(4) of the ITAR) required for the design, development, production, manufacture, assembly, operation, repair, testing, maintenance, or modification of such physical items. 22 C.F.R. § 120.6. Defense services are defined to mean the furnishing of assistance or training related to defense articles by a U.S. person to a foreign person. Providing ITAR-controlled technical data to a foreign person also constitutes furnishing a defense service, as does any military training of foreign persons. 22 C.F.R. § 120.9.

Key Website: http://www.pmddtc.state.gov/index.html

The U.S. Government has long sought to prevent foreign entities from obtaining access to items or technology that could harm U.S. national security. Beginning in the 1930s, Congress and the President focused on achieving this objective through the passage of legislation that placed significant restrictions on the export of defense-related items and technology.

Initially, Congress passed the Neutrality Act of 1935, pursuant to which the Secretary of State was authorized to establish an Office of Munitions Controls that was tasked with registering and issuing licenses to all U.S. entities engaged in defense-related trade.[5] Congress subsequently expanded the U.S. Department of State's role in defense-related exports through the passage of the Mutual Security Act of 1954, the Foreign Military Sales Act of 1968, and the Arms Export Control Act of 1976. To begin with, the Mutual Security Act of 1954 empowered the President to "designate those articles which shall be considered as arms, ammunition, and implements of war" for purposes of controlling the commercial export of such items, which authority the President then delegated to the Secretary of State.[6] Next, the Foreign Military Sales Act of 1968 required, among other things, that the Secretary of State report on all exports "of significant defense articles on the United States munitions list," including those relating to "defense articles and defense services."[7] The Arms Export Control Act of 1976 (AECA),[8] which continues to serve as the primary statutory underpinning for U.S. defense export controls, then was passed to authorize the President to "designate those items which shall be considered as defense articles and defense services . . . and to promulgate regulations for the import and export of such articles and services," with the items so designated "constitut[ing] the United States Munitions List," which authority the President subsequently delegated to the Secretary of State pursuant to Executive Order 11958 of January 18, 1977.[9] In accordance with mandate of the AECA and Executive Order 11958, the U.S. Department of State promulgated the International Traffic in Arms Regulations ("ITAR").[10]

2.2 ADMINISTRATION AND ENFORCEMENT OF THE ITAR

The ITAR are principally administered and enforced by the U.S. Department of State's Directorate of Defense Trade Controls ("DDTC"). Within DDTC, there are four offices with different responsibilities:

---

5. Neutrality Act of 1935, 49 Stat. 108.
6. Mutual Security Act, 68 Stat. 832, 848.
7. Foreign Military Sales Act of 1968, 82 Stat. 1320, 1322-25.
8. Arms Export Control Act of 1976 (AECA), 90 Stat. 744 (codified at 22 U.S.C. § 2778).
9. 42 Fed. Reg. 4311 (Jan. 7, 1977).
10. The International Traffic in Arms Regulations (ITAR) are codified at 22 C.F.R. Parts 120-130.

(1) the Office of Defense Trade Controls Management, which has responsibilities related to the management of defense trade controls operations, including the exercise of general authorities set forth in Part 120 of the ITAR, and the design, development, and refinement of processes, activities, and functional tools for the export licensing regime and to effect export compliance and enforcement activities;

(2) the Office of Defense Trade Controls Licensing, which is responsible for reviewing and adjudicating export applications to ensure compliance with the ITAR and taking into consideration national security and foreign policy concerns, as well as for providing licensing-related guidance and information to the trade community;

(3) the Office of Defense Trade Controls Policy, which has responsibilities related to the general policies of defense trade, including issues referenced under Part 120 and Part 126 of the ITAR and the commodity jurisdiction procedures enumerated under the ITAR; and

(4) the Office of Defense Trade Controls Compliance, which has responsibilities related to violations of law or regulation and compliance therewith, including references contained in Parts 122, 126, 127, 128 and 130 of the ITAR and that portion under Part 129 of the ITAR pertaining to brokering.[11]

Useful information about DDTC's policies and procedures can be accessed at http://www.pmddtc.state.gov/index.html.

With respect to enforcement of the ITAR, DDTC also receives assistance from two agencies within the U.S. Department of Homeland Security: (1) U.S. Customs and Border Protection ("CBP"); and (2) U.S. Immigration and Customs Enforcement ("ICE"), both of which have the authority to investigate, detain, or seize any export or attempted export of ITAR-controlled defense articles or technical data.[12] DDTC also receives enforcement assistance from the Federal Bureau of Investigation ("FBI"), and in cases involving classified technical data or defense articles, advisory assistance from the U.S. Department of Defense's Defense Security Service ("DSS").[13]

2.3 SCOPE OF THE ITAR

The ITAR govern temporary and permanent exports of defense articles and defense services, as well as temporary imports of such items.[14] In order to understand how

---

11. *See* 22 C.F.R. § 120.1.
12. 22 C.F.R. § 127.4.
13. 22 C.F.R. § 127.5.
14. 22 C.F.R. Part 120. Temporary and permanent exports of defense articles and defense services are controlled by the ITAR. In addition, the ITAR govern temporary imports of defense articles and defense services. Permanent imports are regulated by the Attorney General under the direction of the U.S. Department of Justice's Bureau of Alcohol, Tobacco, Firearms, and Explosives (*see* 27 C.F.R. Parts 447, 478, 479, and 555).

broad the scope of the ITAR is, it is necessary to review how certain key terms are defined.

Under the ITAR, a "defense article" is defined to include any item designated on the United States Munitions List ("USML").[15] In addition, any item that is not specifically enumerated on the USML, but which has a substantial military utility and has been specifically designed or modified for military purposes, may be designated as a defense article by DDTC.[16]

The term "defense article" is defined to include "technical data" specified on the USML.[17] Technical data includes information that is required for the design, development, production, manufacture, assembly, operation, repair, testing, maintenance, or modification of defense articles and may take the form of blueprints, plans, diagrams, engineering designs, drawings, photographs, and instructions, among other things.[18] In addition, technical data includes:

- classified information relating to defense articles and defense services;
- information covered by an invention secrecy order; and
- software, as defined under Section 121.8(f) of the ITAR, directly related to defense articles (including, but not limited to, system functional design, logic flow, algorithms, application programs, operating systems, and support software for design, implementation, test, operation, diagnosis, and repair).[19]

However, technical data does not include information concerning: general scientific, mathematical or engineering principles commonly taught in schools; basic marketing information on function or purposes or general system descriptions of defense articles; or information in the public domain, as defined in Section 120.11 of the ITAR (*e.g.*, information which is published and which is generally accessible or available to the public through various means, such as through sale at newsstands or bookstores, through publicly available patents, through unlimited distribution at conferences or meetings, and at libraries open to the public).[20] It also does not include technical data approved for public release by the cognizant government agency provided it is subsequently placed in the public domain.[21]

---

15.   22 C.F.R. § 120.6.
16.   *Id. See also* 22 C.F.R. § 120.3.
17.   *Id.*
18.   22 C.F.R. § 120.10.
19.   *Id.*
20.   *Id.*
21.   The cognizant agency is DoD Office of Security Review, 1155 Defense Pentagon, Washington, DC 20301-1155. See 32 CFR Part 250 and DoD Instruction 5230.29, Security and Policy Review of DoD Information for Public Release (Jan. 8, 2009), http://www.dtic.mil/whs/directives/corres/pdf/523029p.pdf. The Office of Security Review's website contains useful guides for submitting documents for review for public release. See http://www.dtic.mil/whs/esd/osr/ .

Exports of "defense services" also are controlled under the ITAR. A "defense service" is defined as "[t]he furnishing of assistance (including training) to foreign persons, whether in the United States or abroad in the design, development, engineering, manufacture, repair, maintenance, modification, operation, demilitarization, destruction, processing or use of defense articles."[22] In addition, a "defense service" includes the furnishing to foreign persons of any technical data controlled under the ITAR, whether in the United States or abroad, as well as military training of foreign units and forces, regular and irregular, including formal or informal instruction of foreign persons in the United States or abroad.[23] The concept of a "defense service" is not limited to providing ITAR-controlled technical data. If the assistance or training is limited to providing publicly available information, under DDTC's current interpretation of the current definition of defense service, its delivery still constitutes a "defense service" if the purpose of that information is to support the use of defense articles or to train military units.

Under the ITAR, the term "export" is defined to include:

(1) sending or taking a defense article out of the United States in any manner, except by mere travel outside of the United States by a person whose personal knowledge includes technical data;

(2) transferring registration, control or ownership to a foreign person of any aircraft, vessel, or satellite covered by the USML, whether in the United States or abroad;

(3) the United States any defense article to an embassy or any agency of subdivision of a foreign government (*e.g.*, diplomatic mission);

(4) disclosing (orally or visually) or transferring technical data to a foreign person, whether in the United States or abroad, or

(5) performing a defense service on behalf of, or for the benefit of, a foreign person, whether in the United States or abroad.[24]

As can be seen from this broad definition, an export can occur in numerous ways. Significantly, for example, this means if technical data is provided or transferred to a foreign person, including an employee of the company, the information is deemed to have been exported to that person's home country.

The distinction between "U.S. persons" and "foreign persons" is critical under the ITAR. Generally, in the absence of an exemption enumerated under the ITAR, specific authorization from DDTC is required for "U.S. persons" to export ITAR-controlled items and technical data to "foreign persons" or for "foreign persons" to

---

22.   22 C.F.R. § 120.9.
23.   *Id.*
24.   22 C.F.R. § 120.17.

re-export or transfer such items to other "foreign persons." The term "U.S. person" includes: (1) U.S. citizens; (2) lawful permanent residents; (3) protected individuals, as defined by 8 U.S.C. § 1324b(a)(3); (4) any corporation, society, or other entity or group that is incorporated or organized to do business in the United States; and (5) any federal, state, or local government entity in the United States.[25] As such, permanent resident aliens (*i.e.*, green card holders) and persons granted political asylum, under certain circumstances, are treated as U.S. persons. Thus, dual nationals who are also citizens of the United States, and non-U.S. citizens who hold U.S. green cards are U.S. persons for purposes of the ITAR.

The definition of a "foreign person" is anyone who is not a U.S. person.[26] This includes any person who is not a citizen, a lawful permanent resident, or a "protected person" of the United States, any foreign corporation or other entity that is not incorporated or organized to do business in the United States, and any foreign government.[27] Thus, persons who are in the United States under various kinds of visas (*e.g.*, H-1B, L-1, and F-1 visas) are considered foreign persons. In addition, care must be taken to consider dual nationals as well. Under DDTC's interpretation, if they are not U.S. persons, foreign persons can be citizens of more than one country, and DDTC considers country of birth, even in cases where a person does not hold a passport from his country of birth, in addition to countries of subsequent citizenship, as factors in determining the nationality of the foreign persons. When a U.S. company employs a foreign person, the U.S. company is obligated to ensure its compliance with U.S. export control laws and regulations, including the ITAR, with respect to that employee. This means, among other things, that a U.S. company generally would be required to obtain authorization from DDTC before a foreign person employee could be granted access to ITAR-controlled items and technical data regardless of whether that employee is located in the United States.

2.4 DETERMINING WHAT IS SUBJECT TO THE ITAR

As the discussion above indicates, it is critical to understand when an item is subject to the ITAR. The first step in evaluating whether an item is subject to the ITAR is to determine whether the item is identified on the USML. The USML includes the following categories:

Category I:	Firearms, Close Assault Weapons, and Combat Shotguns
Category II:	Guns and Armament
Category III:	Ammunition/Ordnance

---

25.   22 C.F.R. § 120.15.
26.   22 C.F.R. § 120.16.
27.   *Id.*

Category IV:	Launch Vehicles, Guided Missiles, Ballistic Missiles, Rockets, Torpedoes, Bombs, and Mines
Category V:	Explosives and Energetic Materials, Propellants, Incendiary Agents and Their Constituents
Category VI:	Vessels of War and Special Naval Equipment
Category VII:	Tanks and Military Vehicles
Category VIII:	Aircraft and Associated Equipment
Category IX:	Military Training Equipment
Category X:	Protective Personnel Equipment
Category XI:	Military Electronics
Category XII:	Fire Control, Range Finder, Optical and Guidance and Control Equipment
Category XIII:	Auxiliary Military Equipment
Category XIV:	Toxicological Agents, Including Chemical Agents, Biological Agents, and Associated Equipment
Category XV:	Spacecraft Systems and Associated Equipment
Category XVI:	Nuclear Weapons, Design and Testing Related Items
Category XVII:	Classified Articles, Technical Data, and Defense Services Not Otherwise Enumerated
Category XVIII:	Directed Energy Weapons
Category XIX:	[Reserved]
Category XX:	Submersible Vessels, Oceanographic and Associated Equipment
Category XXI:	Miscellaneous Articles[28]

The USML lists "end-items," "components," "accessories and attachments," and "parts," and definitions of these terms are provided under Section 121.8 of the ITAR.[29] Items on the USML that are deemed to be "Significant Military Equipment" (SME) are preceded by an asterisk, and it should further be noted that technical data directly related to the manufacture or production of any defense articles identified as SME shall themselves be designated as SME.[30] Moreover, following the USML itself, there are a number of "interpretations" set forth under the remaining Sections of Part 121 of the ITAR, which often clarify or amplify the items on the USML.[31]

Significantly, Category XXI is broadly defined to include "[a]ny article not specifically enumerated in the other categories of the U.S. Munitions List which has substantial military applicability and which has been specifically designed, devel-

---

28. 22 C.F.R. § 121.1.
29. 22 C.F.R. § 121.8.
30. 22 C.F.R. § 121.1(b).
31. 22 C.F.R. §§ 121.2-121.16.

oped, configured, adapted, or modified for military purposes" and "technical data (as defined in § 1201.10 of this subchapter) and defense services (as defined in § 120.9 of this subchapter) directly related to [such] defense articles."[32]

The decision as to whether any article or service should be included on the USML ultimately rests with DDTC.[33] In making such decisions, DDTC will determine that an item or service should be designated as a defense article or a defense service if it:

(1) is specifically designed, developed, configured, adapted, or modified for a military application; and

(2) does not have predominant civil applications; and

(3) does not have performance equivalent (defined by form, fit and function) to those of an article or service used for civil applications.[34]

DDTC also will determine that an item is ITAR-controlled if it is specifically designed, developed, configured, adapted or modified for a military application, and has significant military or intelligence applicability such that control under the ITAR is necessary.[35]

Significantly, in accordance with the Obama Administration's goal of reforming U.S. export controls to simply and clarify them and make them less onerous, DDTC and the Department of Commerce Bureau of Industry and Security ("BIS") have published several proposed rules that seek to revise the USML in major ways beginning in early December 2010. Pursuant to one of the first notices, which was published in December 2012, DDTC issued a proposed rule that would dramatically revise Category VII (Tanks and Other Military Vehicles), which, if enacted, is projected to reduce the number of items currently requiring export licenses by 74 percent due to the elimination of many lower-level parts and components from the scope of ITAR control.[36] In another early notice from December 2010, DDTC requested the submission of comments relating to how other USML Categories could be streamlined in a manner similar to that proposed for Category VII such that the entire USML would become a "positive list" that would specifically identify what items are controlled by different tiers and that would result in many lower-level systems, parts, and components being freed from control under the ITAR.[37] Subsequently, DDTC has published proposed rules to make significant modifications to USML Categories IV, V, VI, VII, VIII, IX, X, XI, XIII, XVI, XIX, and XX, as well as proposed amendments to the

---

32. *Id.*
33. *Id.*
34. 22 C.F.R. § 120.3(a).
35. 22 C.F.R. § 120.3(b).
36. *See* 75 Fed. Reg. 76,930 (Dec. 10, 2010).
37. *See* 75 Fed. Reg. 76,935 (Dec. 10, 2010).

definitions of "specially designed" and "equipment."[38] As of the time of this writing, no final rules have yet been published to codify any of the proposed amendments to the various USML Categories. If the necessary review by the U.S. Congress can be completed in time, such final rules may be published by mid-2013, and as such, the trade community should vigilantly monitor the *Federal Register* to see when such final rules are actually published.

On a less positive note, DDTC has historically followed a largely unwritten "see through" rule with respect to the evaluation of end-items and their individual components.[39] Under this rule, if there is even a single component subject to the ITAR, this item remains subject to the ITAR even once it is incorporated into a larger non-ITAR controlled system, thus effectively subjecting the entire end-item to ITAR-control pursuant to 22 C.F.R. § 120.3(b). One implication of this rule is that a foreign-origin end-item incorporating ITAR-controlled U.S.-origin components or U.S.-origin technology can be deemed subject to the ITAR. Another implication of this rule is that even a predominantly civil end-item can, in some circumstances, be deemed to be ITAR-controlled. In the absence of a final rule or other official guidance issued by DDTC revoking or modifying the "see through" rule, companies must operate from the presumption that the "see through" rule applies and must act accordingly.[40] This rule, more than any other, has resulted in foreign manufacturers striving to ensure that their foreign origin products are "ITAR-free" – that is, the products do not contain

---

38.   *See* 76 Fed. Reg. 68,694 (Nov. 7, 2011); 76 Fed. Reg. 76,097 (Dec. 6, 2011); 76 Fed. Reg. 76,100 (Dec. 6, 2011); 76 Fed. Reg. 80,302 (Dec. 23, 2011); 76 Fed. Reg. 80,305 (Dec. 23, 2011); 77 Fed. Reg. 25,944 (May 2, 2012); 77 Fed. Reg. 29,575 (May 18, 2012); 77 Fed. Reg. 33,698 (June 7, 2012); 77 Fed. Reg. 35,317 (June 19, 2012); 77 Fed. Reg. 36,428 (June 19, 2012); 77 Fed. Reg. 37,346 (June 21, 2012); 77 Fed. Reg. 70,958 (Nov. 28, 2012); 78 Fed. Reg. 6,269 (Jan. 30, 2013); 78 Fed. Reg. 6,765 (Jan. 31, 2013).

39.   Support in the ITAR for the "see through" rule can be found in 22 C.F.R. §§ 123.9(b) and (e), albeit in far from clear language. 22 CFR 123.9(b) requires the key export control documents contain the following destination control statement: "These commodities are authorized by the U.S. Government for export only to [country of ultimate destination] for use by [end user]. They may not be transferred, transshipped on a non-continuous voyage, or otherwise be disposed of in any other country, either in their original form or after being incorporated into other end items, without the prior written approval of the U.S. Department of State." Likewise, 22 CFR 123.9(e) provides an exemption for NATO and major non-NATO allies of reexports or retransfers of "U.S.-origin components incorporated into a foreign defense article."

40.   On March 15, 2011, DDTC published a proposed rule that would ameliorate the effects of the "see through" rule to some degree. *See* 76 Fed. Reg. 13928 (March 15, 2011). Under the proposed rule, a license from DDTC would not be required for the export or reexport of defense articles incorporated into end-items subject to the EAR when certain conditions are met (e.g., the value of the defense article is *de minimis*, at less than 1% of the end-item's value and the end-item would be rendered inoperable or benign by the removal of the defense article). *See id.* However, DDTC has not yet published a final rule on the subject, and until such time that it does, the trade community must operate from the assumption that the "see through" rule applies with full effect. Moreover, it should be noted that under the proposed rule, the end item must be "subject to the EAR," which effectively means that truly foreign origin products (which are not subject to the EAR) incorporating U.S. ITAR items would *continue* to be subject to a zero percent *de minimis* standard.

ITAR parts or components, and indeed they are using "ITAR-free" as a marketing strategy.

Given the complexities involved in determining whether an item is controlled under the ITAR when it is not specifically identified on the USML and the ramifications of the "see through" rule, companies are well advised to seek a commodity jurisdiction determination (CJ determination) from DDTC if they have any doubt as to whether an item is subject to the ITAR. CJ requests may be submitted to DDTC through an on-line application[41] using the DS-4076 Commodity Jurisdiction (CJ) Request Form with electronic attachments for other relevant data, including brochures, technical specification sheets, and other documentation that provide information relating to the history, design, development, and use of the product.[42] After a CJ request has been submitted, DDTC will consult with the U.S. Department of Commerce Bureau of Industry and Security (BIS), the U.S. Department of Defense (DOD), and other relevant U.S. Government agencies regarding the classification of the article or service, and any disputes among the agencies will be resolved in accordance with established procedures.[43] If a person in unsatisfied with a CJ determination, which often may take DDTC more than 60 days from the date of submission to provide, the person may appeal the CJ determination by submitting a written request for reconsideration to the Managing Director of DDTC, and if the person disagrees with the Managing Director's determination, which must be issued within 30 days from the date on which the request for reconsideration was filed, the person may appeal the decision through the Deputy Assistant Secretary for Defense Trade Controls to the Assistant Secretary for Political-Military Affairs.[44] It is important to note that a CJ determination stating that a product is not covered by the ITAR does not necessarily mean that it can be exported without a license, because there could be EAR licensing requirements. Fortunately, DDTC and BIS have worked together to improve their CJ determinations and now CJ determinations typically include the Export Control Classification Number (ECCN) of the item determined to be subject to the EAR.

In addition, DDTC recently began posting short summaries of their CJ rulings on the DDTC website,[45] with the result that companies seeking to understand the classification of their products can check to see the classification of other similar products. The resource is currently limited in value by its size, and also because CJ determinations can be design specific. Thus, the fact that a product is listed on the CJ web page as EAR-controlled might not be a good precedent for another company's similar

41.   This on line application system is *not* DDTC's D-Trade licensing system and does have some peculiarities. Those who have not tried to use the CJ on line system would be well advised to allot some extra time simply to getting the files in the requisite format to be able to file them successfully.

42.   For more information about how to complete an on-line DS-4076 Commodity Jurisdiction (CJ) Request Form, see http://www.pmddtc.state.gov/commodity_jurisdiction/index.html.

43.   22 C.F.R. § 120.4.

44.   *Id.*

45.   *See* http://www.pmddtc.state.gov/commodity_jurisdiction/determination.html.

product particularly if the latter had been designed for the U.S. military with defense dollars, and contained characteristics that made it militarily more significant.

2.5 REGISTRATION REQUIREMENTS

To ensure that the U.S. Government has current information regarding which entities are involved in the manufacture, export, and brokering of defense articles and services, DDTC maintains certain registration requirements. Specifically, as discussed below, subject to few exceptions, any person who engages in the United States in the business of either manufacturing or exporting of defense articles or furnishing of defense services must register with DDTC, and any person subject to U.S. jurisdiction in any location that is engaged in brokering activities is required to register with DDTC.[46]

The only entities that are exempt from the registration requirement relating to the manufacture or export of defense articles or the furnishing of defense services are:

- officers and employees of the U.S. Government acting in an official capacity;
- persons whose pertinent business activity is limited to the production of unclassified technical data only;
- persons whose manufacturing and export activities are limited exclusively to activities licensed under the Atomic Energy Act of 1954, as amended; and
- persons who engage only in the production of articles for experimental or scientific purposes, including research and development.[47]

With respect to brokering activities, the only persons that are exempt from registering with DDTC are:

- employees of the U.S. Government acting in an official capacity;
- employees of foreign governments or international organizations acting in an official capacity; and
- persons exclusively in the business of financing, transporting, or freight forwarding, whose business activities do not also including brokering defense articles or defense services.[48]

Aside from these exempt entities, any U.S. person that engages in the manufacture or export of defense articles or the furnishing of defense services and any person subject to U.S. jurisdiction that performs brokering activities must register with DDTC.

---

46. Registration requirements for manufacturers and exporters of defense articles or defense services are set for under 22 C.F.R. § 122.1; registration requirements for brokers are enumerated under 22 C.F.R. § 129.3.
47. 22 C.F.R. § 122.1(b).
48. 22 C.F.R. § 129.3.

It is important to note that manufacturers of defense articles are required to register with DDTC, even if they do not export defense articles.[49]

To register, a company must submit to DDTC a Statement of Registration (Form DS-2032), an official document evidencing that the company is authorized to do business in the United States (*e.g.*, a state incorporation certificate or state certificate of good standing), a required transmittal letter, and the applicable registration fee.[50] Pursuant to DDTC guidelines, the parent U.S. legal entity is required to register using the Form DS-2032, which must, among other things, list all wholly-owned or partially-owned subsidiaries that manufacture or export defense articles or furnish defense services and provide information relating to the company's officers and directors, and both the Form DS-2032 and the transmittal letter must be signed by a senior officer of the company.[51]

Typically, it can take DDTC four to six weeks to process a new registration submission but occasionally, particularly recently when DDTC's offices experienced a fire and a flood, the process has taken months. Once it has processed the registration submission, DDTC will issue a letter to the applicant informing it of its registration number and requesting that the applicant provide certain information to DDTC, including who the "empowered officials" will be for the applicant. Such "empowered officials" must be U.S. persons who are:

(1) directly employed by the applicant or a subsidiary in a position having authority for policy or management within the applicant's organization;

(2) legally empowered in writing by the applicant to sign license applications or other export approval requests on behalf of the applicant;

(3) understand the provisions and requirements of U.S. export control laws and regulations, including the AECA and the ITAR; and

(4) have independent authority to enquire into any aspect of a proposed export or temporary import by the applicant, verify the legality of the transaction and accuracy of the information to be submitted, and refuse to sign any license application or other approval request without prejudice or other adverse recourse.[52]

A registrant must renew its registration with DDTC on an annual basis. At least 60 days prior to the expiration date of the current registration, DDTC is supposed to send to the registrant a written notification of the fee to be paid for the registration renewal based on the tiered fee structure that is set forth in Section 122.3 of the ITAR,

---

49.   22 C.F.R. § 122.1(a).
50.   22 C.F.R. §§ 122.2-122.3.
51.   DDTC's guidance regarding preparation of registration submissions is available on DDTC's website at http://www.pmddtc.state.gov/registration/index.html.
52.   22 C.F.R. § 120.25.

which is based on the number of applications to which DDTC has responded during the 12-month period ending 90 days prior to the expiration of the current registration.[53] If a registrant believes an error has been made in calculating its fee, the registrant may submit a written request explaining the basis for the challenge to DDTC. If the registrant's registration is set to expire within 30 days, the registrant should submit the challenge to DDTC with a completed renewal registration submission with a fee of $2,250 to ensure registration does not expire while their inquiry is being resolved to comply with DDTC's registration renewal requirements.[54]

A registrant must notify DDTC of any material change to its statement of registration, such as: (1) a change in senior management; (2) the establishment, acquisition, or divestment of a subsidiary or foreign affiliate; (3) the dealing in an additional category of defense articles or services; or (4) the indictment, debarment, or denial of import-export privileges of a registrant, board member, or senior officer.[55] Registrants must provide such notifications to DDTC by registered mail within five days of the event.[56] A registrant also is required to notify DDTC by registered mail at least 60 days in advance of any intended sale or transfer of ownership or control to a foreign person.[57] In addition, when a new entity is formed when a registrant merges with another company or acquires, or is acquired by, the company must advise DDTC of: (1) the new firm name and all previous firm names being disclosed; (2) the registration number that will survive and those that are to be discontinued (if any); (3) the license numbers of all approvals on which unshipped balances will be shipped under the surviving registration number; and (4) amendments to agreements approved by DDTC to change the name of a party to those agreements.[58] Subsequently, a registrant must provide a signed copy of an amendment to each agreement signed by the new U.S. entity, the former U.S. licensor, and the foreign licensee.[59] DDTC has published guidance on its procedures for the transfer of licenses and agreements which should be followed with care.[60]

It also should be noted that registrants are required to maintain certain records concerning the manufacture, acquisition, and disposal of defense articles, technical

53. 22 C.F.R. § 122.3.
54. *See* 22 C.F.R. § 122.3(b); *see also* http://www.pmddtc.state.gov/registration/faqs_reg.html#2.
55. 22 C.F.R. § 122.4(a).
56. *Id.*
57. 22 C.F.R. § 122.4(b). For purposes of the registration change notification requirements set forth under Part 122 of the ITAR, "ownership" is defined to mean that more than 50 percent of the outstanding voting securities of the firm are owned by one or more foreign persons, and "control" exists when one or more foreign persons have the authority or ability to establish or direct the general policies or day-to-day operations of the firm. 22 C.F.R. § 122.2(c). A presumption of control arises when there is 25 percent control of voting stock and no U.S. person controls an equal or larger percentage. *Id.*
58. 22 C.F.R. § 122.4(c).
59. *Id.*
60. *See* http://www.pmddtc.state.gov/licensing/documents/gl_GCsUSu.pdf and http://www.pmddtc.state.gov/licensing/documents/gl_GCsForeign.pdf.

data, brokering activities, and the provision of defense services.[61] Registrants must store such records in a way that is highly legible and, for electronic information, in a manner that prevents alterations without a record of all changes and who made them.[62] In addition, Registrants must track information regarding political contributions, fees, and commissions, and they must keep such records for five years after the expiration of the registrant's approval.[63]

2.6 EXPORTATION OF DEFENSE ARTICLES

Registration with DDTC, in and of itself, does not confer any right to export, although it may enable the registered company to qualify for and certify ITAR exemptions that authorize particular exports. It is, however, a necessary first step, since DDTC will reject any export authorization requests prior to registration and all available license exemptions enumerated in the ITAR require that the entity seeking to utilize the exemption be registered with DDTC.[64] This is significant, because, as discussed below, every export of a defense article requires a license or other authorization unless an exemption applies.

Pursuant to Section 123.1 of the ITAR, any person who intends to export or temporarily import a defense article must obtain approval from DDTC prior to the export or the temporary import, unless the export or temporary import qualifies for an exemption specified under the ITAR.[65] The ITAR require that applications for the export or temporary import of unclassified defense articles must be made in the following manner:

(1) applications for licenses for permanent export must be made on Form DSP-5;

(2) applications for licenses for temporary export must be made on Form DSP-73; and

(3) applications for licenses for temporary import must be made on Form DSP-61.[66]

The ITAR further specify that applications for the export or temporary import of classified defense articles or classified technical data must be made on a Form DSP-85.[67] With the exception of Form DSP-85 license applications, all of the other above-referenced license applications may be submitted via DTrade (http://www.pmddtc.state.gov/dtrade/index.html), DDTC's electronic defense export licensing system. A

---

61.   22 C.F.R. § 122.5.
62.   *Id.*
63.   22 C.F.R. Part 130.
64.   22 C.F.R. §§ 120.1(c), 122.1(c), and 126.10(b).
65.   22 C.F.R. § 123.1.
66.   22 C.F.R. § 123.1(a).
67.   *Id.*

certification stating that the applicant, its Board members, and senior officers have not been indicted or convicted for violation of certain U.S. statutes and are not subject to any U.S. agency debarment order or denial of import or export privileges must accompany all application submissions.[68]

A DSP-5 application relating to a commercial sale must be accompanied by a copy of a purchase order, a letter of intent, or other appropriate documentation.[69] If the export involves articles or services valued at $500,000 or more being sold commercially to or for the use of the armed forces of a foreign country or international organization, a statement concerning the payment of political contributions, fees and commissions must accompany the export application.[70]

With respect to applications involving defense articles designated as SME or classified defense articles or services, it is important to note that the exporter is required to obtain from the foreign consignee and end-user a Non-transfer and Use Certificate (Form DSP-83), pursuant to which the foreign consignee, the end-user, and the applicant agree not to re-export such equipment outside the authorized country of destination and not to resell or otherwise dispose of the licensed item to any foreign person, except as may be authorized by DDTC.[71] In addition, DDTC may require that the applicant provide a Form DSP-83 for the export of any defense articles to any destination, and when the foreign customer is a non-governmental foreign end-user, DDTC may also require that the foreign government be a signatory to the Form DSP-83.[72]

It is important to note that it is the general policy of the U.S. Government to deny licenses and other approvals for exports and temporary imports of defense articles and defense services destined for or originating in certain countries, frequently referred to as "proscribed countries." This policy applies to all of the countries specified in Section 126.1 of the ITAR, and includes, among other countries, Belarus, Burma, China, Cuba, Democratic Republic of Congo, Eritrea, Fiji, Iraq, Iran, Ivory Coast (Cote d'Ivoire), Lebanon, Liberia, Libya, North Korea, Somalia, Sudan, Syria, and Venezuela.[73] A listing of proscribed countries and countries that are currently subject to restrictive licensing policies is available at http://www.pmddtc.state.gov/embargoed_countries/index.html.

Licenses issued by DDTC are valid for a period of four years.[74] They must be returned to DDTC at the end of the validity period or when the full authorized quantity has been exported, whichever occurs first.[75] Specific procedures for the filing of export information pertaining to licenses via the Automated Export System (AES), as

---

68.   22 C.F.R. § 123.1(c)(3); *see also* 22 C.F.R. § 126.13.
69.   22 C.F.R. § 123.1(c)(4).
70.   22 C.F.R. § 123.1(c)(6).
71.   22 C.F.R. § 123.10.
72.   *Id.*
73.   22 C.F.R. § 126.1.
74.   22 C.F.R. § 123.21.
75.   *Id.*

well as for filing, retaining, and returning licenses are set forth under Section 123.22 of the ITAR.[76]

However, Section 123.22 should be read with care, inasmuch as some of its provisions have never been put into effect. For example, DDTC had intended to set up an electronic notification process for export of technical data that was exported pursuant to license or exemption. This process has never been implemented, and instead exporters notify DDTC of the first export of technical data pursuant to DDTC agreements via a letter of notification which they can upload via DTrade.

Minor amendments to approved licenses can be sought and obtained from DDTC for small changes, such as corrections of typographical errors, a change in the source of commodity, and the addition of a U.S. freight forwarder or U.S. consignor.[77] However, requested amendments for more significant changes, such as additional quantity, changes in the kind of commodity covered, or alterations to the country of ultimate destination, end-use, end-user, or foreign consignee, and/or extension of duration will be rejected: in order for such changes to be granted, a new license must be sought and obtained from DDTC.[78]

DDTC authorization is required for any resale, transfer, transshipment, or disposal to a different end-user, end-use, or destination that is not expressly approved in the license.[79] When seeking such authorization from DDTC, the applicant must file a written submission with DDTC, called a General Correspondence (GC), that contains the following information: the license number under which the defense article was previously authorized for export from the United States; a precise description of the defense article, including quantity and value; a description of the new end-use; and identification of the new end-user.[80] Except as narrowly authorized by applicable exemptions, written authorization from DDTC must be obtained before reselling, transferring, transshipping, or disposing of a defense article in any country other than the country of ultimate destination, anyone other than the authorized end-user or anything but the authorized end-use.[81]

DSP-5 license applications are also used to export technical data since all technical data exports are considered permanent. DSP-5s can be used for:

- Marketing presentations and
- In some cases, the training of foreign persons where it would be impractical to obtain a technical assistance agreement.[82]

---

76. 22 C.F.R. § 123.22.
77. 22 C.F.R. § 123.25.
78. *Id.*
79. 22 C.F.R. § 123.9(a).
80. 22 C.F.R. § 123.9(c).
81. 22 C.F.R. § 123.9(d).
82. However, if instead of a single export of a technical document, your company needs to have a technical interchange such as a design review, an agreement such as a TAA or MLA will be required.

It also is possible to obtain a DSP-5 license to permit the transfer of controlled technical data to foreign persons that are employed by U.S. companies. The license authorizes the U.S. person to transfer technical data and perform limited defense services to the employee(s) on their products, and the license authorizes the foreign person to perform defense services on behalf of the U.S. company. The foreign person employed by a U.S. company does not have to reside in the U.S. to be considered an employee but may reside and perform the job duties outside the United States. If the foreign person is a full time regular employee, directly paid, insured, hired/fired and/or promoted exclusively by the U.S. company, the foreign person is deemed to be "employed" by the U.S. company. The U.S. company must ensure the employee's compliance with U.S. export laws and regulations regardless of where the employee currently resides. A license approved for foreign person employment is valid only for a period of four years or until expiration of their authorized stay from U.S. Department of Homeland Security ("DHS"), whichever is shorter. If the foreign person employee resides outside the United States, the license will be valid for the standard validity of a license. In instances when the authorized stay is longer than four years, or the employee's employment continues beyond the approved validity, the applicant must apply for a renewal of the license.[83]

It also should be noted that a Distribution Agreement is another vehicle through which defense articles can be exported. A Distribution Agreement is an agreement or contract to establish a warehouse or distribution point abroad for defense articles exported from the United States for subsequent distribution to entities in an approved sales territory.[84] Such agreements must be limited to unclassified defense articles, and they must contain conditions for special distribution, end-use, restrictions on re-exporting, and reporting requirements.[85]

There also are a number of exemptions set forth under the ITAR that permit unclassified defense articles to be exported without a license from DDTC. Some pertinent exemptions that are used for such purposes include:

- components or spare parts for a defense article previously exported with DDTC approval so long as the value does not exceed $500 in a single transaction;[86]
- hipments of defense articles conducted by or for use by U.S. Government agencies under specified circumstances;[87]
- unclassified components, parts, tools or test equipment exported to a subsidiary, affiliate, or facility owned or controlled by a U.S. person if the components,

83. *See* DDTC Guidance on Licensing Foreign Persons Employed by U.S. Persons (*available at* http://www.pmddtc.state.gov/licensing/guidelines_instructions.html).
84. 22 C.F.R. § 120.23.
85. *See* 22 C.F.R. Part 124.
86. 22 C.F.R. § 123.16(b)(2).
87. 22 C.F.R. §§ 126.4(a)-(c). Please use this exception with caution as it contains specific requirements that are difficult, if not impossible, to meet.

parts, tools or test equipment are to be used for manufacture, assembly, testing, production or modification subject to certain conditions;[88]

- defense articles being exported in furtherance of an approved technical assistance agreement, manufacturing License Agreement, or distribution Agreement;[89]
- unclassified defense articles exported to any public exhibition, trade show, air show or related event if the article has previously been licensed for such an event and the license is still valid;[90]
- unclassified models or mock-ups of defense articles so long as the models or mock-ups are non-operable, do not reveal controlled technical data, and do not contain USML components;[91]
- reexports and retransfers of U.S.-origin components incorporated into a foreign defense article to a government of a NATO country, or the governments of Australia or Japan to NATO, Australia or Japan;[92]
- certain items on the USML may be exported to Canada without a license when the article is for end-use in Canada by Canadian Federal or Provincial governmental authorities or by Canadian companies that are registered with the Government of Canada under the Defense Production Act, or the item will be returned to the United States;[93]
- exports of defense services for specified items controlled by Category XV(a) or (e) by accredited institutions of higher learning in direct support of fundamental research;[94] and
- temporary exports of certain firearms, ammunition, and body armor for the personal use of a U.S. citizen or permanent resident subject to safeguarding, use, recordkeeping, and other conditions.[95]

It is critical to note that there are often numerous requirements and limitations associated with each of the exemptions referenced above and not all the requirements for use of the exemptions are contained in the same provision of the ITAR as the exemption. Accordingly, companies should carefully review the requirements and limitations before seeking to use the exemptions. Although it is out of date (dating back to January 2004) and does not contain the new exemptions, and some consider it

---

88.   22 C.F.R. § 123.16(b)(9).
89.   22 C.F.R. § 123.16(b)(1). See discussion of TAAs/MLAs infra. Note this exception is of limited utility as DDTC interprets it to permit only one export of defense articles. Thus, most TAAs and MLAs envisioning the export of defense articles will require a series of accompanying DSP-5 licenses.
90.   22 C.F.R. § 123.16(b)(5).
91.   22 C.F.R. § 123.16(b)(4).
92.   22 C.F.R. § 123.9(e).
93.   22 C.F.R. § 126.5.
94.   22 C.F.R. § 125.4(d).
95.   22 C.F.R. §§ 123.17 and 126.1.

to adopt a relatively conservative reading of the exemptions, the Exemptions Handbook (a/k/a the "Pink Book") is a good resource for marshalling the various requirements for the use of exemptions.[96]

2.7 EXPORTATION OF DEFENSE SERVICES AND TECHNICAL DATA

As with the export of defense hardware, the export of defense generally require approval from DDTC, unless an exemption enumerated under the ITAR can be used. In terms of approvals, the ITAR provide for the use of certain kinds of agreements for the export of defense services and technical data. Agreements are generally used in situations in which the exporter anticipates the need for an unrestricted two-way exchange of technical data with a foreign person/entity within certain pre-determined technical parameters. The agreements are generally structured as contracts for the exchange of technical data with mutual rights and obligations based on specific required clauses that are copied directly from the ITAR. These agreements are *not* commercial contracts, and they should not contain the various standard clauses found in commercial contracts. These agreements are approved by DDTC, then signed by all parties (and submitted to DDTC), and subsequently, exports of defense services and technical data may be made pursuant to the agreement without individual licenses. As discussed below, typical agreements may concern the design and development of foreign-origin equipment based on ITAR controlled technical specifications, design drawings or other ITAR controlled technical data, the delivery of overseas maintenance or training support, technical studies or evaluations, and the release of manufacturing data or production rights to foreign parties.

A Manufacturing License Agreement ("MLA") is an agreement whereby a U.S. person grants a foreign person an authorization to manufacture defense articles abroad.[97] An MLA covers the export of technical data or defense articles or the performance of a defense service, or the use by the foreign person of technical data or defense articles previously exported by the U.S. person.[98]

A Technical Assistance Agreement ("TAA") is an agreement for the performance of a defense service or the disclosure of technical data, as opposed to an agreement granting a right or license to manufacture defense articles.[99] Assembly of defense articles may be included in the TAA, provided production rights or manufacturing know-how is not conveyed.[100] Should such rights be transferred, an MLA would be required.

The following information must be included in all proposed agreements.

---

96. *See* http://www.siaed.org/en/catalogs/items/view.asp?catalogid=4.
97. 22 C.F.R. § 120.21.
98. *Id.*
99. 22 C.F.R. § 120.22.
100. *Id.*

- a description of the defense articles to be manufactured and all defense articles (including technical data) to be exported;
- a specific description of any assistance or technical data to be provided (including design and manufacturing know-how) and any manufacturing rights to be granted;
- the duration of the agreement, which can be up to ten years; and
- the specific countries where manufacturing, production, processing, or sale is to be licensed.[101]

Agreements also must include certain specified clauses, including ones relating to the following: a confirmation of any continuing obligation of the parties to the U.S. Government; a waiver of any U.S. Government liability arising from approval of the agreement; and the continuing validity of any undertakings by the U.S. Government after the agreement has been terminated.[102] These clauses are contained in sections 124.8 and 124.9 of the ITAR and must be copied into the Agreements virtually verbatim.

Agreements are submitted electronically via DTrade, using a DSP-5 license application as a vehicle for their submission. Agreements must also include a cover letter (which also must contain specified information in specified order) and a certification. The rules for submitting Agreements using the DSP-5 vehicle are very complicated, and require filling in blanks in the DSP-5 application in a way that is not intuitive, particularly where the MLA has a sales territory or where the foreign parties employ foreign third country and dual nationals of other countries. Because the rules are so complicated, it is essential to review and follow carefully DDTC's essential guidance on preparing and submitting agreements, which can be found in DDTC's *Agreement Guidelines*.[103]

After DDTC approves the agreement, the exporter is required to file with DDTC one copy of the signed MLA or TAA no more than 30 days after the agreement enters into force,[104] or if the approved agreement is ultimately not executed, notification of such non-execution must be provided to DDTC within 60 days of the decision not to execute the agreements.[105] In the case of concluded agreements involving coproduction or licensed production outside of the United States, the filing must include a written statement concerning foreign production, including alternative measures and controls to ensure compliance with restrictions specified in the agreement regarding production quantities and third-party transfers in instances where U.S. access and

---

101.   22 C.F.R. § 124.7.
102.   *See* 22 C.F.R. § 124.8.
103.   *DDTC Agreement Guidelines* (*available at* http://www.pmddtc.state.gov/licensing/agreement.html).
104.   22 C.F.R. § 124.4.
105.   22 C.F.R. § 124.5.

verification is denied.[106] It also should be noted that the U.S. party to an MLA or TAA must provide written notice to DDTC of the impending termination of the agreement at least 30 days prior to the expiration date of such agreement.[107] Additional filing requirements are set forth under Section 123.22 of the ITAR.[108]

In some instances, it may be appropriate to submit a DSP-5 to seek authorization to export technical data. For example, it may be beneficial to submit a DSP-5 application when seeking to allow a U.S. person to be able to disclose ITAR-controlled technical data to foreign persons in connection with a plant visit or an international conference that is not open to the public or when desiring to export technical data for purposes of filing a patent application in a foreign country when the technical data required exceeds that required for a patent application filing in the United States.[109]

There also are a number of exemptions set forth under the ITAR that permit technical data and defense services to be exported without a license from DDTC which are set forth mainly under Section 123.16 and Section 125.4 of the ITAR. Some pertinent exemptions that are frequently used for such purposes include:

- technical data in furtherance of an approved MLA or TAA;[110]
- technical data in furtherance of a contract between the exporter and an agency of the U.S. Government, if the contract provides for the export of the data and such data does not disclose the details of design, development, production or manufacture of any defense article;[111]
- technical data to be disclosed pursuant to an official written request or directive from the DOD;[112]
- copies of technical data previously authorized for export to the same recipient, including revisions provided that the revisions are solely editorial and do not add to the content of the technology previously authorized for export;[113]
- technical data sent by a U.S. corporation to a U.S. employee overseas or to a U.S. Government agency subject to certain limitations;[114]
- technical data in the form of basic operations, maintenance, and training information relating to a defense article lawfully exported or authorized to export to the same recipient;[115]

---

106. *Id.*
107. 22 C.F.R. § 124.6.
108. 22 C.F.R. § 123.22.
109. *See* 22 C.F.R. §§ 125.2(a)-(c).
110. 22 C.F.R. § 125.4(b)(2).
111. 22 C.F.R. § 125.4(b)(3).
112. 22 C.F.R. § 125.4(b)(1).
113. 22 C.F.R. § 125.4(b)(4).
114. 22 C.F.R. § 125.4(b)(9).
115. 22 C.F.R. § 125.4(b)(5).

- technical data for which the exporter has been granted an exemption in writing pursuant to an arrangement with the DOD, DOE, or NASA;[116]
- technical data approved for public release by the cognizant U.S. Government department or agency;[117] and
- defense services and related unclassified technical data necessary to respond to a written request from the DOD for a quote or bid proposal are exempt when transmitted to nationals of NATO countries, Australia, Japan and Sweden.[118]

It is critical to note that there are often numerous requirements and limitations associated with each of the exemptions referenced above. For example, 22 CFR 123.26 requires that the export keep a record of each export of technical data via exemption, including a description of the unclassified technical data, the name of the recipient end user, the date and time of the export, and the method of transmission. This provision is not located anywhere close to the main exemptions for the export of technical data. Accordingly, as noted above, companies should carefully review the requirements and limitations, and consult the SIA Exemptions Handbook, before seeking to use the exemptions.

2.8 BROKERING UNDER THE ITAR

In addition to exports and temporary imports of defense articles and defense services, the ITAR also control the "brokering" of defense articles and defense services. Under the ITAR, a "broker" is defined as "any person who acts as an agent for others in negotiating or arranging contracts, purchases, sales or transfers of defense articles or defense services in return for a fee, commission, or other consideration."[119] The ITAR further specify that "brokering activities" mean acting as a "broker" as defined under Section 129.2(2) of the ITAR and include the "financing, transportation, freight forwarding, or taking of any action that facilitates the manufacture, export, or import of a defense article or defense service, irrespective of its origin."[120]

The ITAR specify that brokering activities can be performed by U.S. persons located in the United States or abroad.[121] While activities by U.S. persons that are limited exclusively to U.S. or domestic sales or transfers (e.g., not for export or retransfer in the United States or to a foreign person) are not considered brokering activities,[122]

---

116.   22 C.F.R. § 125.4(b)(11).
117.   22 C.F.R. § 125.4(b)(13). *Note:* This exemption is used when the company does NOT place the information in the public domain. If the information, once approved for public release, is placed in the public domain, there is no need to use this exemption as the information is no longer technical data subject to the ITAR.
118.   22 C.F.R. § 125.4(c).
119.   22 C.F.R. § 129.2(a).
120.   22 C.F.R. § 129.2(b).
121.   *Id.*
122.   *Id.*

it is clear that U.S persons operating in the U.S. or abroad who facilitate the sale by another person of U.S. defense articles, including technical data, or defense services, or foreign origin goods or technology that would be deemed to be ITAR-controlled defense articles or defense services if exported from the United States, would be deemed to be engaging in brokering activities.

The extent to which the brokering provisions apply to foreign persons, however, is less clear. As stated under Section 129.2(b) of the ITAR, brokering activities include ones performed by foreign persons subject to U.S. jurisdiction.[123] Typically, U.S. courts have construed the term "subject to the jurisdiction of the United States" to require that a foreign person have certain "minimum contacts" with the United States, such as conducting business in the United States.[124] DDTC, however, takes a broader view pursuant to which a foreign person not otherwise subject to U.S. jurisdiction would be subject to U.S. jurisdiction if the foreign person acted as an agent in negotiating the contract for the delivery of U.S. defense articles or defense services irrespective of whether the foreign person actually had access to controlled defense services or technical data. In effect, DDTC's view is that anyone, including both U.S. and foreign persons, who helps to arrange or negotiate contracts, purchases, sales or transfers of defense articles or defense services in return for a fee, is an agent.

In *United States v. Yakou*, the U.S. Court of Appeals for the District of Columbia examined the issue of the applicability of the brokering provisions to foreign persons.[125] In the ruling, in which it affirmed a lower court decision holding that a British citizen had not brokered the sale of military patrol boats to the Iraqi Navy within the meaning of the ITAR, the Court noted:

> In the Brokering Amendment, then, Congress was concerned with both United States brokers of arms and foreign brokers of arms located in the United States, but not with foreign brokers located outside the United States, see id., even though each type of individual could be involved in brokering activities affecting the United States. . . .

> Congress has not expressed with the requisite clarity that it sought to apply the Brokering Amendment and, by extension the ITAR's brokering provisions, in such an extraterritorial manner [i.e., to apply to "non-U.S. persons located and acting outside the United States."] [citations omitted] . . . Accordingly, while the Brokering Amendment and the ITAR have extraterritorial effect for "U.S.

---

123. *Id.*
124. *See International Shoe Co. v. Washington*, 326 U.S. 310 (1945).
125. *United States v. Yakou*, 393 F.3d 231 (D.C. Cir. 2005).

persons," they do not have such effect for "foreign persons," like Yakou, whose conduct occurs outside the United States.[126]

From this language, it seemed fairly clear that the Court believed that Congress did not intend for the brokering amendments to the AECA to apply to foreign persons operating outside of the United States.

However, shortly after the ruling was issued, the U.S. Government requested that the Court clarify that the meaning of "otherwise subject to the jurisdiction of the United States" had not been raised in the case, and the Court subsequently issued an amended order in which it stated that the "D.C. Circuit amends the Yakou decision to clarify that the opinion does not address the provisions of the International Traffic in Arms Regulations (ITAR) regulating foreign persons "otherwise subject to U.S. jurisdiction."[127] Since the issuance of the amended order, DDTC has continued to maintain its expansive view regarding the application of the brokering provisions to foreign persons, as evidenced by a proposed rule that it published in December 2011 that would effectively codify its view.[128] However, numerous groups, including the ABA Section of International Law, raised significant concerns about the proposed rule, including its extraterritorial applications, and subsequently, DDTC issued a "working copy" of a significantly revised version of a proposed rule relating to the brokering provisions in January 2013.[129]

Generally, any U.S. person, wherever located, or any foreign person located in the United States or otherwise subject to the jurisdiction of the United States, who engages in the business of brokering activities, must register with DDTC on an annual basis.[130] The only entities that may perform brokering activities that are exempt from registering with DDTC are:

- employees of the U.S. Government acting in an official capacity;
- employees of foreign governments or international organizations acting in an official capacity; and
- persons exclusively in the business of financing, transporting, or freight forwarding, whose business activities do not also include brokering defense articles or defense services.[131]

---

126. *Id.*
127. *United States v. Yakou*, Amended Order No. 04-3037 (D.C. Cir. May 9, 2005).
128. *See* 76 Fed. Reg. 78578 (Dec. 19, 2011).
129. The ABA Section of International Law's comments regarding DDTC's December 2011 proposed rule on brokering provisions can be found on the ABA Export Controls and Economic Sanctions Committee webpage (*available at* http://apps.americanbar.org/dch/committee.cfm?com=IC716000). The "working copy" of the revised proposed rule, which DDTC posted on its website in January 2013, can be accessed at http://www.pmddtc.state.gov/dtag/documents/plenary_Nov2012_BrokeringWorkingPaperProposedRule.pdf.
130. 22 C.F.R. § 129.4.
131. 22 C.F.R. § 129.3.

Additional details and guidance regarding registration requirements and procedures are set forth below in Section 2.7.

In addition to brokering registration requirements, brokers must comply with the brokering-related prior notification, prior approval, and reporting requirements. Brokers must provide prior notification in writing to DDTC at least 30 days prior to making a brokering proposal or presentation relating to SME valued at less than $1,000,000, except in instances where U.S. persons who are registered with DDTC as both exporters and brokers will provide only basic marketing information (e.g., information that does not include performance characteristics, price, and probable availability for delivery).[132]

Brokers also must obtain prior written approval (e.g., a license) from DDTC before engaging in a wide range of brokering activities. For example, a license must be obtained before engaging in brokering activities to or from any country relating to:

(1) fully automatic firearms and components and parts thereof;

(2) nuclear weapons strategic delivery systems and related components, parts, accessories, and attachments specifically designed for such systems and associated equipment;

(3) nuclear weapons design and test equipment of a nature described by USML Category XVI;

(4) naval nuclear propulsion equipment of a nature described by USML Category VI(e);

(5) Missile Technology Control Regime Category I items (see ITAR § 121.16);

(6) classified defense articles, services, and technical data; and

(7) foreign defense articles or defense services (other than those that are arranged wholly within and destined exclusively for NATO, Australia, Japan, New Zealand, or South Korea).[133]

In addition, except in instances involving Australia, Japan, New Zealand, South Korea, or NATO countries, approval from DDTC must be obtained before engaging in brokering activities involving defense articles or defense services relating to SME valued at $1,000,000 or more when: (i) the identical SME has not previously been licensed for export to the country concerned or approved for sale under the Foreign Military Sales Program (FMS Program); or (ii) the recipient or end-user is not a foreign government or international organization.[134] Requests for approval must be submitted to DDTC in writing by an empowered official of the registered broker and must identify all parties involved in the proposed transaction and their roles, as well as

---

132. 22 C.F.R. § 129.8.
133. 22 C.F.R. § 129.7.
134. *Id.*

outline in detail the defense article and related technical data (including manufacturer, military designation, and model number), quantity, value, security classification (if any), and the specific end-use(s) and end-user(s).[135] The proposed brokering activity may not be engaged in until approval is issued by DDTC, which can be in the form of written statement from DDTC approving the proposed activity or a license or other written approval issued under Parts 123, 124, or 125 of the ITAR provided that the names of all brokers have been identified in an attachment accompanying the submission of the initial application.[136]

If any doubt exists as to whether an activity is a brokering activity within the scope of the ITAR or whether prior notification or prior approval requirements apply, entities can seek written guidance from DDTC.[137] Persons wishing to obtain such guidance should follow the same procedures that are enumerated under Section 126.9 of the ITAR for obtaining advisory opinions from DDTC.[138] As with advisory opinions, however, the guidance issued by DDTC on matters relating to brokering activities is not binding on DDTC and may not be used in future matters before DDTC.[139] Moreover, in the past, DDTC has been slow to issue brokering advisory opinions and those opinions have typically not been very helpful.

Brokers also are subject to certain reporting requirements under the ITAR. Specifically, any person who is required to register as a broker with DDTC must file an annual report with DDTC.[140] Such annual reports, which must be submitted to DDTC by January 31 for the previous year's activities, must describe the brokering activities by quantity, type, value (US$), purchaser(s), recipient(s), and license number(s) for approved activities and any exemptions utilized for other covered activities.[141]

As discussed above, with limited exceptions, entities engaging in brokering activities must register with DDTC, obtain prior written approval from DDTC before actually engaging in brokering activities, and file annual reports with DDTC relating to brokering activities performed during the previous year.[142] In addition, DDTC has interpreted the brokering provisions set forth in the AECA very broadly, and DDTC's attempts to amend the brokering regulations have not, to date, been successful. As such, the brokering provisions are a particularly risky section of the ITAR, and they bear close attention, particularly by exporters who engage representatives outside the United States to assist them in the sale of defense articles and defense services.

---

135. *Id.*
136. *Id.*
137. 22 C.F.R. § 129.10.
138. *Id. See also* 22 C.F.R. § 126.9.
139. 22 C.F.R. § 129.10.
140. 22 C.F.R. § 129.9.
141. *Id.*
142. 22 C.F.R. Part 129.

2.9 ITAR REQUIREMENTS CONCERNING FEES, COMMISSIONS, AND POLITICAL CONTRIBUTIONS

Another area of the ITAR to which special attention is warranted relates to fees, commissions, and political contributions that are paid in connection with the sale of defense articles or defense services. As discussed below, there are important reporting requirements relating to such payments, and significant penalties can be, and have been, imposed by DDTC when companies have filed inaccurate reports or have failed to file reports at all.

The reporting requirements apply to entities that seek licenses or other approvals from DDTC and to suppliers and vendors, as defined under Part 130 of the ITAR. Suppliers are defined to mean any person who enters into a contract with the DOD for the sale of defense articles or defense services valued in an amount of $500,000 under Section 22 of the AECA.[143] Vendors are defined to include: (1) any distributor or manufacturer who, directly or indirectly, furnishes to an applicant or supplier defense articles valued at $500,000 or more that are end-items or major components, as defined under Section 121.8 of the ITAR; or (2) any person who directly or indirectly, furnishes to an applicant or supplier defense articles or defense services valued at $500,000 or more when such defense articles or defense services are to be delivered or incorporated into defense articles or defense services to be delivered to or for the use of the armed forces of a foreign country or international organization under a sale requiring a license from DDTC or a sale with the DOD under Section 22 of the AECA.[144]

When seeking a license or other approval from DDTC in connection with the sale of defense articles or defense services, an applicant must inform DDTC whether it or its vendors have paid or agreed to pay political contributions in an aggregate amount of $5,000 or more or fees and commissions in aggregate amount of $100,000 or more and such entity must file a report with DDTC containing certain information relating to the sale.[145] This requirement applies regardless of whether such political contributions or fees and commissions are paid directly by the applicant or any of its vendors or by anyone on their behalf or at their direction.[146] In addition, in connection with such sales, suppliers must file the same kind of report with DDTC with respect to such political contributions or fees and commissions paid or agreed to be paid by the supplier or its vendors or by anyone on their behalf or at their direction.[147]

The information that must be provided in such reports includes:

(1) the total contract price of the sale to the foreign purchaser;
(2) the name, nationality, address, and principal place of business of the applicant or the supplier, and, if applicable, the employer and title;

---

143. 22 C.F.R. § 130.7.
144. 22 C.F.R. § 130.8.
145. 22 C.F.R. § 130.9.
146. *Id.*
147. *Id.*

(3) the name, nationality, address, and principal place of business, and if applicable, employer and title of each foreign purchaser, including the ultimate end-user involved in the sale;

(4) the amount of each political contribution paid, or offered or agreed to be paid, or the amount of each fee or commission paid, or offered or agreed to be paid;

(5) the date(s) on which each reported amount was paid, or offered or agreed to be paid;

(6) the recipient of each such amount paid, or the intended recipient if not yet paid;

(7) the person who paid, or offered or agreed to pay such amount;

(8) the aggregate amount of political contributions and of fees or commissions, respectively, which shall have been reported.[148]

When providing information regarding each recipient, the following information must be provided: (i) name; (ii) nationality; (iii) address and principal place of business; (iv) its employer and title; and (v) its relationship, if any, to the applicant, supplier, or vendor, and to any foreign purchaser or end-user.[149] It should be noted, however, that such information regarding the recipients need not be provided if the payments do not exceed $2,500 in the case of political contributions or $250,000 in the case of fees or commissions, and in such instances, however, the aggregate amounts of the payments must be reported and identified as miscellaneous political contributions or miscellaneous fees or commissions, as applicable.[150] Any person filing such a report may request that confidential business information contained in the report not be published, divulged, disclosed, or made know in any manner, and no such confidential business information may be made know in any manner unless authorized by law.[151]

It should be noted that applicants and suppliers who file such reports have an obligation to file supplementary reports in certain circumstances. Specifically, such supplementary reports must be filed if, subsequent to the submission of the initial report:

(1) any political contributions aggregating in value at $2,500 or more or fees or commissions aggregating in value at $50,000 or more not previously reported are paid or offered or agreed to be paid by the applicant or supplier or any vendor;

(2) subsequent developments cause the information initially reported to be no longer accurate or complete; or

---

148. 22 C.F.R. § 130.10.
149. *Id.*
150. *Id.*
151. 22 C.F.R. § 130.15.

(3) additional details are requested by DDTC with respect to any miscellaneous payments reported under Section 130.10(c) of the ITAR.[152]

Such supplementary reports must be submitted to DDTC within 30 days after the payment, offer or agreement reported therein, or when requested by DDTC, within 30 days after such request, and they must reference the DDTC license number, if any, and the DOD contract, if any, related to the sale.[153]

In order to determine their reporting requirements, applicants and vendors must determine from each of their applicable vendors a full disclosure by the vendor of all political contributions and fees or commissions paid by the vendor with respect to the sale at issue.[154] Any vendor to whom such a request is made must provide a response within 20 days of the initial request, although if the vendor believes that furnishing the information required would unreasonably risk injury to the vendor's commercial interests, the vendor may provide an abbreviated statement that discloses only the aggregate amount of all political contributions and the aggregate amount of all fees and commissions that have been paid, or offered or agreed to be paid, by the vendor with respect to the sale.[155] If no response is received from the vendor within 25 days of its request to the vendor, the applicant or supplier must file a written submission with DDTC attesting to the applicant's or supplier's attempt to obtain from the vendor the initial statement required under Section 130.10(a) of the ITAR, the vendor's failure to comply with the request, and the amount of time that has elapsed between the date of the applicant's or supplier's request and the date of the signed submission to DDTC.[156] Even in such instances, the applicant or supplier still must file with DDTC the report required pursuant to Section 130.9 of the ITAR.[157]

In addition, in order determine their reporting requirements, applicants, suppliers, and vendors must obtain from each person to whom they have paid, or offered or agreed to pay, a fee or commission relating to a covered sale, a statement containing a full disclosure by such a person of all political contributions paid, or offered or agreed to be paid, by itself or on its behalf, or at its discretion, relating to such sale.[158] Moreover, applicants, suppliers, and vendors also may request that each person to whom a fee or commission is paid to provide periodic reports of its political contributions to the extent that such reports may be necessary for the applicants, suppliers, and vendors to comply with their ITAR reporting requirements.[159] Any person who provides such information may request that confidential business information not be

---

152.   22 C.F.R. § 130.11.
153.   *Id.*
154.   22 C.F.R. §130.12.
155.   *Id.*
156.   *Id.*
157.   *Id.*
158.   22 C.F.R. § 130.13.
159.   *Id.*

published, divulged, disclosed, or made know in any manner, and no such confidential business information may be made know in any manner unless authorized by law.[160]

There are recordkeeping requirements associated with such reports. Specifically, each applicant, supplier, and vendor must maintain a record of any information that it was required to furnish or obtain under Part 130 of the ITAR for not less than five years following the date of the report to which they pertain.[161]

Significant penalties can be imposed by DDTC for the filing of materially inaccurate reports or the failure to file such reports at all. For example, in 2011, UK-based BAE Systems plc (BAE-UK) entered into a settlement agreement with DDTC pursuant to which BAE-UK agreed to pay a $79 million penalty for numerous violations of the ITAR's provisions relating to brokering and reporting of political contributions and fees and commissions.[162] This penalty was on top of nearly $450 million in penalties that BAE-UK agreed to pay to U.S. authorities (approximately $400 million) and UK authorities (approximately 47 million) for violations of various U.S. and UK anti-corruption and fraud laws. In view of the staggering penalties imposed on BAE-UK, it is clear that exporters must carefully follow the ITAR's provisions relating to brokering and reporting of political contributions and fees and commissions.

2.10 PENALTIES AND ENFORCEMENT

Significant penalties can be imposed for violations of the AECA and the ITAR. Civil penalties can be as high as $500,000 per violation.[163] Criminal penalties can be as high as $1,000,000 and/or up to 10 years of imprisonment per violation.[164] DDTC also can debar companies and individuals from participating directly or indirectly in the export of defense articles or the furnishing of defense services.[165] In addition, any attempt to export defense articles in violation of the ITAR can result in the seizure and forfeiture of the defense articles,[166] and DDTC possesses the discretion to deny, suspend, or revoke licenses and registrations on the basis of conviction or indictment under the criminal statutes listed in Section 120.27 of the ITAR or in other circumstances listed in Section 126.7 of the ITAR.[167]

In recent years, DDTC has significantly intensified its enforcement of the AECA and the ITAR. For example, In August 2010, DDTC announced that Xe Services,

---

160.   22 C.F.R. § 130.15.

161.   22 C.F.R. § 130.14.

162.   A copy of the consent agreement between BAE-UK and DDTC can be accessed on DDTC's website at http://www.pmddtc.state.gov/compliance/consent_agreements/baes.html. Significantly, DDTC determined that BAE-UK's U.S. subsidiary, BAE Systems, Inc. (BAE-US), was not involved in the violations, and accordingly, BAE-US was excluded from DDTC's enforcement action.

163.   22 U.S.C. § 2778(e).

164.   22 U.S.C. § 2780(j)-(k).

165.   22 C.F.R. § 127.7.

166.   22 C.F.R. § 127.6.

167.   22 C.F.R. §§ 120.27 and 126.7.

formerly known as Blackwater, had agreed to enter into a consent order pursuant to which it would be subject to a civil penalty of $42 million for various violations of the ITAR, including unauthorized exports of U.S.-controlled commodities and technical data; provision of defense services without a license; and employment of unauthorized foreign nationals.[168] More recently, in June 2012, DDTC imposed a $55 million penalty on United Technologies Corporation ("UTC") primarily for numerous unauthorized exports of defense articles and defense services to China,[169] and as discussed above, in May 2011, DDTC imposed a staggering $79 million civil penalty on BAE-UK, the largest military contractor in Europe, to settle 2,591 brokering and reporting-related violations of the ITAR.[170] Based on remarks made by DDTC officials at recent conferences, it seems likely that the trend of intensified enforcement and staggering fines will continue for the foreseeable future.

2.11 VOLUNTARY DISCLOSURES

Companies can seek to mitigate potential penalty exposure by filing voluntary disclosures with DDTC. It should be noted that in some cases, the disclosures are not, strictly speaking, voluntary. Specifically, 22 CFR 126.1(e) imposes an affirmative obligation on any person who knows or has reason to know of such a proposed or actual sale, or transfer, of such articles, services or data to a 126.1 country to "immediately inform" DDTC. Thus, if a company has committed the error of sending a defense article to China, for example, or releasing technical data to a Chinese national employee, the company is actually required to notify DDTC immediately and failing to do so is a separate violation. In fact, DDTC made such findings in the case involving UTC, and several of its subsidiaries, including Pratt & Whitney Canada Corp. and Hamilton Sundstrand Corporation, that resulted in UTC entering into a consent agreement pursuant to which it agreed to pay $55 million in penalties.[171]

Likewise, there may be many cases where a company has to note in its license application that it has had past exports without a license to the same ultimate consignee because failing to explain this would mean that the company would file a license application with a material omission, which again would be a separate legal violation. In such cases, companies should file a voluntary disclosure, and cross-reference the voluntary disclosure number in the blank in the license application.

In order to initiate the voluntary process, a company typically submits to DDTC an initial disclosure that outlines the suspected or alleged violations and commits to

---

168.   *See* http://www.pmddtc.state.gov/compliance/consent_agreements/XeServicesLLC.html.
169.   *See* http://www.pmddtc.state.gov/compliance/consent_agreements/pdf/UTC_CA.pdf.
170.   *See* http://www.pmddtc.state.gov/compliance/consent_agreements/baes.html.
171.   A copy of the consent agreement between UTC and DDTC can be accessed on DDTC's website at http://www.pmddtc.state.gov/compliance/consent_agreements/pdf/UTC_CA.pdf. It should further be noted that UTC entered into a related deferred prosecution agreement with the DOJ pursuant to which UTC agreed to pay $20.7 million in penalties to the DOJ.

providing a complete report after completing an investigation into the facts. The initial notification need not be more than two or three pages in length and need not lay out the facts in any detail. However, to the extent there is a violation involving a 126.1 proscribed country, it should clearly note sufficient facts to notify DDTC to fulfill the company's obligations to immediately notify DDTC as set forth in 126.1(e).

An initial notification can be a full voluntary disclosure, if the facts are readily available, and there is no reason to file immediately. A full voluntary disclosure should:

- describes with precision the circumstances surrounding the suspected violations (*e.g.*, a detailed explanation of why, when, where, and how the violation occurred);
- give the identities and addresses of all persons known or suspected to be involved in the activities that resulted in the suspected violation;
- identify the kinds of defense articles and defense services involved, including their USML classifications;
- discuss what corrective actions and new compliance initiatives, if any, have been implemented to address the causes of the suspected violations; and
- provide the name of the person making the disclosure and a point of contact, if different, should further information be needed by DDTC.[172]

The full voluntary disclosure should include substantiating documentation, including: licensing documents; shipping documents, and any other relevant documents.[173] Both the initial and full voluntary disclosure must include a certification executed by one of the company's empowered officials stating that all of the representations made in connection with the voluntary disclosure are true and correct to the best of the person's knowledge and belief.[174]

If an initial disclosure is filed, the full disclosure setting forth all of the pertinent facts must be submitted to DDTC within 60 calendar days from the date of the letter from DDTC acknowledging receipt of the initial disclosure was filed, unless an extension is granted by DDTC, or else the initial notification will not be considered to be a voluntary disclosure.[175]

Most voluntary disclosures filed with DDTC do not result in the imposition of fines. Although DDTC fines are, as noted above, very large, in practice DDTC typically imposes fines on only a handful of companies each year. DDTC is more likely to fine where the violations involve exports to a proscribed country such as China or Iran, where DDTC feels the company has a systemic and serious compliance issue

---

172. 22 C.F.R. § 127.12.
173. *Id.*
174. *Id.*
175. *Id.*

or where DDTC wishes to inform the defense industry of a particular issue, such as foreign person access to technical data or exports at the request of a U.S. government agency where ITAR exemption requirements have not been met.

2.12 CONCLUSION

In summary, compliance with the ITAR is of critical importance to U.S. persons and foreign persons (*i.e.*, non-U.S. persons) that are involved in the manufacture and export of defense articles and the furnishing of defense services, as well as to those who are engaged in brokering activities relating to defense articles and defense services. Given that the export control reform initiative initiated by the Obama Administration is resulting in many proposed amendments to the ITAR, it will be essential for all such persons to monitor evolving developments closely by regularly checking out DDTC's website, which can be accessed at http://www.pmddtc.state.gov/, and by participating in the work of key organizations that seek to work collaboratively and constructively with DDTC to effect change that balances appropriately national security concerns with opportunities to promote meaningful growth in U.S. exports, such as the American Bar Association's Section of International Law, whose website can be accessed at http://www.americanbar.org/groups/international_law.html.[176]

---

176. The ABA Section of International Law's Export Controls and Economic Sanctions Committee is especially active in providing education, outreach, and advocacy relating to U.S. export controls. The Committee's website can be accessed at http://apps.americanbar.org/dch/committee.cfm?com=IC716000.

$$\textbf{3}$$

Export Administration Controls

J. Scott Maberry, Thaddeus R. McBride, and Mark E. Sagrans[1]

3.1 INTRODUCTION

This chapter provides an overview of the Export Administration Regulations, known as the EAR.

What Is Regulated? Virtually all items not regulated by the ITAR are regulated by the EAR.[2] Section 3.3 below provides more detail.

Where to Find the Regulations: The EAR are contained in parts 730 through 774 of chapter 15 of the Code of Federal Regulations.[3]

Who Is the Regulator? The regulations are administered by the U.S. Department of Commerce's Bureau of Industry and Security (BIS).

---

1. This chapter was authored by J. Scott Maberry, Thaddeus R. McBride, and Mark E. Sagrans. Scott and Thad are partners in the law firm of Sheppard Mullin Richter & Hampton LLP in Washington, D.C., and Mark is Corporate Counsel, DuPont Legal. This chapter was prepared in the usual manner, *i.e.*, with younger lawyers doing most of the hard work and the listed authors taking most of the credit. Many thanks to our colleagues Mark Jensen, Cheryl Palmeri, and Reid Whitten, who are associates in the international trade practice of Sheppard Mullin. The listed authors take full responsibility for the content of this chapter, including any errors.
2. The EAR are often described as covering so-called "dual-use" items, on the theory that the items subject to the EAR potentially could be used for either civil or military purposes. *See, e.g.,* 15 C.F.R. § 730.3, "General Information" (stating that, "in general, the term dual use serves to distinguish EAR-controlled items that can be used both in military and other strategic uses and in civil applications from those that are weapons and military related use or design and subject to the controls of the Department of State or subject to the nuclear related controls of the Department of Energy or the Nuclear Regulatory Commission."). But the term "dual use" tends to create confusion, and BIS has proposed largely to abandon it as part of its Export Control Reform Initiative. *See* 76 Fed. Reg. 41,971 (July 15, 2011). Therefore, the term is not used extensively in this chapter. The items subject to the EAR are best distinguished from ITAR-controlled items on the grounds that items that are specially designed or modified for military use (or for a few other specialized uses, such as satellite or intelligence applications) are covered by the ITAR (*see* chapter 2); whereas items not specially designed or modified for those applications are generally covered by the EAR. However, the EAR do include some items that may originally have been specially designed or modified for military applications; the number of such items will grow significantly if the current export control reform initiative, which is discussed briefly in section 3.14 below, proceeds as currently anticipated.
3. The statutory authority for the EAR is the Export Administration Act of 1979. That act lapsed on August 21, 2001, and has never been renewed, but Executive Order 13,222 keeps the EAR in effect under the President's authority pursuant to the International Emergency Economic Powers Act (IEEPA). *See, e.g.,* Revision and Clarification of Civil Monetary Penalty Provisions of the Export Administration Regulations, 71 Fed. Reg. 44,189 (Aug. 4, 2006).

How to Get a License: License applications are filed electronically on BIS's website using the SNAP-R system (http://www.bis.doc.gov/snap/index.htm).

Key Website: http://www.bis.doc.gov/index.htm

3.2 STRUCTURE OF THE EXPORT ADMINISTRATION REGULATIONS

The structure of the EAR is described briefly below. It is also the structure of this chapter, which is organized roughly in the order of the steps one takes to determine the export controls applicable to a particular item.[4]

1. Determine if the item is subject to the EAR. Some items are controlled by the ITAR, some items are subject to the jurisdiction of another specialized agency, and some are not controlled at all. This step is outlined in section 3.3 below.

2. Classify the item. The items controlled by the EAR are classified on the Commerce Control List (CCL).[5] Items are described by reference to performance characteristics. This step is outlined in sections 3.5 and 3.6 below.

3. Determine whether the item is controlled to the relevant destination by review of the relevant export control classification number (ECCN), the Commerce Country Chart contained in supplement 1 to part 738 of the EAR and specific sections of the EAR for controls, such as Short Supply, not listed in the Commerce Country Chart. Unlike the ITAR, even if the item is determined to be subject to the EAR, a license often is not required to export the item. Depending on the sensitivity of the item, licenses may or may not be required for certain destinations. That licensing decision is outlined in sections 3.8 and 3.9 below.

4. Determine if there is any other reason that a license may be required in light of the particular parties to the transaction, the end use of the item to be exported, or other factors. If any of several "general prohibitions" applies, a license is required for export to any destination, as outlined in section 3.7 below.

5. If the item is controlled for the particular destination, end user, and/or end use, determine whether any of several "license exceptions" applies, in which case it may not be necessary to obtain a license for the export. This step is outlined in section 3.10 below.

6. Apply for a license if required, as outlined in section 3.11 below.

7. Throughout the export classification and licensing process, during the export itself, and even after the export transaction is completed, it is important to ensure compliance with the EAR. To that end, section 3.12 lays out certain export com-

---

4. The steps described here are somewhat simplified. The EAR section titled "Steps for Using the EAR" describes twenty-nine distinct steps in detail. *See* 15 C.F.R. pt. 732. A helpful graphical summary of the steps for using the EAR is provided at 15 C.F.R. pt. 732, supp. 1, *available at* http://www.bis.doc.gov/policiesandregulations/ear/732.pdf.

5. 15 C.F.R. § 774, supp. 1.

pliance best practices. In the current enforcement landscape, these practices are important to undertake, particularly given the array of penalties that may be imposed for violations. Those penalties, and the enforcement provisions by which those penalties may be imposed, are outlined in section 3.13 below.

8. For many years, various presidential administrations and legislators have talked about reforming the export control regime. The current initiative undertaken by the administration of President Barack Obama is more energetic than most, and is described briefly in section 3.14 below.

3.3 WHAT IS REGULATED? SCOPE OF THE EAR

As noted in section 3.1 above, most items specially designed or modified for military application are subject to the ITAR; most other items are subject to the EAR. A very few items are subject to the exclusive jurisdiction of some other export control agency.[6] Although the coverage of the EAR is broad, a license is not needed for exports of most items to most destinations or end users.[7] License requirements are based on the item's technical characteristics, destination, end user, and end use. In order to determine whether an item or transaction requires a license, it is useful to consider the following questions, often known as the 4 Ws:

- What are you exporting?
- Where are you exporting?
- Who will receive your item?
- What will your item be used for?

With this information, as summarized further in this chapter, it is possible to analyze whether the EAR controls the transaction and whether a license is required.

The EAR applies to several categories of items, as follows:

- items physically located in the United States, regardless of where manufactured
- U.S.-origin items wherever located, whether in or outside the United States

---

6.   Those agencies include the following: U.S. Nuclear Regulatory Commission (NRC). Regulations administered by the NRC control the export and reexport of items related to nuclear reactor vessels. *See* 10 C.F.R. pt. 110; *see also* Atomic Energy Act of 1954, as amended, 42 U.S.C. §§ 2011 *et seq.* U.S. Department of Energy (DOE). Regulations administered by the DOE control the export and reexport of technology related to the production of special nuclear materials. *See* 10 C.F.R. pt. 810; *see also* Atomic Energy Act of 1954, as amended, 42 U.S.C. §§ 2011 *et seq.* U.S. Patent and Trademark Office (PTO). Regulations administered by the PTO provide for the export of unclassified technology in connection with patent applications and related filings. *See* 37 C.F.R. pt. 5. U.S. Department of the Treasury, Office of Foreign Assets Control (OFAC). OFAC administers the U.S. economic sanctions and embargoes contained in 31 C.F.R. ch. V. Exports to embargoed destinations are generally covered by these regulations. (*See* chapter 1.) In large part, these regulations are *concurrent* with the EAR, and violations of OFAC's regulations may simultaneously violate the EAR.

7.   *See* http://www.bis.doc.gov/licensing/exportingbasics.htm.

- foreign-origin items with more than de minimis U.S.-origin content by value, and certain technology related to those items[8]
- foreign-origin items that are considered to be a "direct product" of certain controlled U.S.-origin technology or software[9]

In addition to controls on exports of physical goods (referred to as commodities under the EAR), the scope of the EAR also includes technology and software related to controlled commodities. Controlled "technology" may include plans, specifications, design information, technical data, and manufacturing know-how. The EAR impose controls on exports made in any form, such as by e-mail, by facsimile, or in other soft-copy form.[10]

The EAR also specifically control the "release" of technology or software to a foreign national, including through oral or visual disclosure.[11] Such disclosure of controlled technology to a foreign national is considered a deemed export even if the disclosure takes place within the United States. The disclosure is considered an export even if the foreign recipient of the export is lawfully permitted to be in the United States (e.g., by having a valid visa). This kind of export is commonly called a deemed export if the disclosure takes place in the United States and a deemed reexport if the disclosure takes place outside the United States.

Some items are specifically excluded from the scope of the EAR and thus are not covered by any EAR restriction (but may be subject to certain other restrictions such as U.S. economic sanctions and embargoes). Items not subject to the EAR include the following:[12]

- Most books, newspapers, periodicals, music, and films.
- Most software or technology that is "publicly available" (but not certain software or technology dealing with encryption). Software and technology may be considered publicly available if they have been published.[13] Also considered publicly available is software and technology resulting from "fundamental

---

8. *See* 15 C.F.R. § 734.3, "Items Subject to the EAR." The *de minimis* rule is different depending on the destination of the item. For destinations subject to U.S. embargo, if the controlled U.S.-origin content is valued at 10% or less of the total value of the item, the item is not subject to the EAR. For destinations not subject to embargo, if the controlled U.S.-origin content is valued at 25% or less of the total value of the item, the item is not subject to the EAR. For certain special items, such as certain encryption items, there is no *de minimis* level.

9. *See* 15 C.F.R. § 734.3(a)(4).

10. While posting information on the Internet may also constitute an export, the regulatory treatment of Internet exports is complicated by the fact that items on the open Internet are considered to be publicly available, and thus not subject to the EAR. *See* section 3.3.

11. *See* 15 C.F.R. § 734.2(b)(2)(ii).

12. *See* 15 C.F.R. § 734.3(b) ("Items Not Subject to the EAR").

13. The rules for what constitutes "publication" for these purposes are provided in 15 C.F.R. § 734.7.

research" in science and engineering, where the resulting information is "ordinarily published and shared broadly within the scientific community."[14]

- Information included in a patent application.[15]

3.4 WHO IS REGULATED?

Because the EAR generally control U.S.-origin items wherever located and foreign-origin items containing more than de minimis U.S. content, the actions of both U.S. and non-U.S. persons and companies may be subject to the EAR. Exports of items subject to the EAR from one country outside the United States to another are referred to as reexports.

3.5 CLASSIFICATION: THE EXPORT CONTROL CLASSIFICATION NUMBER

The CCL is divided into ten broad categories, and each category is further subdivided into five item types. Entries on the CCL are identified by an ECCN, which is composed of a single digit, followed by a letter, followed by a three-digit code (e.g., 2B991).

The first digit of the ECCN indicates the CCL category as follows:

0: Nuclear materials, facilities, and equipment (and miscellaneous items)
1: Materials, chemicals, microorganisms, and toxins
2: Materials processing
3: Electronics
4: Computers
5: Telecommunications and information security
6: Sensors and lasers
7: Navigation and avionics
8: Marine
9: Propulsion systems, space vehicles, and related equipment

The letter in the ECCN indicates the product group as follows:

A: Systems, equipment, and components
B: Test, inspection, and production equipment
C: Material
D: Software
E: Technology

14. *See* 15 C.F.R. § 734.8.
15. *See* C.F.R. § 734.3(b)(3)(iv).

The final three digits of the ECCN indicate the basis for control. The three-digit codes 000–099 indicate control for national security, 100–199 for missile technology, 200–299 for nuclear-related technology, 300–399 for chemical and biological weapons, and 900–999 for antiterrorism, crime control, and other reasons. If an item is controlled on more than one basis, the lowest (in terms of absolute numbering) and highest (in terms of control level) applicable "reason for control" group number is typically used in the ECCN.

If the item is not given an ECCN, it falls in a catch-all category known as EAR99, discussed in section 3.6 below.

BIS encourages exporters to self-classify their items and technologies on the CCL in most instances. The agency also provides formal commodity classifications, which are typically used when the classification of an item is ambiguous or when the compliance profile of a particular export requires a high degree of certainty in the classification. To obtain a formal classification, a party must submit an application to BIS containing information about the product, including a description and technical specifications of the product, via BIS's Internet-based licensing/classification system, SNAP-R.[16] BIS then will determine whether the item is subject to the EAR and, if so, what ECCN applies. In particular, BIS issues a formal classification through the Commodity Classification Automated Tracking System (CCATS), with a unique number on which the manufacturer and exporters can rely from that point forward.[17]

As noted in part 3.4, with limited exceptions, the jurisdiction of the EAR extends to all U.S.-origin items wherever they are located and all items in the United States.[18] EAR99 is the designation for items that fit within the scope of the EAR, and are therefore subject to the EAR, but are not assigned an ECCN with specific technical or functional parameters. The EAR99 designation is thus unique in that it is not described on the CCL; instead, it serves as a catch-all classification for commercial items subject to the EAR that have not been identified to pose particular national security concerns.[19] The EAR99 listing appears in a statement at the end of each CCL category, as follows: "[i]tems subject to the EAR that are not elsewhere specified in this CCL category or in any other category in the CCL are designated by the number EAR99."[20]

EAR99 items may be exported to most destinations without a license. Important exceptions include situations where a "general prohibition" applies.[21] For example, EAR99 items may not be exported without a license to embargoed destinations, or for

---

16. *See* http://www.bis.doc.gov/snap/index.htm.
17. Today, many exporters use the term "CCATS" to refer to the BIS classification itself, as opposed to the tracking system.
18. 15 C.F.R. § 734.3(a)(1–2).
19. *See* 15 C.F.R. §§ 732.3(b)(3) and 734.3(c).
20. *See* 15 C.F.R. pt. 774, supp. 1.
21. *See infra* section 3.7.

certain prohibited end uses, or to certain prohibited end users such as those listed on the Denied Persons List[22] and the Entity List.[23] Embargoed destinations are listed in part 746 of the EAR, although exporters also should consult the U.S. sanctions regulations issued by OFAC, described in chapter 1. End-use and end-user-based export restrictions are listed in part 744 of the EAR and should be consulted prior to exporting items to an unfamiliar party or to a party where there are "red flags" that the party may use the product for prohibited end uses or divert the product to embargoed destinations or prohibited end users. Prohibited end uses in part 744 of the EAR are varied, but the core prohibited end uses include the proliferation of weapons of mass destruction: nuclear weapons, unsafeguarded nuclear and fuel cycle activities, chemical and biological weapons, and rockets, missiles, and unmanned aircraft (UAVs). In any event, all exports from the United States must be documented in compliance with the recordkeeping provisions of part 762 of the EAR.

3.6 GENERAL PROHIBITIONS

Part 736 of the EAR lists ten general prohibitions that apply to any transaction subject to the EAR. Any violation of one of the general prohibitions will be subject to possible enforcement and any applicable penalties, as described in part 764 of the EAR.[24]

The general prohibitions are as follows:[25]

1. Export or reexport of controlled items without a required license or license exception.
2. Reexport and export from abroad of foreign-made items incorporating more than a de minimis amount of controlled U.S. content without a required license or license exception.
3. Reexport and export from abroad of the foreign-produced direct product of U.S. technology and software without a required license or license exception.
4. Engaging in actions prohibited by a denial order. From time to time, the Department of Commerce issues orders under part 766 of the EAR. Denial orders are published in the *Federal Register*. Export contrary to the terms of a denial order is prohibited; there are no license exceptions that authorize any such exports.
5. Export or reexport to end uses or end users that are prohibited by part 744 of the EAR.
6. Export or reexport to embargoed destinations as set forth in part 746 without a required license. As of 2012, Cuba, Iran, Sudan, and Syria are subject to comprehensive economic embargoes, such that virtually all exports to those

---

22. U.S. Department of Commerce, Bureau of Industry and Security, Denied Persons List, http://www.bis.doc.gov/dpl/thedeniallist.asp.
23. 15 C.F.R. pt. 744, supp. 4.
24. 15 C.F.R. § 736.1(c).
25. 15 C.F.R. § 736.2(b).

countries require licenses. North Korea is also subject to sanctions, such that most exports require a license. Other countries are subject to somewhat more targeted sanctions. As outlined in more detail in chapter 1, it is important to understand that trade restrictions differ widely by country and evolve regularly based on U.S. policy considerations. Depending on the type of export and the embargoed destination, either BIS or OFAC will have licensing jurisdiction (though, in certain transactions, both agencies may have jurisdiction).

7. Support of proliferation activities, such as certain financing, contracting, service, support, transportation, freight forwarding, or employment activities by a U.S. person where the U.S. person knows the activity will assist in the proliferation of weapons of mass destruction set forth in section 744.6(c) of the EAR.

8. Certain in-transit shipments: For items being exported or reexported via a route that requires the items to be unladen from vessels or aircraft in any of a list of countries,[26] a separate license must be obtained as if the country of unlading were the ultimate destination.

9. Violation of any order, terms, or conditions of a license. All BIS licenses contain terms and conditions limiting their applicability.

10. Proceeding with transactions with knowledge that a violation has occurred or is about to occur.

General Prohibition 10 merits special mention. First, General Prohibition 10 refers to all the other prohibitions; those prohibitions become, in essence, an element of General Prohibition 10. Because a violation under General Prohibition 10 turns on a "transaction" related to a violation, a violation could include not only an export or reexport itself, but also any activity such as transferring, financing, ordering, transporting, forwarding, or even storing an item subject to the EAR within the United States. Another key aspect of General Prohibition 10 is the "knowledge" requirement, which can be met by either actual knowledge or constructive knowledge— that is, when a party "should have known" of a violation. General Prohibition 10 effectively requires exporters seeking to support past illegal exports (for example, to export an item previously exported in violation of U.S. law, or to repair such an item) to file a disclosure with BIS so that they may then seek authorization from BIS to provide such support.[27]

---

26.   The countries subject to this prohibition as of 2012 were Armenia, Azerbaijan, Belarus, Cambodia, Cuba, Georgia, Kazakhstan, Kyrgyzstan, Laos, Mongolia, North Korea, Russia, Tajikistan, Turkmenistan, Ukraine, Uzbekistan, and Vietnam.

27.   Such authorizations are not filed through the normal licensing process of SNAP-R, but instead through a hard copy letter made to the Office of Exporter Services (*see infra* discussion at 3.11).

3.7 REASONS FOR CONTROL

Generally speaking, under the EAR, items are controlled for export in accordance with specified foreign policy aims of the United States. Items on the CCL are assigned one or more reasons for control, which in turn form the basis for licensing requirements for those items.

The reasons for control, and examples (as of 2013) of items controlled for each reason, are as follows:

1. Proliferation of chemical and biological weapons. Examples of items controlled for this reason include animal pathogens (ECCN 1C352) and equipment capable of use in handling toxic materials (ECCN 2B352).
2. Nuclear nonproliferation. Examples include machine tools and any combination thereof for removing or cutting metals, ceramics, or composites, which can be equipped with electronic devices for "numerical control" (ECCN 2B001) and high explosives other than those on the U.S. Munitions List (ECCN 1C239).
3. National security. Examples include equipment for the manufacturing of semiconductor devices or materials (ECCN 3B001), optical equipment and components (ECCN 6A004), and submersible vehicles and surface vessels (ECCN 8A001).
4. Missile technology. Examples include turbojet and turbofan engines (ECCN 9A101) and ceramic base materials (ECCN 1C007).
5. Regional stability. Examples include radar systems and equipment (ECCN 6A998) and certain cameras (6A003).
6. Firearms convention.[28] Examples include shotguns with barrel length 18 inches or over (ECCN 0A984) and optical sighting devices (ECCN 0A987).
7. Crime control. Examples include voice print identification and analysis equipment (ECCN 3A980) and restraint devices (ECCN 0A982).
8. Antiterrorism. Examples include portable electric generators (ECCN 2A994) and certain information security software (ECCN 5D992).
9. Short supply (not on country chart). Examples include horses for export by sea, crude oil and certain petroleum products, and western red cedar.
10. U.N. sanctions (not on country chart). Examples include aircraft and gas turbine engines controlled in ECCN 9A991 and certain discharge arms (e.g., stun guns, electric cattle prods) (ECCN 0A985).
11. Specially designed implements of torture such as those controlled in ECCN 0A983.

---

28. The firearms convention referred to here is the Inter-American Convention Against the Illicit Manufacturing of and Trafficking in Firearms, Ammunition, Explosives, and Other Related Materials (Nov. 14, 1997), governing nations of the Organization of American States.

12. Encryption items such as "information security systems" meeting certain technical criteria in ECCN 5A002 and corresponding technology (ECCN 5E002).

13. Communications intercepting devices such as those primarily useful for surreptitious interception of wire, oral, or electronic communications (ECCN 5A980) and software applying to such devices (ECCN 5D980).

The reason for control appears in the heading of the ECCN entries.[29] Below is an example of such an entry:

A. Systems, Equipment and Components

5A002 Systems, equipment, application specific "electronic assemblies," modules and integrated circuits for "information security," as follows (see List of Items Controlled), and other specially designed components therefor.

License Requirements

Reasons for control: NS, AT, EI

Control(s)	*Country Chart*
NS applies to entire entry	NS Column 1
AT applies to entire entry	AT Column 1

In this example, any systems or equipment meeting the technical specifications of ECCN 5A002 are subject to national security (NS), antiterrorism (AT), and encryption items (EI) controls. In order to determine whether the reason for control would require a license or license exception for a given destination, it is necessary to check the country chart and applicable related regulations in part 742 and 740.17 of the EAR as outlined in section 3.9.

End-user and end-use-based controls, which may apply regardless of the country of destination, are contained in part 744 of the EAR.[30] While those are not identified as "reasons for control" as that label is employed in the EAR, end-use restrictions include but are not limited to certain nuclear end uses, restrictions on chemical and biological weapons end uses, missile, rocket, and unmanned air vehicle end uses, maritime nuclear propulsion end uses, and military end uses in the People's Republic of China.[31]

Separate restrictions on end users include the lists maintained by BIS (the Entity List and the Denied Persons List) and persons designated in certain executive orders and named to the U.S. Department of Treasury's Specially Designated Nationals

---

29.   15 C.F.R. pt. 774, supp. 1.
30.   15 C.F.R. pt. 744.
31.   *See* 15 C.F.R. §§ 744.2, 744.4, 744.5, 744.21.

(SDN) List.[32] BIS maintains a collection of "Lists to Check" on its website that can be used to screen prohibited parties to any transaction.[33]

Once an item's correct ECCN and reason for control are determined, the Commerce Country Chart[34] is generally used to determine whether a license is required to export or reexport that item to a particular destination.[35] Some ECCNs contain self-evident descriptions of the license requirement (e.g., in the rare case where a license is required to all destinations)[36] or refer to another set of controls such as the ITAR.[37] But for most items, the reason for control must be found in the ECCN entry, and then the destination (and intermediate destinations for transshipped items) must be checked in the country chart.[38]

A sample country chart entry (for Uruguay) is reproduced below:

Reasons for Control

Countries	Chemical & Biological Weapons			Nuclear Nonprolif- eration		National Security		Missile Tech	Regional Stability		Firearms Conven- tion	Crime Control			Anti- Terrorism	
	CB 1	CB 2	CB 3	NP 1	NP 2	NS 1	NS 2	MT 1	RS 1	RS 2	FC 1	CC 1	CC 2	CC 3	AT 1	AT 2
Uruguay	X	X		X		X	X	X	X	X	X	X		X		

The checked boxes indicate that a license or applicable license exception is required to export (or reexport) to Uruguay any item controlled under the following reasons for control: Chemical & Biological Weapons Categories 1 and 2, Nuclear Nonproliferation Category 1, National Security Categories 1 and 2, Missile Technology Category 1, Regional Stability Categories 1 and 2, Firearms Convention Category 1, and Crime Control Categories 1 and 3.

As an example, an item classified in ECCN 5A002 (from the example used in earlier in section 3.7) would be controlled for export to Uruguay as follows: by the terms of the ECCN, a 5A002 item is controlled under NS column 1; as shown in the coun-

---

32. *See* 15 C.F.R. pt. 744, supp. 4 (Entity List); U.S. Department of Commerce, Bureau of Industry and Security, Denied Persons List, http://www.bis.doc.gov/dpl/thedeniallist.asp; 15 C.F.R. § 744.12 (referring to SDN List, 31 C.F.R. ch. V, app. A).

33. *See* BIS, Lists to Check, http://www.bis.doc.gov/complianceandenforcement/liststocheck.htm. The Department of Commerce has also published a consolidated list of most other important lists. That consolidated list is available at http://export.gov/ecr/eg_main_023148.asp.

34. 15 C.F.R. pt. 738, supp. 1.

35. *See* 15 C.F.R. § 738.1(b).

36. *See, e.g.,* ECCN 0A983 (specially designed implements of torture—noting that a license is required for all destinations).

37. *See, e.g.,* 15 C.F.R. § 774, supp. 1, ECCN 7A994.

38. 15 C.F.R. § 738.3(a); *see generally* 15 C.F.R. § 738.4.

try chart entry above, items controlled for National Security column 1 are controlled for export to Uruguay.

It is important to note that if any of the reasons for control listed in the ECCN has an "X" in the box for the destination on the country chart, the item is controlled. In this example, 5A002 is controlled for both NS 1 and AT 1, but Uruguay only has an "X" in the box for NS 1. A single applicable reason for control is sufficient to require a license or license exception for the export. The fact that there is no restriction to Uruguay for items controlled for antiterrorism reasons (i.e., there is no "X" in the box for AT 1) does not change the fact that the 5A002 item is still controlled for export to the country.

It is also important to note that the encryption item reason for control does not appear in the country chart. As an example, the ECCN 5A002 entry lists "EI" as one of the reasons for control. But the country chart entry for Uruguay (as with all countries on the chart) does not contain a column for EI controls. For encryption item controls, it is necessary to review the provisions in the notes to the ECCN and the relevant regulations (particularly 742.15 and 740.17) to determine whether a license is needed. There are additional items that are controlled, for example crude oil and other items controlled for short supply, that do not appear in the country chart. If an ECCN identifies a reason for control that does *not* appear as one of the columns in the country chart, you must nonetheless research the reasons for control in the EAR. Typically, part 742 is a good place to start, but some controls have their own special section, e.g., short supply controls, which are addressed in part 754 of the EAR.

The fact that an item is controlled for export to a particular destination means that a license or applicable license exception is required to export the given item to that destination. Note that if there are multiple reasons for control, a license exception is required for each applicable reason for control for the given destination.[39]

Remember too that, as noted above, export controls apply equally to exports physically sent to other countries and to deemed exports—that is, transfers of controlled technology or source code to a non-U.S. national even while in the United States.[40]

The Commerce Country Chart does *not* cover end-use or end-user restrictions and, although it makes reference to U.S. sanctions and embargoes in some country entries (e.g., Cuba), it does not provide full coverage of the end-use and end-user restrictions.[41] Because the end-use and end-user restrictions may impose separate licensing requirements administered by BIS or other U.S. government agencies, it is important to implement a screening process for those restrictions in addition to checking the Commerce Country Chart.

---

39. *See* 15 C.F.R. § 738.4(a)(2)(ii)(A).
40. *See* 15 C.F.R. § 734.2(b)(2)(ii).
41. *See* 15 C.F.R. § 738.4(a)(2)(ii)(B).

3.8 LICENSE EXCEPTIONS

Part 740 of the EAR lists the various license exceptions that are available to export-ers. An applicable license exception provides authorization for a transaction that is controlled for export to a given destination, end user, or end use that would otherwise require a license from BIS. License exceptions are highly fact-dependent and may be limited by the dollar value of a shipment or other factors. Certain license exceptions are only available after certain steps are completed (such as a specific request to BIS or a technical review by BIS).

By way of example, license exceptions are available for certain exports of the following:[42]

- certain lower-technology items of low dollar value (license exception LVS);
- exports of certain items to countries listed in country group B of the EAR, found in 15 C.F.R. § 740 Supp. 1 (license exception GBS);
- baggage as described in 15 C.F.R. § 740.14 (license exception BAG); and
- certain aircraft and vessels on "temporary sojourn" in the United States or through foreign countries (license exception AVS).[43]

As summarized below, several steps will help to determine whether a license excep-tion applies to a given transaction.

1. Determine whether any of the general prohibitions (discussed in section 3.7) apply to the export or reexport.[44] If no prohibition applies, a license or license exception is unnecessary (though you may have specific recordkeeping obliga-tions under parts 758 and 762 of the EAR).
2. Determine whether one or more of the restrictions against using a license excep-tion applies.[45] Be sure to check EAR section 740.2 carefully before proceeding, as it is a trap for the unwary. If a restriction in 740.2 renders a license exception unavailable, a license is required to proceed with the export or reexport.
3. If no restrictions apply, determine whether any of the license exceptions listed in part 740 of the EAR apply. Some license exceptions, such as LVS, GBS, TSR, and others, are available only if they are listed as available in the ECCN of the item to be exported. Other license exceptions are available even if they are not listed in the ECCN. It is therefore necessary to carefully review both the ECCN and the relevant section of part 740 describing the license exception and conditions for its use to determine the applicability of a particular license

---

42.   The full list of license exceptions is contained in 15 C.F.R. pt. 740.
43.   15 C.F.R. § 740.15.
44.   15 C.F.R. § 736.2(b).
45.   15 C.F.R. § 740.2.

exception. Eligibility may depend on the item, destination country, end use, and/or end user of the item as well as any special conditions of the license exception.[46]

4. Comply with all terms and conditions listed in the license exception.

3.9 LICENSING

(a) License Application

When a specific license is required, the exporter must submit a license application to BIS through the agency's electronic application system, known as SNAP-R (an acronym for Simplified Network Application Process Redesign).[47] In order to submit an application using SNAP-R, it is first necessary to register with SNAP-R and obtain an authorizing PIN.

As part of the license application, the exporter must provide information about itself and all other parties to the transaction—for example, the end user and any freight forwarder and/or other intermediate consignees. The application also must provide the applicable ECCN and a description of items to be exported, including the quantity and value of such items.

(b) License

A BIS license typically will contain a number of standard clauses and a term of validity, and may also include specific terms and conditions. All terms, conditions, and restrictions of a license must be complied with; failure to do so would be considered a violation of general prohibition 9.[48] A license authorizes exports only within the terms of the license application. It does not constitute an authorization to engage in other transactions with the country of destination or to continue exports after the license has expired.

(c) 764.5(f) Authorizations

If a company has exported something without a license and now needs to support it in an action that would otherwise *not* require a license, as noted above, that support would be prohibited by general prohibition 10.[49] It is possible to obtain an authorization to provide such support, but this process is not conducted through the SNAP-R

---

46.   License exceptions TMP, RPL, BAG, AVS, GOV, and TSU authorize exports notwithstanding the provisions of the CCL. List-based license exceptions (LVS, GBS, CIV, TSR, and APP) are available only to the extent specified on the CCL. Part 740 of the EAR provides authorization for reexports only to the extent each license exception expressly authorizes reexports. License exception APR authorizes reexports only. For exports under license exceptions GBS, CIV, LVS, APP, TSR, or GOV, you should determine the applicability of certain reporting requirements. 15 C.F.R. § 743.1.

47.   http://www.bis.doc.gov/snap/index.htm.

48.   15 C.F.R. § 736.2(b)(9); *see also supra* section 3.7.

49.   15 C.F.R. § 736.2(b)(10); *see also supra* section 3.7.

licensing process.[50] Instead, it is conducted by filing a letter request with the Office of Exporter Services within BIS after the company has filed a voluntary disclosure with the Office of Export Enforcement (OEE) within BIS (see discussion at 3.12). Unfortunately, the Office of Exporter Services has recently begun restricting what the authorization request letter can contain. Previously, that office had authorized broad-based requests to conduct all operations that were prohibited by general prohibition 10. At present, however, the office is requiring that the request be tailored to the specific actions necessary, making such requests much less useful and likely increasing the number of requests that will need to be filed.

In the event that an exporter discovers that it has violated the EAR, it may decide to voluntarily report the violation to the OEE. Part 764 of the EAR details the procedures involved in making a voluntary self-disclosure to the OEE. Reporting a violation of the EAR is not mandatory, but it is strongly encouraged by the OEE and may mitigate potential penalties.[51] A person disclosing a violation will be given credit only if neither the OEE nor another U.S. government agency has previously learned of the conduct at issue.

The OEE encourages persons submitting a voluntary self-disclosure to follow a two-step process:

(1) submit a brief initial notification with basic information about the parties involved and the conduct at issue, and

(2) submit a subsequent, full narrative report detailing the suspected violations at issue, the review conducted, and measures taken to deter future violations. The EAR contain a list of details to be covered in the narrative report and examples of supporting documentation to accompany the report. Submitting parties are required to certify to the accuracy of the information submitted with the disclosure. The OEE generally discourages oral presentations for disclosures but may agree to them upon request. The OEE also requires that parties retain all records relevant to a transaction until a final decision has been made.

It is important for every exporter to understand the EAR and other relevant export laws and to have an appropriate compliance program in place to prevent and detect violations. While BIS has created an export management system document that provides details of what the agency considers to be essential components of an effective

---

50. Note that if the support would require a license — for example, technical assistance that would require a license — the authorization request is still made via SNAP-R, although the SNAP-R license request should be sure to reference the past export and the pending voluntary disclosure to make sure it is complete.

51. BIS also has published its "Guidance on Charging and Penalty Determinations in Settlement of Administrative Enforcement Cases," 15 C.F.R. pt. 766, supp. 1, which describes BIS's approach to EAR violations. The guidance specifically includes a list of both mitigating and aggravating factors the agency will consider when making a penalty determination.

export compliance program, no one sample policy should be considered sufficient for compliance. Rather, a compliance program must be tailored carefully to the exporter's needs. For example, an exporter whose inventory is limited to EAR99 items and whose sales territory consists solely of the United States and Canada will have a very different risk profile from a company that regularly ships highly controlled items to China, Russia, and the Middle East. A company that employs only U.S. citizens may have less of a need for strict technology transfer controls than a company that has many non-U.S. engineers in its R&D laboratories.

One important component of any compliance program is the ability to identify and respond to "red flags"—that is, any circumstances that indicate an export may be destined for an improper destination, end use, or end user.[52] BIS has developed an extensive list of sample red flags on its website, but any abnormal circumstances may give cause for suspicion.[53] BIS expects that any red flags present will be addressed before any export transaction occurs. Exporters also have a duty not to self-blind with respect to information that may constitute a red flag.[54]

Whatever compliance policy the exporter adopts, it is important that relevant personnel be trained on the applicable law and the company's procedures for complying with it. Records of each export transaction generally are required to be maintained for at least five years from the date of the transaction and must be made readily available to the government at its request. Periodic compliance audits may also be appropriate to review how effectively existing compliance processes are working and to identify areas for improvement.

3.10 PENALTIES AND ENFORCEMENT

Penalties for violations of the EAR can be severe. Criminal penalties against a company can include fines of up to $1 million.[55] Criminal penalties against an individual can include a fine of up to $1 million or imprisonment for up to twenty years, or both, for each violation.[56]

Civil penalties against a company or an individual can include fines of up to the greater of $250,000 or two times the value of the exports for each violation.[57]

In addition to the civil and administrative penalties outlined above, the U.S. government may impose administrative penalties in appropriate cases including the following:

---

52.   15 C.F.R. pt. 732, supp. 3.
53.   *See* BIS, Red Flag Indicators, *available at* www.bis.doc.gov/complianceandenforcement/redflagindica tors.htm.
54.   15 C.F.R. pt. 732, supp. 3.
55.   50 U.S.C. § 1705.
56.   *Id.*
57.   *Id.*

- denial of export privileges
- exclusion from U.S. government contracts
- seizure and forfeiture of goods

The U.S. government continues to aggressively enforce the EAR against companies and individuals both inside and outside the United States. A short list of recent export enforcement actions, including descriptions, is provided below at Section 3.12.

Several trends emerge from these and other recent enforcement matters. First, the government clearly believes that taking action against individuals who violate the export laws, and in certain cases sending people to jail for such violations, is a particularly effective deterrent against violations. Second, recent enforcement actions show that the U.S. government remains especially focused on export violations involving China—many recent enforcement actions, particularly several high-profile matters, involve unauthorized exports to Chinese entities or by Chinese nationals. Finally, settlements increasingly include specific compliance obligations that the settling party has to meet. For example, when settling with individuals, the government is often requiring individuals to attend export compliance training, including certifying to the government as to attendance at such training. With respect to entities, designated officials are also being required to attend training, and entities are being obligated to conduct—and report to the government on the results of—periodic export controls compliance audits.

We think these trends are likely to continue, particularly in light of new tools the government has introduced for investigating and enforcing potential violations. One of these tools is the National Export Control Coordinator, a position created under President George W. Bush in 2007 to coordinate the U.S. Justice Department and other law enforcement agencies in export enforcement.[58] Another tool is the Export Coordination Enforcement Center created under President Barack Obama, designed to coordinate export enforcement among federal agencies.[59]

3.11 SPECIAL TOPIC: EXPORT CONTROL REFORM

In August 2009, President Obama ordered an interagency review of U.S. export controls directed at strengthening national security and the competitiveness of key U.S. manufacturing and technology sectors. That review found the current system to be overly complicated, redundant, and in some cases ineffective.[60]

---

58. U.S. Department of Justice, Justice Department Appoints National Export Control Coordinator as Part of Enhanced Counter-Proliferation Effort (June 20, 2007).
59. Exec. Order No. 13,558 (Nov. 9, 2010).
60. http://export.gov/ecr/eg_main_047329.asp.

In response to this finding, the administration launched the Export Control Reform Initiative (ECR Initiative) aimed at simplifying the U.S. export control system. Three phases are planned: In phases I and II, which are underway, various export control definitions, regulations, and policies are being reconciled among the various regimes. Phase III envisions a single control list, single licensing agency, single information technology system, and single enforcement coordination center.[61]

In July 2011, BIS issued a proposed rule that would create a regulatory structure for harmonizing the ITAR control list (the U.S. Munitions List) (*see* chapter 2) and the CCL and would standardize certain key definitions of the two regulatory systems. The proposed regulatory structure would allow a number of parts and components currently regulated under the ITAR to migrate to EAR control. Such items would be subject to significant control (National Security column 1) and would require a license or applicable license exception to export to all countries other than Canada.[62]

In a subsequent series of proposed rules, BIS has proposed revisions to the EAR relating to items the President determines no longer warrant control under the USML.[63] In addition, the U.S. State Department has issued a series of related proposed rules to revise and establish categories of the USML.[64]

In 2012, BIS revised the EAR by establishing a new ECCN series, 0Y521, on the CCL and making corresponding changes to the EAR. The ECCN 0Y521 series covers items that warrant control on the CCL but are not yet identified in an existing ECCN. This new temporary holding classification is equivalent, with one limitation, to USML Category XXI (Miscellaneous Articles). Items will be added to the 0Y521 ECCNs by BIS, with the concurrence of the Departments of Defense and State, when it identifies an item that should be controlled because it provides a significant military or intelligence advantage to the United States or because foreign policy reasons justify such control.[65]

Under phase III of the ECR Initiative, it is envisioned that the U.S. export control agencies will work with the administration (and Congress, to the extent necessary) to streamline export redundancies by creating what are referred to as the "four singles"—that is, a single control list, single licensing agency, single information technology system, and single enforcement coordination center.[66]

---

61. http://export.gov/ecr/eg_main_047329.asp.
62. *See* 76 Fed. Reg. 41,958 (Jul. 15, 2011).
63. *See* 76 Fed. Reg. 68,675 (Nov. 7, 2011); 76 Fed. Reg. 76,072 (Dec. 6, 2011); 76 Fed. Reg. 76,085 (Dec. 6, 2011); 76 Fed. Reg. 80,282 (Dec. 23, 2011); 76 Fed. Reg. 80,291 (Dec. 23, 2011).
64. *See* 76 Fed. Reg. 68,694 (Nov. 7, 2011); 76 Fed. Red. 76,100 (Dec. 6, 2011); 76 Fed. Reg. 76,097 (Dec. 6, 2011); 76 Fed. Reg. 80,302 (Dec. 19, 2011); 76 Fed. Reg. 80,305 (Dec. 23, 2011).
65. *See* 77 Fed. Reg. 22,191 (Apr. 13, 2012).
66. http://export.gov/ecr/eg_main_047329.asp.

3.12 RECENT EXPORT ENFORCEMENT MATTERS

(a) Recent Enforcement Matters: Individuals

(i) Ping Cheng (March 2012)

Defendant was charged with exporting controlled carbon fibers to China without appropriate BIS authorization. The defendant settled the case in exchange for a civil penalty in the amount of $125,000, though $75,000 of the total was suspended so long as the defendant did not violate the export laws for two years following the date of the settlement. The defendant also agreed to attend export compliance training within one year of the settlement and to provide a certificate of attendance to the government following such training. In addition, the defendant was the subject of a denial order that was suspended for two years so long as the defendant did not commit any further export violations.

(ii) Eric Cohen (June 2011)

Defendant was charged with taking actions to evade the Export Administration Regulations and abetting the unlicensed export of thermal imaging cameras to South Korea. To settle the charges, the defendant agreed to pay a civil penalty of $15,000. In addition, his export privileges were revoked for a period of five years.

(b) Recent Enforcement Matters: Entities

(i) General Technology Services Integration Corporation (June 2012)

Company exported analog-to-digital converters to China without appropriate export authorization. The company agreed to settle the matter for a civil penalty in the amount of $300,000, with $250,000 of that penalty suspended. The company also agreed that it would conduct three export compliance audits to cover the six-year period beginning April 1, 2012. In addition, the company agreed that its officials would complete export compliance training.

(ii) A.M. Castle & Co. (September 2011)

The company was charged with exporting aluminum alloy to China, Malaysia, Mexico, and Singapore without necessary export licenses. The company agreed to settle the matter in exchange for a civil penalty in the amount of $775,000 and also agreed to complete and submit results of an external export controls compliance audit within fourteen months of the settlement.

(iii) Toll Global Forwarding (USA) Inc. (July 2011)

The company was charged with causing, aiding, and abetting the unauthorized export of platinum electronic components and platinum pellets to Indian entities listed on the BIS Entity list. The company agreed to settle the matter by paying a civil penalty in the amount of $200,000 and also agreed to complete an external export controls compliance audit within fourteen months of the settlement.

(iv) Polar Star International Co. Ltd. (March 2011)

The company was charged with reexporting electronic components controlled for antiterrorism (AT) grounds to Al-Faris, a designated entity under General Order

No. 3, without appropriate export authorization. The company settled the matter in exchange for a civil penalty of $50,000 and an agreement to conduct and submit results of an external compliance audit to the government within eighteen months of the settlement.

(v) TW Metals, Inc. (March 2011)

The company was charged with exporting titanium alloy and aluminum bar controlled for nuclear nonproliferation grounds to China (forty-eight violations) and Israel (one violation) without the required authorization. The company agreed to settle the matter in exchange for a civil penalty in the amount of $575,000.

Anti-Money Laundering Controls

Cari N. Stinebower

4.1 OVERVIEW

As with economic sanctions and export controls, covered in the prior chapters, since September 11, 2001, anti-money laundering laws and regulations have dramatically evolved and developed, as has the focus on enforcement. Given the role sanctions, export controls, and anti-money laundering laws and regulations collectively play in protecting the domestic and international financial system, it is not a surprise that once-distinct practice areas now overlap, as do many of the compliance responsibilities and enforcement investigations.

What Is Regulated? Traditional financial institutions and designated nonfinancial businesses and professionals (DNFBPs) are regulated to protect the financial system from exposure to money laundering and terrorist financing. These entities are regulated because they are "gatekeepers" and can help stop illicit financial transactions from entering "clean" commerce.

What Is Money Laundering and Terrorist Financing? Money laundering is the practice of engaging in financial transactions to conceal or attempt to conceal an illegal source of money, the identity of the individual or group to whom the money belongs, the beneficiaries of the funds, and/or the uses to which funds are being put.[1] Money laundering is accomplished by transforming questionable funds into "legitimate funds" by placing them into legitimate financial channels, including annuity contracts, life insurance policies, and brokerage accounts. Terrorist financing provides a person (individual or entity) the opportunity to collect funds with the intention of intimidating a population or compelling a government or international organization to abstain from carrying out an act through the threat of violence. The funding may be derived from criminal activities or legitimate sources.[2]

Who Are the Regulators? U.S. anti-money laundering (AML) laws and regulations are shaped to protect the U.S. financial system from money laundering and terrorist financing threats—but also, as part of an informal association of industry sectors (i.e.,

---

1. *See* Financial Crimes Enforcement Network, *History of Anti-Money Laundering Laws*, http://www.fincen.gov/news_room/aml_history.html.
2. Office of the Inspector General of the Department of the Treasury, Terrorist Financing/Money Laundering: Responsibility for Bank Secrecy Act Is Spread Across Many Organizations 5 (Apr. 9, 2008), http://www.treasury.gov/about/organizational-structure/ig/Documents/oig08030.pdf.

the "gatekeepers") and governments, to protect the international financial network from the same threats. In the United States, while there are close to one dozen domestic organizations[3] that have substantial Bank Secrecy Act (BSA) responsibilities, the Financial Crimes Enforcement Network (FinCEN) maintains primary responsibility for administering the BSA. Internationally, some of the leading international groups focused on money laundering and terrorist financing controls, primarily because the banking sector was a leader in responding to the global AML threat, include:

- the Financial Actions Task Force (FATF);
- the Egmont Group of Financial Intelligence Units; and
- the lead industry sector groups, including the Wolfsberg Group.

Where to Find the Regulations: FinCEN administers the BSA through the Bank Secrecy Act Regulations. *See* Bank Secrecy Act, 31 C.F.R. tit. 31, ch. X (2012) (formerly 31 C.F.R. pt. 103).

How to Get a License: The BSA does not contemplate licenses. Most suspicious activity reports (SARs) are filed electronically through FinCEN's e-filing system at http://bsaefiling.fincen.treas.gov/main.html.

Key Website: For U.S. financial institutions and DNFBPs, see http://www.fincen.gov/.

(a) The International AML Organizations

Because we operate in a global economy, and financial institutions and DNFBPs activities operate across borders, U.S. AML laws and regulations are part of the global gatekeeper initiatives.

(b) The Financial Actions Task Force

Since at least 1989, when the G-7 formed the FATF, global leaders have recognized that money laundering is a serious threat to the stability of the global financial system. The FATF was established at the G-7 Summit to examine money laundering techniques and trends, review the response taken at the national or international level, and establish measures to be taken to combat money laundering.

The FATF established guidelines that, if implemented by member states, are designed to protect the international financial system from money laundering and terrorist financing threats and threats posed by proliferators of weapons of mass

---

3. Within Treasury, in addition to FinCEN and OFAC, the Office of the Comptroller of the Currency and IRS maintain AML duties. Other regulators include the Federal Reserve, Federal Deposit Insurance Corporation, Securities and Exchange Commission, the National Credit Union Administration, and the Commodities Futures Trading Commission. SROs include the Financial Industry Regulatory Authority, the New York Mercantile Exchange, and the National Futures Association.

destruction. While the FATF is an intergovernmental policy-making body with no independent ability to enact laws,[4] it "enforces" its standards through the Mutual Evaluation Process. In addition to the United States, other charter members of the FATF include the United Kingdom, France, Italy, and Germany (and eleven other members). FATF now consists of thirty-six members, comprising thirty-four countries and territories and two regional organizations.[5] In 1990, the FATF issued a report containing a section called 40 Recommendations, which provides a comprehensive plan of action needed to combat money laundering.[6] The 40 Recommendations established (1) an anti-money laundering framework, (2) the role of the national legal system in combating money laundering, (3) the role of the financial system in combating money laundering, and (4) general guidelines for international cooperation.

In response to the attacks on September 11, 2001, the FATF issued 9 Special Recommendations to address terrorist financing threats.[7] The 40 plus 9 Recommendations, taken together with FATF's interpretive notes, constituted the standard for combating money laundering. In June 2006, the FATF evaluated the United States and found the country to have a strong regulatory system but to lack certain key features. Specifically, the FATF noted the following:

- The United States has a comprehensive legal and institutional framework for investigating and prosecuting money laundering and terrorist financing offenses.
- The United States vigorously pursues, seizes, and confiscates the assets of criminals involved in money laundering and terrorist financing.
- The United States has an effective regulatory and supervisory framework for monitoring compliance with AML/CFT measures and has imposed severe financial penalties on financial institutions that do not comply with the measures.
- Customer identification requirements apply to most types of financial institutions; however, these could be strengthened, particularly in relation to the identification of beneficial owners.

---

4. *See* Financial Action Task Force, Mutual Evaluations Programme, http://www.fatf-gafi.org/topics/mutualevaluations/.

5. Argentina, Australia, Austria, Belgium, Brazil, Canada, China, Denmark, European Commission, Finland, France, Germany, Greece, Gulf Co-operation Council, Hong Kong, Iceland, India, Ireland, Italy, Japan, Kingdom of the Netherlands, Luxembourg, Mexico, New Zealand, Norway, Portugal, Republic of Korea, Russian Federation, Singapore, South Africa, Spain, Sweden, Switzerland, Turkey, United Kingdom, and the United States. *See* Financial Actions Task Force, FATF Members and Observers, http://www.fatf-gafi.org/pages/aboutus/membersandobservers/.

6. The original 40 Recommendations are available at Financial Action Task Force, FATF 40 Recommendations (Oct. 2003), http://www.fatf-gafi.org/media/fatf/documents/recommendations/pdfs/FATF%20Recommendations%202003.pdf.

7. The 9 special Recommendations are available at Financial Action Task Force, 9 Special Recommendations (SR) on Terrorist Financing, http://www.fatf-gafi.org/document/9/0,3343,en_32250379_32236920_34032073_1_1_1_1,00.html.

- AML/CFT measures presently apply to a broad range of financial institutions; however, the FATF recommends that comprehensive AML/CFT measures should also apply to a wider range of nonfinancial businesses and professions.
- Company formation procedures and reporting requirements are such that the information on beneficial ownership of legal persons may not, in most instances, be adequate, accurate, or available on a timely basis.[8]

As addressed in greater detail below, customer identification procedures (CIP), customer due diligence (CDD), and the definition of and implementation of beneficial ownership identification procedures remain on the forefront of developing U.S. AML policies and procedures—across multiple industry sectors.

To further assist private industry sectors in addressing money laundering and terrorist financing threats, the FATF has begun to issue industry-by-industry guidance on recommended best practices. To date, the FATF has issued risk-based guidance for legal professionals, trust and company service providers, accountants, real estate agents, dealers in precious metals and stones, the life insurance sector, money services businesses, the securities sector, and commercial website and Internet payment systems.[9]

On February 16, 2012, after a year-long consultation process, the FATF published a revised 40 Recommendations, incorporating the 9 Special Recommendations and reorganizing the Recommendations into seven sections: (1) AML/CFT Policies and Coordination, (2) Money Laundering and Confiscation, (3) Terrorist Financing and Financing of Proliferation, (4) Preventative Measures, (5) Transparency and Beneficial Ownership of Legal Persons and Arrangements, (6) Powers and Responsibilities of Competent Authorities and Other Institutional Measures, and (7) International Cooperation.

In order to draft the revised 40 Recommendations, the FATF called for participation of the private sector and received considerable response. Nonetheless, the response to the private sector participation in the consultation process was a mere nine pages.[10] The FATF consultation process continues, and industry sectors on the domestic and international scale should actively contribute to the conversation with FATF. Moreover, the same industry groups also have an opportunity to craft the next generation of U.S. AML efforts, whether risk- or rules-based.

---

8. *See* Financial Action Task Force, Mutual Evaluation of the United States, http://www.fatf-gafi.org/topics/mutualevaluations/documents/mutualevaluationoftheunitedstates.html.

9. *See* Financial Action Task Force, http://www.fatf-gafi.org/documents/guidance/.

10. Financial Action Task Force, FATF's Response to the Public Consultation on the revision of the FATF Recommendations (Feb. 16, 2012), http://www.fatf-gafi.org/media/fatf/documents/publicconsultation/FATF%20Response%20to%20the%20public%20consultation%20on%20the%20revision%20of%20the%20FATF%20Recommendations.pdf.

(c) The Egmont Group

As addressed above, a key component to the success of the global AML infrastructure is cooperation between jurisdictions: where a money laundering enterprise crosses international borders, so must enforcement authorities. A key means through which to share information and cooperate during cross-border investigations is the domestic Financial Intelligence Unit (FIU) (FinCEN is the United States FIU). Recognizing the benefits inherent in the development of a FIU network, in 1995, a group of FIUs met at the Egmont Arenberg Palace in Brussels and established an informal group for the stimulation of international cooperation.[11] The Egmont Group meets regularly to address cooperation through the exchange of information, training, and the sharing of expertise.[12]

(d) The Wolfsberg Group

In addition to the FATF and the Egmont Group, the financial sector identified a need to address money laundering threats. Perhaps the most prominent of the industry sector groups is the Wolfsberg Group, an association of eleven global banks (ABN AMRO NV left the group in 2007) established to develop financial services industry standards, and related products, for Know Your Customer, AML, and Counter Terrorist (CT) Financing policies.

The group came together in 2000 to draft anti-money laundering guidelines for private banking. The Wolfsberg Anti-Money Laundering Principles for Private Banking were subsequently published in October 2000 (and revised in May 2002).[13] Following September 11, 2001, in January 2002, the group published the Statement on the Financing of Terrorism and, in November 2002, released the Wolfsberg Anti-Money Laundering Principles for Correspondent Banking.[14] The group released the Wolfsberg Statement on Monitoring Screening and Searching in September 2003, and, in 2004, the Wolfsberg Group developed the due diligence model for financial institutions, in cooperation with Banker's Almanac.[15] Since then, the group has published two sets of guidance: Guidance on a Risk-Based Approach for Managing Money Laundering Risks, and AML Guidance for Mutual Funds and Other Pooled Investment Vehicles.[16] Also published were FAQs on AML Issues in the Context of Investment and Commercial Banking and FAQs on Correspondent Banking, which complement the

---

11. *See* Egmont Group of Financial Intelligence Units, http://www.egmontgroup.org/about.
12. *See id.*
13. Wolfsberg Group, Wolfsberg Anti-Money Laundering Principles on Private Banking, http://www.wolfsberg-principles.com/privat-banking.html.
14. Wolfsberg Group, Wolfsberg Anti-Money Laundering Principles for Correspondent Banking, http://www.wolfsberg-principles.com/corresp-banking.html.
15. Wolfsberg Group, International Due Diligence Repository, http://www.wolfsberg-principles.com/diligence.html.
16. Wolfsberg Group, Anti-Money Laundering Guidance for Mutual Funds and Other Pooled Investment Vehicles, http://www.wolfsberg-principles.com/pdf/mutual-funds.pdf.

other sets of FAQs available on the site on Beneficial Ownership, Politically Exposed Persons, and Intermediaries.[17]

4.2 U.S. ANTI-MONEY LAUNDERING LAWS AND REGULATIONS

Domestically, following September 11, 2001, the U.S. government passed the USA PATRIOT Act, a portion of which amended the Bank Secrecy Act (originally passed in 1970) to strengthen domestic anti-money laundering laws and regulations. Although there are close to one dozen organizations[18] that have substantial Bank Secrecy Act (BSA) responsibilities, the Financial Crimes Enforcement Network (FinCEN) maintains primary responsibility for administering the BSA through the Bank Secrecy Act Regulations.[19]

To add to the enforcement focus, in late 2010, the Department of Justice (DOJ) announced the establishment of the new Money Laundering and Bank Integrity Unit (MLBIU) within the Asset Forfeiture and Money Laundering Section of the Criminal Division at the DOJ.[20] At the time, the DOJ indicated that the newly formed MLBIU would focus on three categories of potential fraudsters: (1) banks and other financial institutions, including their officers and employees, (2) professional money launderers who sell their services to criminal operations, and (3) those using the latest technology to practice money laundering, such as mobile payment systems and virtual currency. The MLBIU investigates and prosecutes complex domestic and international criminal cases involving violations of the money laundering statutes, the Bank Secrecy Act, and other related statutes.

The BSA Regulations apply to traditional financial institutions as well as to other industry sectors identified as at risk for exposure to money laundering. Covered industry sectors include depository institutions, broker dealers in securities, money services businesses, casinos, insurance companies offering certain covered products, and dealers in precious metals, gems, and stones. Not all industries covered by FATF's Recommendations are subject to the BSA Regulations, but, based on the February 2012 Announced Notice of Proposed Rule Making, it would appear that the BSA Regulations may be amended to incorporate other industry sectors as well. That document announces FinCEN's intentions to develop consolidated customer due diligence (CDD) rules for banks, brokers or dealers in securities, mutual funds, futures commissions merchants, and introducing brokers in commodities. The notice also

---

17.　Wolfsberg Group, Frequently Asked Questions, http://www.wolfsberg-principles.com/faq.html.

18.　Within Treasury, in addition to FinCEN and OFAC, the Office of the Comptroller of the Currency and IRS maintain AML duties. Other regulators include the Federal Reserve, Federal Deposit Insurance Corporation, Securities and Exchange Commission, the National Credit Union Administration, and the Commodities Futures Trading Commission. SROs include the Financial Industry Regulatory Authority, the New York Mercantile Exchange, and the National Futures Association.

19.　*See* Bank Secrecy Act, 31 C.F.R. tit. 31, ch. X (2012) (formerly 31 C.F.R. pt. 103).

20.　*See* U.S. Dep't of Justice, http://www.justice.gov/criminal/afmls/forfeiture-fellowship.html.

signals that these CDD rules are likely to be extended to other covered industries and that FinCEN may also bring within its jurisdiction (through legislation) other industry sectors.[21] These other sectors could include, for example, lawyers, persons engaged in real estate transactions, and trust and company service providers not subject to the BSA Regulations but covered by FATF's Recommendations.[22] As addressed below, while some of these industries are not covered by the BSA Regulations, many have implemented risk-based (rather than rules-based) AML Good Practices tailored to protect the industry from money laundering and terrorist financing threats.

Other relevant laws include the Money Laundering Control Act of 1986, which criminalizes money laundering and structuring or the attempt to structure a financial transaction to avoid the reporting requirement,[23] and the USA PATRIOT Improvement and Reauthorization Act of 2005, which enhances penalties for terrorist financing, amends the Racketeer-Influenced and Corrupt Organizations Act by adding illegal money transmitters to the definition of racketeering activity, and closes a loophole concerning money laundering through informal money transfer networks.[24]

4.3 COMPLYING WITH U.S. AML LAWS AND REGULATIONS

In general, the BSA Regulations require that covered entities (1) conduct a risk assessment addressing potential exposure to money laundering threats, (2) develop a risk-based AML program in response to the identified threats, (3) respond to inquiries from FinCEN under section 314 of the USA PATRIOT Act, and (4) maintain appropriate records.

(a) The Risk Assessment

In general, an entity covered by the BSA Regulations is expected to conduct a comprehensive evaluation of the level of risk for its (1) products, (2) services, (3) customers, and (4) geographic exposure. Each of the four categories should be rated as low, moderate, or high risk.

When reviewing products and services, the Federal Financial Institutions Examination Council's (FFIEC) *Bank Secrecy Act/Anti-Money Laundering Examination Manual* (*BSA/AML Exam Manual*)[25] (primarily focused on depository institutions)

---

21. *See* Customer Due Diligence Requirements for Financial Institutions, 77 Fed. Reg. 13,046 (Mar. 5, 2012) (FinCEN announcing a Notice of Proposed Rule Making).

22. In addition to these entities specifically addressed by the FATF Recommendations, the USA PATRIOT Act contemplates regulating pawnbrokers, travel agencies, sellers of vehicles, private bankers, commodity pool operators, and investment companies. For now, these entities are exempt from BSA Regulations mandating AML programs. *See, e.g.,* 31 C.F.R. § 1010.205(b).

23. Money Laundering Control Act, Pub. L. No. 99-570, § 1352, 100 Stat. 3207 (codified as amended at 18 U.S.C. §§ 1956–1957 (2009)).

24. USA Patriot Improvement and Reauthorization Act of 2005, Pub. L. No. 109-177, §§ 402-403, 405, 120 Stat 192 (2006).

25. Federal Financial Institutions Examination Council, Bank Secrecy Act/Anti-Money Laundering Examination Manual, http://www.ffiec.gov/bsa_aml_infobase/pages_manual/manual_online.htm.

identifies as higher risk electronic services, private banking, monetary instruments, trade finance, foreign correspondent accounts, trust and asset management services, and, inter alia, services provided to a third-party payment processor or sender.[26] Applying these types of activities to other covered industry sectors, a higher risk for exposure to money laundering appears wherever the entity and the customer are not face-to-face, where the entity "touches the money" for the customer, and where transactions occur across borders. Of particular concern should be services or products offered over the Internet. Also considered higher risk are products or services offered in large volume to non-customers.

The *BSA/AML Exam Manual* also provides examples of higher-risk customers. Higher-risk customers can be those located in a separate jurisdiction from the service provider; senior foreign government officials and their immediate family members and close associates (i.e., politically exposed persons, or PEPs); cash-intensive businesses; nongovernmental organizations and charities; and professional service providers including lawyers, accountants, doctors, or real estate brokers.[27]

In order to determine the appropriate risk posed by particular geographic exposure, an entity can refer to the State Department's International Narcotics Control Strategy Report, Volume II: Money Laundering and Financial Crimes, which ranks jurisdictions by potential money laundering risks.[28] Other resources for geographic risk rankings include Transparency International's Corruption Index, the list of countries targeted for sanctions administered by the Department of the Treasury's Office of Foreign Assets Control; jurisdictions determined to be "of primary money laundering concern" by FinCEN pursuant to section 311 of the USA PATRIOT Act; countries identified as supporting international terrorism under § 6(j) of the Export Administration Act of 1979; countries identified in section 126.1 of the International Traffic in Arms Regulations (ITAR);[29] and the FATF's High Risk and Non-Cooperative Jurisdictions list.[30]

Where a geographic risk is identified, the compliance program is expected to include additional due diligence processes to mitigate against that risk.

---

26. *See* Federal Financial Institutions Examination Council, BSA/AML Risk Assessment – Overview, http://www.ffiec.gov/bsa_aml_infobase/pages_manual/OLM_005.htm.

27. *See id.*

28. U.S. Dep't of State, 2012 Int'l Narcotics Control Strategy Report (Mar. 7, 2012), http://www.state.gov/r/pa/prs/ps/2012/03/185364.htm.

29. 22 C.F.R. §§ 120–129 (2012).

30. Transparency Int'l, Corruption Perception Index 2011, http://www.transparency.org/research/cpi/overview; Financial Action Task Force, High Risk and Non-Cooperative Jurisdictions, http://www.fatf -gafi.org/topics/high-riskandnon-cooperativejurisdictions/. Section 126.1 countries are identified in the ITAR, 22 C.F.R. § 126.1 (2012) and U.S. Department of State, Country Policies and Embargoes, http://www.pmddtc.state.gov/embargoed_countries/index.html. FinCEN's list of 311 jurisdictions is available at Financial Crimes Enforcement Network, Special Measures for Jurisdictions, Financial Institutions, or Int'l Transactions of Primary Money Laundering Concern, http://www.fincen.gov/statutes_regs/patriot/section311.html.

(b) The Compliance Program

Once a covered entity has conducted its risk assessment and rates its risks, the entity develops written policies, procedures, and processes to address how it will protect itself, its customers, and the financial system from exposure to money laundering and terrorist financing. The BSA Regulations and the bank examiners mandate that the AML Compliance Program (1) is in writing, (2) is approved by senior management, (3) contains sufficient internal controls to ensure ongoing compliance, (4) identifies an individual or individuals responsible for managing BSA compliance, (5) offers training to relevant personnel, and (6) is subject to independent auditing and testing to ensure the program remains effective in mitigating potential exposure to money laundering and terrorist financing threats.[31] Because some of the higher risks from an AML perspective are similar to those from a sanctions or anti-bribery/anticorruption perspective, there are often opportunities to streamline an entity's compliance programs.

During any regulatory or enforcement review of an entity's AML compliance program, one of the first objectives is to determine whether the entity maintains a corporate commitment to compliance—that is, is a good corporate citizen. An indicator of this commitment includes top-level support for a strong compliance program. This typically comes in the form of a written management statement in favor of compliance. Other indicia of the good corporate citizen include elevating the AML compliance officer to a senior management position with entity-wide visibility and access to senior management.

Also inherent to a good compliance program are well-trained personnel so that potentially problematic transactions can be identified at multiple stages within an organization. For example, where an insurance industry offers a covered product (i.e., life insurance), it is helpful to have well-trained agents, brokers, underwriters, and compliance personnel—each acting as a backstop for the other so that a problematic policy may be identified *before* the paper is written. Establishing such a program means that personnel who "touch the money" are kept up to date on specific industry risks or red flags. FinCEN publishes industry SAR Reports, FATF publishes industry-specific guidance, and many industry-specific trade associations also publish specific AML guidance containing recent AML good practices. Examples of specific industry guidance are identified in the bibliography to this chapter.

A third pillar to a good compliance program is "knowing your customer," or KYC. In KYC, an entity ensures that the customers that it brings in are who they say they are, are conducting legitimate business, and are using legitimate funds. Typically, these assurances are provided during the on-boarding process and by continued transaction monitoring. During the initial stages of bringing on a new customer, there is an expectation that the entity will engage in CDD. During the CDD process, the entity

---

31.   31 C.F.R. tit. 31, ch. X.

verifies the customer's identity through documentary or nondocumentary means. For an individual, this can mean collecting:

- the customer's complete name (including former names and aliases);
- a copy of valid government-issued photo identification;
- date of birth;
- current street address;
- proof of current address (i.e., utility bill, bank or credit card statement);
- place of birth; and
- nationality/ies.

For a privately held entity, the following information may be collected:

- complete name of the entity;
- complete name of contact person;
- address for entity and for contact person;
- certified true copy of certificate of incorporation or registration or other document evidencing establishment;
- details of registered office and place of business; and
- due diligence documents as identified for shareholders/directors holding more than 20 percent of an interest in the entity.

Lesser due diligence is appropriate for publicly traded entities or other regulated entities; greater due diligence is appropriate for entities comprising senior government officials, their families or associates—or for instances where red flags are present.

There also is an expectation that similar procedures are in place for other business relationships (i.e., agents and vendors).

Also within a good compliance program's policies and procedures are steps for filing SARs, as appropriate. In order to ensure that suspicious activity is identified promptly, relevant employees must know what to look for and must know to whom to report. An established reporting chain is essential to ensure that potentially suspicious activity is escalated to the appropriate AML compliance officer(s) and, where appropriate, SARs are filed.

Finally, in addition to the role the AML compliance officer will play in developing and evolving the entity's compliance program, an entity must ensure that the program is independently reviewed and audited to ensure effectiveness. Independent review does not require an outside party to conduct the review—only that someone other than the compliance officer or someone in his or her chain of command conduct the review. Of course, records for the review, including recommendations and steps taken to implement the recommendations, should be maintained.

Whereas an AML compliance program may look and operate in a manner consistent with sanctions and export controls compliance programs, the concept of a voluntary self-disclosure differs. The BSA Regulations do not contain enforcement guidelines providing for mitigating credit where a covered financial institution detects and self-reports an AML program deficiency. Rather, an entity must first decide whether the entity is required to disclose potential AML program deficiencies resulting in potential violations of AML laws and regulations to the entity's other regulators. For example, an entity regulated by the Federal Reserve may notify that regulator during a routine exam that the entity has identified a potential problem and is in the process of amending procedures. Entities regulated by the SEC and FINRA must consider whether they are required to report a potential Bank Secrecy Act violation under the relevant rule and, if not, whether a disclosure will provide cooperating credit.[32]

(c) Compliance Program Pitfalls

A common pitfall of a compliance program occurs when policies and procedures are too stringent to implement and personnel create work-arounds or other informal processes to address practical issues. When a regulator or enforcement officer reviews the entity's policies and procedures, one of the first items typically to be examined will be compliance with those written policies and procedures; many entities have found themselves to be out of compliance with their own policies and procedures. To help mitigate against this pitfall, the AML program should be periodically tested to ensure that the policies and procedures strike the appropriate balance between protecting against money laundering risks and conducting a productive business. Where relevant, testing should include ensuring that automated screening software is neither creating so many false positive matches that compliance officers suffer from screening fatigue (and miss the few true hits), nor tuned so high that it misses close matches

---

32. For example, the SEC Enforcement Manual (Mar. 9, 2012) identifies four broad measures for a company's cooperation: (1) self-policing prior to the discovery of the misconduct, including establishing effective compliance procedures and an appropriate tone at the top; (2) self-reporting of misconduct when it is discovered, including conducting a thorough review of the nature, extent, origins, and consequences of the misconduct, and promptly, completely, and effectively disclosing the misconduct to the public, to regulatory agencies, and to self-regulatory organizations; (3) remediation, including dismissing or appropriately disciplining wrongdoers, modifying and improving internal controls and procedures to prevent recurrence of the misconduct, and appropriately compensating those adversely affected; and (4) cooperation with law enforcement authorities, including providing the Commission staff with all information relevant to the underlying violations and company's remedial efforts. *See* 6.1.2. Framework for Evaluating Cooperation by Companies, *available at* http://www.sec.gov/divisions/enforce/enforcementmanual.pdf.FINRA rule 4530(b), requires a member firm to report to FINRA within thirty days after the firm has concluded, or reasonably should have concluded, on its own that the firm or an associated person of the firm has violated any securities-, insurance-, commodities-, financial-, or investment-related laws, rules, regulations, or standards of conduct of any domestic or foreign regulatory body or self-regulatory organization. *See* FINRA Regulatory Notice 11-06, *available at* http://www.finra.org/web/groups/industry/@ip/@reg/@notice/documents/notices/p122888.pdf.

to sanctioned parties. Other common pitfalls include failing to obtain management support for the program; understaffing the compliance function so that higher-risk transactions pass through undetected; failing to adequately train (or provide periodic updated training to) all relevant personnel; and failing to maintain adequate records so that compliance personnel are not able to retrace a decision-making process at a later date when asked by an examiner (or the Department of Justice).

(d) Financial Intelligence Unit (FIU) Inquiries

On occasion, an entity may receive from FinCEN or another law enforcement agency a request to produce certain information for use in a law enforcement investigation related to terrorist activity or money laundering. Such requests in the United States are made pursuant to section 314(a) of the USA PATRIOT Act. When FinCEN requests the information, FinCEN should provide the entity with:

- a statement that each individual, entity, or organization about which the law enforcement agency is seeking information is engaged in, or is reasonably suspected based on credible evidence of engaging in, terrorist activity or money laundering;
- specific identifying information such as date of birth, address, and social security number so that the entity can differentiate between common or similar names; and
- a contact person at the law enforcement agency who can respond to any questions relating to the request.[33]

Such requests for information generally require that the entity search its records to determine whether it maintains or has maintained accounts for, or has engaged in transactions with, any specified individual, entity, or organization.

In responding to a 314(a) request, an entity should be prepared to provide, where available:

- the name of such individual, entity, or organization;
- the relevant account number(s);
- any social security number, taxpayer identification number, passport number, date of birth, address, or other similar identifying information provided by the individual, entity, or organization when each such account was opened or each such transaction was conducted;
- when the account(s) was established; and
- the date(s) and type(s) of transaction(s).[34]

---

33. *See, e.g.,* 31 C.F.R. § 1010.520(b) (2012).
34. *See, e.g., id.*

(e) Recordkeeping

Consistent with export controls and OFAC's economic sanctions regulations discussed in prior chapters, records covered by the AML program also should be retained for at least five years from the cessation of the relevant underlying contract, business relationship, or transaction.

(f) Sample Industry-Specific Risks

In general, an AML program will train personnel to identify risks typical to money laundering and terrorist financing, and specific to the particular industry sector. General red flags include customers who use unusual or suspicious identification documents that cannot be readily verified; customers with multiple aliases or spelling variations; contact information that is not valid (i.e., a business or home telephone number is disconnected); the customer's background differs from what is typical for others similarly situated in the industry; and the customer engages in transactions atypical for the industry.[35]

(i) Risks for Broker Dealers

Like other covered industries, broker dealers are expected to maintain tailored anti-money laundering programs after risk assessments. The Securities and Exchange Commission, in March 2012, published its AML Source Tool for Broker Dealers, which cites, in relevant part, the National Association of Security Dealers (NASD) Notice 02-21 to Members: Anti-Money Laundering Guidance. Within the guidance is a list of some customer-focused risks particular to the industry sector. These red flags include but are not limited to instances where the customer:

- is unusually concerned with the company's compliance policies and procedures (including AML reporting requirements);
- wishes to engage in transactions that appear to lack legitimate business purpose;
- provides false information (i.e., false source of income, false identifying information);
- refuses to disclose source of funds or party on whose behalf he or she is acting;
- has a higher-risk profile (i.e., is subject of press reports relating to possible illegal activity);
- appears to lack general knowledge of his purported industry sector;
- makes frequent deposits of cash or cash equivalents or appears to structure deposits, keeping each under $10,000;
- has an account that appears to have unusual or unexplained activity;

---

35. Federal Financial Institutions Examination Council, Bank Secrecy Act/Anti-Money Laundering Examination Manual, Appendix F – Money Laundering and Terrorist Financing "Red Flags," http://www.ffiec.gov/bsa_aml_infobase/pages_manual/OLM_106.htm.

- for no apparent business reason, maintains multiple accounts with a large number of inter-account or third-party transfers; and
- for no apparent reason or in conjunction with other red flags, engages in transactions involving certain types of securities, such as penny stocks, Regulation "S" stocks, and bearer bonds, which although legitimate, have been used in connection with fraudulent schemes and money laundering activity.[36]

(ii) Risks for Casinos and Card Clubs

FinCEN has identified risks specific to this industry, some of which are identified below:

- Two or more customers each purchase chips with currency in amounts under $10,000, engage in little gaming, and then cash out the chips for a casino check.
- A customer pays off a large credit debt (i.e., over $20,000) over a short period of time through a series of currency transactions, none of which exceeds $10,000.
- A customer receives a payout in excess of $10,000 and asks for currency of less than $10,000 and asks for the remainder in chips. The customer then redeems the chips in an amount less than the currency transaction report requires.
- A customer bets both sides of a game or event.
- A customer requests casino checks below the $3,000 threshold to be made out to a third party.[37]

(iii) Risks for Money Services Businesses (MSBs)

As with other industry sectors, FinCEN publishes guidance specific to MSBs.[38] Identified red flags for MSBs include but are not limited to the following:

- **Customer:** customer uses false identification; two or more customers use similar identification; customer alters transaction upon learning that he or she must show identification; customer uses multiple variations of his or her name; two or more customers work together to break one transaction into two or more transactions in order to evade the BSA reporting or recordkeeping requirement; customer uses two or more locations or cashiers in the same day in order to break one transaction into smaller transactions and evade the BSA reporting or recordkeeping requirement; customer offers bribes or tips.[39]

---

36. *See* Nat'l Ass'n Sec. Dealers, Special NASD Notice to Members 02-21, at 10–11 (Apr. 2002), http://www.sec.gov/about/offices/ocie/aml2007/nasd-ntm-02-21.pdf.

37. Financial Crimes Enforcement Network, Guidance: Recognizing Suspicious Activity – Red Flags for Casinos and Card Clubs (Aug. 1, 2008), http://www.fincen.gov/statutes_regs/guidance/html/fin-2008-g007.html.

38. Financial Crimes Enforcement Network, A Money Services Business Guide, http://www.fincen.gov/financial_institutions/msb/materials/en/prevention_guide.html#Red Flags.

39. *Id.*

- **Services:** currency exchanges just under $1,000; cash sales of money orders or traveler's checks of just under $3,000.[40]

(iv) Risks for Insurers

Insurers offering covered products are subject to the BSA Regulations and must maintain an AML program. Covered products include (1) permanent life insurance policies (other than group life), (2) annuity contracts (other than group annuity contracts), or (3) any other insurance product with features of cash value or investment. FinCEN has identified the following customer-based insurance-specific red flags:

- purchase of an insurance product inconsistent with customer's needs;
- unusual payment methods;
- early termination of a product;
- payment by or to, or transfer of benefit to, an apparently unrelated third party;
- insured who shows little concern for investment performance but is focused on early termination features;
- reluctance to provide identifying information or provides fictitious identifiers;
- purposeful obscuring of source of funds;
- insured who borrows the maximum amount available soon after purchasing the product;
- insured/cedent purchases insurance products using a single, large premium payment, particularly when payment is made through unusual methods such as currency or currency equivalents;
- policies are purchased that allow for the transfer of beneficial ownership interests without the knowledge and consent of the insurance issuer; and
- an insured is known to purchase several insurance products and uses the proceeds from an early policy surrender to purchase other financial assets.[41]

(v) Risks for Lawyers

Though lawyers are not covered under the BSA Regulations, the FATF has identified certain designated nonfinancial businesses and professionals (DNFBPs), including lawyers, for inclusion in domestic AML laws and regulations. There also have been attempts to include lawyers within the BSA. For example, in 2002, FinCEN published the Advanced Notice of Proposed Rule Making, which intended to mandate AML programs for persons involved in certain real estate transactions.[42] Because

---

40. *Id.*

41. Federal Financial Institutions Examination Council, Bank Secrecy Act/Anti-Money Laundering Examination Manual, Appendix F – Money Laundering and Terrorist Financing "Red Flags," http://www.ffiec.gov/bsa_aml_infobase/pages_manual/OLM_106.htm.

42. *See* Anti-Money Laundering Program Requirements for Persons Involved in Real Estate Closings and Settlements, 68 Fed. Reg. 17,569 (Apr. 10, 2003) (FinCEN announcing an Advanced Notice of Proposed Rule Making).

of the response, however, the final rule has yet to be published. The American Bar Association (ABA) has resisted formal inclusion of lawyers under the BSA or the BSA Regulations and has, instead, promoted a risk-based approach to protecting the sector from money laundering and terrorist financing threats. As a result, on April 23, 2010, the ABA Task Force on Gatekeeper Regulation and the Profession, together with other ABA committees and organizations, drafted the Voluntary Good Practices Guidance for Lawyers to Detect and Combat Money Laundering and Terrorist Financing.[43] Activities covered by the guidance (i.e., the high-risk services) include those five categories identified in the FATF's RBA Guidance for Legal Professionals (October 23, 2008). To keep in (voluntary) line with the FATF guidance, the ABA's Good Practices identify they covered activities including (1) buying and selling of real estate; (2) managing a client's money; (3) management of a bank, savings, or security account; (4) organization of contributions for the creation, operation, or management of companies; and (5) creation, operation, or management of legal persons or arrangements, and buying and selling of business entities.[44] In order to be more useful than the broad FATF guidance, the ABA Good Practices modifies the FATF red flags (below) by adding practice pointers. The FATF risk factors include:

- **Geographic risk:** transactions involving sanctioned countries; countries ranked as higher risk for corruption.
- **Client risk:** politically exposed persons (i.e., individuals who are or have been entrusted with prominent functions in a foreign country); clients conducting their relationship or requesting services in unusual or unconventional circumstances, where the structure or nature of the client entity or relationship makes it difficult to identify the true beneficial owner or controlling interests; clients that are cash-intensive businesses; charities and other nonprofits that are not subject to monitoring or supervision; clients using financial intermediaries, financial institutions, or legal professionals not subject to AML laws and regulations; clients convicted of proceeds-generating crimes; clients with no address or multiple addresses without a legitimate reason; clients who change their settlement or execution instructions without appropriate explanation.
- **Service risk:** transactions where the lawyer touches the client's money; services designed to improperly conceal beneficial ownership from relevant legal authorities; services requested by a client for which the client knows the lawyer does

---

43.   Voluntary Good Practices for Lawyers to Detect and Combat Money Laundering and Terrorist Financing (adopted Aug. 9–10, 2010), http://www.americanbar.org/content/dam/aba/migrated/leader-ship/2010/annual/pdfs/116.authcheckdam.pdf.
44.   The FATF lawyer guidance identifies these five categories as activities that should be regulated under domestic anti-money laundering laws and regulations. *See* Financial Action Task Force, RBA Guidance for Legal Professionals (Oct. 23, 2008), http://www.fatf-gafi.org/dataoecd/5/58/41584211.pdf.

not have the expertise; transfers of real estate between parties in an accelerated fashion (and lacking legitimate business reasons for the expedited treatment); payments for services from unassociated or unknown third parties; transactions where it is apparent to the lawyer that there is inadequate consideration (and there appears to be no legitimate business reason for the lower consideration); administration of estates where the decedent was known to be a person convicted of proceeds generating crimes.[45]

Of course, as the ABA's Good Practices emphasizes, the risk factors will vary depending on size of the firm, types of clients, sophistication in addressing money laundering threats, and nature of the client relationship, among others.[46] The expectation unless and until lawyers fall under the BSA Regulations is that lawyers will take tailored and risk-based steps to mitigate exposure to identified money laundering and terrorist financing threats.

(vi) Risks for Charities

Charities—particularly those operating in disaster zones—can be a higher risk for exposure to money laundering and terrorist financing. Soon after September 11, 2001, recognizing this exposure, the Department of the Treasury, working with representatives from the charities sector, drafted the Anti-Terrorist Financing Guidelines: Voluntary Best Practices for U.S.-Based Charities.[47] These Best Practices were not well received by some in the charities sector. In response, the Treasury Guidelines Working Group of Charitable Sector Organizations and Advisors drafted the Principles of International Charity (March 2005).[48] While neither document identifies red flags specific to the charitable sector, the Treasury document reminds U.S.-based charities that, as U.S. persons, they are subject to the economic sanctions regulations, discussed in prior chapters, administered by the U.S. Department of the Treasury's Office of Foreign Assets Control (OFAC). While no compliance program is required under OFAC's regulations, a risk-based program (as described earlier in this chapter) is appropriate to mitigate terrorist financing and money laundering threats. The Treasury document further recommends that U.S.-based charities operate transparently, disclose relevant employees' and controlling officers' identities, engage in due diligence for potential recipients, and engage in periodic audits and other appropriate controls.

---

45. Voluntary Good Practices, *supra* note 43.
46. *Id.*
47. U.S. Department of the Treasury Anti-Terrorist Financing Guidelines: Voluntary Best Practices for U.S.-Based Charities, http://www.treasury.gov/press-center/press-releases/Documents/0929%20final revised.pdf.
48. Treasury Guidelines Working Group of Charitable Sector Organizations and Advisors, Principles of International Charity (Mar. 2005), http://www.usig.org/PDFs/Principles_Final.pdf.

4.4 REPRESENTATIVE ENFORCEMENT ACTIONS

In 2011, the number of enforcement actions predicated on violations of the Bank Secrecy Act (BSA) and anti-money laundering statutes (AML) increased across the board. FinCEN fines for AML and BSA violations doubled from five in 2010 to ten issued in 2011. The ten fines FinCEN issued in 2011 were levied against banks, bank employees, financial institutions, and a casino. The three other major bank regulators, including the Federal Deposit Insurance Corporation (FDIC), the Office of the Comptroller of the Currency (OCC), and the Office of Thrift Supervision (OTS), which has since been folded into the OCC, issued a collective forty-four enforcement actions related to violations of the BSA in 2011. DOJ also prosecuted or settled a number of money laundering cases.

(a) Representative FinCEN Fines During 2011

In 2011, FinCEN fined Ocean Bank, based in Miami, Florida, $10.9 million in civil penalties for violations of the BSA and AML.[49] At the time he announced the fine, the director of FinCEN, James H. Freis, Jr., said that Ocean Bank had systematically failed to respond to and mitigate risks and to report transactions involving activity traditionally associated with money laundering. Freis noted that Ocean Bank had particular issues with direct foreign account relationships in high-risk jurisdictions like Venezuela.[50]

Zions First National Bank in Salt Lake City, Utah, was concurrently fined $8 million by the OCC and FinCEN for violations of the BSA and the USA PATRIOT Act. The fine relates to an electronic remote deposit program that was marketed to high-risk customers during 2006 and 2007.

FinCEN fined the Lower Sioux Indian Community, doing business as Jackpot Junction Casino Hotel of Morton, Minnesota, for $250,000 for violations of the BSA's requirements for casinos. The violations stemmed from the casino's failure to establish internal controls to facilitate the gathering and recording of information required for BSA reporting, the failure to train and test employees, and multiple failures to file timely and accurately Currency Transaction Reports by Casino forms and Suspicious Activity Report by Casino forms.

FinCEN assessed a $25,000 civil money penalty against Victor Kaganov of Oregon for making more than 4,200 funds transfers within the United States, involving more than $172 million without registering with FinCEN as a money services business as required by the BSA. Kaganov typically received foreign wire transfers into an

---

49. *See* Assessment of Civil Monetary Penalty, *In re Ocean Bank*, No. 2011-7, http://www.fincen.gov/news_room/ea/files/08222011_OceanBank_ASSESSMENT.pdf.
50. *Id.*

account he controlled and then instructed his bank to transfer the funds to a third party, who was frequently located in Europe or Asia.[51]

(b) Other Significant AML Cases

Consistent with the practice in the export controls and economic sanctions front, the DOJ continues to pursue financial institutions for AML violations.

(i) Wachovia

In March 2010, Wachovia Bank, N.A., entered into a deferred prosecution agreement with the U.S. Attorney's Office of the Southern District of Florida and the Assets Forfeiture and Money Laundering Section of the Criminal Division of the DOJ to resolve charges that it willfully failed to establish an AML program.[52] As part of the agreement, Wachovia agreed to forfeit to the United States $110 million, which, according to the Southern District of Florida's press release, represents proceeds of illegal narcotics sales that were laundered through the bank. According to the press release, Wachovia was aware of the high risk that drug money was being laundered through Mexican exchange houses (*casas de cambio*) but did not institute appropriate safeguards to mitigate this risk. Moreover, according to the court documents, Wachovia did not monitor these transactions and did not report potential money laundering activities.

(ii) HSBC

On October 7, 2010, the Federal Reserve Board announced that it had, on October 4, issued a consent cease and desist between HSBC North America Holdings, Inc.[53] (HNAH), New York, New York, a registered bank holding company, and the Federal Reserve Board. The order required HNAH to take corrective action to improve its firm-wide compliance risk-management program, including its anti-money laundering compliance risk management. Concurrent with the Federal Reserve Board's announcement of its enforcement action, the Office of the Comptroller of the Currency announced its October 10, 2010, issuance of a cease and desist order against HSBC Bank USA, N.A., McLean, Virginia (HBUS, a subsidiary of HNAH), for vio-

---

51. *See* Assessment of Civil Monetary Penalty, *In re Victor Kaganov*, No. 2011-2 (Mar. 7, 2011), http://www.fincen.gov/news_room/ea/files/03-07-2011KaganovASSESSMENT.pdf. In a similar matter, Omar Abukar Sufi and Mohamed Abukar Sufi were fined $40,000 by FinCEN for violations of the money transmitter registration requirements of the BSA. The Sufi brothers ran a money transmission business out of their grocery store in Michigan, sending funds to beneficiaries in Yemen, Somalia, Sudan, Kenya, Saudi Arabia, Uganda, Ethiopia, Qatar, Europe, and the United Arab Emirates.

52. *See* Deferred Prosecution Agreement, *United States v. Wachovia Bank, N.A.*, No. 10-20165-CR-LEONARD (S.D. Fla. Mar. 16, 2010), http://www.justice.gov/usao/fls/PressReleases/Attachments/100317-02.Agreement.pdf; *see also* Press Release, United States Attorney's Office, Wachovia Enters into Deferred Prosecution Agreement (Mar. 17, 2010), http://www.justice.gov/usao/fls/PressReleases/100317-02.html.

53. Cease and Desist Order, *In re HSBC North America Holdings, Inc.*, No. 10-202-B-HC (Oct. 4, 2010), http://www.federalreserve.gov/newsevents/press/enforcement/enf20101007c1.pdf.

lating the Bank Secrecy Act and its underlying regulations.[54] The OCC found that the bank's BSA compliance program had deficiencies with respect to suspicious activity reporting, monitoring of bulk cash purchases and international funds transfers, customer due diligence concerning its foreign affiliates, and risk assessment with respect to politically exposed persons and their associates. These findings resulted in violations by the bank of statutory and regulatory requirements to maintain an adequate BSA compliance program, file suspicious activity reports, and conduct appropriate due diligence on foreign correspondent accounts.

---

54.   Consent Order, *In re HSBC Bank U.S.A., N.A.*, No. AA-EC-10-98 (Sept. 24, 2010), http://www.occ. gov/news-issuances/news-releases/2010/nr-occ-2010-121a.pdf.

Antiboycott Measures

Michael L. Burton[1]

5.1 OVERVIEW

Since the 1970s, the United States has maintained two antiboycott laws that prohibit or penalize U.S. companies and individuals from supporting or participating in boycotts of countries friendly to the United States. Although these laws are drafted without reference to any particular boycott, their principal target is the Arab League's long-standing economic boycott of Israel. These laws impose far-reaching restrictions on boycott-related actions and agreements, and even the furnishing of information. Penalties for violations can include civil and criminal fines, imprisonment, and the loss of tax credits or export privileges.

What Is Regulated? Virtually any transaction within U.S. jurisdiction (see below) involving official foreign government boycotts or restrictive trade practices that the United States does not support.

Where to Find the Regulations: The U.S. antiboycott regulations and statutes are contained primarily in (1) part 760 of chapter 15 of the Code of Federal Regulations, (2) section 999 of the Internal Revenue Code, and (3) Department of the Treasury Guidelines: Boycott Provisions (section 999) of the Internal Revenue Code (IRC).

Who Is the Regulator? The U.S. antiboycott laws are administered by the U.S. Department of Commerce's Bureau of Industry and Security (BIS) and Office of Antiboycott Compliance (OAC), and the U.S. Treasury Department's Internal Revenue Service (IRS).

How to Get a License/File a Report: No licenses are granted under the antiboycott regulations. Persons receiving boycott requests, however, are required to report them to the OAC and the IRS. For the OAC, reports of receipts of boycott requests must be filed quarterly on form BIS 621-P for single transactions or BIS 6051-P for multiple transactions received during the same calendar quarter (see http://www.bis.doc.gov/complianceandenforcement/antiboycottcompliance.htm#requestform). Reports under section 999 of the IRC are filed with annual tax returns on IRS form 5713. This form is available from local IRS offices.

Key Website: http://www.bis.doc.gov/complianceandenforcement/antiboycottcompliance.htm. See also section 5.8 below.

---

1. Michael L. Burton is Managing Member of Joiner Burton PLLC in Washington, D.C.

This chapter is intended to provide the reader with an introduction to and basic understanding of the U.S. antiboycott laws. These laws are complicated and sometimes counterintuitive. Whether a particular action is permissible can often turn on very subtle variations in language and circumstances. For this reason, it is critical that you consult the regulations for answers to specific antiboycott issues. The information here is not intended nor may it be relied on as legal advice.

5.2   U.S. ANTIBOYCOTT LAWS

Although the United States recognizes the sovereign right of each country not to trade with countries to which they are hostile, the U.S. antiboycott laws are designed to (1) monitor foreign boycotts the United States does not support and (2) to prohibit or penalize individuals and entities subject to U.S. law from acting in furtherance of more trade distortive forms of boycott activity.

Understanding the differences among primary, secondary, and tertiary boycotts is helpful in conceptualizing the framework of U.S. antiboycott law.

- Primary Boycott   =   Boycotting country prohibits imports from or exports to the boycotted country.
- Secondary Boycott =   Boycotting country prohibits companies contributing to the economic or military strength of the boycotted country from trading with the boycotting country.
- Tertiary Boycott   =   Boycotting country prohibits business with companies that conduct business with individuals or entities identified as having a business relationship with the boycotted country (e.g., blacklisted persons).

Generally speaking, the U.S. antiboycott laws do not prohibit or penalize persons subject to U.S. law from acting in furtherance of primary boycotts. Participation in secondary or tertiary boycotts, however, is prohibited and penalized. Further, unless an exception applies, the U.S. government requires reporting of the request, regardless of the level of the boycott. Thus, even if not prohibited or penalized, primary boycott requests often need to be reported. The U.S. government has an interest in monitoring the boycott and reviewing how persons subject to U.S. law handle those requests, even in those situations where the requested action is within the boycotting country's rights under international law.

While understanding the level of boycott at issue is useful as a conceptual framework, exceptions abound. Whether a specific boycott-related request is prohibited/penalized or reportable depends on (1) the facts of a particular transaction, (2) the transaction being subject to U.S. jurisdiction, (3) which of the two (or both) U.S. antiboycott laws is implicated, and (4) a detailed review of the relevant regulations, which are replete with sometimes idiosyncratic examples reflecting U.S. foreign policy considerations as applied to a range of actual business scenarios.

(a) The Commerce Department's Antiboycott Law

As noted above, the more sweeping of the two U.S. antiboycott laws is maintained by the Commerce Department in part 760 of the U.S. Export Administration Regulations (EAR).[2] The substantive prohibitions and the reporting requirements of the Commerce Department's antiboycott law apply if (1) the person taking the action in question is a "U.S. person" and (2) the activity is in the "interstate or foreign commerce of the United States."[3] Jurisdiction will be discussed further below.

Under the Commerce Department's antiboycott provision, the following types of actions are prohibited:[4]

- refusing to do business with boycotted countries, companies of a boycotted country, nationals of a boycotted country, or "blacklisted" companies;
- furnishing boycott-related information, including information about one's business relationships with a boycotted country, companies of a boycotted country, nationals of a boycotted country, or "blacklisted" companies;
- discriminating against any U.S. person on the basis of race, religion, sex, or national origin; and
- evasion of the antiboycott provisions of the EAR.

The Commerce Department's antiboycott provisions also require U.S. companies each calendar quarter to report the receipt of requests to take any action that has the effect of furthering or supporting the boycott. Boycott-related requests—whether oral or written—are generally reportable regardless of whether the requested action is prohibited or permitted *and regardless of whether the recipient complies with the request*. Certain exceptions to the reporting requirements, however, are provided for in the EAR.

The Office of Antiboycott Compliance (OAC) within the Bureau of Industry and Security of the U.S. Department of Commerce administers and enforces part 760 of the EAR. OAC is aggressive in its enforcement actions and investigations. Violations of the Commerce Department's antiboycott regulations are subject to the full range of civil and criminal penalties available under the EAR, including fines, imprisonment, and the denial of export privileges. (See the discussion in chapter 3, section 3.10.)

---

2.   15 C.F.R. §§ 760.1–760.5.
3.   15 C.F.R. § 760.1. "U.S. persons" include owned or controlled foreign affiliates of U.S. companies.
4.   15 C.F.R. § 760.2.

(b) The Treasury Department's Antiboycott Law

In addition to the EAR's antiboycott rules, under section 999(a)(1) of the Internal Revenue Code, any person (or any member of a "controlled group" including such person) must file reports with the Internal Revenue Service (IRS) if that person has operations in, or relating to, (1) a boycott-listed country (or the government, a company, or a national of such country) or (2) any other country (or the government, a company, or a national of such country) if such person knows or has reason to know that participation in a boycott is a condition of conducting operations in such other country.[5] The U.S. Treasury Department publishes a list of countries believed to be engaged in boycotts and other restrictive trade practices on a periodic basis.[6] The IRS requires persons with operations "in or relating to such" countries to file a boycott report on form 5713, listing such operations.

Under section 999(a)(2), a taxpayer also must report whether it, or any member of a "controlled group" of which it (or such foreign corporation) is a member, has participated in or cooperated with an international boycott or has been requested to participate in or cooperate with an international boycott.[7] When entered into or requested, *as a condition of doing business with a boycotting country or its companies or nationals*, the following types of agreements are subject to tax penalties and IRS reporting requirements:[8]

- agreements to refuse to do business directly or indirectly within a country that is the object of the boycott or with the boycotted country's government, companies, or nationals;
- agreements to refuse to do business with U.S. persons who do business in a boycotted country or with its government, companies, or nationals;
- agreements to refuse to do business with companies owned or managed by individuals of a particular race, religion, or nationality;
- agreements to refrain from employing persons of a particular race, religion, or nationality; and
- agreements to refuse to ship or insure products on carriers owned or operated by persons who do not participate in or cooperate with the boycott.

---

5. I.R.C. § 999(a)(1).
6. Currently, the countries listed by the Treasury Department as boycotting countries for tax purposes are Iraq, Kuwait, Lebanon, Libya, Qatar, Saudi Arabia, Syria, United Arab Emirates, and Yemen. List of Countries Requiring Cooperation with an International Boycott, 77 Fed. Reg. 49,864 (Aug. 17, 2012). However, "operations" in other countries or with any company or government may be implicated if participation in a boycott is an express or implied condition of conducting such operations.
7. I.R.C. § 999(a)(2).
8. All listed at I.R.C. § 999(b)(3).

In analyzing antiboycott issues under section 999, it is important to determine whether (1) there is some agreement or request to agree and (2) that agreement is a condition of doing business with a boycotting country, its companies, or its nationals. Both elements must be met. That being said, agreements may be inferred from course of conduct and the circumstances surrounding a given transaction.

Like the Commerce Department's antiboycott regulations, reports are required even if the requested agreement is never reached. Unlike the EAR, however, form 5713 is filed with the IRS on an annual basis rather than quarterly.

Taxpayers who willfully fail to make a required boycott report may be fined up to $25,000 or imprisoned for not more than one year, or both.[9] Taxpayers that agree to impermissible boycott-related actions may be subject to significant tax penalties by being prohibited from claiming favorable tax treatment with respect to boycott-related income. Depending on a taxpayer's operations and corporate structure, the tax consequences can be wide reaching.

(c) Distinctions between the Two U.S. Antiboycott Laws

It is important to note that part 760 of the EAR and section 999 of the IRC contain a number of significant distinctions relating to jurisdiction as well as substance. The U.S. government has provided an unofficial summary of the key distinctions in a chart available at http://www.bis.doc.gov/complianceandenforcement/comparison-antiboycott-laws.pdf. *See* Appendix G. It is important to note that subtle variations in the wording of boycott-related requests can result in different legal outcomes between section 760 of the EAR and section 999 of the IRC, requiring case-by-case review.

5.3 APPLICATION OF U.S. ANTIBOYCOTT LAWS

(a) Part 760

The EAR's antiboycott provisions apply to all "U.S. persons" acting in the interstate or foreign commerce of the United States. According to OAC, "The term 'U.S. person' includes all individuals, corporations and unincorporated associations resident in the United States, including the permanent domestic affiliates of foreign concerns. U.S. persons also include U.S. citizens abroad (except when they reside abroad and are employed by non-U.S. persons) and the 'controlled in fact' foreign affiliates of domestic concerns."

Section 760.1(c) of the EAR sets forth a multifactor test for determining when a foreign subsidiary or affiliate of a U.S. domestic concern is deemed to be owned or controlled in fact by the U.S. domestic concern. Subject to rebuttal by competent evidence, a foreign affiliate is presumed to be controlled in fact, and thus a U.S. person, when:

---

9.   I.R.C. § 999(f).

- the domestic concern beneficially owns or controls (whether directly or indirectly) more than 50 percent of the outstanding voting securities of the foreign subsidiary or affiliate;
- the domestic concern beneficially owns or controls (whether directly or indirectly) 25 percent or more of the voting securities of the foreign subsidiary or affiliate, if no other person owns or controls (whether directly or indirectly) an equal or larger percentage;
- the foreign subsidiary or affiliate is operated by the domestic concern pursuant to the provisions of an exclusive management contract;
- a majority of the members of the board of directors of the foreign subsidiary or affiliate are also members of the comparable governing body of the domestic concern;
- the domestic concern has authority to appoint the majority of the members of the board of directors of the foreign subsidiary or affiliate; or
- the domestic concern has authority to appoint the chief operating officer of the foreign subsidiary or affiliate.

To satisfy the jurisdictional requirements of part 760 of the EAR, the transaction not only must involve a U.S. person but also be within the interstate or foreign commerce of the United States. "U.S. commerce" is broadly defined to include activities relating to the sale, purchase, or transfer of goods or services (including information) within the United States or between the United States and a foreign country. Such activities include importing, exporting, financing, freight forwarding, and shipping.

(b) Section 999

The penalty provisions of the Treasury Department's antiboycott regulations—which are self-imposed by taxpayers when they file their returns—apply only to U.S. taxpayers. In comparison, the reporting requirements of section 999 are broader and cover not only U.S. taxpayers and U.S. shareholders, but also a range of foreign affiliated companies in which the U.S. ownership can be as little as 10 percent.

The reporting requirements of section 999 require U.S. taxpayers (i.e., any legal or natural person filing a U.S. tax return) to report their own activities as well as the activities of all members of their "controlled groups."[10] The term *controlled group* is defined under the Internal Revenue Code to include parent-subsidiary controlled groups in which a common parent holds a majority interest in one or more "chains of corporations connected through stock ownership."[11] Because the reporting require-

---

10.   I.R.C. § 999(a).
11.   I.R.C. § 999 (defining "controlled group" by referencing I.R.C. § 993(a), which in turn references with modifications I.R.C. § 1563(a)); *see also* Income Tax Regs. § 1.1563-1 (1998).

ments extend to all members of a U.S. taxpayer's controlled groups, U.S. taxpayers are required to report on the activities of their foreign parent companies as well as on the activities of other foreign companies in which their foreign parent holds a majority interest. This reporting requirement as to foreign entities applies even if the U.S. taxpayer does not itself hold a direct interest in the foreign company and the foreign company is not involved in U.S. commerce.[12]

The extraterritorial impact of these reporting requirements is mitigated somewhat by a limited waiver under which U.S. taxpayers are excused from having to report the activities of foreign parent and sister corporations that are not otherwise required to report. To qualify for this waiver, however, the U.S. taxpayer must forfeit all deferral, domestic international sales corporation (DISC), foreign sales corporation (FSC), and foreign tax credit benefits related to operations in countries with unsanctioned boycotts, or show that the benefits derive from operations "separate and identifiable" from boycott-related activities.[13] Even where this waiver is possible, the U.S. taxpayer must still report (1) its own activities, (2) the activities of all other U.S. members of its controlled groups, and (3) the activities of all foreign corporations in which it is a U.S. shareholder (as defined below).[14]

In addition to the controlled group reporting requirements of section 999, U.S. shareholders are required to report the boycott-related activities of all foreign companies in which they hold the requisite ownership interest. U.S. shareholders are defined with respect to foreign companies as U.S. persons owning at least 10 percent of a foreign company's total combined voting stock.[15] Recognizing that minority shareholders may not be able to secure information from foreign companies, this shareholder-based reporting requirement applies only to information that is "reasonably available" to the U.S. shareholder.[16]

5.4 REPORTING REQUIREMENTS

Section 760.5 of the EAR requires U.S. persons (including U.S. companies and, in many cases, their foreign subsidiaries) to report the receipt of requests to take any action that has the effect of furthering or supporting the boycott on a *quarterly* basis. The specific deadline for reporting depends on whether the request was received in the United States or abroad. If the request was received in the United States, the report must be filed within one month following the end of the quarter during which the request was received. If received outside the United States, the U.S. person receiving the request has one additional month to report.

---

12. *See, e.g.,* Prop. Treas. Reg. § 1.999-1 (guideline A-18), 43 Fed. Reg. 3454, 3457 (1978).
13. *See, e.g.,* Prop. Treas. Reg. § 1.999-1 (guideline A-14A), 43 Fed. Reg. 3454, 3456 (1978).
14. *Id.*
15. I.R.C. § 951(b).
16. *See* Prop. Treas. Reg. § 1.999-1 (guideline A-18), 43 Fed. Reg. 3454, 3457 (1978).

- Boycott request received in United States   =   Report within *1 month* following the end of the quarter during which request received.

- Boycott request received abroad   =   Report within *2 months* following the end of the quarter during which request received.

Boycott-related requests—whether oral or written—are generally reportable regardless of whether the requested action is prohibited or permitted and regardless of whether the recipient complies with the request. A number of exceptions to the reporting requirements are set forth in the EAR. These exceptions are listed below, along with additional guidance regarding the reporting requirements of section 760.5 of the EAR.

Section 999 of the Internal Revenue Code requires U.S. taxpayers and members of their controlled groups to report any operations in or with any of the following boycotting countries: Iraq, Kuwait, Lebanon, Libya, Qatar, Saudi Arabia, Syria, the United Arab Emirates, and Yemen. In addition, such taxpayers must report the receipt of any request to enter into an impermissible boycott-related agreement, as defined below, whether or not the request came from one of the above-mentioned countries. Reports are filed in conjunction with the filing of the taxpayer's annual return.

5.5 REPORTING A BOYCOTT-RELATED REQUEST

EAR reports are filed quarterly. Form BIS 621-P is used for single requests, and form BIS 6051-P is used for multiple requests. The forms are available from the Department of Commerce's Office of Antiboycott Compliance (OAC). To obtain these forms, call OAC's Report Processing Unit at (202) 482-2448 or mail a request to U.S. Department of Commerce, BIS/Office of Antiboycott Compliance, Room 6098, Washington, DC, 20230. The forms are also available on the OAC website at http://www.bis.doc.gov/complianceandenforcement/ anti-boycottcompliance.htm.

Reports pursuant to section 999 are filed annually with a U.S. taxpayer's tax return using IRS form 5713. This form is available at any IRS office or at http://www.irs.gov.

5.6 PENALTIES AND ENFORCEMENT

(a) Commerce Department

Violations of the EAR's antiboycott provisions are subject to the full range of civil and criminal penalties available under the EAR, including fines, imprisonment, and denial of export privileges. Criminal violations of the EAR can result in penalties of up to $1 million and/or imprisonment for up to twenty years. The maximum civil penalty for an antiboycott violation under the EAR is $250,000 per violation or twice the value of the exports involved, whichever is greater. OAC's penalties typically do not reach these levels on a per count basis, but they are significant, and compliance breakdowns often involve numerous counts. Multiple violations may be asserted based on a single document. For example, each separate response to an eight-point boycott questionnaire may be treated as a separate count of furnishing boycott-related information.

The Commerce Department recognizes a formal voluntary self-disclosure procedure to self-report antiboycott violations, which is detailed in section 764.8 of the EAR. Though similar to section 764.5 of the EAR, the antiboycott voluntary disclosure procedure is distinct from the process for disclosing violations of the export control provisions of the EAR. Section 764.8(a) sets forth BIS's policy on voluntary disclosures and provides, "BIS strongly encourages disclosure to the Office of Antiboycott Compliance (OAC) if you believe that you may have violated the antiboycott provisions. Voluntary self-disclosures are a mitigating factor with respect to any enforcement action that OAC might take."

Voluntary self-disclosures to OAC are valid only if OAC receives the disclosure "before it commences an investigation or inquiry in connection with the same or substantially similar information it received from another source." OAC's receipt of a mandatory boycott report pursuant to section 760.5 is treated as information from another source. Fortunately, violations revealed during requests for advice from OAC are not treated as information from another source, but the revelation is not treated as a voluntary self-disclosure. Thus, OAC provides an opportunity to make a voluntary self-disclosure and potentially obtain mitigation after receiving advice from OAC that the conduct in question violated part 760 of the EAR.

Additional information regarding OAC's penalty practices may be found in supplement no. 2 to part 766 of the EAR: Guidance on Charging and Penalty Determinations in Settlement of Administrative Enforcement Cases Involving Antiboycott Matters. It is important to note that OAC operates under separate penalty guidelines than BIS's Office of Export Enforcement.

OAC regularly pursues enforcement actions against companies and individuals for violations of part 760 of the EAR. Recent cases illustrating the types of violations and range of penalties include the following:

- *SteelSummit International Inc.* – April 13, 2012. OAC assessed a civil penalty of $14,400 to settle allegations that on four occasions, SteelSummit furnished information about business relationships with boycotting countries or blacklisted persons in connection in violation of section 760.2(d) of the EAR. The alleged violations related to the furnishing of negative certificates of origin to persons in Saudi Arabia.
- *Samuel Shapiro & Company, Inc.* – March 8, 2012. OAC assessed a $10,000 civil penalty against Samuel Shapiro & Company for five alleged failures to report

the receipt of a request to engage in a restrictive trade practice or foreign boycott against a country friendly to the United States in violation of section 760.5 of the EAR. The alleged violations related to vessel eligibility certificates received in connection with exports to the United Arab Emirates.

- *Parfums de Coeur, Ltd.* – January 12, 2012. OAC assessed a $27,000 civil penalty against Parfums de Coeur to settle allegations of three prohibited furnishings of information and six failures to report the receipt of boycott-related requests. The alleged violations related to vessel eligibility certificates from the United Arab Emirates.

- *JAS Forwarding (USA), Inc.* – October 6, 2011. A civil penalty of $19,200 was levied against JAS to settle three counts of furnishing boycott-related information to persons in Kuwait and Lebanon. Two of the counts related to negative certificate of origin, and the third involved certifying in an insurance certificate that the company had a duly appointed agent or representative in Kuwait.

- *Bank of New York Mellon (Shanghai Branch)* – August 19, 2011. The bank paid a $30,000 civil penalty to settle allegations that its Shanghai branch furnished prohibited boycott-related information on fifteen occasions.

- *Chemguard, Inc.* – August 18, 2011. Chemguard agreed to pay $22,000 to settle allegations of two counts of furnishing prohibited boycott-related information and five failures to report boycott-related requests in connection with vessel eligibility certificates from the United Arab Emirates and Oman.

- *GM Daewoo Auto & Technology Company (Korea)* – January 8, 2010. GMDAT (a wholly owned Korean subsidiary of General Motors Company) paid $88,500 to settle allegations that on fifty-nine occasions it furnished prohibited boycott-related information to entities in Libya in connection with the shipment of Korean origin goods to Libya, involving the sale and transfer of title to those goods through a U.S. affiliate of General Motors for resale through an Egyptian distributor to Libya.

- *Baxter International, Inc.* – March 1993. This is the leading criminal antiboycott case, though it also resulted in a significant civil penalty and limited export denial order. Two affiliates of Baxter and one of its officers agreed to pay a total of $6,060,600 in civil penalties to settle allegations of violating part 760 of the EAR in connection with their efforts to be removed from the Arab League's blacklist. Baxter, its affiliates, subsidiaries, and employees were also subject to a limited denial order prohibiting them from "entering into, negotiating, or extending contracts to export goods or technology to Syria and Saudi Arabia from March 1993 until March 1995." Baxter also pled guilty to a single felony count and was fined $500,000. A corporate whistle-blower brought the matter to the U.S. government's attention.

Information regarding other Commerce Department antiboycott enforcement actions may be found at http://efoia.bis.doc.gov/antiboycott/violations/tocantiboycott .html and http://efoia.bis.doc.gov/antiboycott/warningletters/warningletters.htm.

(b) Treasury Department

Impermissible agreements to participate in or cooperate with an unsanctioned foreign boycott may result in the denial of certain tax privileges, including denial of foreign tax credits, denial of foreign tax deferral, and denial of the benefits of ETI, FSC, and DSC with respect to boycott-related income. Taxpayers are required to calculate these penalties in connection with the preparation of their tax returns. Detailed guidance on the rather complicated tax penalty calculation methodology is provided in the Department of the Treasury Guidelines: Boycott Provisions (section 999) of the Internal Revenue Code. Willful failures to make required reports are punishable by criminal fines up to $25,000 or imprisonment up to one year, or both. The Internal Revenue Service enforces civil violations of section 999, and the U.S. Department of Justice prosecutes criminal tax law violations.

Section 999 does not provide for a voluntary disclosure process distinct from disclosing other errors on a tax return. Because boycott-related agreements penalized under section 999 are enforced through the imposition of tax penalties, which are treated as confidential taxpayer information, civil cases are not reported.

5.7 LIST OF "BOYCOTTING" COUNTRIES

The Department of Treasury publishes this list on a periodic basis. The current list is composed of Iraq, Kuwait, Lebanon, Libya, Qatar, Saudi Arabia, Syria, the United Arab Emirates, and Yemen. This list is not exhaustive, and it is not uncommon to receive boycott-related requests from countries not on the official list, such as Bangladesh, Pakistan, Indonesia, Malaysia, and Nigeria. A current list of countries with a reputation for generating boycott-related requests is provided in Appendix D.

The Commerce Department does not publish any list of boycotting countries, and the requirements of part 760 of the EAR do not depend on a list.

5.8 LEGAL RESOURCES/WHERE CAN I FIND ADDITIONAL INFORMATION?

The primary legal resources for U.S. antiboycott compliance are as follows:

- part 760 of the U.S. Export Administration Regulations (15 C.F.R. § 760);
- parts 762 (Recordkeeping), 764 (Enforcement and Protective Measures), 766 (Administrative Enforcement Proceedings) of the EAR;
- section 999 of the Internal Revenue Code (26 U.S.C. § 999); and

- Department of the Treasury Guidelines: Boycott Provisions (section 999) of the Internal Revenue Code.[17]

Additional information and guidance may be found on the OAC website at http://www.bis.doc.gov/complianceandenforcement/antiboycottcompliance.htm.

OAC provides general or transaction-specific guidance on antiboycott compliance to the public. They may be contacted at:

U.S. Department of Commerce
BIS/Office of Antiboycott Compliance, Room 6098
1401 Constitution Ave, NW
Washington, DC 20230

Antiboycott Advice Line: (202) 482-2381

The Treasury Department will provide copies of form 5713, the current list of boycotting countries, section 999, and copies of all guidelines. Please contact:

Mr. David Joy, Office of the General Counsel
Room 2015 – Main Treasury Building
Department of the Treasury
1500 Pennsylvania Avenue, NW
Washington, DC 20220

Mr. Joy can also be reached at (202) 622-1945 for informal, nonbinding answers to questions concerning section 999 of the Internal Revenue Code. His e-mail address is david.joy@do.treas.gov.

5.9 COMPLIANCE TOOLS AND ANALYTICAL FRAMEWORK

Because antiboycott law is so dependent on specific examples and complicated concepts, the explanation of which would make for a rather long chapter indeed, Appendixes A through G elaborate on this chapter and provide some useful compliance tools to the practitioner. It bears reiterating, however, that there is no substitute for carefully analyzing a given set of facts under part 760 of the EAR and section 999 of the IRC (including the Treasury Department guidelines). Though dense and somewhat tedious, these sources should answer the lion's share of questions you and your

---

17. The 999 guidelines may be found in the *Federal Register* (look under the topic "Treasury" on the following dates: 1/25/78, for the original guidelines; 11/19/79, for supplemental guidelines; and 4/26/84, for additional guidelines). The guidelines are also available in compilations such as CCH, Standard Federal Tax Reports, in the notes under I.R.C. section 999 and BNA (Tax Management) Portfolio 345.

clients are likely to confront. In closing, I offer the following framework to help guide your analysis.

Framework for Analyzing Boycott-Related Requests

COMMERCE	TREASURY
1. Is there a U.S. person (or an owned or controlled foreign affiliate of a U.S. person)?	*Is there a U.S. taxpayer or member of its controlled group?*
2. Is the transaction within the interstate or foreign commerce of the United States?	*Does the taxpayer claim U.S. foreign tax credits or other tax benefits enumerated in section 999?*
3. Does the request fall within a prohibition?	*Did the taxpayer agree to or receive a request to enter into a boycott agreement?*
4. Does the request meet an exception to the prohibitions?	*Does the agreement meet an exception to section 999, or has it been deemed not penalized under the Treasury Department Section 999 Guidelines?*
5. Even if not prohibited, is the request reportable?	*All penalizable agreements or requests to agree are also reportable.*
6. Does the request meet an exception to the reporting requirements?	

Handling Violations

Internal Investigations, Voluntary Disclosures, Global Settlements, and Possible Defenses

Wendy L. Wysong and Adam Klauder

6.1 OVERVIEW

Given the complexities of the U.S. system of economic sanctions and export controls, violations are perhaps inevitable. What may come as a shock for companies and their employees, however, are the serious financial and reputational consequences that could result from these violations. Administrative monetary penalties have risen in recent years, as has the likelihood of criminal prosecution, accompanied by heavy corporate fines and imprisonment for individuals. Equally significant are the possible collateral consequences arising from violations, including suspension or denial of export privileges—a threat that overhangs all negotiations with the government in these cases.

The manner in which a company addresses a potential violation is, in many ways, as important to the outcome as the severity of the underlying conduct. Potential violations need to be investigated quickly and thoroughly, keeping in mind that a key determinant of the level of liability will be whether the violation was willful. A finding of willfulness may very well transform an administrative or regulatory matter into a criminal case in federal court, particularly when a national security concern is implicated. Thus, a company needs to conduct its internal investigation with an eye on the possibility of either administrative or criminal resolution, or both.

This chapter provides an overview of the numerous agencies that are responsible for the enforcement of export controls and economic sanctions; the steps involved in conducting a thorough internal investigation of potential export control violations; how voluntary self-disclosures should be utilized and the process for submitting them; strategies to consider when crafting a global settlement; possible defenses to export control allegations; and case studies that highlight these issues.

6.2 EXPORT CONTROL ENFORCEMENT OVERVIEW

Multiple agencies within the U.S. government are responsible for the regulation and enforcement of export controls and economic sanctions. The primary regulatory agencies include:

- Department of Commerce's Bureau of Industry and Security (BIS), which administers the Export Administration Regulations (EAR),[1] pursuant to the International Emergency Economic Powers Act (IEEPA);[2]
- Department of State's Directorate of Defense Trade Controls (DDTC), which administers the Arms Export Control Act (AECA),[3] and International Traffic in Arms Regulations (ITAR);[4] and
- Department of Treasury's Office of Foreign Assets Control (OFAC), which is responsible for implementing economic sanctions regulations,[5] pursuant to the Trading with the Enemy Act (TWEA)[6] and IEEPA.

The primary agencies with export control and economic sanctions enforcement authority include:

- BIS, through its Office of Export Enforcement (OEE);
- DDTC, through the Enforcement Division of the Office of Defense Trade Controls Compliance (DTCC);
- Department of Homeland Security, through U.S. Customs and Border Protection (CBP) and U.S. Immigration and Customs Enforcement (ICE);
- Department of Justice (DOJ), in coordination with the Federal Bureau of Investigation (FBI) and the U.S. Attorney's offices around the country.
- OFAC, through its Sanctions Compliance & Evaluation Division (for financial institution respondents) and Enforcement Division (for all other respondents); and
- Census Bureau, through its own enforcement mechanism and CBP.

These agencies have wide-reaching jurisdiction, which can impact both U.S. and foreign companies. Jurisdiction among the agencies is often overlapping and concurrent, which can lead to inconsistency in enforcement due to competing priorities and differing interpretations of the relevant laws and regulations. Moreover, multiple agencies may have an interest in investigating and penalizing the same violation under different regulations. When a violation is discovered, a company should consider and address all the agencies that may have jurisdiction. A company must be careful to ensure that violations of each regime are uncovered and, where appropriate, disclosed to and resolved with all the relevant agencies. Overlooking an agency and having to face additional penalties and collateral consequences later can be disastrous. In response to calls to address the inefficiencies inherent in overlapping jurisdiction, the

---

1. 15 C.F.R. pts. 730–774 (2012).
2. 50 U.S.C. § 1705(b).
3. 22 U.S.C. § 2778.
4. 22 C.F.R. §§ 120–130 (2012).
5. 31 C.F.R. §§ 500–598 (2010).
6. 50 U.S.C. app. § 16(a).

potential for inconsistent enforcement, and burden of addressing multiple agencies, President Obama initiated a broad-based interagency review of the existing export control framework in August 2010.[7] The administration concluded that, with respect to export enforcement, "[a] multitude of agencies with overlapping and duplicative authorities currently enforce our export controls, creating redundancies and jeopardizing each other's cases."[8] To address this problem, the administration proposed several reforms, including an increased focus on enforcement efforts by "building higher walls around the most sensitive items,"[9] having additional end-use assurances against diversion from foreign consignees, increasing outreach and on-site visits domestically and abroad, and enhancing compliance and enforcement.

President Obama signed Executive Order 13,558 on November 9, 2010, which established an Export Enforcement Coordination Center that will "coordinate and strengthen the U.S. Government's enforcement efforts—and eliminate gaps and duplication—across all relevant departments and agencies."[10] Although these reforms will take time to implement, a company should monitor any developments that could signal changes in the U.S. government's enforcement priorities and likely areas of focus for prosecution. These changes will affect the nature and conduct of any corresponding internal investigations.

For example, Under Secretary for Industry and Security Eric Hirschhorn stated in 2011 that BIS will adjust "how [it] penalize[s] those who violate U.S. export controls."[11] He explained that "BIS has typically imposed penalties on companies involved in export violations. Now, where a violation is the deliberate action of an individual, we consider seeking penalties against that individual."[12]

Thus, in conducting an investigation, companies should take into account not only the priorities of all agencies with regulatory and enforcement authority, but should, in light of recent developments, also consider the risk that individual conduct will face heightened scrutiny.

6.3 INTERNAL INVESTIGATIONS

(a) Preliminary Steps

There are many ways in which a potential export control or economic sanction violation can be uncovered, including through a routine internal audit, from a whistle-

---

7. *See* Press Release, The White House, Office of the Press Secretary, President Obama Lays the Foundation for a New Export Control System to Strengthen National Security and the Competitiveness of Key U.S. Manufacturing and Technology Sectors (Aug. 30, 2010), *available at* http://www.whitehouse.gov/the-press-office/2010/08/30/president-obama-lays-foundation-a-new-export-control-system-strengthen-n.

8. *Id.*

9. *Id.*

10. Exec. Order No. 13,558, 75 Fed. Reg. 69,573 (Nov. 15, 2010).

11. Eric L. Hirschhorn, Under Secretary for Industry and Security, Dept. of Commerce, Bureau of Industry and Security, Remarks of Eric L. Hirschhorn at Update 2011 Conference (Jul. 19, 2011) (transcript *available at* http://www.bis.doc.gov/pagetwo.html).

12. *Id.*

blower report, a media investigation, the receipt of a subpoena, or the execution of a search warrant by government agents. When a potential violation is uncovered, a company should begin to address the issue by taking several initial steps: (1) ensuring that any potential violations are stopped, (2) assessing the scope and significance of any potential violations, (3) preserving relevant documents, and (4) determining how to conduct an internal investigation of the facts, including whether to retain outside counsel and/or forensic investigators.

During this initial stage, a company should also consider the possibility of government involvement. In some cases, the government may already be aware of the potential violation, while in others, the company may ultimately consider voluntarily disclosing it, as described in section 6.5. In either case, the company's preliminary actions will be subject to scrutiny and will impact, and perhaps determine, the success of the ultimate resolution.

(i) Stopping the Potential Violations

The most important step a company should take upon discovering a violation is to ensure that any potentially unlawful conduct is stopped. At a minimum, any shipments of goods that are the subject of the potential violation should be stopped. Depending on the facts and circumstances of the investigation, a company may also need to recover any items that have been shipped illegally and/or terminate the trade relationship it has with any counterparties that are implicated by the allegations of misconduct. A company may also need to temporarily suspend any employees who were involved in the violative conduct or remove them from positions within the company where they could continue to engage in illegal activity, pending further investigation.

These initial company responses serve two primary purposes: (1) they are critical steps in stopping any illegal conduct quickly and in preventing any further violations and (2) they demonstrate the company's commitment to compliance. This latter point is particularly important in the context of any scrutiny by regulatory or enforcement authorities. One of the first questions the regulatory/enforcement authorities will often ask is whether the company took measures to protect against any further misconduct. A company's ability to demonstrate that it responded comprehensively and in a timely manner when it became aware of the potential violations will aid in establishing that the company is committed to remediation and ongoing compliance.

The manner in which a company initially responds to knowledge of a potential violation is also important when a company employee raises the initial complaint. If the company can demonstrate that it took the allegation seriously, it can decrease the likelihood that the complainant will report the conduct outside the company, either to the media or to the government. Keeping knowledge of a complaint or a potential violation internal enables the company to maintain control over the initial investigation steps, rather than allowing third parties, such as enforcement agencies, to drive the scope and timing of the investigation.

(ii) Initial Evaluation of Alleged Conduct

In parallel with its efforts to stop any potentially illegal conduct, a company should evaluate the facts against the applicable export control regulations to determine the likelihood that a violation occurred and whether a more comprehensive internal investigation is, in fact, warranted. The company may conclude that an informal inquiry is all that is required to understand the full scope of the issue. It should be cautious, however, in deciding whether to conduct an investigation that could be perceived by a regulator or enforcement authority as too narrow to address the allegations with sufficient analysis.

In order to ensure that the initial evaluation is thorough and complete, the company should, among other things:

- determine the scope of the misconduct;
- ascertain whether it was systemic or the work of a rogue employee;
- understand how the violation occurred;
- evaluate the credibility of the information provided;
- identify compliance mechanisms that did not work; and
- attempt to establish whether the violation was willful or negligent.

A company must analyze the facts gathered through the investigation under the appropriate export control and economic sanctions regime. This analysis is often difficult because the regulations are subject to frequent amendment, the same terms are used and defined inconsistently across the different regulations, and agencies sometimes apply the regulations differently to the same conduct. Ideally, the analysis should therefore be undertaken by someone with specialized knowledge of export controls and economic sanctions.

Once a company has completed its initial evaluation, it will be in a better position to determine whether and how to proceed. Regardless of the decision, a company should document its reasons for either concluding the investigation after an initial inquiry or continuing with a further internal investigation. This will be particularly important if regulators or enforcement agencies scrutinize a company's decision not to conduct a full internal investigation.

If a company decides to proceed with an informal internal inquiry, every effort should be made to keep the details of the investigation closely held until the company determines whether it will disclose its findings to the government. Thus, a company should not disclose more information than is necessary in company-wide communications, such as document preservation notices, and personnel involvement should be kept to a minimum during this period of preliminary investigation.

(iii) Deciding Who Will Lead the Investigation

After deciding to conduct an internal investigation, a company must next determine which party should conduct the investigation. In making this decision, a company should weigh questions of expertise, resources, confidentiality, independence and objectivity (and the perception thereof), and cost.

It may be appropriate for in-house counsel, compliance staff, or internal auditors to lead the investigation if the alleged violations are limited in nature and number and were clearly the result of inadvertent mistakes. In-house counsel often has a strong understanding of the applicable export control laws and should have the advantage of a deep knowledge of the company's personnel, systems, and operation. If there are indications, however, that the conduct at issue is widespread or criminal in nature (i.e., deliberate and willful) or if there is evidence that management is implicated, a company should consider retaining outside counsel to conduct the investigation.

First, the attorney-client privilege and work-product doctrine protect strategic communications and investigative materials most effectively when they are prepared by or with the assistance of outside counsel. This is especially relevant in cross-border investigations involving countries where the attorney-client privilege does not apply to communications with in-house counsel.

Second, a company can demonstrate the independence and objectivity of its investigation to the government most easily when outside counsel leads the investigation. By hiring outside counsel that the government believes is independent and objective, a company can credibly assert that it should be allowed to proceed with the investigation without being subjected to an intrusive and disruptive government investigation, which often involves the use of search warrants or the grand jury process.

Third, outside counsel can serve as a buffer between the company and the government and provide a single point of contact for all stakeholders. Using outside counsel as the primary interlocutor with the government can also achieve certain strategic goals, particularly during settlement negotiations where counsel's statements are not necessarily considered to be those of the company.

Fourth, outside counsel with expertise in export controls, perhaps gained through government experience in the area, may have a better understanding of the regulatory nuances and intricacies than local prosecutors with limited experience in this area or federal agents on a rotation detail. Although training of prosecutors and agents has improved with the implementation of the multi-government agency National Export Control Initiative, experienced export control practitioners may be better able to negotiate potential charges. Similarly, if the case is being prosecuted criminally, a company should make sure to consult expert criminal counsel.

Finally, almost by definition, export control violations involve non-U.S. legal jurisdictions, thereby implicating data privacy statutes, bank secrecy regulations, employment laws, blocking statutes, and other relevant local laws. Outside counsel can help determine whether non-U.S. legal issues will need to be addressed and can coordinate this advice with qualified local counsel.

(iv) Preserving Documents

With regard to document preservation—another crucial initial step—a company should develop a plan to ensure that relevant documents are not destroyed. It should immediately suspend the automatic document destruction process/procedure/policy to preserve all electronic communications and documents and take steps to ensure the preservation of such information on servers, back-up tapes, hard drives, and other similar locations. Failure to do so could result in obstruction of justice charges.

A company should also identify employees who may possess relevant documents and distribute document protection notices to them. These notices should be carefully worded in order to keep details about the investigation closely held. These instructions should direct employees not to destroy any documents (both hard copy and electronic) in their offices or elsewhere that are in their possession and control. The notices should also require an acknowledgment and certification of compliance by the custodians, which should be maintained in the investigation files. In the event that relevant documents are not maintained, it will be important for a company to demonstrate that it did everything possible to prevent their destruction. Document collection is described in further detail in section 6.3(b)(ii) below.

(b) Conducting the Investigation

If the initial analysis demonstrates a real likelihood of violations of law such that an internal investigation is warranted, a company should consider implementing the following steps.

(i) Attorney-Client Privilege and Attorney Work-Product Doctrines

Prior to conducting any investigation, a company should consider how to preserve legally privileged materials throughout the investigation.

The attorney-client privilege protects confidential communications from a client to a lawyer made to obtain legal assistance from the lawyer in his or her capacity as a legal adviser, and the advice given by the lawyer to the client in the course of representing the client. In order for the attorney-client privilege to apply, the primary purpose of the communication must be to seek or provide legal advice. Communications are not privileged if the sole or dominant purpose of the communication is business advice. It should also be noted that dual-purpose (i.e., business/legal) communications may not be protected.

The attorney work-product doctrine protects from discovery documents prepared by a party or its representatives in anticipation of litigation. This doctrine is not a privilege, but a qualified immunity from disclosure. Courts apply a balancing test in assessing whether the doctrine protects against the disclosure of attorney work product by weighing the public interest in disclosure against the privacy rights of the party. This doctrine applies to oral and written communications and is not limited solely to lawyers. For example, paralegals, assistants, clerks, staff, and others are covered if their work product is done at the direction of a lawyer on behalf of the lawyer's client in anticipation of litigation.

The following are some practical recommendations for preserving privilege and work product:

- Always mark privileged documents "Privileged & Confidential" and include, where appropriate, (a) "Lawyer-Client Communication" to reflect communications between outside counsel and the company or between the in-house counsel and employees of the company; (b) "Work Product" for documents prepared in connection with the investigation or in anticipation of litigation; or (c) both. The markings should be clear on the face of the document, bolded and obvious, to make inadvertent disclosure less likely.

- When communicating with inside or outside counsel, be clear that the person sending the communication is seeking a legal opinion. One means of doing so would be to state explicitly, "I am seeking your legal opinion on . . ." This is particularly important where communication is by e-mail, which is often characterized by an informal style. Similarly, when forwarding e-mails, voicemails, or other documents to inside or outside counsel, always make it clear in the communication that it is being done for the purpose of obtaining legal advice.

- Whenever possible, have outside counsel, rather than company lawyers, prepare any necessary documents, including memoranda, drafts, e-mails, and/or notes of conversations or interviews.

- Counsel should be present at all interviews, and no one other than the subject and outside or in-house counsel should be present. Only counsel should take notes at the interview to ensure that they are protected by the attorney-client privilege and work-product doctrine. The *Upjohn* warning should be provided at the beginning of the interview, indicating that (1) counsel represents the company and not the individual, (2) the interview is protected by the attorney-client privilege, which is held by the company and not the employee, and (3) the company can waive such privilege at its discretion and disclose information from the interview to third parties, including the government.

- Privileged documents should not be voluntarily disclosed to a government agency without first (1) drafting an appropriate reservation of rights to assert privilege, (2) receiving recognition from the recipient agency of such reservation, (3) requesting confidentiality, and (4) receiving assurance from the agency recipient of confidential treatment. The foregoing should first be achieved informally and verbally with the agency. It should then be confirmed in a formal letter to the agency (perhaps a cover letter forwarding privileged documents as attachments).

- To the extent that counsel retains the services of outside vendors or consultants to assist in any investigation being undertaken for purposes of providing legal advice or developing information in anticipation of litigation, the vendor or consultant should execute an appropriate confidentiality agreement with counsel (not the client), obligating it to maintain the confidentiality of any work-product materials.

(ii) Document Control, Collection, and Analysis

The documents that were preserved during the initial analysis and assessment should now be collected, reviewed, and analyzed. The document custodians who were initially identified, and any others subsequently identified, should be sent written notices to preserve and collect all responsive documents in their possession and to turn them over to a central point of contact. Consider every department that might be involved in an export violation, including sales, marketing, finance, shipping, human resources, facility security, travel, and logistics. The company should also conduct initial scoping interviews to ensure that all possible custodians are identified and all documents arguably relevant to the investigation are collected. Also consider the effect of non-U.S. data protection laws, which could be implicated by the mere act of collecting the documents even before their analysis, and obtain local counsel opinions where necessary as to the appropriate method for collecting the documents (e.g., whether the custodian's consent must be sought).

Analysis of the documents may require the services of a litigation support company to electronically scan and upload hard-copy documents, along with the electronic documents. A search methodology will need to be developed, perhaps using a list of keywords, which may ultimately need to be shared with the government to ensure that the document search and analysis were suitably comprehensive and thorough.

Once the documents are analyzed and the relevant documents identified, they can be used as the basis for substantive interviews.

(iii) Conducting Interviews

Counsel should conduct substantive interviews of all employees involved with the transactions at issue. Additionally, individuals who can provide information about the export compliance program in general should be interviewed to determine a company's level of commitment to compliance and corporate knowledge of export controls and economic sanctions. High-level officials and senior management may also be interviewed to determine, among other things, whether they understood their responsibility for setting the "compliance tone at the top."

If the government is or will be involved, there is a potential that any interview memoranda will be disclosed during the course of the investigation, although the government is restricted from conditioning cooperation credit on waiver of the attorney-client privilege. Accordingly, the memoranda should not include editorial comments and case strategy.

To prevent any misunderstanding that company counsel represents the employee/interviewee in connection with the investigation, the interview memoranda should document that the *Upjohn* warning was provided and that the employee/interviewee acknowledged that he/she understood. If an employee's interests are at all adverse to the company's interests, the individual should retain separate counsel.

At a minimum, counsel should address the following topics during the interview. First, the interviewer should inquire about the facts surrounding the transaction, including the identities of everyone involved, to gain an overall understanding of the issue and determine whether any other parties should be questioned in relation to the investigation. Next, information should be gathered about the potentially export-controlled item or transaction at issue, including any technical specifications, components, and licensing history. Most important, the interviewer must determine the extent to which the parties involved have knowledge of export control and economic sanctions laws and the company's relevant compliance procedures, particularly as they relate to the specific transaction at hand. Interviewees should also be questioned about any advice they relied on in causing the transaction. Finally, the questioning should reveal what remedial measures were taken following discovery of the violation, including how additional violations were prevented, what attempts were made to recover the item(s) at issue, and whether any disciplinary actions occurred or were planned. An understanding of the remedial measures taken by the company will be vital in the event that the company decides to disclose the violation to the government.

Interviews conducted overseas present their own unique challenges. The interview process must recognize and accommodate local customs, history, and cultural traditions, as well as different languages and dialects. As such, local employment laws overseas might require local counsel or may limit the conditions under which the interview may take place. Logistics such as witness safety and comfort, recordkeeping, and document handling will also present challenges.

6.4 REMEDIATION

The sufficiency of the remedial measures a company takes to correct violations and prevent them from recurring are as important to the government as the rigor of the investigation into the historic conduct. This is clear from DOJ's explicit inclusion of a corporation's remedial efforts, including the implementation of an effective compliance program, replacement of responsible management, and discipline of wrongdoers, in the DOJ Principles of Federal Prosecution of Business Organizations.[13]

Once its internal investigation is complete, a company should make sure that all internal control deficiencies are addressed. A company should update all its policies and procedures to address violations that occurred. A company should also document its heightened efforts to ensure that the relevant regulations are effectively communicated to employees through regular training or other means.

---

13. *See* United States Attorneys' Manual, ch. 9-28.000 (2008), http://www.justice.gov/usao/eousa/foia_reading_room/usam/.

Where the investigation reveals that particular individuals are responsible, a company should take disciplinary action in order to demonstrate that it takes such misconduct seriously. In cases of serious illegality, a company should consider terminating the employment of such individuals, keeping in mind the effect that termination would have on the investigation in terms of that individual's willingness to continue to cooperate.

In most cases, the government includes in its settlement documents a description of the mitigation given to a company in recognition of the remediation undertaken as a result of the discovery of the violation. For example, BAE received significant credit in its settlement with DDTC in recognition of the extensive remedial compliance measures it implemented after its discovery of export violations.[14]

6.5 VOLUNTARY SELF-DISCLOSURE

Companies should evaluate whether to voluntarily disclose a violation to the government at various points during an investigation, including as early as completion of the preliminary evaluation if a company concludes it is likely that a violation occurred. The government generally gives maximum mitigation credit for voluntary self-disclosure (VSD)—as high as 50 percent of the maximum penalty—and the opportunity should not be lost.

The first question to ask in determining whether to make a VSD is whether the VSD is in fact required by law. In the export control area, VSDs are required by law in several circumstances, including the following:

- Where the underlying conduct involves a potential violation of the ITAR, and a proscribed country is involved. In such cases, the ITAR imposes a requirement to immediately notify DDTC.[15]
- Where the underlying conduct involves a potential violation of the EAR, and the company would violate general prohibition 10 if it proceeded with a particular transaction (e.g., the company has been requested to fix any item that was illegally exported).[16]
- Where the company is required by contract to export additional items or undertake additional tasks requiring a license, and the company needs to apply for a license for these additional tasks.[17] In such a case, failure to note in the license application that some of the exports/tasks requiring a license have already been undertaken without a license would constitute a material omission.[18]

14. BAE Systems PLC, Proposed Charging Letter 1-2 (U.S. Dep't of State 2011) (describing the mitigation, including senior management and Board of Directors changes and remedial compliance measures), http://www.pmddtc.state.gov/compliance/consent_agreements/pdf/BAES_PCL.pdf.
15. *See* 22 C.F.R. § 126.1(e)(1).
16. *See* General Prohibition 10, 15 C.F.R. §§ 736, 764.2(e) and 764.5(f).
17. *See* 15 C.F.R. § 764.5(f)(1).
18. *See* 18 USC § 1001 and 15 C.F.R. § 746.2(g).

From the beginning, a company must also carefully analyze the possible risk that the government will discover the violation on its own and whether such discovery is imminent. Such government-initiated discovery can negate a company's chance to obtain full credit for voluntary disclosure. For example, if a disgruntled employee or industry competitor is about to tip the government or media, immediate disclosure is advisable to preserve any mitigative benefit. Or, if nondisclosure could create a national security risk (e.g., if government assistance is required to recover a sensitive item destined for dangerous hands), disclosure should be immediate.[19]

In some circumstances, however, where the transaction at issue is an isolated instance involving a nonsensitive item where there is no chance of recurrence, a company may consider whether disclosure may not be warranted. It is also possible that the violation may never come to the government's attention. In such cases, a company should consider carefully the potential downside to disclosure, as the fines and penalties imposed even on voluntarily disclosed violations can be substantial. It is by no means a free pass. On the other hand, disclosure of even minor violations that are unlikely to generate large fines can demonstrate the effectiveness of a company's auditing and reporting program.

In order to encourage voluntary disclosures, agency officials have stated that they would not refer, and Department of Justice lawyers have confirmed that they would not accept, a case disclosed voluntarily for criminal prosecution if they determine that the disclosure was truthful, complete, and voluntary.[20] These qualifications are discretionary with the government and somewhat subjective, leaving it to the government to decide whether a disclosure is full and complete, truthful or voluntary.[21] Accordingly, companies should make disclosures to the regulatory agency knowing that there is a very real possibility of criminal prosecution. Despite the government's assurances of lenient treatment for voluntary disclosures, the government will investigate and criminally prosecute cases where the government believes that it can make a compelling criminal case, based on whether it can prove criminal intent at high levels within the company. Even if no penalties are imposed, the government keeps a record of the violation, which will affect the treatment of future violations.

---

19.   It should be noted that there are also disclosure obligations under the securities laws and state regulations if business with sanctioned countries would be material to investors or if potential violations of export controls and economic sanctions would be financially material for shareholders.

20.   Steven W. Pelak, the Deputy Chief of the Counterespionage Section, National Security Division, DOJ and National Coordinator for Export Enforcement, has stated as recently as December 11, 2012, that DOJ wants to encourage voluntary self-disclosures and thus, DOJ will not prosecute a company that comes forward with a voluntary self-disclosure as long as the disclosure is "truthful, complete, and voluntary." Steven W. Pelak, Remarks at Practicing Law Institute: Coping with U.S. Export Controls 2012 (December 11, 2012). Mr. Pelak also made similar statements at this annual conference in 2010 and 2011.

21.   *See* discussion of criminal resolutions against United Technologies Corporation and ITT below, section 7.5.

A company may waive the attorney-client privilege by its submission of a voluntary self-disclosure, not only as to the voluntary self-disclosure itself, but potentially to the entire subject matter of the voluntary self-disclosure. In addition, in order to prevent disclosure of the voluntary self-disclosure filing to outside parties under a Freedom of Information Act ("FOIA") request, the filing should indicate that it includes confidential proprietary commercial and/or financial information, and be marked accordingly.

In preparing a voluntary self-disclosure, the company should consult the relevant agency's specific procedures and evaluative methodologies set forth in the agency's regulations and on their websites.[22]

(a) OFAC

If OFAC determines that a self-disclosure is "voluntary," the potential administrative penalty amount will be reduced by 50 percent, as discussed in more detail in chapter 1.[23]

OFAC narrowly defines *voluntary*, excluding information that would otherwise be available to OFAC, or contained in a report that is required of another participant in a transaction (such as an intermediary bank in a funds transfer), regardless if and when the report is ultimately filed. Nonetheless, any level of cooperation with OFAC may lead to very substantial mitigation of a penalty—nearly as much as a voluntary self-disclosure.

If a company decides to file a VSD, it is generally advisable to notify OFAC of the issue as soon as it is discovered by making an initial filing. This avoids the possibility that OFAC or a third-party participant in the transaction will become aware of the issue first, potentially negating the potential for VSD mitigation credit. If an initial VSD is filed, OFAC requires that it be followed up with a final report containing full details required for the case's adjudication within "a reasonable time." What is reasonable depends on the circumstances, as OFAC does not have a regulatory deadline, but generally it should be within sixty to ninety days. If there are special circumstances, they should be discussed on an ongoing basis with the OFAC case officer. The VSD should address all relevant factors present in the case that could affect the severity of a potential civil penalty, including the parties and transactions involved and the results of the transaction.

---

22. *See* Export Administration Regulations, 15 C.F.R. § 766, supp. no. 1 (2012); International Traffic in Arms Regulations, 22 C.F.R. § 127.12 (2012); Economic Sanctions Enforcement Guidelines, 31 C.F.R. § 501, app. A (2012); *see also* chapter 1 U.S. Economic Sanctions Law: Voluntary Self-Disclosures, Enforcement, and Penalties.

23. This and other potentially substantial reductions in the amount of a civil penalty are contained in the guidelines' ten general factors. *See* 74 Fed. Reg. 57,593, 57,602 (Nov. 9, 2009) (to be codified at 31 C.F.R. app. § 501).

If negotiation of a settlement is intended following the filing of a final VSD, the respondent should request that OFAC not issue a pre-penalty notice (PPN), and that settlement negotiations immediately commence so that the potential charges can be discussed. Negotiation of a settlement may also occur if a PPN has been issued, provided that the time for a penalty notice has not expired. Other potential outcomes for an OFAC-enforcement investigation include the following: no action; an administrative subpoena where further information is required; a cautionary letter warning the respondent to be more vigilant; a formal "finding of violation" that documents the determination but without further penalty; criminal referral; or other administrative actions, such as an OFAC license denial, suspension, modification, or revocation, or an OFAC cease and desist order.

(b) BIS

BIS provides "great weight" to disclosures—at least 50 percent of the calculated penalty—as long as they are determined to be voluntary. Unlike OFAC, however, BIS does not define the base on which the 50 percent mitigation is imposed in light of the value of the transaction. Accordingly, even for violations involving small values (exports of less than $10,000 for example), BIS can impose its 50 percent mitigation on the maximum fine level of $250,000, whereas OFAC would impose its 50 percent mitigation on the export transaction value. As a consequence, BIS, more than OFAC, is apt to temper its fine level by looking to past average fines for similar export transactions.

To be deemed voluntary, the disclosure must be received before any government agency obtains knowledge of the "same or substantially similar information from another source and has commenced an investigation or inquiry in connection with that information."[24] Though BIS provides great weight to VSDs, consideration will be given to all other factors in a given case, and the VSD credit may be outweighed by other aggravating factors.

According to BIS, an initial notification should be submitted by the disclosing party "as soon as possible after violations are discovered."[25] The initial notification should include the identification of the disclosing party and a description of the general nature and extent of the violations. Upon submitting the initial notification, the disclosing party should then conduct a thorough review, which BIS recommends should cover a period of five years prior to the date of the initial notification. Once the review is completed, the disclosing party must then submit a final VSD, which must include a narrative account of the violations, supporting documentation, and a certification of truth and accuracy by the disclosing official with authority to bind the company. BIS has proposed a 180-day deadline for persons who have submitted

---

24.   15 C.F.R. § 764.5(a)(3).
25.   15 C.F.R. § 764.5(c).

an initial notification to complete and submit the final narrative report to OEE.[26] The Director of OEE could extend this 180-day time deadline, at his or her discretion, if U.S. government interests would be served by an extension or upon a showing by the party making the disclosure that more time is reasonably necessary to complete the narrative account.[27] BIS provides a list of what the narrative account should address, including (1) the nature of the review conducted and measures that may have been taken to minimize the likelihood that violations will occur in the future; (2) the kind of violation involved; (3) an explanation of when and how the violations occurred; (4) the identities and addresses of all parties involved; (5) license numbers; (6) a description, quantity, value, and ECCN of the item(s) involved; and (7) any mitigating circumstances. Upon review of a VSD, BIS may take the following actions: no action, a warning letter, a proposed charging letter and settlement, or referral of the matter to the DOJ for criminal prosecution.

(c) DDTC

In order for a disclosure to be considered voluntary by DDTC, the disclosing party must submit its disclosure before any government agency "obtains knowledge of either the same or substantially similar information from another source and commences an investigation or inquiry that involves that information, and that is intended to determine whether the [AECA] or the [ITAR] or any other license, order or other authorization issued under the [AECA] has been violated," prompting an investigation.[28] In addition, DDTC "strongly encourages" disclosure and may consider the submission of a VSD a mitigating factor.[29] Unlike OFAC and BIS, however, DDTC will consider the failure to submit a VSD an aggravating factor when determining the disposition of a case. Unlike OFAC and BIS, DDTC often resolves VSDs without imposing any penalties at all—saving the imposition of penalties for more egregious cases threatening national security, cases demonstrating some important legal issue to notify the defense industry of its interpretation, or cases where DDTC believes that the exporter willfully violated the ITAR or demonstrated gross negligence or lack of respect for DDTC's authority or interpretation of the ITAR.

---

26. See Time Limit for Completion of Voluntary Self-Disclosures and Revised Notice of the Institution of Administrative Enforcement Proceedings, 77 Fed. Reg. 66,777 (proposed Nov. 7, 2012) (to be codified at 15 C.F.R. pts. 764 and 766).

27. The Proposed Rule sets forth some illustrative examples of circumstances that might warrant additional time, including: (1) records or information from multiple entities and/or jurisdictions are needed to complete the narrative account; (2) material changes occur in the business, such as a bankruptcy, large layoffs, or a corporate acquisition or restructuring, and present difficulties in gaining access to, or analysis of, information needed to complete the narrative account; and (3) a pending U.S. government determination (such as a commodity jurisdiction determination or a classification request) is needed to complete the narrative account.

28. 22 C.F.R. § 127.12(b)(2).

29. 22 C.F.R. § 127.12(a).

DDTC requires that the disclosing party submit an initial notification "immediately after a violation is discovered," followed by a thorough review and final disclosure within sixty calendar days of the initial disclosure.[30] While DDTC will consider granting an extension after the disclosing party provides a justification in writing, any unreasonable delay may result in the disclosure not qualifying as "voluntary."

DDTC provides specific instructions regarding what should be included in a VSD, including (1) identification of the disclosing party and a point of contact; (2) a precise description of the violations and the exact circumstances surrounding the violations; (3) the complete identities and addresses of all parties involved; (4) license numbers, exemptions, or other applicable authorizations; (5) a description, quantity, and USML category of the hardware, technical data, or defense service involved; and (6) corrective actions taken and how they are designed to prevent similar violations from occurring in the future. DDTC also provides a list of factors to be addressed in the VSD, including whether the violation was intentional or inadvertent, the parties' familiarity with the laws and regulations; prior AECA administrative or criminal action, and the compliance measures that were in place at the time of the violation. In addition, the VSD must include any supporting documentation and a certification of truth and accuracy by an empowered official or senior officer, depending on the severity of the violations.

When more than one agency is involved, such as when there are potentially both EAR and ITAR charges, disclosure of all the violations to each of the relevant agencies should be done simultaneously. Coordinating investigation status updates among the various government agencies will help facilitate a global resolution. By serving as a communication conduit, counsel can also control the flow of information to some degree. Interagency communication may be limited—but one should not assume that the agencies are not sharing information.

Regardless of the procedures and methodologies required by the respective government agency, any disclosures that are made to the government should be truthful and complete, as any false or misleading statements can serve as the basis for separate criminal charges that are unrelated to the underlying conduct. Further, all voluntary self-disclosures should present every applicable mitigating circumstance and preemptively address any aggravating factors. A company does not want to end up in a situation where numerous aggravating factors are discovered by DDTC and used against it in assessing the final penalty. In addition, any voluntary self-disclosure should include what remedial measures have been taken since discovering the violation. Finally, during the investigation and at the time of determining whether to disclose, the company should consider any violations in related subject areas (i.e., anti-money laundering, financial sanctions, and/or anti-bribery).

---

30.   22 C.F.R. § 127.12(c)(i).

Counsel representing a company who has made a disclosure should maintain an ongoing dialogue with government counsel and enforcement agents. Through that dialogue, information about the scope of the investigation, the potential targets, and the government's point of view can often be obtained, which can inform the course of the company's internal investigation. It may be helpful to meet with all the relevant agencies to ensure that their review is coordinated and that a simultaneous resolution with each is possible.

However a company decides to proceed on the question of disclosure, it should ensure that its policies and procedures will prospectively prevent a recurrence of the violations. It should also retain its detailed investigation and remediation records in the event that the government does discover the violation.

6.6 GLOBAL SETTLEMENTS

In settling cases involving export controls and economic sanctions, companies and their counsel must consider all relevant agencies, administrative and criminal, that may be involved given the overlap in regulatory authority. Settlement negotiations may include DDTC, BIS, OFAC, and in some cases, even Census, in addition to the DOJ. Each agency has its own agenda, interests, priorities, and timing, which will determine whether it will defer to another agency's fine or insist on an additional penalty. Moreover, companies and their counsel must be very aware of the collateral consequences of any conviction or settlement, even without imprisonment or a minimal fine. For example, a criminal conviction may result in federal contract debarment or denial of export privileges—consequences that counsel unfamiliar with export controls may be unaware of until they jeopardize a carefully structured settlement.

Throughout the investigative phase and during settlement discussions, companies should try to communicate with all relevant agencies, as these agencies may or may not be communicating among themselves. Defense counsel should coordinate the global settlement, as agencies will not negotiate among themselves and do not have authority to bind each other—or even to bind departments within the same agency. Thus, representations made by one enforcement authority regarding another's position on resolution should not be relied on and should be separately confirmed. However, including all the agencies in the settlement discussions may result in a single fine joined by all the agencies, or even suspension of one agency's fine in light of the penalty exacted by another. No agency can speak for another, but some agencies can be encouraged to utilize their leverage to obtain a final resolution with all the relevant government agencies.

On the other hand, not including a relevant agency in the settlement discussions can have disastrous consequences. A successfully negotiated settlement among several entities can be threatened by a late arrival who was not invited to the initial discussions and who insists on separate fines and consequences.

The maximum penalties set forth in the statutes and regulations are the starting point for a company's calculations as to the possible penalties. Keep in mind that the ultimate fines could be multiples of the maximum or twice the value of each transaction, depending on the number of violations and other factors. However, counsel should also compare the case at hand with previous settlements reached with the relevant agencies. The agencies publish their settlements on their websites and/or in the *Federal Register*.[31] BIS and OFAC have set forth the factors on which they will focus in determining appropriate penalties and how those penalties are calculated, thereby providing a framework for settlement negotiations.[32]

When considering how to structure a settlement, a company should consider all potential outcomes, including suspension of all or part of any penalty in recognition of the company's fiscal realities. The agency may suspend part of the penalty if that amount is directed to improving compliance measures. If the agency insists on denial of export privileges, a company should ensure that the denial be tailored to the particular risk posed by the specific item, country, or business unit involved. However, the company must recognize the reality that appearing on a denial list, even in a limited way, can still have a potential for business harm, as ultra-compliant customers and suppliers will not deal with a listed company at all. Compliance monitors may also be part of the settlement package and must be carefully considered before agreement is reached.

6.7 POSSIBLE DEFENSES AND MITIGATION

In some ways, the complexities of the laws and regulations governing export controls and economic sanctions can work in favor of a company seeking a defense. As a company learns the facts during an investigation, it may become clear that the potential violation was caused by an inadvertent mistake due to an honest misunderstanding of complex, inconsistent, and oft-amended laws. It may even become evident that there was no violation at all, due to a misinterpretation of the company's conduct by the government, a mistaken licensing determination or classification, or an overlooked amendment to the denied parties lists or the regulations. It is critical to review the regulations that were in place at the time of the violation as well as subsequently, as a case will have little appeal to a jury and is a questionable use of scarce enforcement resources if the restriction the company is accused of violating has been lifted. Jurisdiction, definitions, classifications, and the various agency lists all should be considered in mounting a defense.

---

31. *See* http://www.treasury.gov/resource-center/sanctions/CivPen/Pages/civpen-index2.aspx;
      http://efoia.bis.doc.gov/exportcontrolviolations/tocexportviolations.htm;
      http://www.pmddtc.state.gov/compliance/consent_agreements.html;
      http://www.justice.gov/nsd/docs/export-case-fact-sheet.pdf.
32. *See* Guidance on Charging and Penalty Determinations in Settlement of Administrative Enforcement Cases, 15 C.F.R. pt. 766, supp. no. 1 (2012); Economic Sanctions Enforcement Guidelines, 31 C.F.R. § 501, app. A (2012).

(a) Challenges to the Charges
(i) Government Missteps and Misinterpretations

In developing a defense to a possible export control violation, a company should review the government's investigation, including how the alleged violation was discovered and how it was determined to be a violation. Experience and familiarity with this complex regulatory area varies among the agencies, as some investigations are undertaken by agents that are on a rotational system and do not spend their careers enforcing this body of law. On the other hand, some career export control agents have little experience with criminal investigative procedures because so many cases are the result of voluntary disclosures that are settled quickly with minimal court proceedings.

The Government Accountability Office reported in 2006 on a case in which the FBI, without coordinating with BIS or ICE, pursued an investigation, arrested an exporter, and prevented shipment of items despite a BIS determination that a dual-use item in question did not require a license.[33] Ultimately, criminal charges were never filed because the items did not require a license. The FBI had relied on the National Security Agency's determination that the items were a high risk for national security, without recognizing that the NSA had no authority to determine whether the items required a license. Apparently, the FBI did not understand the exclusive jurisdiction of the Department of Commerce over the items.

Counsel should carefully examine search and arrest warrants, interview memoranda, criminal complaints, and indictments. Again, due to the complexity of the laws and, until recently, the rarity of these cases in federal court, drafting mistakes can be detected and used to protect against overreaching. In one case, known to the authors, an indictment was dismissed after the jury was sworn because the drafter somehow excluded the mundane element of intent, while carefully explaining the intricacies of the applicable law, its lapse, and continuing authority.

Finally, a careful review of the applicable regulations themselves is important, particularly when they have been recently amended, as typographical and clerical errors sometimes appear. In 1996, in the last major revision of the EAR, certain categories of items were mistakenly lost between a shift from the USML to the Commerce Control List and thus were left uncontrolled for a period of time. Exports of such items could not be prosecuted, as there was no law to support the prohibition. Possible lapses may occur again during this period of export control reform, as the regulations undergo significant amendments.

(ii) Licensing Determinations and Classifications

Cases arising under the EAR and ITAR frequently rise and fall on a determination by the relevant agency that a license was required but not obtained. Determining

---

33. U.S. Gov't Accountability Office, Export Controls: Challenges Exist in Enforcement of an Inherently Complex System 13–14 (Dec. 2006), *available at* http://www.gao.gov/new.items/d07265.pdf.

whether an item requires a license involves a mix of engineering and legal analysis, which must be confirmed in order to assess whether a violation occurred.

Independent assessment is discouraged by the line of authority that establishes that the classification of an item by the agency is not subject to challenge.[34] However, that authority only limits challenges to the underlying classification of a type of item but not the applicability of that classification to the particular item involved in the transaction.[35] For example, although the USML includes some chemical detection units, the determination as to whether the technical specifications of a particular unit's configuration may subject it only to commerce control is challengeable. Accordingly, counsel should always request the underlying rationale for any licensing determination.

As technology changes, so too does the basis for licensing determinations, as the export reform measures move many parts from the USML to the Commerce Control List. An original determination may no longer be valid because of these changes in the perceived sensitivity of the item or an all-too-frequent regulatory amendment, such that it is not a worthwhile use of enforcement resources to pursue the case whether or not the basis for the violation was solid at the time.

Over the course of years, there is a chance that the government can make inconsistent licensing determinations and classifications for a particular type of item, particularly if different parties submit the requests. Licensing officers within the same agency have issued inconsistent opinions as to whether a particular item requires a license. To the authors' knowledge, this has led parties in at least one instance to deliberately seek numerous determinations for the same item in an attempt to generate inconsistent classifications. Another disturbing example of the problems caused by inconsistent government licensing determinations occurred in the *Roth* case, discussed below. In that case, four separate expert witnesses for the government testified to four different interpretations of the AECA's application to the defendant's conduct.[36]

---

34. *See* International Traffic in Arms Regulations, 22 C.F.R. § 120.3 ("The Arms Export Control Act (22 U.S.C. § 2778(a) and 2794(7)) provides that the President shall designate the articles and services deemed to be defense articles and defense services for purposes of this subchapter . . . Such designations are made by the Department of State with the concurrence of the Department of Defense."); *see also* United States v. Martinez, 904 F.2d 601, 602 (11th Cir. 1990) (*citing* Baker v. Carr, 369 U.S. 186, 217 (1962) ("The question whether a particular item should have been placed on the Munitions List possesses nearly every trait that the Supreme Court has enumerated traditionally renders a question 'political.'"); United States v. Helmy, 712 F. Supp. 1423, 1434 (E.D. Cal. 1989) and cases cited therein (given the sensitive national security concerns involved ". . . congressional failure to codify a meaningful opportunity to challenge the listing determinations made under the AECA or the EAA either before or after prosecution is not a violation of the defendants' constitutional rights."); *but see* United States v. Pulungan, 569 F.3d 326, 328 (7th Cir. 2009). (The agency's "claim of authority to classify any item as a 'defense article,' without revealing the basis of the decision and without allowing any inquiry by the jury, would create serious constitutional problems.")

35. *See* United States v. Pulungan, 569 F.3d at 328 (explaining that the ITAR "deals with attributes rather than names"; therefore, the authority to designate articles and services only applies to those attributes listed on the USML and not specific names or models of those items).

36. Petition for Writ of Certiorari at 8, United States v. Roth, 2011 WL 1336432 (U.S. Apr. 5, 2011).

Because the licensing officer will be a crucial expert witness at trial, defense counsel should seek to speak with the officer and examine the notes from the licensing determination at the earliest opportunity to test its validity. Counsel should also locate expert witnesses, perhaps former employees of the relevant licensing agency, to examine the licensing determination as early as possible, even possibly halting a government investigation at its inception.

It should also be noted that early in the investigation stage, parties have the possibility of filing their own classification requests with BIS and commodity jurisdiction requests with DDTC. By filing their own requests early in the case—prior to the agency itself making a licensing determination—the parties ensure that they present all the evidence needed to support a favorable licensing determination. Moreover, the parties get the opportunity to interact more directly with the classification personnel and sometimes even supply additional information when the classification decision appears to be "heading south."

(iii) Denied Party or Entity List Transactions

When the alleged violation is a transaction with a restricted party included on one of the various government lists,[37] possible defenses may be based on the frequent amendments to the lists, the inaccurate identification of the parties, and the sometimes limited nature of the prohibitions, which are subject to interpretation.

Defense counsel should closely scrutinize the particular entity's listing, including all the surrounding details, the date of listing in comparison to paperwork underlying the transaction, how the party was described, and the rationale for the listing. A company should be able to describe the measures it took to avoid dealing with a prohibited party, including its screening procedures for business partners and customers. If the prohibited party misled the company as to its identity or restricted status, the company may have a valid defense for any criminal charges. Transacting business with a prohibited party is, however, a strict liability offense, and a company is subject to administrative penalties regardless of knowledge. Accordingly, cooperation with the government may be the best mitigative option.

(b) Culpability Challenges

If it is clear that a violation of the export control and economic sanctions regulations occurred, every effort must be made to determine whether the company or particular individuals acted "willfully" in violating those laws. If the government feels that the violations were deliberate or willful, the case could be prosecuted criminally and would involve much higher penalties and the possibility of imprisonment. By contrast, liability in administrative cases does not turn on intent as violations are subject to a strict liability standard.

---

37. *See* BIS website, Lists to Check, http://www.bis.doc.gov/complianceandenforcement/liststocheck.htm.

In criminal cases, where the government must prove intent and willfulness, its burden of proof is heavy, particularly in view of the complexity of the export control laws. Currently, there is a split in the circuits as to how heavy that burden is.

Though the Supreme Court has not ruled on the meaning of "willfulness" in the criminal provisions of export control statutes, the Court in *Bryan v. United States*,[38] a case involving a federal firearms licensing statute, held that the defendant's knowledge that his conduct was unlawful—and not that he knew of specific federal licensing requirements—was all that was required to prove willfulness.[39] Some federal appellate courts have applied the intent standard set forth in *Bryan* in export control cases,[40] and the DOJ has taken the position that the standard in *Bryan* should be applied in this context.[41] Thus, a criminal prosecution can be based solely on an employee's knowledge that he or she was doing something unlawful. Other appellate courts have, however, adopted a heightened standard that requires the government to prove that the defendant had the specific intent to violate a known legal duty.[42] Generally, the trend among the federal courts has been away from a heightened standard. Nevertheless, given the lack of guidance from the Supreme Court and the lack of clarity

---

38.   524 U.S. 184 (1998).

39.   *Id.* at 196.

40.   *See* United States v. Electro Glass Prods., No. 07-3191, 2008 WL 4597217, at *2 (3d Cir. Oct. 16, 2008) (*quoting* United States v. Tsai, 954 F.2d 155, 160 n. 3, *cert. denied*, 506 U.S. 830 (1992) (holding that the willfulness element of the AECA is established "if the defendant knew that the export was in violation of the law. The Government does not need to prove the basis of that knowledge, or that the defendant was aware of the licensing requirement."); United States v. Brodie, 403 F.3d 123, 147 (3d Cir. 2005) (holding that the government "need not prove the defendant had knowledge of the *specific regulation* governing the conduct engaged in—in other words, a defendant 'cannot avoid prosecution by claiming that that [he or she] had not brushed up on the law'"); United States v. Homa Int'l Trading Corp., 387 F.3d 144, 147 (2d Cir. 2004) (holding "[T]o establish a 'willful' violation of a statute, the Government must prove that the defendant acted with knowledge that his conduct was unlawful."); United States v. Tsai, 954 F.2d at 162 (holding that the jury could convict if it found that defendant knew only that the export was illegal).

41.   *See* Steven W. Pelak, "Willfully" and "Knowingly" in Export Control Prosecutions, The Export Practitioner (Feb. 2006); *see also* Ronald J. Sievert, *The Special Importance and Challenge of Export Control Cases*, 44 USA Bulletin No. 5, at 45 (Oct. 1996), *available at* http://www.usdoj.gov/usao/eousa/foia_reading_room/usab4405.pdf (analyzing intent in export control prosecutions pre-*Bryan*).

42.   *See* United States v. Piquet No. 09-12760, 2010 WL 1267162, at *49 (11th Cir. 2010) (holding that "the government must prove specific intent for a substantive offense under §2778" and that the "requirement of willfulness connotes a voluntary, intentional violation of a known legal duty," and thus does not cover "innocent or negligent errors."); United States v. Elashyi, No. 06-10176, 2008 WL 5392122, at *16–17 (5th Cir. Dec. 29, 2008) (holding that the *Bryan* standard applies in considering willfully dealing in property of an SDT, while requiring the government to prove that the defendants knew licenses were required with respect to the EAR violations); United States v. Al-Arian, 308 F. Supp. 2d 1322, 1340 (M.D. Fla. 2004) (holding that "[w]hile knowledge of IEEPA, the Executive Order, or the regulations thereunder is not necessary to support a conviction, some 'bad purpose' must be demonstrated by the government"); United States. v. Huynh, 246 F.3d 734, 743 (5th Cir. 2001) (holding that the government must prove the defendant had specific intent to circumvent its requirements); United States v. Covarrubias, 94 F.3d 172, 175 (5th Cir. 1996) (holding that the government must prove "that the defendant acted with specific intent to violate a known legal duty"); United States v. Cardoen, 898 F. Supp. 1563 (S.D. Fla. 1995), *aff'd sub. nom.*; United States v. Johnson, 139 F.3d 1359 (11th Cir. 1998), *cert. denied*, 527 U.S. 1021 (1999) (holding that a substantive understanding of the law is required to establish willfulness); United States v. Macko, 994 F.2d 1526, 1532 (11th Cir. 1993) (holding that willfulness in the export control context requires a finding of specific intent to violate the trade provisions).

in some circuits, an argument could still be made that the export control laws and regulations are "highly technical statutes," and a heightened intent standard should therefore apply.

Regardless of the standard applied, the following factors remain relevant to the determination of intent: a company's licensing history for a particular item, the quality of the training a company provides to its employees, an employee's experience in export controls, the sophistication of the employee, and the complexity of the licensing requirements. To demonstrate how difficult it is for the average person to understand the regulations, much less "intend" to violate them, one need only look at the Sudanese sanctions regime. In order to avoid violating the Sudanese sanctions, an exporter must determine whether the ultimate destination is within the "non-specified areas of Sudan," the "marginalized areas," and the "specified areas," or a location in "Southern Sudan," all of which have different levels of restrictions. Or, worse, it is doubtul that a defendant could possibly know intuitively that the night-vision goggles he bought at Sports Authority could not be shipped to his brother in China.

Beyond the very real possibility of a misinterpretation of these complex laws, a defendant's reliance on flawed legal advice would indicate a lack of willfulness and diminish the appeal of a case in a prosecutor's eyes, as well as in the eyes of the judge and jury. In addition, although they have been decided in a circuit that has applied a heightened intent standard, several cases involving TWEA and the Cuban sanctions program demonstrate the willingness of courts to take into account the context of the defendants' activities in assessing intent.[43] The extremely restrictive yet non-security-related Cuban sanctions have caused considerable problems for prosecutors, as courts are reluctant to penalize exports of dental equipment, wooden pallets, and pepper plants.

(c) Mitigating Circumstances

In administrative cases where a company knows that it has committed a violation of the export control or economic sanctions laws and is unable to defend its conduct, there are several mitigating factors that the relevant regulations recognize and defendants should be sure to raise, including:[44]

- the submission of a voluntary self-disclosure;
- having an effective export compliance program in place or instituting a program to reduce the likelihood of future violations;

---

43. *See* Macko, 994 F.2d at 1532 (reasoning that the defendants' engagement in exporting, the fact that the regulations were widely and publicly available, and the defendants' attempts to hide their contacts with Cuba were illustrative in finding willfulness to violate the statutes); United States v. Frade, 709 F.2d 1387, 1391–92 (11th Cir. 1983) (reversing convictions of priests for assisting Cuban refugees in the Mariel boat lift because general awareness of unlawfulness was insufficient under TWEA).

44. *See* Export Administration Regulations, 15 C.F.R. pt. 766, supp. no. 1 (2012); International Traffic in Arms Regulations, 22 C.F.R. § 127.12 (2012); Economic Sanctions Enforcement Guidelines, 31 C.F.R. 501, app. A (2012).

- the violation was an isolated occurrence or good-faith misinterpretation;
- an authorization would likely have been granted if requested;
- no prior violations, settlements, warnings, etc.;
- cooperation with the government investigation; and
- the violation did not cause the type of harm at which the regulations were aimed.

Although all these factors have a mitigating effect on the penalties imposed by the various agencies, some are given greater weight than others. For example, BIS gives "great weight" to the submission of a voluntary self-disclosure. It will also extend great weight mitigation credit if the party involved had an effective export compliance program in place before the violation was discovered.[45] Therefore, beyond preventing violations, an effective export compliance program will allow a company to discover violations before the government does and to disclose them immediately, thereby gaining the benefit of great weight mitigation when, or if, it comes time to impose penalties.

6.8 CASE STUDIES

The following are several recent export control prosecutions that highlight particular issues discussed above.

(a) *United States v. BAE Systems PLC*

The investigation and prosecution of British defense contractor BAE Systems PLC (BAE) provides an illustration of how the U.S. government enforces the export control laws, the risks that companies face when charged with violations of those laws, and how a global settlement should and should not be handled. One part of the case was handled jointly by the DOJ and the UK's Serious Fraud Office (SFO). Another part, which was resolved a year after the first settlement, involved the U.S. Department of State, which was not a party to the original settlement. Ultimately, the company paid over $479 million in criminal and administrative fines.

The 2010 U.S. and UK criminal settlements arose from a six-year investigation by U.S. and British authorities of bribery allegations dating back more than two decades. The U.S. criminal information, which charged one count of conspiracy to make false statements to the Department of Defense and to the Department of State, had two prongs. The first involved payments made to "marketing advisors" through offshore shell companies in order to evade the Foreign Corrupt Practices Act's (FCPA) due diligence and compliance measures that BAE had represented were in place in a letter to the Secretary of Defense concerning its newly acquired defense businesses in the United States.[46] The second prong involved false export applications, filed by

---

45. *See* Export Administration Regulations, 15 C.F.R. pt. 766, supp. no. 1 (2012).
46. Information at 7–8, United States v. BAE Systems PLC, No. 10-cr-00035 (D.D.C. Feb. 4, 2010), *available at* http://www.justice.gov/criminal/pr/documents/03-01-10BAE-information.pdf.

the Swedish government in connection with their leases of fighter jets to the Czech Republic and Hungary. BAE caused the filing of the false export applications by not disclosing to the Swedish government the $29 million in payments it made to secure the leases.[47] As part of the DDTC license application process, an applicant must disclose whether fees or commissions aggregating $100,000 were paid by the applicant or its vendors to secure the transfer of defense articles. On March 1, 2010, BAE pleaded guilty and agreed with the DOJ and SFO to pay $400 million and £30 million, respectively.

Immediately after the plea agreement was announced, DDTC issued on its website a temporary administrative hold on BAE export licenses so it could consider whether to take additional action against the company. Although the hold was withdrawn, for the next year, DDTC delayed on its issuance of licenses to BAE until May 16, 2011, when BAE entered into a consent agreement with DDTC, agreeing to pay $79 million over the next four years.

In the case brought by DDTC against BAE, DDTC charged BAE with 2,591 violations of the AECA and ITAR, all of which were related to the brokering regulations under the ITAR.[48] According to the charging letter, BAE marketed and sold a variety of aircraft and aircraft parts to several countries between 1997 and 2011, which required BAE to register as a broker and obtain DDTC approval prior to its activities.[49] The charging letter alleged that BAE not only failed to obtain approval for its brokering activities, but also failed to register as a broker with DDTC altogether.[50] In addition, DDTC alleged that BAE caused others to engage in brokering activities by providing financing through payments to brokers, totaling no less than one hundred payments to brokers between 1998 and 2007.[51]

The case is notable because it demonstrates international enforcement cooperation, a reality that companies must take into account when undertaking an investigation, considering whether to disclose, and structuring a settlement. The case also demonstrates a recent trend in criminal enforcement actions by aggressive prosecutors who recognize that compliance deficiencies are seldom confined to one regulatory regime. Charging under one set of regulations rather than another may have certain prosecutorial advantages, such as fewer proof problems and higher penalties. For example, the ITAR intersect with the FCPA due to the required fees and commissions disclosure under part 130 of the ITAR, the use of brokers and third parties in arms deals, and the registration requirements of non-U.S. brokers, and may be easier to prove. As this case demonstrates, counsel should cast a wide net across the compliance spectrum when conducting an internal investigation.

---

47. *Id.* at 6–7.
48. BAE Systems PLC, Proposed Charging Letter 1 (U.S. Dep't of State 2011), at 1–2, http://www.pmd-dtc.state.gov/compliance/consent_agreements/pdf/BAES_PCL.pdf.
49. *Id.* at 5–10.
50. *Id.* at 5.
51. *Id.* at 8.

The case also illustrates how pleas can be structured to avoid the effect of collateral consequences of which a company is aware. In this case, although the conduct clearly involved bribery, the criminal convictions were based on other charges, perhaps so as to avoid triggering the consequential EU prohibition on contracting with companies convicted on corruption charges.

The case also illustrates the importance of understanding which agencies should be involved in the settlement, who has authority to speak for which agency, and all the collateral consequences that might arise from a conviction. Whether or not the DDTC licensing hold and subsequent settlement was a surprise to the company and its counsel, it resulted in prolonging the investigation and resolution of the case and also generated an additional fine.

Finally, it should be noted that despite the extensive bribery scheme alleged and the more than 2,500 export control violations, BAE was ultimately not subject to statutory debarment, and only certain of its subsidiaries were made subject to the denial of export licensing privileges. While DDTC stated in the consent agreement that the lack of a broad policy of denial resulted from a determination that BAE took "appropriate steps to address the causes of the violations and to mitigate any law enforcement concerns,"[52] it may also be a sign of DDTC's apprehension in implementing such a sweeping denial against a defense contractor as large as BAE.

Ultimately, the BAE case is instructive as to the risk of ignoring the reality of today's comprehensive enforcement environment.

(b) *United States v. ITT Corporation* and *United States v. TW Metals*

The cases against ITT and TW Metals are instructive with respect to dealing with the government following discovery of violations.

The government's criminal investigation of ITT Corporation began when Department of Defense agents discovered that a classified U.S. military document relating to night-vision technology had been illegally sent by ITT employees to foreign nationals in the UK. According to the government, ITT initially chose not to cooperate, entering into joint defense agreements with employees, making multiple assertions of questionable privilege, and essentially trying over the next three years to run out the clock on the statute of limitations.[53] When the government informed the board of directors that it intended to seek an indictment, the newly appointed CEO changed course, hired new outside counsel, and instructed the company to fully cooperate, potentially saving the company from what a DOJ press release described as "permanent ruin."

---

52.   BAE Systems PLC, Consent Agreement 20 (U.S. Dep't of State, May 16, 2011), http://www.pmddtc. state.gov/compliance/consent_agreements/pdf/BAES_CA.pdf.

53.   *Id.*

In March 2007, the company pleaded guilty to two felony charges and the deferred prosecution of a third count, agreed to pay $100 million in penalties and forfeitures, and subjected itself to independent monitoring and an extensive remedial action program. It is notable that while one count of the criminal information against ITT related to the unlawful exports, the second count involved the willful omission of material facts to the Department of State.[54] Specifically, letters submitted in April and May 2000 by outside counsel on ITT's behalf that were certified to be accurate by an ITT manager characterized certain consignment license violations as "recently discovered," despite the fact that a number of employees and managers were actually aware of some of the violations since the mid-1990s.[55]

While the case illustrates the risks a company takes if it decides not to cooperate with a criminal investigation, it also demonstrates what it can do to repair the damage done.

On April 12, 2011, the court granted the DOJ's motion to dismiss the remaining deferred criminal charge against ITT. The assistant U.S. attorney stated that "the extensive efforts undertaken by ITT's management team to work with the government and the Independent Monitor to reform ITT's compliance program is a model of how a company can take a very bad situation and turn it into something positive for the company and the security of the United States."[56] According to the DOJ, "when a company admits its wrongdoing, reforms its internal processes, and brings its activities into compliance with the law, the government will recognize these efforts."[57]

The concept of the government recognizing a company's efforts to admit its wrongdoing and reform its conduct to comply with the law is further illustrated by the case against TW Metals. On March 11, 2011, TW Metals entered into a settlement agreement with BIS for violations based on forty-eight exports of titanium alloy through Canada to China without the required export license and one export of aluminum bar through Canada to Israel without the required export license.[58] According to BIS, "TW Metals voluntarily disclosed the violations and cooperated fully with the investigation,"[59] resulting in a reduced administrative fine of $575,000. According to the settlement agreement, TW Metals was subject to a maximum administrative penalty of up to the greater of $250,000 per violation or twice the value of the transaction

---

54.   Information at 1–2, United States v. ITT Corp., No. 07-CR-00022 (W.D. Va. Mar. 28, 2007).
55.   *Id.* at 4–7.
56.   Press Release, Office of the U.S. Attorney, Court Grants Government's Motion to Dismiss Deferred Count Against ITT Corp. (Apr. 12, 2011) (on file with author), *available at* http://www.bloomberg.com/apps/news?pid=conewsstory&tkr=ITT:US&sid=aNxfpvUn8bCM.
57.   *Id.*
58.   TW Metals, Settlement Agreement 2 (U.S. Dep't of Commerce, Mar. 11, 2011), http://efoia.bis.doc.gov/exportcontrolviolations/e2201.pdf.
59.   Press Release, Bureau of Industry and Security, Pennsylvania Company Fined for Export Violations Involving China and Israel (Mar. 15, 2011) (on file with author), *available at* http://www.bis.doc.gov/news/2011/bis_press03152011.htm.

that is the basis of the violation.[60] This could have resulted in a maximum fine for TW Metals of $12.25 million. BIS "applaud[ed] TW Metals for coming forward to report these violations" and reinforced that "a voluntary self-disclosure is a significant mitigating factor when [BIS] consider[s] administrative settlements."[61]

The ITT and TW Metals cases, when read together, highlight the importance of full and immediate disclosure of violations of the U.S. export control laws as well as subsequent cooperation with any government investigation.

(c) *United States v. Latifi*[62] and *United States v. Roth*[63]

In both the case against Alex Latifi and his company, Axion Corp., and the case against Professor John Reece Roth, the defense challenged the government's assertion of willfulness. The trial of Latifi and Axion ultimately resulted in an acquittal and is an example of how to mount an effective defense at trial. Professor Roth's challenge on the issue of intent was ultimately unsuccessful at trial and on appeal to the Sixth Circuit. The Supreme Court refused to review the case.

Alex Latifi, the owner of Axion Corp., was charged with knowingly and willfully exporting technical drawings of a component of the UH 60 Black Hawk helicopter to China without a license from DDTC, making material false and fraudulent representations regarding the part to the U.S. Army, and submitting test reports containing false statements and misrepresentations.[64] In October 2007, Latifi waived a jury trial, and after several days of witness testimony, the judge hearing the case granted the defense's motion for acquittal.

According to Latifi's defense counsel, the dismissal was granted because the technical drawings given to Latifi by the government that were allegedly illegally transferred to China did not contain AECA warnings to put contractors on notice that they contained sensitive information. The drawings that had been sent to the bidders, including Axion, were labeled "unclassified" and "uncontrolled." The government's experts acknowledged that the drawings were improperly marked and that nothing indicated that distribution of the documents was restricted in any way. Language on the drawings did not indicate that the Department of Defense owned the drawings, but rather that they came from the manufacturer. Finally, evidence was introduced that the U.S. government had sold the Black Hawk helicopters and their components

---

60. TW Metals, Inc., Proposed Charging Letter 2 (U.S. Dep't of Commerce 2011), http://efoia.bis.doc.gov/exportcontrolviolations/e2201.pdf.

61. Press Release, Bureau of Industry and Security, Pennsylvania Company Fined for Export Violations Involving China and Israel (Mar. 15, 2011) (on file with author), *available at* http://www.bis.doc.gov/news/2011/bis_press03152011.htm.

62. No. 07-cr-00098-IPJ-PWG (N.D. Ala. Oct. 31, 2007).

63. 628 F.3d 827 (6th Cir. 2011), *cert. denied*, 132 S. Ct. 94 (2011).

64. Gov't Trial Memorandum 7–10, United States v. Latifi, No. 07-cr-00098-IPJ-PWG (N.D. Ala. Oct. 31, 2007).

to China, and thus the drawings were unnecessary for reverse engineering, and the drawings themselves were widely available on the Internet.

The government's documents failed to put Latifi on notice and may have misled him into thinking that they were unrestricted, so the government could not carry its burden of proving intent. This case highlights the importance of conducting a thorough investigation of the facts and of challenging the government's contention that an item is controlled under the export laws.

The case against Professor Roth had the opposite result, as Roth was convicted for exporting data to China related to a U.S. Air Force defense research project involving plasma technology for use on military drone aircraft and allowing two foreign national students from China and Iran to access technical data and equipment related to the project. Roth began serving a four-year prison sentence on January 18, 2012.

Roth challenged his conviction, appealing to the Sixth Circuit Court of Appeals and arguing that the district court incorrectly instructed the jury as to willfulness.[65] According to Roth's defense counsel, the prosecution should have had to prove that the defendant knew that items being exported were on the USML, rather than simply knowing that the underlying action was unlawful in order prove willfulness under the relevant export control statutes. The Sixth Circuit disagreed, holding that the AECA "does not require a defendant to know that the items being exported are on the Munitions List. Rather, it only requires knowledge that the underlying action is unlawful."[66] According to the court, "willfulness can be 'a word of many meanings' whose construction is often dependent on the context in which it appears."[67] Therefore, the court reasoned that because "Congress did not instruct courts to apply the willfulness requirement to any specific provision, let alone the Munitions List, even though it could have," the AECA only requires that someone knew that they were violating some provision of the Act, not which specific provision they were violating.[68] Further, the court contrasted export control laws to confusing tax laws, which require specific intent to violate the law due to their complexity. Unlike tax laws, which the court reasoned can be unintentionally violated by uninformed citizens, "exporting defense articles can only be achieved by educated parties with atypical access to proprietary military weapons, systems, and data."[69]

The *Roth* decision applies only to the Sixth Circuit, and the Supreme Court has yet to decide on the meaning of willfulness in the export control context, so an argument still can be made that the export control laws and regulations are "highly technical statutes" and a heightened intent standard should therefore apply. The complexity of

---

65. *Id.* at 831.
66. *Id.* at 835.
67. *Id.* at 833.
68. *Id.* at 835.
69. *Id.*

the export control regulatory scheme and the potential for criminalizing what would otherwise be considered innocent conduct support such an argument. Furthermore, it can be argued that "willfully" should have a different meaning depending on which export control statute is at issue.

Additional arguments that can be used by defense lawyers when arguing for a heightened standard of intent can be found in Roth's recent writ of certiorari to the Supreme Court, which Roth's lawyers filed on April 5, 2011,[70] and which was denied on October 3, 2011. Roth's lawyers cited the varying interpretations of the law by government expert witnesses as it applied to Roth's situation and the continued and unresolved split between the circuits regarding the issues of willfulness in export control cases. Further, the petition argued that if the regulations are to remain flexible in order to protect national security, as Roth's counsel believes they should, then defendants should not be the ones to "bear the brunt of the regulations' opacity."[71] This, the petition argued, contradicts the Rule of Lenity. Therefore, if the regulations are to remain flexible, the government should be required to satisfy a heightened standard of proof of intent. Finally, the petition argued that, not only are the individual regulations themselves complex, but individuals must be able to navigate a "patchwork of often-confusing, overlapping statutes."[72] The petition was denied, so the issue remains undecided at the Supreme Court level.

(d) *United States v. PPG*

In an investigation that exemplifies BIS's announced intention of "imposing penalties not only on the companies involved, but also on individuals," BIS did not conclude a recent investigation of PPG Industries (PPG) and its wholly owned Chinese subsidiary by imposing only corporate fines, but instead also went after the parent company's sales manager and the subsidiary's managing director.

According to court documents, the subsidiary, PPG Paints Trading (Shanghai) Co., Ltd. (PPG Paints), contracted with a company to supply high-performance coatings for application at a nuclear power plant in Pakistan that was under the control of the Pakistan Atomic Energy Commission (PAEC). Because PAEC is on the Entity List, PPG submitted a license application to BIS, which was denied. In order to circumvent the EAR licensing requirements, PPG Paints arranged to sell the coatings to a third-party distributor in China, which in turn would deliver the coatings to Pakistan. In its purchase order, PPG Paints falsely stated that the coatings were to be used at a nuclear power plant in China, which would not require a license from BIS.[73]

---

70. Petition for Writ of Certiorari, United States v. Roth, 2011 WL 1336432 (U.S. Apr. 5, 2011), *cert. denied*, 132 S. Ct. 94 (2011).

71. *Id.* at 28.

72. *Id.* at 29.

73. *Id.* at 2–4.

PPG Paints pled guilty to conspiring to violate the IEEPA and the EAR, agreed to pay a criminal fine of $2 million, serve five years of corporate probation, and forfeit $32,319 in gross proceeds it received for its illegal exports.[74] The parent company, PPG, signed an agreement conditioning its non-prosecution on the payment of the above fine by PPG Paints, continuing cooperation with the DOJ, and maintenance of an export compliance program with mandatory reporting of all violations. In separate settlement agreements with BIS, PPG and PPG Paints agreed to pay administrative penalties of $750,000 and $1 million, respectively, and also agreed to complete two external export compliance audits.[75] While this would normally signify the end of the investigation and enforcement by BIS, in accordance with BIS's individual prosecution policy, BIS recently entered into a settlement agreement with Curtis Hickcox, a former sales manager of PPG.[76] BIS imposed a $500,000 administrative fine on Hickcox and a five-year denial of export privileges for his involvement in causing the unlicensed export of EAR99 coatings by informing PPG that the coatings were for a "mock-up" and would not be used by PAEC, even though Hickcox had knowledge that there was no "mock-up" and that the shipment was to be used at the PAEC facility. Xun Wang, a former managing director of PPG Paints, plead guilty to conspiring to violate the IEEPA and faces a maximum jail sentence of five years and up to a $250,000 fine.[77] Wang separately settled with BIS, agreeing to pay an administrative penalty of $200,000, with $50,000 suspended, and being placed on the Denied Persons List for five years with five years suspended.[78]

(e) *United States v. Pulungan*[79]

Doli Syarief Pulungan was convicted for willfully attempting to export defense articles (riflescopes) without a license in violation of the AECA. In 2009, the Seventh Circuit overturned the conviction based on a faulty licensing determination by DDTC, confirming that the classification of an item by an agency is subject to challenge. On appeal, Pulungan argued that the prosecution had failed to prove the riflescopes were "manufactured to military specification" as required by the applicable DDTC regu-

---

74.   *See* PPG Industries, Inc., Cooperation and Non-Prosecution Agreement 1 (Office of U.S. Attorney, Dec. 21, 2010), http://lib.law.virginia.edu/Garrett/prosecution_agreements/pdf/ppg.pdf.

75.   *See* PPG Paints Trading (Shanghai) Co., Ltd, Settlement Agreement (U.S. Dep't of Commerce, Dec. 20, 2010), http://efoia.bis.doc.gov/exportcontrolviolations/e2193.pdf.

76.   *See* Order Relating to Curtis L. Hickcox (U.S. Dep't of Commerce, Jun. 20, 2011), http://efoia.bis. doc.gov/exportcontrolviolations/e2210.pdf; Curtis L. Hickcox, Settlement Agreement (U.S. Dep't of Commerce Jun. 17, 2011), http://efoia.bis.doc.gov/exportcontrolviolations/e2210.pdf.

77.   Press Release, U.S. Attorney's Office, Former Managing Director of PPG Paints Trading (Shanghai) Co., Ltd., Pleads Guilty to Conspiring to Illegally Export High-Performance Coatings to Nuclear Reactor in Pakistan (Nov. 15, 2011) (on file with author), *available at* http://www.justice.gov/usao/dc/news/2011/nov/11-503.html.

78.   *See* Order Relating to Xun Wang (U.S. Dep't of Commerce, Nov. 16, 2011), http://efoia.bis.doc.gov/exportcontrolviolations/e2241.pdf; Xun Wang, Settlement Agreement (U.S. Dep't of Commerce, Nov. 15, 2011), http://efoia.bis.doc.gov/exportcontrolviolations/e2241.pdf.

79.   569 F.3d 326 (7th Cir. 2009).

lation and also that he lacked the required mental state. The prosecution relied on a DDTC expert, who testified that the agency had concluded that the riflescopes were "manufactured to military specifications," though he would not say what those specifications were or why DDTC believed the riflescopes were "manufactured" to them. DDTC's decision itself was not produced.

The Seventh Circuit reversed Pulungan's conviction, casting doubt on the government's position concerning the validity of DDTC's classification of the riflescopes *in dicta*. The court did not need to decide the case on this issue because it ruled for Pulungan on the grounds that he lacked the requisite intent. Nevertheless, the court stated that the agency's "claim of authority to classify any item as a 'defense article,' without revealing the basis of the decision and without allowing any inquiry by the jury, would create serious constitutional problems."[80] The court also expressed concern that an unnamed official using unspecified criteria "that is put in a desk drawer, taken out only for use at a criminal trial, and immune from any evaluation by the judiciary, is the sort of tactic usually associated with totalitarian regimes" and stated that the government "must operate through public laws and regulations."[81]

This case highlights the importance of both regulatory and legal arguments in defending an export control case, and it offers avenues for the defense to attack an agency's licensing determination or classification decision where it lacks proper foundation.

(f)   *United States v. United Technologies Corporation*

The case against United Technologies Corporation (UTC) is full of lessons learned, including (1) the importance of a company properly classifying its products, (2) the level of due diligence required when determining the end use and end user, (3) developing an export compliance program adequate to address the complexities of a decentralized business, and (4) ensuring truthfulness and accuracy when drafting voluntary self-disclosures.

After UTC submitted several voluntary self-disclosures over a period of six years related to the export of helicopter engine control software to China, the U.S. Department of State charged UTC with 576 violations of the ITAR, resulting in a global settlement between UTC, the U.S. Department of State, and the U.S. Department of Justice totaling $75 million. The proposed charging letter divided the charges into three categories: "(1) unauthorized exports and reexports, resulting from the failure to properly establish jurisdiction over defense articles and technical data; (2) unauthorized exports, resulting from the failure to exercise internal controls over technical data; and (3) failure to manage Department-authorized agreements."[82]

---

80.   *Id.* at 328.
81.   *Id.*
82.   United Technologies Corporation, Proposed Charging Letter 4 (U.S. Dep't of State 2012), http://www.pmddtc.state.gov/compliance/consent_agreements/pdf/UTC_PCL.pdf.

UTC's failure to properly establish jurisdiction over defense articles and technical data involved two UTC subsidiaries, Pratt & Whitney Canada (P&W Canada; a Canadian subsidiary of UTC) and Hamilton Sundstrand Corporation (HSC; a U.S. subsidiary of UTC). According to the proposed charging letter, P&W Canada entered into a contract with the China Aviation Industrial Corporation II (China AVIC II) of the People's Republic of China (PRC) to develop and sell helicopter engines and related software for use in the civilian variant of the Chinese Z-10 helicopter. Internal P&W Canada documents showed that P&W Canada was aware of the potential that China AVIC II may use the engines in its military variant of the Z-10 helicopter and, during a visit to China, observed the engines being utilized on the military variant. The related software was provided by HSC, who electronically exported the software to P&W Canada without proper authorization. P&W Canada later reexported the controlled software to China AVIC II. Two years after the export of the controlled software, UTC disclosed the violation to DDTC, but failed to mention the company's early awareness of the software's use on military variants of the Z-10 helicopter and mischaracterized several corrective measures.

UTC outsourced several engineering tasks to foreign person contractors whom it co-located at Pratt & Whitney U.S. (P&W U.S.) facilities. The foreign person contractors had access to ITAR-controlled technical data documents without proper authorization as a result of UTC's failure to exercise internal controls over technical data (e.g., an effective technology control plan and work space restrictions). P&W U.S. voluntarily self-disclosed the violations and continued its investigation, which resulted in additional disclosures. One of the additional disclosures involved an HSC contract engineer who traveled to the PRC on business with an HSC-issued laptop containing ITAR-controlled technical data. The contract engineer left the laptop at a Shanghai airport upon his return and failed to retrieve it.

Finally, P&W U.S., as well as HSC, failed to properly manage department-authorized agreements by violating several provisos, exceeding the scope of the agreements, and allowing unauthorized access by foreign persons not authorized under the agreements.

Under the consent agreement between the U.S. Department of State and UTC, UTC agreed to pay a penalty in the amount of $55 million, $20 million of which was suspended if it was used for remedial compliance measures.[83] Pursuant to a deferred prosecution agreement, UTC agreed to pay an additional $20.7 million in criminal penalties and forfeitures.[84]

More important than UTC's failure to properly classify its products or comply with its agreements was UTC's failure to truthfully and accurately report its viola-

---

83. United Technologies Corporation, Consent Agreement 17 (U.S. Dep't of State 2012), http://www.pmddtc.state.gov/compliance/consent_agreements/pdf/UTC_CA.pdf.
84. United Technologies Corporation, DOJ Press Release, *available at* http://www.justice.gov/opa/pr/2012/June/12-nsd-824.html.

tions in its voluntary self-disclosures. While its voluntary self-disclosures did provide some mitigating effect, the fact that they were inaccurate, missing critical information, and untimely in some cases caused UTC to face criminal penalties on top of its administrative penalties and also prevented UTC from gaining full mitigation from its disclosures. This case should be a lesson to companies that a vigorous investigation of any potential violations should be conducted quickly and reported immediately in order to avoid additional penalties. Even if the investigation is not complete, companies should consider reporting the potentially violative conduct immediately and follow up with supplemental information as the investigation progresses.

6.9 CONCLUSION

A company attempting to navigate the labyrinth of economic sanctions and export controls must also be prepared with a plan to deal with the consequences of virtually inevitable violations. Quick and thorough investigations and informed analysis of the regulations and relevant statutes are key. Particularly in light of the export initiatives driven by the Obama administration, companies need to be aware of the increased coordination by the agencies responsible for enforcing economic sanctions and export controls to ensure that their resolution of violations is comprehensive and addresses the priorities and interests of each agency. Further, if a company decides to go down the road of a voluntary disclosure or settlement, attention should be paid to the intricacies of each regulatory regime to ensure the most advantageous result. Finally, in mounting a challenge to the charges, analyzing the highly complex statutory and regulatory framework, examining the assumptions made by the government, investigating the factual underpinnings of intent, and creating a record of compliance are all important elements of an effective defense strategy.

Reexport Controls–Intersection of EU and U.S. Measures

John Grayston

7.1 INTRODUCTION

The European Union (EU) has consistently criticized the United States of America for its determination in not only adopting but also enforcing extraterritorially the application of trade and economic sanctions. The implication would seem to be that the EU neither adopts nor seeks to enforce its own rules on an extraterritorial basis. As this chapter seeks to underline, whereas the EU (and its member states) may fall short in terms of third-country enforcement, it has not failed to introduce laws and regulations that provide the legal base for such enforcement.

7.2 OVERVIEW

In the preceding sections of this work, we have seen how the United States of America seeks to assert control over exports of U.S.-origin controlled items from third countries. In this way, the U.S. seeks to ensure that U.S. policies and procedures are applied to reexports of controlled items of U.S. origin as well as of goods manufactured in a third country incorporating more than minimum percentages of U.S.-controlled parts or technology. The question up for discussion in this chapter is to what extent such reexport controls are applied by the EU.

We must start by defining what we mean when we say "by the EU." We understand this phrase to refer to the work of the EU as the federal body governing the member states. As in many areas of EU policy, the regulation of export control in the EU is complicated because the EU and member states in practice still share powers in relation of even those areas of export control law that fall within the overall competence of the EU. So when we try to answer the question "Does the EU apply reexport controls?" we will focus on the federal aspects of this question rather than providing a review for each of the national laws of the twenty-seven member states.

By way of general introduction, it is helpful to note the following:

What Is Regulated by the EU? The EU is responsible for adopting measures dealing with the control of exports of dual-use items.

The EU is also responsible for adopting regulations dealing with trade sanctions and embargoes.

Although in general terms the EU is not competent to deal with issues concerning the control of military goods, this has not stopped the EU from being used to agree to measures that provide a common list for military goods and for rules dealing with controls on intra-EU movements of military goods.

Where to Find the Regulations: References to specific legislation are given in the footnotes to this chapter.

For general reference, the following websites of the EU Commission and Council provide access to all relevant documents:

Export Control – Dual Use and Military:

http://ec.europa.eu/trade/creating-opportunities/trade-topics/dual-use/

http://www.consilium.europa.eu/eeas/foreign-policy/non-proliferation,-disarma ment-and-export-control-/security-related-export-controls-ii?lang=en

EU Sanctions:

http://eeas.europa.eu/cfsp/sanctions/index_en.htm

Who Is the Regulator? In almost all cases, the regulator is the national authority responsible for export control or sanctions in the member state(s) concerned.

7.3 EU OBJECTIONS TO REEXPORT CONTROLS

Given that the EU has actively objected to U.S. reexport controls as amounting to an unnecessary regulatory burden and direct barrier to trade, one might assume, incorrectly as it turns out, that the EU clearly applies no similar provisions itself.

In the European Commission's 2006 annual trade barriers report, a whole section was devoted to the trade distortions of U.S. reexport controls. The Commission noted as follows:

A comprehensive system of export controls for dual-use items under the Export Administration Act of 1979 and the Export Administration Regulations was established to prevent trade to unauthorised destinations. This system, among other things, requires companies incorporated and operating in the EU to comply with U.S. reexport controls, including compliance with U.S. prohibitions on reexports for reasons of national security and foreign policy. The extraterritorial nature of these controls has repeatedly been criticized by the EU, given the fact that it has active members of all international export control regimes: the Nuclear Suppliers Group, the Australia Group, the Missile Technology Control Regime and the Wassenaar Arrangement.[1]

The EU objection is based, in addition to the general infringement of the principle of extraterritorial application of U.S. laws, on the grounds that the U.S. controls are

---

1. European Commission, United States Barriers to Trade and Investment Report for 2006 12, *available at* http://trade.ec.europa.eu/doclib/html/133290.htm.

not necessary when the EU and its member states are members of the same international agreements that the U.S. reexport controls seek to implement.

There are weaknesses in this argument—not least of which is that it is not entirely correct to say that all member states are members of all international export control regimes. More important, it is accepted by the EU Commission itself in relation to dual-use controls that in practice the EU system, which leaves substantial discretion to individual member states, results in EU rules being applied strictly in some member states whereas in others a much more liberal approach to compliance is adopted.[2]

7.4 THE EUROPEAN UNION (EU)

The EU currently has twenty-seven individual member states. The EU works through the institutions set up under the treaty creating the EU—currently called the Treaty on the Functioning of the European Union (TFEU). For these purposes, the two most important institutions are the EU Council and the EU Commission.

Decisions of the EU are adopted in a number of different legal forms. Legislative measures may derive force of law as a matter of EU (federal) law, which is the case for regulations, or they may simply give instructions (directives) to the member states to adopt specific measures in their own national laws. In addition, the EU institutions may also issue nonbinding statements of good practice or mere recommendation.

In simple terms, the subject matter of EU action is limited to those areas in which powers are specifically allocated to it by the TFEU. The control of exports is an area in which the legal base or right to take action at the EU level has been contested, and despite considerable changes over the years, remains partial rather than complete.

Jurisdiction in the EU over export controls can be summarized as follows:

- Control of exports of military goods remains a matter for national jurisdictions.
- In relation to dual-use goods, prior to 1995, member states relied on the same reasoning to exclude the EU from competence to deal with dual-use goods. However, following two judgments of the European Court of Justice,[3] the exclusive competence of the EU to legislate on dual-use goods was confirmed.
- In relation to sanctions, prior to the adoption of the Treaty of Lisbon in 2009, developments of EU common foreign and security policy were organized under a separate "pillar" of action. Lisbon in effect brought this function within the

---

2.   This point was most recently highlighted in the Commission's Green Paper on the future of dual-use controls, where the Commission noted that differences in the administrative, substantive, and operational rules applied by each member state lead to situations where an export of a specific item from one Member State may be significantly delayed or even prohibited, while the export of the same items from another Member State may be completed without any problems. See Commission Green Paper. The dual-use export control system of the European Union: ensuring security and competitiveness in a changing world. Brussels, 30.6.2011 COM (2011) 393 final.

3.   *See* case C-70/94 – Fritz Werner Industrie-Ausrüstungen GmbH v. Federal Republic of Germany and case C-83/94 – criminal proceedings against Peter Leifer, Reinhold Otto Krauskopf, and Otto Holzer.

EU structure. The Common Foreign and Security Policy (CFSP) is now used as the means through which EU member states coordinate their implementation of both international United Nations sanctions as well as, increasingly, the adoption of additional unilateral sanctions measures.

The European Union is first and foremost a customs union. Within the customs union, goods move freely across national borders without any customs event arising. Outside the EU, a uniform common external tariff is applied to all imports into the EU. This means that the same customs rules govern trade to and from third countries to all its current twenty-seven member states. While all customs procedures are established at an EU level, actual imports and exports are managed by national customs services in each of the member states.

Thus, for EU purposes, where goods move between member states, there will be no export and therefore no export control[4]—whereas, for U.S. purposes, each such internal movement will be considered to be a reexport.

In general, the term *export* is defined in relation to the provisions of the Community Customs Code (CCC)—being an export procedure as defined in Article 161 CCC, together with a reexport within the meaning of Article 182 CCC, "but not including items in transit."

It is often overlooked that Article 79 of the CCC provides the essential distinction between goods that are in free circulation (goods produced in the EU and those for which import procedures and all duties have been paid) and those that are not (goods produced in third countries that have not cleared import procedures and for which duties have not been paid). Article 161 CCC confirms that an export takes place when an export declaration is made (subject to exceptions) and when the export formalities are completed, the duties (if any) have been paid, and the goods leave the customs territory of the EU. The CCC thus confirms the procedures to get non-Community goods into free circulation (import) and those in free circulation out into the world of non-Community goods (export).

7.5 MILITARY GOODS

Controls on the export of military goods are in principle outside the scope of this chapter, as they remain an issue for individual member states. This situation is expressly confirmed in Article 346(b) of the TFEU, which provides that:

> any Member State may take such measures as it considers necessary for the protection of the essential interests of its security which are connected with the production of or trade in arms, munitions and war material; such measures shall

---

4.   A limited set of exceptions to this rule is set out in Annex IV of the DU Regulations.

not adversely affect the conditions of competition in the internal market regarding products which are not intended for specifically military purposes.

For the purposes of this chapter, therefore, the conclusion is simply that at this time, export controls, in relation to military goods, do not form part of EU law. Such controls are applied on a national basis, and national rules and procedures are different.

However, even here the dividing lines between national and EU competence are becoming increasingly blurred. The problems of lack of legal base have not stopped the EU from developing, with the support of member states, new rules designed to improve the efficiencies of the EU defense industry. The EU has therefore been able to adopt specific measures providing some degree of harmonization in relation to the procedures to be followed for the authorization of internal movements of defense items between EU member states.[5]

Directive 2009/43/EC distinguishes between exports of "defence related products"—i.e., exports to destinations outside the EU—from transfers between member states of the EU. In addition, specific rules are applied in relation to the intra-EU "passage through" of such items.

Article 4 of the directive confirms that internal transfers of defense-related products shall be subject to a prior authorization only in the member state of dispatch. The passage through a member state of such items on their way to a final destination shall no longer require the authorization of the transiting member states.

Here then is another small but critically important development in EU export control laws, under which a decision to authorize a transfer in one member state in effect provides a form of mandatory reexport authorization in other member states.

As with other areas of EU export controls, the nature of the prior authorization—be it individual or general—will depend on the position taken by the member state in question. The provisions of the directive had to be transposed into national law and therefore available for use from June 30, 2012.

7.6 DUAL-USE GOODS

The EU's first regulation on dual-use goods was adopted in 1994 (Council Regulation [EC] No 3381/94 of 19 December 1994, setting up a Community regime for the control of exports of dual-use goods). The current DU Regulation is set out in Council Regulation (EC) No 428/2009, setting up a Community regime for the control of exports, transfers, brokering, and transit of dual-use items.

---

5. *See* DIRECTIVE 2009/43/EC OF THE EUROPEAN PARLIAMENT AND OF THE COUNCIL of 6 May 2009 (simplifying terms and conditions of transfers of defence-related products within the Community OJEU L 146/1 10/06/2009).

The DU Regulation creates directly applicable EU law. However, very few provisions actually impose mandatory EU rules, and many of the provisions simply confirm that member states either must or may take action on a given issue but without specifying the actions in detail. As a result, the EU-DU Regulation sets out the basic principles and common rules at the EU level but leaves a considerable degree of discretion to the member states to decide on how such principles should be implemented in practice.

The implementation of EU rules does not presuppose the removal or prevention of the adoption of additional national measures. Such additional national rules and procedures can be applied provided member states do so in areas in which they retain national powers and provided that these additional rules do not conflict with existing regulation. Such additional measures or powers are therefore to be considered not as part of EU law but as part of national law.

In terms of the potential scope of extraterritorial application of the DU Regulation, there are two questions to ask:

- To whom do the rules apply?
- In what geographical locations do the rules apply?

7.7 TO WHOM DO THE RULES APPLY?

The DU Regulation applies when an export is made from the EU. The person responsible for all authorizations for such an export is the person (natural or legal) who either:

1. "holds the contract with the consignee in the third country and has the power for determining the sending of the item out of the customs territory of the Community," or
2. where this person acts for another, the person who has the "power for determining the sending of the item out of the customs territory of the Community."[6]

Thus, for goods/items exported from the EU, jurisdiction is based on the place of export and not on the nationality of the exporter or the origin of the item in question being exported from the EU.

7.8 TRANSIT AND TRANSSHIPMENT

In simple terms, since EU Treaty rules generally only apply to matters internal to the EU, the question arises as to whether the DU Regulation applies to goods that are not in free circulation—that is, are outside the EU but are physically present at a port or

---

6. *See* Article 2(3) DU Regulation: definition of "exporter."

in transit through the EU. The inclusion of the term *non-community* in the definition of "transit" as set out in the DU Regulation[7] confirms that this means something other than the EU customs internal transit procedure, used where goods in free circulation move between two member states but via the territory of a third country, preventing the need for an export followed by a new import declaration.

For these purposes, "transit" therefore covers goods arriving on a vessel that docks at an EU port (e.g., Antwerp) but that are then dispatched for delivery to a customer in another country outside the EU (e.g., Ukraine). Here, recital 16 of the DU Regulation[8] makes clear that though such goods are not in free circulation within the EU, the regulation authorizes member states to take action to prevent the onward supply of such goods to a third country—i.e., the physical presence of the goods rather than their customs status determines jurisdiction.

Article 6 of the regulation provides three specific rules regarding transit:

- Article 6(1) permits (but does not oblige) member states in which the transit occurs to prohibit transit of goods where they decide that the goods are to be used for a Weapons of Mass Destruction (WMD) program as defined in Article 4(1).[9]
- Article 6(2) confirms that member states may decide to authorize their national authority to grant individual licenses to permit such transits.
- Article 6(3) confirms that member states can extend the scope of such licenses to cover goods that they have added to the Annex I list (i.e., goods that are not dual-use goods at an EU level), as well as to dual-use goods intended for military use and for goods in transit to a country for which an arms embargo has been agreed to at the EU or international level.

The point to note is that, absent such specific provisions, there is no EU obligation to control the transit of dual-use goods. Article 6.3 was included in the 2009 regulation at the insistence of certain EU member states who did not want to limit the

---

7. "Transit" as defined in the Regulation (Art. 2) means: "a transport of non-community dual use items entering and passing through the customs territory of the Community with a destination outside the Community."

8. "(16)This Regulation includes items which only pass through the territory of the Community, that is, those items which are not assigned a customs-approved treatment or use other than the external transit procedure or which are merely placed in a free zone or free warehouse and where no record of them has to be kept in an approved stock record. Accordingly, a possibility for Member States' authorities to prohibit on a case-by-case basis the transit of non-Community dual-use items should be established, where they have reasonable grounds for suspecting from intelligence or other sources that the items are or may be intended in their entirety or in part for proliferation of weapons of mass destruction or of their means of delivery."

9. Article 4(1) defines a WMD programme as one in which:

"the items in question are or may be intended, in their entirety or in part, for use in connection with the development, production, handling, operation, maintenance, storage, detection, identification or dissemination of chemical, biological or nuclear weapons or other nuclear explosive devices or the development, production, maintenance or storage of missiles capable of delivering such weapons."

scope of the transit control and prohibition possibility to only dual-use goods listed in Annex I or to those to be used in a WMD program.

7.9 BROKERING

The DU Regulation now contains specific provisions on brokering, which extends its scope of application to transactions implemented outside the EU. Brokering is defined as "the negotiation or arrangement of transactions for the purchase, sale or supply of dual-use items from a third country to any other third country, or the selling or buying of dual-use items that are located in third countries for their transfer to another third country."[10]

Ancillary services (in relation to such goods) are excluded. Such services include the provision of transportation, financial services, insurance or re-insurance, or general advertising or promotion.

Here the EU asserts control over such exports made from a country outside the EU by limiting the scope of application to only "EU brokers." The definition of *broker* makes clear the need for a direct link to the EU:

> "broker" shall mean any natural or legal person or partnership resident or established in a Member State of the Community that carries out services defined under point 5 from the Community into the territory of a third country.[11]

So the provision is not applicable to non-EU nationals or companies operating outside the EU.

7.10 LICENSING

As the title of the DU Regulation underlines, its scope of application now extends beyond mere exports, covering both brokering and transits. Article 3(1) of the DU Regulation requires an authorization for the export of dual-use items listed in Annex I.[12] There are three types of licenses that can be granted: general, global, or individual. A further important distinction is whether the license is granted as a result of EU law, under the DU Regulation, or by national measures. Once again, strictly speaking, national authorizations are not part of EU law in that their nature, scope of application, and terms of issue are not consistent across all member states.

7.11 EU END-USE UNDERTAKINGS

These differences are particularly evident in relation to the use of end-use undertakings. Licensing decisions for the export of dual-use goods are taken on the basis

---

10. *See* Article 2(5) DU Regulation: definition of "brokering services."
11. *See* Article 2(6) DU Regulation: definition of "broker."
12. Annex I (as amended) is now set out in Regulation (EU) No 388/2012 of 19 April 2012, OJEU L 129/12.

of information on the identity of the end user and the country of destination. Any changes to these two elements can and will impact the assessment of the risk profile of the export. As a result, EU rules provide that member states may require additional information and commitments as to the destination and use of these items on arrival in the country of export.

There is no mandatory form of end-use undertaking that member states are required to use. Instead, the only EU document is a council working group recommendation adopted in 2009.[13] Some member states follow the language set out in this EU template. Others do not. Of greatest significance in relation to reexport controls is that the EU recommendation contains as an optional clause the following provision:

> "If required: The Customer shall not re-export the goods to third countries without the consent of [the issuing national authority]. Re-exportation to EU-countries or countries listed in Annex II of [DU Regulation] do not require any consent of [the issuing national authority]."

This serves to underline that we have guidance as to what end-use controls should cover, but there is no binding EU measure that directs member states as to their content. Exporters will therefore face differences in end-use undertakings across the EU.

7.12 NATIONAL END-USE UNDERTAKINGS

Differences exist in national end-use undertakings both in terms of their scope and the procedures used. The central differences arise in relation to whether a subsequent sale or reexport by the acquiring customer is required to be approved by the EU national authority who issued the initial export license.

Variations in the terms of the end-use undertaking also vary depending on whether the items are sold to an end user or to a local distributor.

In the absence of any binding EU measure, the form and content of end-use undertakings remains an issue for national law and procedure.

(a) UK

Since July 2010, the UK has included a requirement that all end-user undertakings supplied in support of applications for standard individual export licenses contain a revised undertaking declaration. This explicitly states that the end user will not reexport or transfer goods to a destination subject to an embargo imposed by the United Nations, EU, or Organisation for Security and Cooperation in Europe (OSCE). The current UK standard end-user undertaking provides as follows:

---

13. *See* OJEU C11/1 of 16.1.2009. Available by searching under "Official Journal" at http://eurlex.europa.eu/.

We—the person or body named at 1(e)—certify that we are the end-user of the goods described in Section 2, which are to be supplied by the exporter named in 1(a). We further certify that we shall use the goods for the purposes described in Section 3; that the goods will not be used for any purpose connected with chemical, biological or nuclear weapons, or missiles capable of delivering such weapons; that they will not be re-exported or otherwise re-sold or transferred if it is known or suspected that they are intended or likely to be used for such purposes; that the goods will not be re-exported or otherwise re-sold or transferred to a destination subject to UN, EU or OSCE embargo where that act would be in breach of the terms of that embargo; and that the goods, or any replica of them, will not be used in any nuclear explosive activity or unsafeguarded nuclear fuel cycle.[14]

Where the export is not to the final end user but to a consignee, the required commitment is as follows:

We—the person or body named at 1(c)—certify that we are the importer of the goods described in Section 2. We further certify that the goods are intended for stock to be held against future orders and EITHER (delete i or ii)

i. Will not be re-exported, sold for export or otherwise transferred from the country where we are based, namely _____ OR

ii. Are likely to be transferred to the following countries[15]

(b) Germany

The Federal Office of Economics and Export Control's (BAFA) standard form end-use undertaking[16] contains a more general restriction on reexport of controlled goods. The twelve versions of the form cover a variety of export possibilities. At their core, however, is a basic commitment from the end user as follows:

We (I) certify that we (I) will not re-export the goods to third countries without the approval of the Federal Office of Economics and Export Control (BAFA) of the Federal Republic of Germany.

In relation to certain dual-use exports, such authorization is deemed to be not required when made to an approved country (an EU member state plus Australia, Canada, Japan, New Zealand, Switzerland, and the U.S.).

---

14. *See* http://www.businesslink.gov.uk/bdotg/action/detail?itemId=1086976804&type=RESOURCES.
15. *See* http://www.gov.uk/end-user-and-consignee-undertakings-for-siels-and-oiels.
16. *See* http://www.ausfuhrkontrolle.info/ausfuhrkontrolle/de/antragstellung/endverbleibsdokumente/eve_muster.pdf.

In cases where the export is of technology, the commitment goes further, covering any export of the technology transferred, as well as exports of any derived goods produced as a result of using the technology.

In addition, BAFA seeks by contractual commitment to ensure that the commitments set out in the original end-use undertaking must be accepted by any transferee company or third party as a condition of receiving the goods. Thus, in principle this would see BAFA seeking control over the whole supply chain for the derived goods and further sale of the technology.

(c) Belgium
Belgium essentially follows the format of the EU recommendation.

(d) Spain
Spain's Ministry of Economy and Competitiveness is the home for the national dual-use administration.[17] The standard end-use undertaking includes the following commitment to be given by the named end user:

> We further certify that we shall use the goods for the purposes described in Sections 9b and 11; and that the goods will not be used for any purpose connected with chemical, biological or nuclear weapons, or missiles capable of delivering such weapons; that they will not be re-exported or otherwise re-sold or transferred if it is known or suspected that they are intended or likely to be used for such purposes; and that the goods, or any replica of them, will not be retransferred without prior consent in writing of the Spanish Authorities. We also certify that the goods or any replica of them will not be used in any nuclear explosive activity or unsafeguarded nuclear fuel cycle activity.[18]

7.13 UNION GENERAL EXPORT AUTHORIZATION (UGEA)

UGEAs establish as a matter of EU law general authorizations to export items to specified third countries. They are an example of pure EU export control law because they derive their force of law from the DU Regulation itself and do not require any national transposition measures. They are automatically valid across all twenty-seven member states.[19] There are now seven UGEAs, numbered EU001 to EU007.[20] In formal terms, the UGEAs are all part of Annex II of the DU Regulation.

---

17. *See* http://www.comercio.mityc.es/en/comercio-exterior/informacion-sectorial/material-de-defensa-y-de-doble-uso/Pages/documentos-control.aspx.
18. *See id.*
19. Not all member states follow this logic in practice, and it is not uncommon to find attempts to introduce national procedural or substantive variations to the application of the UGEAs.
20. REGULATION (EU) No 1232/2011 OF THE EUROPEAN PARLIAMENT AND OF THE COUNCIL of 16 November 2011 amending Council Regulation (EC) No 428/2009 setting up a Community regime for the control of exports, transfer, brokering, and transit of dual-use items O.J. L 326/26 of 8.12.2011. This Regulation amended Annex II by introducing EU002-007.

For example, the first UGEA, EU001, provides a general authorization to export all dual-use items listed in Annex I to the United States of America.[21] All that is required in order to rely on EU001 is (1) for the exporter to notify the relevant national authority and (2) to ensure that the specific exports meet all the conditions and requirements set up for the use of the UGEA in question. There can be no mixing and matching. Each UGEA defines a set of circumstances in which the UGEA is to apply and then specifies the third countries to which exports are permitted. If these conditions are not met, an individual license will still be needed.

The conditions of the UGEAs include provisions that directly concern requirements of end use and in some instances expressly require forms of reexport controls. For example, all UGEAs provide that the authorization is not applicable where the export is to a customs-free zone or free warehouse located in an authorized country, on the theory that the goods may well then be exported on from such customs-free zone or free warehouse to other more sensitive locations, which would require a case-by-case review.

In general terms, in cases where the exporter who seeks to rely on a given UGEA is aware that the goods are likely to or will be reexported, the UGEA will not be available.

7.14 INTERNAL REEXPORT CONTROLS

As we have stated above, movements of goods within the EU are not considered exports, and so, in theory, we conclude that such movements do not involve any issue of reexport. However, we have also seen how even under the DU Regulation, a significant role remains for the member states to determine policies and procedures.

Under Article 9(2), the national authority in the member state in which the exporter is established issues authorizations for exports by that company. Notably, this means that the member state in which the goods are located or will be exported from does *not issue the authorization*. National authorizations are valid for exports made from any other member state of the EU.

This means that a particular member state may authorize an export from another member state, when that second member state may not have issued the authorization. To address this potential problem of conflicting licensing views, Article 11 provides a balancing provision requiring the national authority to seek the opinion of any and all other member states in which the goods to be exported are or will be located. The views of these member states are binding on the national authority issuing the authorization. This too leads to difficulties.

Let us imagine as an example an EU subsidiary of a U.S. corporation having three manufacturing facilities, in the UK, Germany, and Italy. Let us also imagine that all

---

21. EU001 also authorizes exports to Australia, Canada, Japan, New Zealand, Norway, and Switzerland, including Liechtenstein.

imports and exports are organized through a distribution facility in the Netherlands. Some of the items manufactured and distributed are dual use.

If the exporter in question is the UK company—central administration located in England—then the UK Export Control Organisation (ECO) will be in charge of issuing the export license for all three manufacturing locations (UK, Germany, and Italy) and the distribution center (Netherlands). As a result of Article 11, the ECO would need to inform its Dutch counterpart in relation to any application for an authorization to export where the goods are or will be located in the Netherlands, and its German and Italian counterparts for any exports of the goods from Germany or Italy. It is simply a matter of time before ECO would find applications accepted by one or more of the member states (e.g., the Netherlands and Germany) but refused by another (e.g., Italy). On the assumption that the home member state authority remains positive toward the authorization of the exports, this would mean that a company would seek to ensure that goods are exported only from those member states that are willing to grant export authorization but not from those where such authorizations may be refused.

7.15 EU SANCTIONS

Since the entry into force of the TFEU in December 2009, measures adopted under the CFSP have broadened the scope of action taken by the EU well beyond that of implementing measures agreed on at an international level (e.g., by the United Nations). EU sanctions now include unilateral measures.

Each sanctions instrument sets out its scope of application, and by and large this is in identical terms. EU sanctions apply globally in respect to the acts of EU nationals. They also apply to any third-country person or entity where it does business at least "in part" in the EU.[22] The place from which goods, services, or funds are provided is therefore not the sole consideration as to the scope of EU sanctions.

Of course, the fact that EU sanctions are applicable to actions taking place outside the EU does not necessarily translate to any actual enforcement by the EU, as the EU does not enforce its sanctions regulations. Instead, enforcement of sanctions is a matter for national law and for individual member states.

Thus, an infringement by a Community national or entity would be prosecuted under the laws and procedures of their home member state. Individual member states will and do have different thresholds of concern in relation to sanctions in general and often with sanctions in relation to a specific third country. These factors explain

---

22. This regulation shall apply: (a) within the territory of the Union, including its airspace; (b) on board any aircraft or any vessel under the jurisdiction of a member state; (c) to any person inside or outside the territory of the Union who is a national of a member state; (d) to any legal person, entity, or body that is incorporated or constituted under the law of a member state; and (e) to any legal person, entity, or body in respect of any business done in whole or in part within the Union.

in part why it is difficult to discern an "EU" policy and standard for enforcement of sanctions.

In conclusion, on the issue of sanctions, there are two specific points to note:

- first, it is necessary to consider the national implementing rules to determine to what extent such sanctions rules are intended to apply extraterritorially; and
- second, these same rules may not distinguish between offenses committed in the home member state and other member states of the EU. Typically the *actus reus* of the offense would be an export from a member state in breach of sanctions to the third country. This suggests that it might be possible for proceedings to be brought in one member state (in which there is a high level of enforcement) for violations that took place in another member state that imposes lower levels of penalty and has a lower level of enforcement.

To make the point more clearly, imagine that either intentionally or negligently, a company incorporated in Member State A exports goods to Iran in breach of EU sanctions. Imagine that the three officers/executives of the company involved in reviewing and approving the transaction are of three different nationalities—Member States A, B, and C. Each of those member states could likely claim competence in relation to the acts of its nationals. The differences in implementation and enforcement mean that each of A, B, and C could very easily face different risks of prosecution and completely different penalties.

Though such outcomes may be considered, in commercial terms, another example of the proverbial un-level playing field in criminal law terms, it would perhaps be more correctly characterized as plainly unfair.

7.16 EU CONCLUSIONS

The working proposition at the start of this chapter is that this summary will underline all the situations in which the United States finds itself alone in terms of seeking to extend the scope of its export controls outside its national territory. Having completed the overview, it becomes clear that in practice the United States is only alone in one specific respect: the application of reexport controls over dual-use items that are purchased and used in the manufacture of goods in a third country.

In all other respects, the EU at the very least either maintains rules that are similar (if not as effective) or enables member states to pursue such policies to control reexports. If we look at the position of internal movements within the EU, we can see that the DU Regulation is based on a basic principle of reexport controls—that is, decisions on licenses taken by the member state in which a company has its central administration and not in which the goods are located.

The big—or even huge—difference between the United States and the EU is in the ability of the United States to actually enforce such rules in third countries.

Reexport Controls–Intersection of Canadian and U.S. Measures

John Boscariol

8.1 OVERVIEW

Because Canada and the United States are each other's largest trading partners, there is significant intersection of the two countries' trade control regimes. Chapters 2 and 3 include discussions of U.S. reexport controls under the Export Administration Regulations and the International Traffic in Arms Regulations. This section focuses on certain issues and challenges specific to the intersection of Canadian and U.S. trade controls, including export controls and economic sanctions.

What Is Regulated? In the case of export controls, goods and technology transferred from a place in Canada to a place outside Canada are covered. Economic sanctions can overlap export controls and cover other goods and technologies; however, they generally apply more broadly to the activities of persons in Canada and Canadian individuals and entities outside Canada.

Where to Find the Regulations: As is further discussed below, Canada's export controls are implemented pursuant to the Export and Import Permits Act and its regulations. Economic sanctions are set out under Canada's United Nations Act, Special Economic Measures Act, Freezing of Corrupt Foreign Officials Act, the Criminal Code, and their regulations. Canada's Defence Production Act and its regulations set out the requirements and prohibitions in respect of the possession, examination, and transfer in Canada of defense items.

Who Is the Regulator? Canadian export controls and economic sanctions are administered by Foreign Affairs and International Trade Canada and enforced by the Royal Canadian Mounted Police and the Canada Border Services Agency. Controls under the Defence Production Act are also administered by the Controlled Goods Directorate of Public Works and Government Services Canada.

8.2 INTRODUCTION TO CANADIAN TRADE CONTROLS

In Canada, the control of exports and cross-border technology transfers falls within the mandate of the federal government. These controls apply not just to physical shipments, but also to transfers by intangible means, including through the provision of services or training, uploads, downloads and other electronic file transfers, e-mails, faxes, telephone conversations, and face-to-face meetings.

Exports of goods and technology may be controlled by means of the Export and Import Permits Act (EIPA),[1] the United Nations Act (UNA),[2] the Special Economic Measures Act (SEMA),[3] and other sectorial regimes.

8.3 EXPORT AND IMPORT PERMITS ACT

Canada maintains controls on exports and transfers of certain goods, services, and technology pursuant to the EIPA. This includes controls based on the nature of the goods and technology as well as their destination. Permit applications for the transfer of such goods and technology are made to the Export Controls Division of Foreign Affairs and International Trade Canada (ECD). The Royal Canadian Mounted Police (RCMP) and the Canada Border Services Agency (CBSA) are responsible for the enforcement of these requirements.

(a) Export Control List

Established under the EIPA, the Export Control List (ECL)[4] identifies those goods and technology that may not be exported or otherwise transferred from Canada by tangible or intangible means without first obtaining an export permit, subject to exemptions for certain destination countries.

The ECL is not product-specific, but instead provides a set of technical specifications that are technology-neutral for the most part and that are functional in their description. Listed goods and technology are categorized into groups as follows:[5]

- dual-use items (Group 1)
- munitions (Group 2)
- nuclear nonproliferation items (Group 3)
- nuclear-related dual-use goods (Group 4)
- miscellaneous goods, including all U.S.-origin goods and technology and certain medical products, forest items, agricultural and food products, prohibited weapons, and nuclear-related and strategic items (Group 5)
- missile equipment and technology (Group 6)
- chemical and biological weapons and related technology (Group 7)

---

1. R.S.C. 1985, c. E-19.
2. R.S.C. 1985, c. U-2.
3. S.C. 1992, c. 17.
4. SOR/89-202.
5. Each group is set out in Department of Foreign Affairs and International Trade, A Guide to Canada's Export Controls (June 2010).

(b) Area Control List

Under the authority of the EIPA, Canada maintains an Area Control List (ACL),[6] on which prohibited destination countries are identified from time to time. No goods or technology may be exported or transferred to these countries—currently Belarus and North Korea—without first obtaining an export permit. Such permits are only issued by ECD in rare circumstances—for example, where the transfer is for humanitarian purposes.

(c) General Export Permits

Goods listed on the ECL, or destined for a country listed on the ACL, may not require an application for an individual export permit provided they meet certain terms and conditions set out in a General Export Permit (GEP).

If the particular exportation in issue satisfies the conditions set out in a GEP, there is no requirement to apply for an export permit, nor is it necessary to seek any authorization from the ECD. However, the GEP number must be provided on the customs export declaration so that CBSA officials are in a position to verify and to satisfy themselves that the particular exportation meets the terms and conditions of the GEP. Some GEPs also contain specific requirements for reporting export volumes and specific final consignees.

At the present time, there are approximately a dozen GEPs in force. These include GEPs for the export of nuclear-related items,[7] industrial dual-use goods,[8] personal computers and software,[9] and dual-use goods returned to Canada for repair or for the repair of goods previously exported under a valid permit.[10]

8.4 UNITED NATIONS ACT AND SPECIAL ECONOMIC MEASURES ACT

Under the UNA and the SEMA, Canada can restrict the export of goods and technology, as well as the movement of people and money and the provisions of services, to any country against which the United Nations or Canada has imposed economic sanctions.

Permits may be available to allow activities otherwise prohibited under these economic sanctions programs to proceed. The Economic Law Division of Foreign Affairs and International Trade Canada is responsible for the issuance of such permits. The RCMP and CBSA are responsible for the enforcement of sanctions programs.

---

6.   SOR/81-543.
7.   General Export Permit No. Ex. 27 — Nuclear-Related Dual-Use Goods, SOR/93-580.
8.   General Export Permit No. Ex. 29 — Eligible Industrial Goods, SOR/94-735, and General Export Permit No. Ex. 30 — Certain Industrial Goods to Eligible Countries and Territories, SOR/94-734.
9.   General Export Permit No. Ex. 18 — Portable Personal Computers and Associated Software, SI/89-121.
10.   Export of Goods for Special and Personal Use Permit, C.R.C., c. 611.

Most regulations promulgated under the UNA and the SEMA also identify "designated persons"—which can include entities, associations, governments, and individuals—that are subject to asset freezes. Persons in Canada and Canadians outside Canada are generally prohibited from engaging in dealings with designated persons regardless of whether such dealings involve a sanctioned country. All transactions should be screened to ensure that designated persons are not involved in any way—including as purchasers, suppliers, creditors, or freight forwarders—or otherwise benefitting from the transaction. Screening based on denied party lists under U.S. or other laws is not sufficient for these purposes.

At the present time, Canada currently imposes trade controls of varying degrees on activities involving the following countries (and in many cases, individuals and entities associated with them): Belarus, Burma (Myanmar), Côte d'Ivoire, the Democratic Republic of the Congo, Cuba, Egypt, Eritrea, Guinea, Iran, Iraq, Lebanon, Liberia, Libya, North Korea, Pakistan, Sierra Leone, Somalia, Sudan, Syria, Tunisia, and Zimbabwe. Any involvement of these countries or any "designated person" in proposed transactions or other activities should raise a red flag for further investigation to ensure compliance with economic sanctions.

8.5 FREEZING OF CORRUPT FOREIGN OFFICIALS ACT

Pursuant to the Freezing of Corrupt Foreign Officials Act (FCFOA),[11] Canada has also implemented economic sanctions measures targeting activities involving certain "politically exposed foreign persons." These are defined as persons who hold or have held certain identified offices or positions in or on behalf of a foreign state. They can include heads of state, members of legislatures, deputy ministers, ambassadors, military officers, presidents of state-owned companies or banks, heads of government agencies, judges, or political party leaders. They can also include any person who, for personal or business reasons, is or was closely associated with such persons, including family members.

The measures prohibit dealing directly or indirectly in any property of such persons, entering into or facilitating a related financial transaction, and providing financial services or other related services in respect of such property. Regulations implemented under the FCFOA provide for specific measures to be taken against former Tunisian and Egyptian leaders and senior officials, as well as their associates and family members, suspected of misappropriating state funds or obtaining property inappropriately.[12]

---

11.   S.C. 2011, c. 10.
12.   Freezing Assets of Corrupt Foreign Officials (Tunisia and Egypt) Regulations, SOR/2011-316.

8.6 DEFENSE TRADE CONTROLS

Canada's Defence Production Act (DPA)[13] and Controlled Goods Regulations[14] set out requirements and prohibitions in respect of the possession, examination, and transfer in Canada of "controlled goods and technology," which include defense and other items covered by the ITAR.[15] Companies engaged in such activities must be registered with and approved by the Controlled Goods Directorate of Public Works and Government Services Canada (CGD) and satisfy a number of significant obligations, including the implementation of a security plan and the screening of employees who are to have access to covered items.

For the export or transfer of DPA goods or technology from Canada (e.g., an ECL Group 2 munitions item), evidence must be provided to ECD that the applicant is registered with the CGD before obtaining a permit.

Specific challenges in the implementation of these controls under applicable Canadian and U.S. laws are discussed further below.

8.7 OTHER

In addition to the EIPA, other Canadian legislation regulates import and export activity, including in respect of rough diamonds,[16] cultural property,[17] wildlife,[18] nuclear goods and technology,[19] hazardous products,[20] and environmentally sensitive items.[21]

8.8 CURRENT EXPORT ENFORCEMENT ISSUES

As noted above, implementation and enforcement of Canadian trade controls are the responsibility of Foreign Affairs and International Trade Canada (the ECD and the Economic Law Section), the RCMP, and the CBSA.

The CBSA continues to exercise its broad authority under the Customs Act and the EIPA to engage in numerous searches, detentions, seizures, ascertained forfei-

---

13. R.S.C. 1985, c. D-1.
14. SOR/2001-32.
15. The Schedule to the DPA defines "controlled goods" for these purposes by reference to certain goods and technology on the ECL: most items in Group 2 (munitions list), item 5504 (strategic goods and technology, including satellite and space-related items and any U.S.-origin items determined under the ITAR "as having substantial military applicability, and which have been specially designed or modified for military purposes"), and all items in Group 6 (missile technology).
16. Export and Import of Rough Diamonds Act, S.C. 2002, c. 25.
17. Cultural Property Export and Import Act, R.S.C. 1985, c. C-51.
18. Wild Animal and Plant Protection and Regulation of International and Interprovincial Trade Act, S.C. 1992, c. 52.
19. Nuclear Safety and Control Act, S.C. 1997, c. 9.
20. Export and Import of Hazardous Waste and Hazardous Recyclable Material Regulations, SOR/2005-149, under the Canadian Environmental Protection Act, 1999, S.C. 1999, c. 33.
21. Ozone-Depleting Substances Regulations, 1998, SOR/99-7, under the Canadian Environmental Protection Act, 1999, S.C. 1999, c. 33.

tures, investigations, and other enforcement activities to ensure that exports from Canada are in full compliance with Canadian legislation. In addition to the EIPA, this includes UNA and SEMA sanctions regulations and Customs Act export reporting obligations.[22]

Continued reports of U.S. authorities' dissatisfaction with Canadian enforcement of export controls appear to be at least part of the reason for increasingly aggressive CBSA enforcement in this area.[23] Historically, Canada does not have as extensive an enforcement record as that of the United States regarding export controls and economic sanctions. However, Canadian officials point to a "continuum of successes" recently, in addition to prosecutions and convictions, in addressing export violations; these include detentions and seizures, which delay and disrupt shipments and can result in lost contracts.[24]

Areas in which Canadian exporters are facing significant compliance and enforcement challenges include the following.

(a) Dealings with "Designated Persons"

Regardless of the destination country, exporters should be routinely screening all parties they deal with against the lists of companies, organizations, and individuals established under the numerous SEMA and UNA sanctions regulations, the FCFOA, and the Criminal Code provisions regarding dealings with terrorist entities. Canadian exporters are prohibited from engaging in dealings with these listed parties.

(b) Information Security Items

Canada's export controls over goods, software, and technology designed or modified to perform encryption or to work with such items (as identified on the ECL) are more cumbersome than their U.S. counterparts. Often, exporters first discover that their products are subject to control when they are detained or seized by the CBSA, and the delays in responding to the enforcement action and obtaining a permit result in costly commercial disruption and lost sales.

In an effort to level the playing field for Canadian exporters, the ECD has recently issued two GEPs for certain cryptographic item. General Export Permit No. 45 (Cryptography for the Development or Production of a Product)[25] allows for the export of controlled cryptographic items, subject to some exceptions, that are used for

---

22.   Reporting of Exported Goods Regulations, SOR/2005-23.

23.   *See, e.g., Fronts in Canada Set Up to Ship Banned Goods Abroad: Secret Cable,* The Globe and Mail, Nov. 23, 2011.

24.   Oct. 31, 2011, Testimony of Geoff Leckey, CBSA Director General, Intelligence and Targeting, before the Standing Senate Committee on National Security and Defence at http://www.parl.gc.ca/content/sen/committee/411/SECD/02EVC-49153-E.htm.

25.   *See* Foreign Affairs and International Trade Canada Notice to Exporters No. 182, http://www.international.gc.ca/controls-controles/systems-systemes/excol-ceed/notices-avis/182.aspx?lang=eng&view=d.

the development or production of a product without having to apply for an individual export permit provided certain conditions are satisfied. The transfer must be made to a non-government entity in one of twenty-nine designated countries or a non-government entity in any country (other than sanctioned or ACL countries) if the entity is controlled by a Canadian resident or a non-government affiliated entity located in one of the twenty-nine designated countries. The exporter must notify ECD prior to the first transfer in each calendar year and then report on transfers made during the previous calendar year by January 31. ECD information requests must be responded to within fifteen days. In the case of physical exports, "GEP-45" must be specified on the export report filed with the Canada Border Services Agency.

ECD has also issued General Export Permit—GEP No. 46 (Cryptography for Use by Certain Consignees)—which allows for the transfer of finished products containing controlled cryptography to affiliates without having to apply for an individual export permit.[26]   This permits transfers to a consignee in another country that is controlled by a resident of Canada or is controlled by an entity that has its head office in one of twenty nine designated country and controls the resident of Canada who is undertaking the transfer. This GEP also has similar notification and reporting requirements as GEP No. 45.

The ECD has also made available several types of "multidestination" export permits (MEPs) for cryptographic items. Although they still require exporters to apply to the ECD and meet reporting and other conditions depending on the applicable MEP, they may be obtained without having to specify consignees in the application. This avoids having to apply for individual export permits for different consignees. The ECD has made six such MEPs available with varying terms and conditions.[27]

(c) "Catch-All" Controls

Pursuant to a "catch-all" provision in the ECL, exports of all goods and technology are prohibited without a permit if "their properties and any information made known to the exporter . . . would lead a reasonable person to suspect that they will be used" in connection with chemical, biological, or nuclear weapons and their delivery systems or missiles (WMDs) or used in any WMD facility.[28] Accordingly, exporters must

---

26.   *See* Foreign Affairs and International Trade Canada Notice to Exporters No. 186, http://www.international.gc.ca/controls-controles/systems-systemes/excol-ceed/notices-avis/186.aspx?lang=eng&view=d.

27.   *See* Foreign Affairs and International Trade Canada, Export Permits for Cryptographic Items, http://www.international.gc.ca/controls-controles/export-exportation/crypto/Crypto_Intro.aspx?lang=eng&view=d.

28.   ECL Item 5505. *See* ECD Notice "Export Controls over Goods and Technology for Certain Uses" (Mar. 2011, Serial No. 176) at http://www.international.gc.ca/controls-controles/systems-systemes/excol-ceed/notices-avis/176.aspx?lang=eng&view=d. This does not apply if the goods or technology are intended for end use in, and the final consignee (and any intermediate consignee) is located in, one of twenty-nine listed allied countries.

exercise due diligence to ensure that their uncontrolled goods and technology are not destined for a WMD facility.

(d) Iran

The supply of any goods and related technology to Iran for use in the petrochemical, oil, or natural gas industry or for nuclear-related purposes is prohibited under SEMA and UNA regulations, which also contain an extensive list of other prohibited items.[29] Canada has also imposed a financial services ban, which can significantly complicate matters for exporters to Iran.[30] Further, no U.S.-origin goods or technology can be transferred to Iran without an export permit, which can only be obtained in limited circumstances.[31] Exporters should be aware that the CBSA is also closely scrutinizing exports to locations that are commonly used for transshipment to Iran, including the United Arab Emirates, Malaysia, and Hong Kong.

(e) Syria

There is a ban on the export to Syria of any goods or technology identified on the ECL as well as any goods or technical data for use in the monitoring of telecommunications.[32] Canada has prohibited the supply to Syria of luxury goods as well as certain listed items that can be used for internal repression or chemical or biological weapons. Canada has also imposed a financial services ban on Syria.[33] As is the case with transfers to Iran, all U.S.-origin goods and technology are prohibited from being transferred to Syria without a permit, which can only be obtained in very limited circumstances.

(f) Cuba

Canada does not restrict exports or transfers to Cuba unless the goods or technology are of U.S. origin or otherwise controlled on the ECL, in which case a permit must first be obtained. However, pursuant to an order issued under the Foreign Extraterritorial Measures Act[34] (FEMA), companies and individuals are prohibited from complying with the extraterritorial U.S. trade embargo of Cuba and are required to advise the Canadian attorney general forthwith of any communications related to the U.S. trade embargo received from a person in a position to influence their policies in Canada. Failure to comply with the order is punishable with criminal penalties.

---

29. Special Economic Measures (Iran) Regulations, SOR/2010-165, and Regulations Implementing United Nations Resolutions on Iran, SOR/2007-44.
30. Effective Nov. 21, 2011.
31. As discussed further below, ECL item 5400 controls all U.S.-origin goods and technology for export or transfer from Canada. General Export Permit No. 12 allows for the shipment of goods to any destination other than Belarus, North Korea, Cuba, Syria, and Iran.
32. Special Economic Measures (Syria) Regulations, SOR/2011-114.
33. Effective Mar. 5, 2012.
34. Foreign Extraterritorial Measures (United States) Order, 1992, SOR/92-584.

How FEMA might apply to U.S.-origin goods and technology to be transferred from Canada is discussed further below and also in chapters 1 and 9.

(g) Belarus and Burma (Myanmar)

Canada's sanctions against Belarus are more aggressive than those imposed by other countries, including those of the United States and the European Union. They prohibit the export or transfer of all goods and technology to Belarus, and permits are available in only very limited circumstances (e.g., for humanitarian purposes).[35]

Effective April 24, 2012, Canada repealed most of its sanctions against Burma (Myanmar). However, persons in Canada and Canadians outside Canada are still prohibited from engaging in various dealings involving a large number of designated persons, and a military goods, services, and technology embargo remains in place.[36]

(h) Other Destinations of Concern

In addition to the ECL product- and technology-specific controls and the sanctions in place against the countries already mentioned above, exporters should be aware that Canada also currently imposes trade restrictions of varying degrees on activities involving Côte d'Ivoire, the Democratic Republic of the Congo, Egypt, Eritrea, Guinea, Iraq, Lebanon, Liberia, Libya, North Korea, Pakistan, Sierra Leone, Somalia, Sudan, Tunisia, and Zimbabwe. These include controls that are enforced by the CBSA as part of its role in monitoring exports from Canada.

8.9 MITIGATING RISK AND SENSITIVITIES TO U.S.-CANADA ISSUES

Failure to comply with these requirements exposes Canadian exporters to significant financial and operational costs arising from penalty assessments, as well as delayed, detained, or canceled export shipments. In many cases, there can also be disastrous reputational consequences for the company as a whole.

In order to mitigate risk, exporters should be in a position to demonstrate effective due diligence by designing and implementing a robust trade controls compliance strategy. A Canadian exporter's internal compliance program should include measures such as:

- a clearly articulated and readily accessible written manual that is regularly reviewed and updated;
- appointing senior officer(s) responsible for the implementation and enforcement of the policies and procedures;

---

35.   Belarus, along with North Korea, is listed on the ACL.
36.   See Special Economic Measures (Burma) Regulations, SOR/2007-285, and the regulations amending the Special Economic Measures (Burma) Regulations, SOR/2012/85.

- education and training of frontline sales and other employees and executives;
- procedures for reporting potential violations internally and externally (e.g., voluntary disclosure) and for providing protection against retaliation;
- internal disciplinary procedures for violations;
- destination and party screening, including the screening of customers, suppliers, freight forwarders, and other involved service providers or agents;
- end-use screening, including written certification from customers; and
- regular reviewing, testing, and enhancement of processes and procedures to ensure full compliance.

There is no "one-size-fits-all" compliance program, as these measures will differ depending on the size of the company; the nature of the exporter's goods, services, and technology; and its markets, customers, and end users, among other factors. In particular, companies should be sure that their compliance policies explicitly reflect the requirements of Canadian law and not simply graft their U.S. parent's or affiliate's trade control program onto their Canadian operations.

As exporters face increasing CBSA scrutiny of their shipments, it is important to pay careful attention to trade control obligations in order to minimize noncompliance risk and avoid the financial and reputational costs associated with CBSA enforcement and delayed or canceled orders.

8.10 SPECIFIC U.S.-CANADA TRADE CONTROL ISSUES

As each other's most important trading partner, the transfer of goods and technology between the United States and Canada proceeds, for the most part, without concerns for cumbersome trade controls. There are, however, a number of key issues arising from the interaction of each country's trade control regime that U.S. and Canadian companies need to address.

(a) Export of U.S.-Origin Goods and Technology

Canada has implemented special rules for the transfer of U.S.-origin goods and technology. Failure to comply can result in the delay and detention of shipments, the imposition of administrative monetary penalties, seizure or ascertained forfeiture, and criminal prosecution.

(i) The ECL Item 5400 Control

Item 5400 of the ECL controls for transfer from Canada all goods and technology that originate in the United States and that are not elsewhere identified on the ECL. The item specifically excludes "goods that have been further processed or manufactured outside the United States so as to result in a substantial change in value, form or use of the goods or in the production of new goods."

In the past, there has been a practice that allowed exporters to make this determination simply on the basis of whether the U.S. content exceeded 50 percent of the value of the item to be transferred. In the author's experience, this is not the only factor to be considered, and exporters should also be carefully considering whether U.S. inputs have gone through a sufficient transformation in form or use when incorporated into the new item to be exported from Canada, even if the U.S. content is below 50 percent.

(ii) General Export Permit No. 12

In most cases, exporters of U.S.-origin goods may rely on an exemption from this control, which allows them to transfer U.S.-origin goods or technology without having to apply for and obtain a permit. GEP No. 12[37] allows for the export from Canada of any goods or technology of U.S. origin, other than those listed elsewhere on the ECL, to any destination other than an ACL country or certain U.S.-sanctioned countries.

At the present time, GEP No. 12 may not be used for transfers to Belarus, Cuba, Iran, Syria, and North Korea. Canada strictly controls the export of U.S.-origin goods and technology to certain U.S.-sanctioned countries in order to ensure that Canada does not act as a conduit for avoiding the application of U.S. trade embargoes.

(iii) Individual Export Permit

If U.S.-origin items are to be transferred to Belarus, Cuba, Iran, Syria, or North Korea, the exporter must apply to the ECD for an individual export permit.

It is within the ECD's discretion as to whether to grant a permit, and this may depend on many factors, including the nature of the goods or technology and the destination country. Experience indicates that such permits are issued on relatively rare occasions, including where the transfer is for humanitarian purposes, the exporter has obtained a U.S. license or can show that it could benefit from a licensing exemption under U.S. law, the U.S.-origin part will be for repair or replacement of a U.S.-origin item that was previously permitted to be exported, the goods are "replacement parts" for non-U.S. origin items, the goods relate to a previously lawfully exported good of Canadian origin, the goods are part of a turnkey operation, or where the transfer is to support permissible Canadian operations in the destination country.

(iv) FEMA and Transfers of U.S.-Origin Items to Cuba

As discussed in more detail in chapter 9, an order issued under FEMA[38] (the FEMA Order), inter alia, prohibits Canadian corporations—and their directors, officers, managers, and employees in a position of authority—from complying with the extraterritorial measures constituting the U.S. trade embargo of Cuba.

The FEMA Order broadly defines these extraterritorial measures to include the U.S. Cuban Assets Control Regulations and any law, guideline, or other enactment or communication having a similar purpose to the extent that "they operate or are likely to operate so as to prevent, impede, or reduce trade or commerce between Canada and

---

37. General Export Permit No. 12 — United States Origin Goods, SOR/97-107.
38. Foreign Extraterritorial Measures (United States) Order, 1992, SOR/92-584.

Cuba."[39] These measures can include reexport provisions of the U.S. Export Administration Regulations (EAR), which generally prohibit reexports of U.S.-origin goods from Canada to Cuba.

The EAR apply to the reexport of items to Cuba where the U.S. content is 10 percent or more of the total value of the item being exported. Although license applications to the U.S. Bureau of Industry and Security (BIS) for U.S.-origin items to be exported or reexported to Cuba are subject to a general policy of denial, licenses may be granted in limited circumstances. One such circumstance will be of particular interest to companies that incorporate U.S. components into products assembled or manufactured in Canada. For companies that are not owned or controlled by U.S. persons and that are seeking to export from a third country to Cuba nonstrategic, foreign-made products that contain an insubstantial proportion of U.S.-origin materials, parts, or components, BIS will generally consider license applications favorably on a case-by-case basis provided that (1) the local law requires, or policy favors, trade with Cuba and (2) the U.S.-origin content does not exceed 20 percent of the value of the item to be exported from the third country.[40]

How does FEMA apply to Canada's control over the export of U.S.-origin items to Cuba (ECL item 5400) and to these EAR reexport provisions? The Regulatory Impact Analysis Statement accompanying the FEMA Order provides that "it is important to note that the Order does not displace Canadian rules prohibiting or controlling the re-export of U.S.-origin goods and technology." A Canadian company that refuses to transfer U.S.-origin technology to Cuba because it is unable to obtain a permit from the ECD should not be considered to be in violation of its noncompliance obligation under the FEMA Order. In this case, the company should be viewed as complying with Canadian law, not U.S. law.

Circumstances, however, are rarely this straightforward. What if the company receives an order to export goods to Cuba but believes that its U.S. components are not sufficiently further processed in Canada to result in the production of new goods? Or what if the company was requested to export 100 percent U.S.-origin goods to Cuba? In these situations, can the company make its own determination that a Canadian export permit would likely not be issued and therefore refuse to engage in the sale without fear of contravening the FEMA Order? Under the EAR, if the U.S. content exceeds 20 percent, a reexport license application to BIS would be subject to a general policy of denial. Accordingly, it could appear that one of the reasons for the Canadian company's refusal to supply is the requirements of the U.S. EAR and therefore raise the risk of FEMA violation.

In such circumstances, the Canadian authorities have taken the view that to be certain that it is not exposed to prosecution under FEMA, this Canadian company

---

39.   *Id* at sec. 2.
40.   Export Administration Regulations, 15 C.F.R. § 746.2(b)(3).

should first apply for an export permit from Canadian authorities. Only if the company applies for and is denied the Canadian permit may it then refuse to export the goods to Cuba without being considered to have breached the noncompliance requirements in the FEMA Order.

(v) Exports of ITAR-Controlled U.S.-Origin Goods and Technology

U.S.-origin goods and technology that are controlled on the ECL other than under item 5400 require a permit regardless of their origin. For items that are identified in the DPA and regulated under the Controlled Goods Program,[41] a U.S. export authorization must be provided to the ECD before a permit will be issued. Generally speaking, these DPA items are the same goods and technology that are controlled under the ITAR.

The ECD's policy of requiring a U.S. export authorization prior to issuing an export permit applies to DPA items that are of U.S. origin, items incorporating any DPA items that are of U.S. origin, or items manufactured in Canada using any DPA items that are of U.S. origin.

Depending on the circumstances, such a U.S. export authorization can include any of the following approvals issued under the ITAR: an export license, a warehouse and distribution agreement, a technical assistance agreement, a manufacturing license agreement, a reexport authorization letter, or a U.S. export license exemption.

It should be noted that if a DPA item to be transferred from Canada is not of U.S. origin but contains U.S.-origin components that are not subject to the ITAR, a U.S. export authorization is not required.

(b) Exports of Controlled Items to the United States

Most controlled goods and technology on the ECL do not require a permit if they are being transferred to a final consignee located in the United States.

ECL items that do require a permit include certain weapons in Group 2; all items in Groups 3 and 4 (nuclear); certain wood, agricultural products, and military and strategic items in Group 5; missile delivery systems in Group 6; and certain chemical and biological weapons agents in Group 7. These items are described on the ECL with a reference to "all destinations."

Exports from Canada that transit the United States to third-country destinations do not qualify as exports to the United States for these purposes.

---

41. The schedule to the Defence Production Act refers to certain goods and technology on the Export Control List: most items in Group 2 (munitions list), item 5504 (Strategic Goods and Technology, including satellite and space-related items and any U.S.-origin items determined under the ITARs "as having substantial military applicability, and which have been specially designed or modified for military purposes"), and all items in Group 6 (Missile Technology Control Regime List).

(c) Goods and Technology in Transit from the United States

Generally, controlled goods and technology originating outside Canada and moving through Canada, whether in bond or cleared through customs, are subject to permit requirements.[42] There is an exception for goods or technology that are in transit on a through journey on a billing that originates outside Canada, if the billing indicates that the ultimate destination is a country other than Canada.

There is an additional requirement in order for goods or technology shipped from the United States to qualify for this exception. In such cases, the billing must also be accompanied by a certified true copy of the U.S. Shipper's Export Declaration, and the declaration cannot contain terms that conflict with the billing.

(d) U.S. ITAR Dual and Third-Country National Rule

Until recently, Canadian firms have faced numerous difficulties with U.S. ITAR rules that prohibited employees of certain nationalities or born in certain ITAR-proscribed countries (e.g., China) from accessing ITAR-controlled defense goods and technology in Canada. To comply with these restrictions, Canadian companies have had to risk violating Canadian provincial and federal antidiscrimination laws and subject themselves to human rights complaints when denying employees access to projects involving ITAR-controlled items because of their nationality or country of birth. Companies in affected sectors have had to address, defend, and settle costly, and in some cases public, antidiscrimination claims arising from ITAR compliance.

In an effort to address these concerns arising under the employment and human rights regimes in Canada and the jurisdictions of other U.S. trading partners, on May 16, 2011, the U.S. Department of State amended the ITAR to add a new § 126.18, effective August 15, 2011.[43] The new provision allows for the transfer of unclassified defense articles to dual and third-country nationals employed by foreign consignees or end users if such individuals have a government security clearance or if they have been screened for substantive contacts with ITAR-proscribed countries.[44]

On October 1, 2011, the CGD began implementing its Enhanced Security Strategy, which is intended to strengthen security screening in Canada and assure Canadian companies qualifying under the Controlled Goods Program (CGP) that they should also meet the requirements of ITAR § 126.18.[45]

A CGP registrant's designated official (DO) must now conduct thorough enhanced background screenings of employees, officers, and directors requiring access to con-

---

42.   Item 5401, ECL.

43.   76 Fed. Reg. 28,174 (May 16, 2011) (adding 22 C.F.R. § 126.18).

44.   22 C.F.R. § 126.18.

45.   See CGD, Notice to Controlled Goods Program Registrants Regarding International Traffic in Arms Regulations Amendment (Sept. 13, 2011), http://ssi-iss.tpsgc-pwgsc.gc.ca/dmc-cgd/actualites-news/itar-eng.html; CGD, Overview of the Enhanced Security Strategy, http://ssi-iss.tpsgc-pwgsc.gc.ca/dmc-cgd/actualites-news/apercu-overview-eng.html.

trolled goods and technology. This screening, which can only be conducted once the individual has consented to the sharing of personal information with Canadian and foreign governments, includes an extensive review of detailed personal information through the completion of a CGD questionnaire.[46] Using this information, the DO must assess the honesty, reliability, and trustworthiness of the individual and the extent to which the individual poses a risk of transferring a controlled good to an unauthorized company or individual.

This review by the DO includes factors similar to those examined in "substantive contact" reviews under the new ITAR rule,[47] such as contacts with government officials, agents, or proxies, business and family contacts, continuing allegiances to foreign countries, relationships with foreign country governments, frequent travel, residences, and bank accounts in foreign countries, and other affiliations within or outside Canada.[48] Unlike the ITAR substantive contact review, CGP screening is not limited to contacts with ITAR-proscribed countries—it applies in respect of all countries other than the United States.

Initially, the CGD stated that notwithstanding the exemption in ITAR § 126.18 for individuals who have obtained a government security clearance,[49] individuals possessing such security clearance were still required to be security screened under the CGP before accessing controlled items in Canada.[50] The CGD has since indicated they will change this policy so that possession of a government security clearance will exempt an individual from CGP screening.

Notably, ITAR § 126.18 does not contain an exemption for individuals who have been cleared under Canada's CGP.[51] However, pursuant to an exchange of letters with Public Works and Government Services Canada in August 2011, the U.S. Department of State Directorate of Defense Trade Controls (DDTC), which administers the ITAR, stated that it has "high regard for the CGP as a means to mitigate the risks of diversion" and recognizes that CGD has enhanced its program through "augmented

46.   See CGD, Controlled Goods Program—Security Assessment Application, *available at* http://ssi-iss. tpsgc-pwgsc.gc.ca/pdf/dmc-cgd/dmc-cgd-es-sa.pdf.
47.   See 22 C.F.R. § 126.18(c)(2).
48.   *See* CGD, Information on Security Assessments Performed by Designated Officials (Oct. 1, 2011), http://ssi-iss.tpsgc-pwgsc.gc.ca/dmc-cgd/form/rd-do/info-eng.html. With this information in hand, and using a "Risk Matrix Assessment Procedures" tool provided by CGD, the DO must determine the risk threshold and make a decision to grant or deny access to controlled goods. Based on a risk threshold of "medium" or "high," the DO may request that the CGD perform a further assessment if there are significant concerns with the results.
49.   *See* 22 C.F.R. § 126.18(c)(1).
50.   *See* CGD, Notice to Controlled Goods Program Registrants Regarding International Traffic in Arms Regulations Amendment (Sept. 13, 2011), http://ssi-iss.tpsgc-pwgsc.gc.ca/dmc-cgd/actualites-news/itar -eng.html.
51.   *See* 22 C.F.R. § 126.18.

security assessment procedures."[52] The DDTC letter states that if the DDTC intends to review the technology security/clearance plans and screening records of Canadian companies pursuant to ITAR § 126.18(c)(2), such a request is to be made through the CGD.[53] It also notes that this does not in any way hinder the DDTC's authority or ability to conduct ITAR-enforcement action.[54]

Whether ITAR § 126.18 and the new enhanced CGP screening procedures will alleviate human rights, employment, and privacy concerns in Canada or elsewhere remains to be seen. One can expect some difficulties and challenges as these new regimes, including enhanced screening by DOs of sensitive employee information, are implemented over the next few years.

---

52. Exchange of Letters Between the Department of Public Works and Government Services Canada and the U.S. Department of State Directorate of Defense Trade Controls (Aug. 25, 2011), *available at* http://ssi-iss.tpsgc-pwgsc.gc.ca/pdf/dmc-cgd/lttr-eng.pdf.
53. *Id.*
54. *Id.*

9

Extraterritoriality and Foreign Blocking Statutes

Paul M. Lalonde (Canada) and Anahita Thoms and Glen Kelley
(European Union)

9.1 OVERVIEW

The introduction of extraterritorial trade controls has led some countries to enact "foreign blocking" legislation designed to counter what they view to be the objectionable application of trade restrictions extraterritorially. These blocking measures help to protect the interests of these countries against the intrusion of foreign trade and commerce policies on their domestic actions and citizens.

The interaction of these measures poses compliance challenges, as the restrictions often directly conflict with foreign blocking laws which impose penalties on compliance with extraterretorial trade sanctions. This chapter provides an overview of the foreign blocking legislation enacted by Canada and the European Union, as well as the legal implications for companies operating in those countries whose business operations may be subject to extraterritorial trade legislation.[1]

What Is Regulated? The blocking statutes seek to prohibit local compliance with certain foreign extraterritorial measures (in practice, U.S. extraterritorial sanctions on Cuba and Iran).

Where to Find the Regulations: The measures are contained in the Canadian Foreign Extraterritorial Measures Act (FEMA),[2] the EU Blocking Regulation,[3] and the Common Action 96/668CFSP of the Council of the European Union.[4]

---

1. Mexico's blocking statute, the Law of Protection of Commerce and Investments from Foreign Policies That Contravene International Law (often referred to as the "Antidote Law"), is not examined in detail in this handbook but is briefly described in chapter 1, above, at page 30.
2. Foreign Extraterritorial Measures Act, R.S.C. 1985, c. F-29.
3. Council Regulation (EC) No 2271/96 of 22 November 1996 protecting against the effects of the extraterritorial application of legislation adopted by a third country, and actions based thereon and resulting therefrom, OJ L 309, 29.11.1996, p. 1.
4. Joint Action of 22 November 1996 adopted by the Council on the basis of Articles J.3 and K.3 of the Treaty on European Union concerning measures protecting against the effects of the extraterritorial application of legislation adopted by a third country, and actions based thereon or resulting therefrom (96/668/ CFSP), OJ L 309, 29.11.1996, p. 7–7. Pursuant to Article 1, each member state shall take the measures it deems necessary to protect the interests of any person protected by the EU Blocking Regulation.

Who Is the Regulator? In Canada, the FEMA is enforced by the Attorney General of Canada. As regards the EU Blocking Regulation, the European Commission administers the reporting requirements while enforcement is left to the individual Member States.

9.2 U.S. EXTRATERRITORIAL MEASURES

The United States maintains several trade restrictions that apply outside its borders.

(a) Extraterritorial Cuba Sanctions

The U.S. Cuban Assets Control Regulations (CACR)[5] extend U.S. trade restrictions with Cuba, or Cuban companies and citizens, to companies designated as "special designated nationals," meaning the U.S. Treasury's Office of Foreign Assets Control (OFAC) views them as acting on behalf of Cuban authorities in international trade.[6]

The Cuban Liberty and Democratic Solidarity (Libertad) Act of 1996 (the "Helms-Burton Act")[7] purports to apply to all companies carrying on business in or with Cuba, including Canadian and other non-U.S. companies. It prohibits trade between Cuba and foreign subsidiaries of U.S. corporations and provides civil penalties for violations, including fines and the forfeiture of property. These provisions in the Act are implemented through the CACR.

Title III of the Helms-Burton Act gives U.S. citizens with claims to Cuban property confiscated by the Castro regime the right to sue any person or entity that traffics in confiscated property. Although Title III of the Helms-Burton Act has been suspended by various U.S. presidents ever since it was enacted, the suspension applies only to the right to sue and does not relieve a person of potential future liability. If a future president were not to continue the suspensions, it is possible that persons dealing in confiscated property would be liable retroactively.

Title IV of the Helms-Burton Act directs the U.S. government to deny entry to a non-U.S. citizen (and his or her spouse, minor child, or agent), if the non-U.S. citizen converts or traffics in confiscated property or is an officer or principal or controlling shareholder of an entity that converts or traffics in confiscated property.[8] These sanctions have been applied only very rarely, but since the law remains on the books, it could be used in the future.[9]

---

5.   U.S. Cuban Assets Control Regulations, 31 C.F.R. pt. 515.
6.   John W. Boscariol, *An Anatomy of a Cuban Pyjama Crisis: Reconsidering Blocking Legislation in Response to Extraterritorial Trade Measures of the United States*, 30 Law & Pol'y Int'l Bus. 439, 446 (1999), citing CACR § 305.
7.   Helms-Burton Act, 22 U.S.C. §§ 6021–6091, supp. 3 (1998).
8.   Helms-Burton Act, 22 U.S.C. § 6091.
9.   Notably, these sanctions have been used against a Canadian company and its directors and senior officers, Sherritt International, a mining company with operations in Cuba. The public securities filings of Sherritt International describe in detail the U.S.-Cuba-related sanctions that apply to it. *See, e.g.,* Sherritt Annual Information Form, *available at:* http://www.sherritt.com/getattachment/f8185db3-8a8b-49ac-9e22-c48f8105a5de/2011-Annual-Information-Form. For further discussion on these extraterritorial measures, *see* chapter 1, above, pages 1–30.

(b) Extraterritorial Iran Sanctions

As regards Iran sanctions, in 1996 extraterritorial provisions were enacted in the *Iran and Libya Sanctions Act of 1996 ("ILSA")*,[10] which over the following decade was extended, amended and broadened several times. Initially, ILSA applied to certain investments related to Iran's energy sector as well as to certain investments related to Libya's energy sector and its weapons or aviation capabilities.

In 2006, the *Iran Freedom and Support Act*[11] removed the provisions applicable to Libya, renamed the Act as the *Iran Sanctions Act ("ISA")* and made several adjustments to the remaining provisions. The *Comprehensive Iran Sanctions, Accountability and Divestment Act of 2010 ("CISADA")*[12] significantly expanded the activities sanctionable under the ISA, added new types of penalties and generally increased the minimum number of sanctions to be imposed (from two to three). In August 2012, the *Iran Threat Reduction and Syria Human Rights Act ("Threat Reduction Act")*[13] further expanded the list of activities involving the Iranian energy sector for which non-US persons could be subject to penalties under the ISA.

9.3 CANADA–THE FOREIGN EXTRATERRITORIAL MEASURES ACT

(a) Overview of the FEMA

Canada has implemented blocking legislation specifically aimed at reducing the impact of the U.S. extraterritorial measures. Introduced in 1985, Canada's FEMA was originally designed to blunt the impact of U.S. antitrust legislation. However, it has only ever been used to protect Canadian interests against the U.S.-Cuban embargo laws.[14]

(b) The Principal FEMA Countermeasures

FEMA contains four principal countermeasures against the extraterritorial application of U.S.-Cuban embargo laws.

(i) Restriction of Production of Records to a Foreign Tribunal

The first countermeasure allows Canada's attorney general to order Canadian records and/or information not to be produced or disclosed to a foreign tribunal, as well as prohibit or restrict the giving of evidence by a Canadian citizen or resident in foreign proceedings.[15]

(ii) Blocking the Judgment of Specific Foreign Trade Laws

The second countermeasure empowers the attorney general to maintain a schedule of foreign trade laws deemed contrary to international law or international comity and

---

10.   H.R. 3107, 104th Congress.
11.   H.R. 6198, 109th Cong.
12.   H.R. 2184, 111th Cong.
13.   H.R. 1905, 112th Cong.
14.   Peter Glossop, *Recent US Trade Restrictions Affecting Cuba, Iran and Libya—A View from Outside the US*, 15 Journal of Energy & Natural Resources 212, 227.
15.   FEMA, s. 3.

to block any judgment made pursuant to legislation listed in that schedule.[16] Currently, the only foreign trade law included in the schedule is the Helms-Burton Act. The Canadian government has taken the additional precautionary measure of specifying that no judgment given under the Helms-Burton Act shall be recognized and enforceable in Canada.[17] As such, no additional order is required to block the enforcement of a Helms-Burton Act judgment.

(iii) "Claw-Back" Provisions to Recover Damages

The third countermeasure is a "claw-back" provision that allows a Canadian defendant in foreign proceedings brought under an instrument listed in the FEMA schedule to sue in a Canadian court to recover the judgment sum, expenses, and consequential loss or damage suffered by reason of the enforcement of the foreign judgment.[18]

A defendant also has the right, at any point during a proceeding instituted pursuant to an instrument listed under the FEMA schedule, to sue for the recovery of costs incurred in defending that proceeding even before a final judgment is made.[19] Moreover, where a Canadian court makes an order in favor of the Canadian defendant, the court is authorized, in addition to any other means of enforcing judgment, to order the seizure and sale of any property in which the foreign plaintiff has a direct or indirect beneficial interest, notwithstanding that such property may be located outside Canada.

(iv) Notification Obligations and Noncompliance Orders

The fourth countermeasure is the notification obligations and noncompliance orders. Where a foreign state or tribunal takes measures affecting Canadian interests in international trade or infringing on Canadian sovereignty, the attorney general may issue orders requiring a person in Canada to notify the attorney general of "any directives, instructions, intimations of policy or other communications relating to such measures from a person who is in a position to direct or influence the policies of the person in Canada."[20] In addition, the attorney general may also prohibit any person from complying with any such directive or communication from a person who is in a position to direct or influence the policies of the person in Canada.[21]

(c) The FEMA Order

To specifically address notification and noncompliance obligations in respect of the U.S.-Cuban legislative embargo measures and under its authority granted by FEMA

---

16.   FEMA, ss. 2.1, 8.
17.   FEMA, s. 7.1.
18.   FEMA, s. 9(1)(a).
19.   FEMA, s. 9(1.1).
20.   FEMA, s. 5(1)(a).
21.   Foreign Extraterritorial Measures Act, R.S.C. 1985, c. F-29, s. 5(1)(b).

under section 5, the attorney general issued the Foreign Extraterritorial Measures (United States) Order (1996) (the 1996 FEMA Order).[22]

The 1996 FEMA Order requires every Canadian corporation and every director and officer of a Canadian corporation to "forthwith give notice" to Canada's attorney general of any directive or communication relating to an "extraterritorial measure" of the United States in respect of any trade or commerce between Canada and Cuba received by the Canadian corporation from a person who is in a position to direct or influence the policies of the Canadian corporation in Canada.[23] The term *extraterritorial measure* is very broadly defined, so as to cover the Helms-Burton Act plus any other instruments designed to enforce the U.S. embargo against Cuba.[24]

The 1996 FEMA Order also contains specific obligations prohibiting compliance with an extraterritorial measure of the United States by a Canadian corporation, including its directors, managers, and employees in a position of authority.[25] These noncompliance obligations apply in "respect of any act or omission constituting compliance," irrespective of whether "compliance with the extraterritorial measure or communication is the only purpose of the act or omission."[26]

This broad application of the noncompliance order places corporations with a number of legitimate reasons for not trading with Cuba in a precarious situation.[27] Canadian companies who refuse to trade with Cuba for legitimate business reasons might still be viewed as acting in compliance with the U.S. measure if one of the reasons for the company's act or omission was the existence of a U.S. measure. The actual degree of reliance placed on the existence of the U.S. embargo (as opposed to another legitimate business reason) in the decision-making process seems to be irrelevant, and the existence of legitimate business reasons does not shield the company from criminal prosecution under FEMA.

Though the notification obligation under the 1996 FEMA Order applies only to the Canadian corporation and its directors and officers, the noncompliance obligation also includes managers and employees in a position of authority. Accordingly, managers and employees in positions of authority are not obliged to notify the attorney

---

22.   Order Requiring Persons in Canada to Give Notice of Communications Relating to, and Prohibiting Such Persons from Complying with, an Extraterritorial Measure of the United States That Adversely Affects Trade or Commerce between Canada and Cuba, SOR/96-84.

23.   1996 FEMA Order, SOR/96-84, s. 3(1).

24.   See s. 2 of the 1996 FEMA Order where "extraterritorial measure" is defined as including the CACR and any law, statute, regulation, by-law, ordinance, order, judgment, ruling, resolution, denial of authorization, directive, guideline, or other enactment, instrument, decision, or communication having a purpose similar to that of the CACR, to the extent that they operate or are likely to operate so as to prevent, impede, or reduce trade or commerce between Canada and Cuba.

25.   1996 FEMA Order, s. 5.

26.   1996 FEMA Order, s. 6.

27.   Deborah Senz & Hilary Charlesworth, *Building Blocks: Australia's Response to Foreign Extraterritorial Legislation,* 2 Melb. J. Int'l L. 69, 113 (2001). *Id.* citing Glossop, *supra* note 10, at 232, 237.

general of communications from their superiors, but they are subject to the noncompliance obligation with respect to the content of those communications.[28]

(d) Enforcement of and Penalties under FEMA
(i) Enforcement of FEMA

It is challenging to assess risk under FEMA, as there are very few enforcement statistics under the legislation. No prosecutions under the legislation have been brought in front of the Canadian courts. Investigations by Canadian authorities into allegations of Canadian companies following directives from U.S. parent corporations to cease engaging in business relationships with Cuba are not generally publicized, and their results are not reported.[29] Furthermore, neither Canada's Foreign Affairs and International Trade (DFAIT) nor the Department of Justice (DOJ), which oversee the administration and enforcement of FEMA, have published any policy statements or information bulletins with respect to the application of FEMA.

(ii) Penalties under FEMA

FEMA authorizes the Canadian government to prosecute violations of FEMA orders made under sections 3 and 5 either by indictment or summary conviction. Under indictment, the maximum fines are CAN $1.5 million for a corporation and CAN $150,000 for an individual. An individual may also face up to five years of imprisonment.[30] In the case of a summary conviction, the maximum fines are CAN $150,000 for a corporation and CAN $15,000 for an individual. Moreover, an individual may be liable to imprisonment for a term not exceeding two years.[31] The penalties under section 7 apply irrespective of whether the violation of the notice or noncompliance order occurred in Canada or outside Canada.[32]

In considering the actual sentence to be imposed for an offense contrary to FEMA, a court may take into account a number of factors, including (1) the degree of premeditation in the commission of the offense; (2) the size, scale, and nature of the offender's operations; and (3) whether any economic benefits have, directly or indirectly, accrued to the offender as a result of having committed the offense.[33]

The term *premeditation* relates to the mental element of the offense, such as the planning and deliberation. Although the prosecutor does not have to establish pre-

---

28. John W. Boscariol, *An Anatomy of a Cuban Pyjama Crisis: Reconsidering Blocking Legislation in Response to Extraterritorial Trade Measures of the United States*, 30 Law & Pol'y Int'l Bus. 439, 457 (1999).
29. Such investigations purportedly targeted large conglomerates such as Pepsi, American Express, Heinz, Eli-Lilly, and Red Lobster. John W. Boscariol, *An Anatomy of a Cuban Pyjama Crisis: Reconsidering Blocking Legislation in Response to Extraterritorial Trade Measures of the United States*, 30 Law & Pol'y Int'l Bus. 439, 461 (1999), citing the *Special Session of the Commission on Foreign Affairs*, House of Commons (Sept. 26, 1996) (statement of Professor John Kirk). It is noteworthy that no official enforcement statistics exist with respect to investigations launched after 1996.
30. FEMA, s. 7(1)(a).
31. FEMA, s. 7(1)(b).
32. FEMA, s. 7(2).
33. FEMA, s. 7(4).

meditation to obtain a conviction, the court is directed to impose a higher penalty if premeditation can be established.[34]

Although FEMA does not clarify the "size, scale, and nature of the offender's operations" criterion, there is a strong chance that companies with relatively large-scale dealings or operations in Cuba will be subjected to more severe penalties than those companies whose operations are on a smaller scale. This is predicated on the view that the larger the size and scale of the Canadian offender's operations, the greater the profile and impact of its conduct on public awareness, and correspondingly the greater the effect the U.S. extraterritorial measures would have had in violating Canadian sovereignty.[35]

It is unclear how the courts might quantify the economic benefit obtained by the offender in complying with the U.S. extraterritorial measure. Ostensibly, the larger the net economic benefit accruing to a company by virtue of compliance with the U.S. measure, the larger the sentence and fine to be imposed on the offender;[36] however, it is difficult to imagine a scenario where compliance with U.S. sanctions would generate a measurable net benefit. Rather, compliance with U.S. sanctions is more likely to lead to lost business opportunities, rather than to any revenue-generating transactions.

(e) The Interaction of FEMA and the Extraterritorial Measures
(i) The Conflict between FEMA and the Extraterritorial Measures

Although independent Canadian-owned businesses are unlikely to be caught by the overlap between the application of FEMA and the U.S. extraterritorial trade restrictions with respect to the CACR, Canadian entities with U.S. affiliates are at risk of being in scenarios that expose them to liability under either the U.S. trade embargo regime or the Canadian measures.

In the event a Canadian subsidiary places the U.S. parent in breach of the Cuba embargo regulations, the U.S. parent is likely to issue a communication or directive to the Canadian subsidiary to halt all business activities pertaining to Cuba. Pursuant to the 1996 FEMA Order, the existence and content of such communications would have to be reported to Canada's attorney general, and the Canadian subsidiary would be obliged not to comply with such a directive. Where the Canadian subsidiary elects not to comply with the directive, the U.S. parent will be subjected to the sanctions applicable under the U.S. regime.

Walmart Canada (a wholly owned subsidiary of the U.S. corporation) faced this dilemma when, after it became aware that some of the pajamas being sold in its Canadian stores were manufactured in Cuba, it took the merchandise off its shelves to

---

34. Andrew C. Dekany, *Canada's Foreign Extraterritorial Measures Act: Using Canadian Criminal Sanctions to Block U.S. Anti-Cuban Legislation*, 28 Can. Bus. L.J. 210, 213 (1997).
35. *Id.* at 214.
36. *See id.* at 214–215.

avoid legal action against its U.S. parent. DFAIT referred the matter for investigation by the Canadian DOJ. However, two weeks after pulling the merchandise off the shelf, Walmart Canada recommenced distributing the pajamas in its Canadian stores after concluding, following legal consultation, that it did not contravene U.S. law because the pajamas were purchased from a Canadian distributor.[37] Though OFAC announced that it was launching an investigation into this matter and that it was intent on enforcing the Cuban embargo, no criminal prosecution materialized initially.[38] Later, OFAC levied a $50,000 fine against Walmart Canada. After consultations with government lawyers, Walmart paid the fine voluntarily without any determination that a violation had been committed.[39]

(ii) FEMA and Helms-Burton

Companies and individuals may also face challenges in relation to the application of the Helms-Burton Act to any Canadian individual and company trafficking in confiscated property. When Sherritt, Inc., the largest Canadian private investor, refused to divest itself of Cuban property after receiving exclusion notices related to Title IV of Helms-Burton, a ban from entering the United States was enacted on nine of its executives.[40] Since then, as Sherritt continued its expansions into Cuba, the ban was expanded to include some of Sherritt's new officers.[41] Apart from the Sherritt case, however, the U.S. government has rarely even threatened to apply the entry ban, thereby leaving it as a real, but low, risk for non-U.S. companies doing business in Cuba.[42]

In contrast to Title IV (the entry ban), Title III of Helms-Burton (allowing companies to be sued for trafficking in expropriated property) has been suspended. Should a future president determine not to continue this suspension, however, Canadian entities carrying on business in Cuba (especially where such entities have U.S. assets) may face substantial risk. Such entities will have to consider whether to cease dealing in confiscated property and face sanctions under FEMA, or open themselves to civil lawsuits.

(iii) Complying with Export Administration Regulations

Compliance with licensing regulations under the Export Administration Regulations (EAR)[43] may also attract liability under FEMA. The EAR are administered by the

---

37. Neil Campbell & Edward Akkawi, Canada and U.S. "Cuba" Laws: The Risks of Getting Caught in the Crossfire (Mar. 10, 1998) (unpublished paper presented to the AIJA Winter Seminar on Extraterritorial Application of U.S. Laws, Vail, Colorado) at 5.

38. John W. Boscariol, *An Anatomy of a Cuban Pyjama Crisis: Reconsidering Blocking Legislation in Response to Extraterritorial Trade Measures of the United States*, 30 Law & Pol'y Int'l Bus. 439, 463 (1999). For more discussion on this event, *see* David E. Sanger, *Wal-Mart Canada Is Putting Cuban Pajamas Back on Shelf*, N.Y. Times, Mar. 14, 1997, at D4.

39. *U.S. Fines Sanctions-Busting Firms*, BBC News (Apr. 15, 2003), http://news.bbc.co.uk/2/hi/business /2948553.stm; Philippe Cicchini, *U.S.-Cuban Relations and the Helms-Burton Act*, 18:1 Mich. Int'l Law. 14, 19 (2006).

40. Shoshana Perl, *Whither Helms-Burton: A Retrospective on the 10th Year Anniversary*, 6 Jean Monnet/ Robert Schuman Paper Series, 8 (Feb. 2006).

41. *Id.* at 11.

42. *Id.* at 8, lists three examples where the ban was threatened (STET, Grupo Domos) or applied (Sherritt).

43. Export Administration Regulations, 15 C.F.R. ch. VII § 742.1.

U.S. Department of Commerce's Bureau of Export Administration and regulate the export and reexport from third countries of goods originating from the United States through licensing requirements, such as where the goods are U.S. origin, where the goods are foreign origin but the U.S. content exceeds 10 percent of the total value of the goods exported, and where the goods are foreign origin but are the direct product of certain U.S. technology.[44] In fact, the EAR require a license for the export to Cuba even of goods subject to the EAR that are *not* on the Commerce list—that is, EAR99 goods—in all but a very few circumstances where license exceptions are available.

Canada's export licensing authority, the Export Controls Division (ECD) of DFAIT, acknowledges to a limited extent the application of U.S. regulations to the reexport of U.S.-origin products to Cuba by requiring Canadian exporters of U.S.-origin items to apply for an export permit to Cuba.[45] However, no export permit is required where U.S.-origin goods have undergone transformation resulting in a substantial change in value.[46]

Canada's DFAIT has taken the view that, to the extent the EAR hinder trade relations between Canada and Cuba, they are an extraterritorial measure that falls under the scope of FEMA.[47] As such, compliance with the licensing permit requirements may place a Canadian company in contravention of FEMA. The mere act of complying with an American regulation that imposes obligations on Canadian entities with no direct connection to the United States is a violation of Canadian sovereignty and may be targeted for sanction under FEMA.

Where U.S.-origin content exceeds the substantial transformation threshold, a Canadian company will need to apply for a permit to export the goods to Cuba. Only where the permit is denied by Canadian authorities can the Canadian company safely refuse to export such goods to Cuba.[48]

The reality, however, is that there are instances where Canadian export authorities actually *do* grant permits for Canadian companies to export U.S.-origin goods to Cuba, thereby placing Canadian companies in violation of their obligations under the

---

44.   Export Administration Regulations, 15 C.F.R. ch. VII § 746.2(a).

45.   Section 5400 of the Export Control List requires a permit for the export from Canada of "all goods that originate in the United States...other than goods that have been further processed or manufactured outside the United States so as to result in a substantial change in value, form or use of the goods or in the production of new goods." Whereas under general Export Permit No. 12, Canada generally permits the reexport of U.S.-origin goods, reexports to certain countries such as Cuba, North Korea, Iran, and Burma (Myanmar) require a permit.

46.   In the past, it was generally understood that exporters could make this determination simply on the basis of whether the U.S. content exceeded 50% of the value of the item to be transferred. Recent experience shows that a simple value calculation is not sufficient and that U.S. value content is not the only factor to be considered. Exporters should also be carefully considering whether U.S. inputs have gone through a sufficient transformation in form or use when incorporated into the new item to be exported from Canada permit-free, even if the U.S. content is below 50%.

47.   John W. Boscariol, *An Anatomy of a Cuban Pyjama Crisis: Reconsidering Blocking Legislation in Response to Extraterritorial Trade Measures of the United States*, 30 Law & Pol'y Int'l Bus. 439, 458 (1999).

48.   *Id.* at 459 (citing an interview with an unnamed Department of Foreign Affairs and International Trade (DFAIT) official (June 30, 1998)).

EAR, a set of regulations that was not the target of the 1996 FEMA Order. Although there exists no formal government of Canada policy on the matter, it appears from experience that permits to export U.S.-origin goods to Cuba may be granted (even where no U.S. reexport authorization is granted) in the following circumstances:

- if the goods are "replacement parts" for non-U.S.-origin items;
- if the goods relate to a previously lawfully exported good of Canadian origin;
- if the goods are part of a turnkey operation (i.e., if a Cuban hotel is ordering a complete kitchen and it contains an appliance made in the United States, on the grounds that the "majority" of the shipment is not U.S. made); and
- if there is a humanitarian reason for the export.[49]

(iv) Consideration of FEMA in the U.S. Courts

Whereas FEMA has received no judicial consideration in Canada, a U.S. decision has discussed the application of FEMA in the context of the obligations imposed on foreign corporations by the Trading with the Enemy Act of 1917 (TWEA)[50] and the CACR.

In *United States of America v. Brodie,*[51] the Pennsylvania district court convicted James Sabzali, a Canadian citizen, on twenty-one counts of conspiracy to violate the TWEA and the CACR.[52] From 1992 through 1996, Sabzali worked as a sales representative in Canada selling U.S.-made water purification supplies to Cuba. He operated out of the Hamilton office of Purolite Canada, the Canadian subsidiary to Bro-Tech (a U.S. chemical company). During that time, he made more than twenty trips from Canada to Cuba on behalf of U.S. and Canadian chemical companies.[53]

The *Brodie* case is significant in a Canadian context for two reasons: (1) it is the first time that a Canadian citizen was convicted for violating the CACR, and (2) it clarifies the U.S. position with respect to the availability of the defense of foreign sovereign compulsion in relation to liability under the U.S.-Cuba trade embargo regulations.

In *Brodie,* the court rejected the argument that a blocking statute such as FEMA could form the basis of a foreign sovereign compulsion defense. The court read FEMA

---

49.   For a more detailed review of the application of U.S. reexport controls in Canada, see chapters 1 and 8.

50.   50 U.S.C. apps. 1–44 (1994 & Supp. III 1998).

51.   United States of America v. Stefan E. Brodie, Donald B. Brodie, James E. Sabzali, Bro-Tech Corporation d/b/a "The Purolite Company," 2001 U.S. Dist. LEXIS 10533 (E.D. Pa. June 19, 2001) (*Brodie* main decision).

52.   It is noteworthy that only thirteen of these twenty-one convictions stemmed from activities that occurred while Sabzali was a resident of the U.S. The other eight convictions pertained to Sabzali's dealings with Cuba while he was a Canadian resident. *See* John Boscariol, *Exposure of Canadians under the U.S. Trade Embargo of Cuba: The Case of James E. Sabzali,* 37 Can. Bus. L.J. 419, 424 (2002).

53.   Sabzali was promoted to marketing director of Bro-Tech and in 1996 moved with his family to Philadelphia. Although he did not travel to Cuba after becoming a U.S. resident, Sabzali continued to be involved in Bro-Tech's sales to Cuba, which were made through the company's foreign subsidiaries.

as prohibiting persons from "not trading with Cuba" if the decision to do so was exclusively because of the CACR. For the defendant to mount a successful foreign sovereign compulsion defense, it would have to prove that its motivation for trading with Cuba was based on fear of prosecution under Canadian law and that it could not have legally refused to accede to the Canadian government's wishes.

Though this view is consistent with previous U.S. court decisions denying a conflict where it is possible to comply with both foreign and U.S. law,[54] it appears to be at odds with the broad scope of the noncompliance obligation imposed by the 1996 FEMA Order that provides that, as long as U.S. law is one of the reasons for ceasing to engage in business with or in Cuba, a Canadian company is in breach of this obligation.

Sabzali was also unable to establish that compliance with the Canadian laws was basic and fundamental to the alleged behavior because the alleged offenses to which FEMA may have applied occurred prior to the introduction of the 1996 FEMA Order. Prior to the time, the noncompliance obligation was only imposed on corporations and did not include directors, officers, managers, and employees in positions of authority as under the 1996 FEMA Order.

While *Brodie* gave cross-border companies a better understanding of the interaction between FEMA and the U.S. anti-Cuba measures, the Pennsylvania district court later overturned the guilty verdict citing grievous prosecutorial misconduct.[55] Though a new trial was ordered for Sabzali, a plea bargain was reached before the new trial took place.[56] As a result, the state of the law remains unclear. Furthermore, even if *Brodie* had not been overturned, it could be argued that, due to the coming into force of the 1996 FEMA Order, the *Brodie* case is distinguishable from any new case dealing with post-1996 acts.[57]

---

54.   *See* Timberlane Lumber Co. v. Bank of America, 549 F.2d 597 (9th Cir. 1977), and Hartford Fire Ins., 509 U.S. 764 (1993).

55.   United States v. Brodie, 268 F. Supp. 2d 420, 423–424 (E.D. Pa. 2003) (*Brodie* 2002 motion).

56.   Sabzali pleaded guilty to a superceding information charging a violation of 18 U.S.C. § 2 (aiding and abetting) and § 545 (smuggling goods into the U.S.) and was sentenced to one year probation and fined $10,000.

57.   A final point of interest is that the goods being shipped by Sabzali to Cuba were of U.S. origin. As discussed above, under section 5400 of the Canadian Export Control List, it is illegal to export U.S.-origin goods from Canada without first applying for and obtaining an export permit. It is generally understood that such export permits are granted only if an applicant provides evidence to the Canadian authorities that permission has been obtained from U.S. authorities to export U.S.-origin goods, although, as explained above beginning 190, in practice we have seen otherwise. A breach of these rules could lead to fines of up to $25,000 and/or imprisonment for a term of up to ten years. In Sabzali's case, it is unclear whether an application for an export permit was ever made or whether a permit was ever issued by the Export Control Division of DFAIT; however, no charges have ever been brought by Canadian authorities against Sabzali for an alleged breach of these export regulations. For a more detailed discussion, *see* John Boscariol, *Exposure of Canadians under the U.S. Trade Embargo of Cuba: The Case of James E. Sabzali*, 37 Can. Bus. L.J. 419, 433–434 (2002).

(f)   Shielding Companies from Liability

There are a variety of measures and practices that, depending on the circumstances, may help cross-border companies manage risk sensibly. Canadian experts have suggested the following best practices to help avoid a conflict between the application of the 1996 FEMA Order and the CACR:

(1)   Brief the U.S. parent corporation managers about the Canadian legal implications of foreign directives before they are sent.

(2)   Maintain Canadian-specific export control manuals, policies, and training programs at the Canadian subsidiary's registered office.

(3)   Employ careful wording of all written and verbal communications from persons in authority at U.S. parent corporations to ensure that they cannot be characterized as foreign directives.

(4)   Limit or eliminate embargo communications between U.S. parents and Canadian subsidiaries.

(5)   Where appropriate given the nature of the communications, have all relevant communications from U.S. parent corporations sent through lawyers to shield them with solicitor-client privilege.

(6)   When withdrawing from Cuba or declining to pursue a trade or investment opportunity in Cuba for legitimate business reasons, ensure that those reasons are well documented.

(7)   Employ various corporate restructuring methods to spin off Cuban investments into separate entities.

(8)   Review for FEMA exposure any intercompany agreements and the Canadian subsidiary's contracts, purchase orders, etc., with unrelated parties.

(9)   Consider whether any provincial business practices legislation is applicable.[58]

With respect to potential liability under the Helms-Burton Act, the advice is much simpler. Before investing in Cuban property, it is essential to carefully investigate whether such Cuban property may be potentially confiscated property under Title III.[59]

(i) Actions to Take Following a Potential Contravention

If a Canadian company is caught in the crossfire of conflicting obligations under FEMA and a U.S. extraterritorial measure, the first step is to ascertain whether the U.S. measure falls within the ambit of the 1996 FEMA Order. If so, the company

---

58.   *See* John W. Boscariol, Managing Conflicting Obligations: Compliance with Canadian Law and Policy on Trade with U.S.-Sanctioned Countries (May 15–17 2007) (unpublished presentation to the American Conference Institute's 10th National Forum on Export Controls and Global Compliance Strategies), at 30–31; Campbell & Akkawi, at 6.

59.   *Id.* at 30–31.

needs to determine whether the measure operates to reduce or impede trade or commerce between Canada and Cuba.[60] It is also essential to establish whether the Canadian subsidiary is in fact a "Canadian corporation" under the 1996 FEMA Order.[61]

With respect to communications between U.S. parents and Canadian subsidiaries, the Canadian subsidiary should determine (1) whether the communication is in the nature of a "directive" or "intimation of policy" and (2) whether the source of the communication is in "a position to direct or influence the policies of the Canadian corporation in Canada."

As for the noncompliance obligation, the next step is to establish whether the Canadian company's act or omission constitutes "compliance" under the 1996 FEMA Order. This analysis involves establishing the principal reason for the Canadian company's act or omission. Is the act or omission carried out to comply with Canadian law, or are there other business reasons?[62]

Last but not least, if goods are to be supplied to Cuba, the Canadian company needs to ascertain the U.S.-origin content of the merchandise to determine whether such goods have been sufficiently transformed outside the United States.

9.4 EUROPEAN UNION: THE EU BLOCKING REGULATION

(a) Overview

In 1996, the EU held the view that the extraterritorial aspects of the above-mentioned U.S. sanctions laws infringed public international law.[63] Therefore, as a reaction, the EU passed two legal acts: the EU Blocking Regulation, and Common Action 96/668/CFSP of the Council of the European Union.

(b) Rationale of the EU Blocking Regulation

The rationale of the EU Blocking Regulation, as outlined in its preamble, aligns with the objectives of the EU, including "contributing to the harmonious development of free trade and to the progressive abolition of restrictions on international trade" and "the objective of free movement of capital between Member States and third countries." In the European Council's view, these objectives are impeded by the extraterritorial application of laws, regulations, and other legislative instruments enacted by third countries that purport to regulate the activities of natural and legal persons under the jurisdiction of EU member states.[64]

---

60. *Id.* at 19–20.
61. *Id.*
62. *Id.*
63. For a detailed discussion of the EU view on the extraterritoriality of the U.S. measures, including the public international law aspects, *see* Werner Meng, *Wirtschaftssanktionen und staatliche Jurisdiktion – Grauzonen im Völkerrecht*, Zeitschrift für ausländisches öffentliches Recht und Völkerrecht 1997, 270–327.
64. *See* paras. 4 to 7 of the preamble of the EU Blocking Regulation.

Although the EU Blocking Regulation was a direct reaction to specific U.S. sanctions laws, it was designed in a manner that allows its application to any other laws with extraterritorial effects once added to the annex of the EU Blocking Regulation.

(c) Scope of Application

The scope of application of the EU Blocking Regulation mirrors the principles of territorial and personal jurisdiction recognized under international law.[65] Pursuant to Article 11, the EU Blocking Regulation applies to:

- any natural person who is resident in the EU *and* is a national of a member state;
- any legal person incorporated within the EU;
- any natural or legal person referred to in Article 1(2) of Regulation (EEC) 4055/86(5);
- any other natural person who is resident in the EU, unless that person is in the country of which he or she is a national; and
- any other natural person within EU territory acting in a professional capacity.

The EU Blocking Regulation only applies when such persons are engaged in international trade and/or the movement of capital and related commercial activities between the EU and third countries.[66]

The material scope of the EU Blocking Regulation is set forth in Article 1. According to this provision, the EU Blocking Regulation applies only to the extraterritorial application of the laws specified in its annex, including regulations and other legislative instruments and of actions based thereon or resulting therefrom. The following statutes and regulations are listed in the annex:

- the National Defense Authorization Act for the Fiscal Year 1993, Title XVII Cuban Democracy Act 1992, sections 1704 and 1706;
- the Cuban Liberty and Democratic Solidarity Act of 1996;
- the Iran and Libya Sanctions Act of 1996; and
- 31 C.F.R. ch. V (7-1-95 edition) pt. 515 – Cuban Assets Control Regulations, subparts B (Prohibitions), E (Licenses, Authorizations, and Statements of Licensing Policy), and G (Penalties).

The European Commission can add or delete, where it deems appropriate, references to regulations or other legislative instruments deriving from the laws speci-

---

65.   Meng, *supra* note 59, at 315.
66.   Article 1, para. 1 of the EU Blocking Regulation; *see* August Reinisch, *Blockiermaßnahmen der EU gegen extraterritoriale Rechtsakte*, Ecolex 900, 901–902 (1997).

fied in the annex.[67] However, the annex to the EU Blocking Regulation has not been amended since it was first enacted in 1996, while U.S. sanctions relating to Iran have undergone frequent revision. This leads to legal uncertainty, discussed below, as to whether the EU Blocking Regulation automatically takes into account changes in foreign laws, such as the amendments to the Iran and Libya Sanctions Act.[68]

(d) The Principal Countermeasures

The EU Blocking Regulation contains four principal countermeasures against the extraterritorial application of the listed U.S. sanctions laws.

(i) Obligation to Inform the Commission

According to Article 2 of the EU Blocking Regulation, EU persons and companies are obliged to inform the European Commission within thirty days if their economic and/or financial interests are affected, directly or indirectly, by the listed U.S. sanctions laws. Insofar as the interests of a legal person are affected, the obligation applies to its directors, managers, and other persons with management responsibilities.[69] The information can also be submitted to the European Commission through the competent authorities of a member state.[70]

(ii) Prohibition of Enforcement and Recognition

Article 4 of the EU Blocking Regulation stipulates that no judgment of a court or tribunal or decision of an administrative authority located outside the EU giving effect directly or indirectly to the listed U.S. sanctions laws shall be recognized or be enforceable in any manner. With this provision, the EU and its member states insist on their territorial sovereignty.[71] The broad language of the provision explicitly includes decisions of administrative authorities, such as administrative sanctions available under the ILSA.[72]

(iii) Prohibition of Compliance

Whereas Article 4 aims at blocking the enforcement of decisions that have already been taken by the relevant authorities outside the EU, Article 5 of the EU Blocking Regulation is directed at persons subject to both the regulation and U.S. sanctions laws. It expressly prohibits affected persons from complying directly or through a subsidiary or other intermediary persons with any requirement or prohibition based on or resulting from the listed laws. The European Commission may authorize

---

67. Article 7, lit. c of the EU Blocking Regulation.
68. For a detailed discussion, see below at 9.4. (f).
69. Article 2, para. 1, sentence 2 of the EU Blocking Regulation.
70. Article 2, para. 3 of the EU Blocking Regulation.
71. Christoph Vedder & Stefan Lorenzmeier, *Das Recht der Europäischen Union*, 35th edition, Art. 133 EGV, para. 248 (Eberhard Grabitz & Meinhard Hilf eds., 2008).
72. Joachim Kayser, Gegenmaßnahmen im Außenwirtschaftsrecht und das System des Europäischen Kollisionsrechts 124 (2000); Jürgen Huber, *The Helms Burton Blocking Statute of the European Union*, 20 Fordham Int'l L.J. 699, 704 (1996).

exceptions to the extent that noncompliance would seriously damage their interests or those of the EU.[73] With this provision, the EU imposes a legal obligation on the protected persons, which is diametrically opposed to the listed U.S. sanctions laws. It *prohibits what is prescribed* by the listed U.S. laws and *prescribes what is prohibited* by the listed U.S. laws. Thereby it intends to allow for the invocation of the foreign state compulsion doctrine[74] before U.S. courts.[75]

(iv) "Claw-Back" Clause

Finally, Article 6 of the EU Blocking Regulation, the so-called "cornerstone"[76] and "core piece"[77] of the EU Blocking Regulation, goes a step further and provides for a claw-back of damages. According to Article 6 of the EU Blocking Regulation, persons affected by the listed U.S. sanctions laws shall be entitled to recover any damages, including legal costs, caused by the application of the listed laws or actions based thereon. The recovery may be obtained from the person that caused the damages.[78]

This provision aims at a complete neutralization of the effects of the U.S. sanctions imposed by Title III of the Helms-Burton Act by creating a tort claim that is based on the U.S. administrative and judicial decisions as the event constituting the claim.[79] (For the content of Title III of the Helms-Burton Act, see chapter 9.2, section [a]). It is more extensive than typical claw-back clauses, as it is not only directed against judgments, but designed as a general damage claim that encompasses punitive damages, and compensatory damages, including ancillary claims and legal costs. Thus, the claimant may retrieve anything that was lost in previous U.S. proceedings.[80]

In order to facilitate the enforcement of the damages claims, Article 6 even allows for initiating judicial proceedings in the courts of any member state where the person causing damages holds assets.[81] Finally, Article 6, para. 4 of the EU Blocking Regulation highlights how extensively the provision is drawn. In order to give greater effect

---

73. Article 5, para. 2 of the EU Blocking Regulation.

74. *See* Restatement (Third) of the Foreign Relations Law of the United States (1987), § 441 (1): "In general, a state may not require a person (a) to do an act in another state that is prohibited by the law of that state or by the act in another state of which he is a national; or (b) to refrain from doing an act in another state that is required by the law of that state or by the law of the state of which he is a national."

75. Martin Gebauer, *Kollisionsrechtliche Auswirkungen der U.S.-amerikanischen Helms-Burton Gesetzgebung*, IPrax 145, 153 (1998); Meng, *supra* note 59, at 315–316; Vedder & Lorenzmeier, *supra* note 67; Reinisch doubts whether the foreign state compulsion doctrine may indeed be invoked, *see* Reinisch, *supra* note 62, at 902–903.

76. Huber, *supra* note 68, at 705.

77. Werner Meng, *Extraterritoriale Jurisdiktion in der U.S.-amerikanischen Sanktionsgesetzgebung*, EuZW 423, 425 (1997).

78. Article 6, para. 2 of the EU Blocking Regulation.

79. Meng, *supra* note 59, at 315–316; Reinisch, *supra* note 62, at 903; Gebauer, *supra* note 71, at 154.

80. Kayser, *supra* note 68, at 126.

81. Article 6, para. 3 of the EU Blocking Regulation. This additional basis for jurisdiction exceeds the jurisdiction allowed for by the Brussels Convention of Sept. 27, 1968 on jurisdiction and the enforcement of judgments in civil and commercial matters, *see* Jacques H.J. Bourgois, in Hans von der Groeben/Jürgen Schwarze, "Kommentar zum EU-/EG-Vertrag, (2003), 6th edition, Art. 133 para. 146; Kayser, *supra* note 68, at 127; Huber *supra* note 68, at 706.

to the claw-back, the recovery can take the form of seizure and sale of assets held by the persons and entities causing the damages and persons acting on their behalf or intermediaries in the EU, including shares held by a legal person incorporated within the EU.

(e) Penalties and Enforcement

Since provisions relating to criminal and administrative penalties can only be adopted by the member states of the EU, the penalties available in the event of a breach of an obligation under the EU Blocking Regulation depend on the national legislation of the respective member state. Whereas, for example, Austrian law also explicitly provides for a penalty for the breach of the obligation to inform the European Commission as stipulated in Article 2 of the EU Blocking Regulation,[82] the German statutory law only provides a penalty for the breach of Article 5. In Germany, the infringement of Article 5 is punishable by a fine of up to 500,000 euro.[83]

Because publicly available information is limited, it is difficult to assess the actual enforcement of the EU Blocking Regulation. So far there has not been any reported judicial decisions in criminal matters. However, member states have proven themselves willing to take action and pursue investigations of EU-based companies complying with U.S. sanctions laws. The following cases have been discussed in publicly available sources.

In the most high-profile case, the Austrian government initiated a legal enforcement procedure against one of its largest banks, BAWAG P.S.K., which in 2007 had reportedly closed accounts held by around a hundred Cuban clients in order to comply with U.S. laws and thereby not to put at risk the expected takeover by an American private equity firm. When BAWAG applied for and was apparently granted a specific license from OFAC to reinstate the accounts of the Cuban nationals, the Austrian government dropped the charges against BAWAG.[84]

More recently, in the UK in 2010, Lloyds TSB reportedly refused to cash checks that were issued by Cuba-based banks. According to press reports, Lloyds modified its practice after the UK government's Department for Business, Innovation & Skills became informally involved.[85]

In 2011, a German online seller initiated civil proceedings before a German civil court after the Internet payment company PayPal closed his account, reportedly

---

82. Bundesgesetzblatt zur Festlegung von Sanktionen bei Zuwiderhandlungen gegen die Verordnung (EG) Nr. 2271/96.

83. §§ 19, para. 4, sentence 1, no. 1 and para. 6, sentence 1 German Foreign Trade and Payments Act (AWG as amended on Jan. 31, 2013, and in force summer 2013), 70 para. 5 lit. f German Regulation Implementing the Foreign Trade and Payments Act Foreign (AWV).

84. „Plassnik: Strafverfahren gegen BAWAG eingeleitet", Krone, 27 April 2007.

85. Roland Gribben, *Banks Action on Cuban Sanctions Hits UK Companies*, The Telegraph, Oct. 18, 2010; Roland Gribben, *UK Banks Warm to Cuba but Are Wary of U.S. Reproach*, The Telegraph, Nov. 8, 2010.

because the German online seller had been selling Cuban rum among other products. However, the court did not render a judgment as the parties reportedly reached a settlement under which PayPal reopened the account of the seller, who in turn refrained from using PayPal with respect to payments for Cuban goods.[86]

(f)   The Blocking Regulation, CISADA and the Threat Reduction Act

After global political pressure on Iran increased in 2010, the United States passed the Comprehensive Iran Sanctions, Accountability, and Divestment Act (CISADA) and the Threat Reduction Act, each of which significantly expanded the ISA and other U.S. sanctions measures targeting Iran. Because the annex to the EU Blocking Regulation has not been amended since its enactment in 1996, it does not specifically refer to CISADA or the Threat Reduction Act. Therefore, it is unclear whether CISADA and the Threat Reduction Act are encompassed by the EU Blocking Regulation. The principal issue is whether the references in the annex to the EU Blocking Regulation are static and thus relate only to the version of the legislation at the time of the drafting, or whether the references need to be interpreted as dynamic and thus automatically take into account amendments.

This question has not yet been answered by the European authorities. However, the wording of Articles 1, 2, 4, 5, and 7 of the EU Blocking Regulation suggests that the annex is static because the Articles refer only to the specific legal texts in the annex. Although the object and purpose of the EU Blocking Regulation—to counter the extraterritorial effects of foreign legislation—might argue for another conclusion, it appears unlikely that the drafters intended to make the annex dynamic. Being fully aware that sanction laws are subject to periodical renewals and often adapted to political changes, the drafters could have easily added a clause to the effect that the Blocking Regulation applies to the latest version of each listed law. However, instead, they included the comitology procedures as stipulated in Article 8 of the EU Blocking Regulation, which sets forth a simplified (less formal) procedure to add or delete references to regulations or other legislative instruments deriving from the laws specified in the annex and falling within the scope of the EU blocking Regulation. Thus, the EU Blocking Regulation provides for an instrument to react to changes and, in particular, extensions of the extraterritorially applicable legislation. Against this background, there are very good grounds to argue that the references in the annex are not to be interpreted as dynamic.

Any other interpretation would set the European principle of sufficient clarity at risk—especially in light of the possible criminal and administrative consequences for persons subject to the EU Blocking Regulation. If the annex were dynamic in its scope, persons subject to the EU Blocking Regulation would not be certain whether

---

86.   *See Ebay setzt Kuba-Embargo auch in Deutschland durch*, Welt Online, July 28, 2011; *Vergleich im Kuba-Streit mit PayPal erzielt*, n-tv, Nov. 1, 2011.

the regulation protects them if they do not comply with U.S. sanctions against Iran not expressly listed in the annex. They would therefore face a situation in which they might not comply with current U.S. law because of the provisions in the EU Blocking Regulation, but may at the same time not be protected by the EU Blocking Regulation. Therefore, it seems clear that if the EU legislator wants to protect EU persons from the extraterritorial effects of the newer U.S. sanctions laws, it needs to amend the EU Blocking Regulation by either including the latest versions of the respective laws or by clarifying that the annex is dynamic.

$$\textbf{10}$$

Export Compliance in the M&A Context

Meredith Rathbone and Amy J. Lentz

10.1 INTRODUCTION

Acquiring or merging with another company can present extraordinary business opportunities, but M&A activity also can present significant risks to the acquirer or surviving company. Among those risks are potentially severe penalties for non-compliance with export controls and economic sanctions laws and regulations. Assessing and addressing international regulatory compliance risks in an M&A context requires an upfront investment of time and resources, but can pay dividends by allowing the acquiring/merging companies to take proactive steps to minimize the likelihood of an undesirable – and potentially costly – outcome. This chapter is intended to provide the reader with an overview of the various actions that should take place in the export controls/sanctions context when a company is seeking to acquire or merge with another company.

If one is acquiring or merging with a company engaged in international business transactions, or with a company that utilizes or manufactures sensitive goods or technology, it is wise to conduct careful and targeted due diligence regarding international trade compliance. Discovering a potential problem before a deal closes gives a company the opportunity to decide whether and under what terms the deal should move forward. In addition, regardless of whether significant regulatory concerns arise during the due diligence process, there may be a requirement for companies engaged in certain types of manufacturing or exporting to provide notification to the U.S. Government prior to closing a transaction, and to seek novation or transfer of relevant licenses and other authorizations. In some cases it is wise to seek prior approval from the U.S. Government through the CFIUS process, particularly when a non-U.S. company intends to acquire a U.S. company involved in the design, manufacture, or export of sensitive goods or technology, or when the target is otherwise in an industry that affects U.S. national security.

Finally, companies involved in M&A activity should take steps to ensure that they establish consistent and integrated international regulatory compliance programs, processes and procedures throughout the corporate family. Companies often experience growing pains throughout this process, which requires a dedicated effort on the part of compliance personnel, managers, and others. The failure of a newly-acquired company to adhere to corporate procedures can increase the likelihood of infractions and enforcement actions. Moreover, activity undertaken by a newly-acquired company that is inconsistent with existing corporate policies and procedures potentially could be viewed by enforcement authorities as an "aggravating factor" in an enforcement action.

In short, companies that take proactive steps to address export controls and sanctions compliance issues early on in a potential transaction typically fare better than those who ignore such issues. Early identification of significant concerns that may threaten or delay the deal allows the parties to take mitigating steps, including implementing corrective actions, filing disclosures, and seeking any necessary government approval, giving both parties an increased comfort level with the transaction.

10.2 ENFORCEMENT

(a) Overview

Over the course of the past decade, it has become abundantly clear that the Department of Commerce's Bureau of Industry and Security (BIS), the Department of State's Directorate of Defense Trade Controls (DDTC), and the Treasury Department's Office of Foreign Assets Control (OFAC) are willing to hold an acquiring company liable for a target company's export controls and sanctions violations, even when those violations occurred prior to the transaction and wholly without the acquiring company's knowledge or involvement. Accordingly, the importance of determining whether the target company is in compliance with export controls and sanctions laws and regulations cannot be overstated.

As discussed in more detail in the next section, the acquiring company should engage in careful due diligence early on, and require that the target company address any export controls and sanctions issues prior to closing. Companies may be able to negotiate indemnity provisions that reduce the potential financial exposure to the acquiring company due to unknown or unquantifiable export controls and sanctions risks of the target company. However, such provisions would not shield the acquiring company from other non-monetary penalties – *e.g.*, requiring the acquiring company to retain a compliance monitor, subjecting the acquiring company to a policy of license denial, or denying the acquiring company export privileges altogether.

(b) Department of Commerce

The case that serves as the foundation for the broad imposition of successor liability by BIS is *Sigma-Aldrich*.[1] In April 1997, three Sigma-Aldrich entities acquired certain assets of, and partnership shares in, Research Biochemicals Limited Partnership (RBLP).[2] Specifically, Sigma-Aldrich Research Biochemicals, Inc. acquired RBLP's

---

1. Order Denying Respondents' Motion for Summary Judgment, August 29, 2002, *available at* http://www.bis.doc.gov/enforcement/casesummaries/sigma_aldrich_alj_decision_02.html.
2. *Id.*

assets, property, and liabilities, while two other Sigma-Aldrich entities acquired RBLP's partnership interests.[3] BIS alleged that RBLP had been making unauthorized exports of controlled biological toxins to Europe and Asia since 1995 (prior to the acquisition by Sigma-Aldrich), and that these unlicensed exports had continued for more than a year after the acquisition.[4] In other words, Sigma-Aldrich failed to discover the prior unlicensed exports during its pre-acquisition due diligence review, and then failed to correct the export violations for a year following the completion of the acquisition. Thus, BIS sought to impose liability against Sigma-Aldrich, both as a successor for violations occurring prior to the acquisition, and as the actual wrongdoer for violations that occurred after the transfer.[5] Although only one of the Sigma-Aldrich entities actually acquired RBLP's assets and liabilities, BIS maintained that all three Sigma-Aldrich entities were liable for the pre-acquisition violations.[6]

In its motion for summary judgment Sigma-Aldrich asserted three primary defenses to the imposition of successor liability. First, the company argued that there was no statutory provision for successor liability underlying the EAR.[7] Second, it maintained that liability could not be imposed because RBLP remained a viable target for the enforcement action.[8] Third, Sigma-Aldrich argued that liability could not be imposed on the two entities that acquired only partnership shares in RBLP, without any assets or liabilities.[9]

The administrative law judge (ALJ) hearing the case rejected all three of Sigma-Aldrich's arguments. First, the ALJ found that the underlying statute does permit the imposition of successor liability under the EAR.[10] Second, the ALJ determined that successor liability could be imposed on the acquiring company even where the predecessor entity was not charged.[11] (The ALJ also found that because RBLP had transferred all of its assets, contracts and liabilities to Sigma-Aldrich, it was no longer a viable target for an enforcement action.[12]) Third, the ALJ acknowledged that entities that acquired only partnership interests in a company would generally not be subject to potential successor liability. However, in this case, the ALJ was not convinced that all that was transferred to the two relevant Sigma-Aldrich entities were partnership units.[13] Accordingly, the ALJ denied Sigma-Aldrich's motion for summary judgment.

---

3. *Id.*
4. *Id.*
5. *Id.*
6. *Id.*
7. *Id.*
8. *Id.*
9. *Id.*
10. *Id.*
11. *Id.*
12. *Id.*
13. *Id.*

Following the ALJ's decision, Sigma-Aldrich agreed to pay BIS $1.76 million to settle the case.[14]

(c) Department of State

DDTC, too, has not hesitated to impose liability on a successor company for alleged violations of an acquired company that took place prior to the acquisition. For example, shortly after the *Sigma-Aldrich* settlement, DDTC issued a charging letter to the Boeing Company alleging violations of the International Traffic in Arms Regulations (ITAR) by Hughes Space and Communications (Hughes).[15] Boeing had purchased Hughes in 2000, and the charging letter alleged violations with respect to Hughes' launch of satellites from the People's Republic of China in the mid-1990s.[16] In March 2003, Boeing and Hughes settled these charges for $32 million.[17]

In its settlement agreement with General Motors (GM)/General Dynamics (GD) the following year, the State Department indicated that a company may be able to reduce the penalties levied against it under the successor liability theory if it discovers export control violations during its due diligence investigation in connection with a proposed acquisition, and discloses those violations to the government. While there was divided liability between GM and GD for export violations involving GM units that were acquired by GD after the violations occurred, GD was required to pay $5 million of the $20 million fine.[18] Furthermore, GD was allowed to spend that $5 million over a five-year period on the implementation of export compliance enhancement measures specifically directed at the acquired GM units.[19] This lesser penalty may well have been the result of GD's discovery of GM's export control violations, and the actions it took in response to that discovery.

The State Department's recent settlement with AAR International likewise suggests that pre-closing due diligence and cooperation may have significant mitigating effects in successor liability cases. AAR International purchased Presidential Airways

---

14. Two years later, BIS used the doctrine of successor liability to extract a $1.54 million civil settlement from ProChem Proprietary Ltd. (ProChem) for 220 violations of the EAR committed by another company, Protea, which ProChem had acquired. *See* http://efoia.bis.doc.gov/exportcontrolviolations/e924.pdf.
15. Investigation of Hughes Electronics Corporation and Boeing Satellite Systems (formerly Hughes Space and Communications) Concerning the Long March 2E and Long March 3B failure investigations, and other satellite-related matters involving the People's Republic of China, December 26, 2002, *available at* http://www.pmddtc.state.gov/compliance/consent_agreements/pdf/HughesElectronic_LetterRegardingInvestigation.pdf.
16. *Id.*
17. Consent Agreement: Hughes Electronics Corporation and Boeing Satellite Systems, March 2003, *available at* http://www.pmddtc.state.gov/compliance/consent_agreements/pdf/HughesElectronic_ConsentAgreement.pdf.
18. Consent Agreement: General Motors Corporation and General Dynamics Corporation, 2004, *available at* http://www.pmddtc.state.gov/compliance/consent_agreements/pdf/GeneralMotorsCorp_ConsentAgreement.pdf.
19. *Id.*

(Presidential), which was subsequently charged with thirteen violations of the ITAR and the Arms Export Control Act.[20] In its Charging Letter, the State Department acknowledged that AAR International met with the Department prior to the purchase of Presidential to assist in resolving the export control violations.[21] The Consent Agreement resolving the dispute contained no monetary penalties.[22]

(d) Office of Foreign Assets Control

In recent years OFAC has relied on the doctrine of successor liability to impose penalties on acquiring companies for sanctions violations committed by acquired companies prior to acquisition. The monetary penalties imposed by OFAC have in the past tended to be significantly smaller than those imposed by BIS or DDTC. However, OFAC penalties have grown larger in recent years, and the amount of the potential penalties that OFAC can impose has increased dramatically since the enactment of the IEEPA Enhancement Act.

For example, in 2008, Zimmer Dental Inc., successor to Centerpulse Dental Inc., paid $82,850 to settle allegations that Centerpulse had been exporting goods and services to Iran without an OFAC license. The alleged violations occurred prior to the acquisition of Centerpulse Dental Inc. by Zimmer Dental's parent company, and Zimmer Dental voluntarily disclosed the violations to OFAC.[23]

Similarly, in 2007, GE Security agreed to pay $1,900 to settle alleged violations of the Cuban Assets Control Regulations by a wholly-owned foreign subsidiary of InVision Technologies, Inc. OFAC alleged that InVision's foreign subsidiary acted without an OFAC license by exporting goods and services to Cuba, and these alleged violations occurred prior to the acquisition of InVision by GE Security. InVision had voluntarily disclosed the matter to OFAC.[24]

(e) Conclusions on Enforcement

All of these cases suggest that the penalties imposed on the basis of successor liability potentially could be mitigated when the acquiring company discovers export control and sanctions violations in the course of its due diligence review and discloses those violations to the Government. The risk of imposition of a monetary penalty on a

---

20.   Regarding Violations of the Arms Export Control Act and the International Traffic in Arms Regulations, July 14, 2010, *available at* http://www.pmddtc.state.gov/compliance/consent_agreements/pdf/AAR-PCL.pdf.

21.   *Id.*

22.   Consent Agreement: AAR International, Inc., July 2010, *available at* http://www.pmddtc.state.gov/compliance/consent_agreements/pdf/AAR-ConsentAgreement.pdf.

23.   *See* http://www.treasury.gov/resource-center/sanctions/OFAC-Enforcement/Documents/01112007.pdf.

24.   *See* http://www.treasury.gov/resource-center/sanctions/OFAC-Enforcement/Documents/09072007.pdf.

successor company may increase when an acquiring company fails to undertake a thorough international regulatory compliance review, and only discovers after the fact that the company it acquired was in violation of export controls or sanctions laws. This is particularly true when the violations continued to occur after the acquisition. The following section offers suggestions for conducting a thorough export controls and economic sanctions due diligence review.

10.3 DUE DILIGENCE

(a) Overview

Undertaking a due diligence review is standard practice in corporate mergers and acquisitions, but the focus has long been on the financial condition of the target company, while the need to conduct a comprehensive review of international regulatory compliance is frequently overlooked. As discussed herein, the U.S. Government increasingly holds acquiring companies liable for export controls and sanctions violations by a target company that occurred prior to the acquisition. The Government has imposed significant fines and other mandatory compliance measures on these acquiring companies, even when the company seemingly had no knowledge of the past violations of the company it acquired. These cases make clear that when an acquiring company fails to conduct a substantive review of a target company's international regulatory compliance history and practices, it takes on a significant and (largely) avoidable risk.

The exact nature of the export compliance review that should be undertaken by an acquiring company will necessarily depend on the industry involved, the type of transaction, and the nature of the target company's business activities. For example, companies in certain industries, such as technology, telecommunications, energy, defense, software, electronics, and government contracts, are likely to be subject to more stringent regulatory regimes. If a target company is involved in one of these industries, and does business overseas, the necessary export compliance review will be more in-depth than if the target company operates in a less regulated industry with little international activity.

The information collected during export compliance due diligence should allow the acquiring company to accurately assess the following: (1) the nature and footprint of the target company's business and workforce; (2) the nature of the target company's compliance program and the manner in which that program is implemented; (3) the Government agencies which have jurisdiction over the target company's business and the target company's license posture before any relevant agencies; (4) the existence of any past or present export controls or sanctions violations; and, (5) the target company's recordkeeping procedures. Collecting this information before closing will help the acquiring company identify compliance risks in order to ensure that the transaction is properly valued and the future liability is minimized.

(b) Conducting the Review
(i) Collecting Documents

Due diligence in the context of export and sanctions compliance is like due diligence in any other area of the target company's business, in that the first step of the review is to request and collect relevant documents. The failure of an acquiring company to conduct sufficient export controls and sanctions due diligence frequently stems from not asking the right questions at the outset. As discussed above, the exact nature of the export controls and sanctions review will necessarily depend on the industry involved and the specifics of the transaction, but generally speaking, documents should be collected that allow the acquiring company to answer the following types of questions:

- **Structure of the Company's Business:** Does the company's business involve products/technologies that are controlled under U.S. export laws? What percentage of the company's sales are to international markets? To which countries has the company exported over the past five years? With which companies has the company engaged in business, financing, support, or other transactions over the past five years? How is the company structured? Does the company have international operations, and of what type and with whom? How does the company sell – through international distributors or with the assistance of agents? Does the company outsource aspects of its product development? Does the company employ foreign persons?

- **Compliance Policy and Procedures:** Does the company have a written export controls and sanctions compliance policy? Does the compliance policy establish a clear chain of command with respect to export and sanctions compliance decisions? Does the policy provide for adequate training for the employees involved in the company's export and sanctions operations? Does the policy establish an adequate procedure for screening potential overseas customers, suppliers, distributors, agents, and other business partners? Does the policy establish a procedure for screening employees? What does the policy provide with respect to document retention? What is the company's procedure for determining whether a particular transaction is subject to export controls or sanctions restrictions? How does the company determine the jurisdiction and classification of its products and technology? What export licenses does the company have from the relevant government agencies? If the company exports defense articles or defense services, is the company registered with DDTC?

- **Export Control Violations:** Has the company ever submitted a voluntary disclosure or been subject to an investigation regarding export controls or sanctions violations? If so, has the company ever been subject to any penalties as a result of such an investigation? What was the cause of the violation(s)? What changes were made within the company to ensure that similar violations did not recur? Is the company aware of any other potential infractions of export controls laws or regulations that have not been disclosed, and if so, how were these addressed?

- **Recordkeeping:** Has the company maintained copies of its export documents for at least five years (where "export documents" is defined broadly to include all records of export, such as proposals, applications, licenses, contracts, specifications, correspondence, shipping records, and other export control documents)?

These questions are examples: at the end of this chapter we provide a sample preliminary export control compliance document request list.

As the acquiring company is conducting its initial document collection, a clear red flag is a target company that does a substantial amount of business overseas, but lacks a comprehensive compliance policy and maintains inadequate records. Other red flags are when the target company does not know the export control classification of its products, or has sold to embargoed or high risk countries over the past five years. However, in many instances, potential export controls and sanctions compliance problems will be far less obvious, and it is only when the target company's documents are reviewed by persons with expertise in the area that deficiencies become clear.

(ii) Reviewing Documents

Reviewing documents as part of the export and sanctions compliance due diligence effort may be complicated by the fact that the documents themselves are regulated by export control laws. Thus, one of the first steps that must be undertaken by the parties to the transaction is to ensure that adequate authorization exists for the acquiring company to review the documents that it has identified, particularly if the acquiring company is not a U.S. company, or if persons reviewing the documents on behalf of the acquiring company are themselves foreign persons. In addition, if a U.S. person employee of a foreign company is reviewing documents on behalf of his or her employer, access by that person to controlled technical data may be viewed as a transfer of that technical data to the foreign employer.

Once any appropriate authorizations are in place, an export and sanctions compliance due diligence review must involve a substantive review of the documents, not just a confirmation that a certain set of documents has been provided in response to a request. For example, in order to determine whether the target company has "adequate procedures" for screening employees, overseas customers, suppliers, distributors, agents, and other business partners, the acquiring company will need to actually review the target company's screening process in order to ensure that it effectively flags the following persons or entities: (1) any person or entity located in a restricted or embargoed country; (2) any person or entity on OFAC's list of Specially Designated Nationals (SDNs) or any entities owned or controlled by an entity on this list; and, (3) any person or entity denied export privileges or otherwise restricted by BIS or DDTC. It is not enough for an acquiring company to know that there are screening procedures in place without examining the efficacy of those procedures. Indeed, one method frequently used in export compliance due diligence is to obtain a complete list of all customers of the target company for the preceding five years and run those customers against all of the restricted party lists.

The questions above provide an example of some of the initial questions that an acquiring company will want to address. More examples are provided in the checklist found at the end of this chapter. In many instances, the responses to these questions should lead to a substantial number of follow-up questions. For example, "deemed exports" constitute a compliance area that is frequently overlooked, particularly by companies that only sell their products domestically. If a company employs foreign persons, the acquiring company will want to ensure that those foreign persons do not have access to source code, technology, defense articles, or anything else that would require an export license if it were being exported to that foreign national's country or countries of nationality. If foreign persons do have such access, then the acquiring company will need to ensure that the appropriate authorizations are in place.

Follow-up questions may also be appropriate even when the initial response would seem to suggest that there is no more information to be obtained. For example, the target company may say in response to an initial questionnaire that it has never submitted a voluntary disclosure or been subject to an investigation for export control violations. If the target company does not employ many foreign persons and has limited export business, this may be reasonable. But if the target company produces controlled products and has a significant number of overseas customers, this should raise a red flag. It is certainly possible that the target company has a perfect record of export and sanctions compliance, but it also may be the case that the company's compliance policies and procedures are ineffective, or worse, that the company is actively trying to conceal past problems.

Finally, gathering and reviewing all of the relevant documents is not the end of the export controls and sanctions compliance due diligence process. It is extremely helpful if the reviewing team from the acquiring company is able to take the time to actually meet with the target company's compliance managers and personnel, sales and marketing representatives, contracts management team, shipping department personnel, information technology management team, and/or human resources personnel in order to ensure that the compliance policies that exist on paper are both fully understood and actually being implemented on the ground. These interviews may also alert the acquiring company to potential ongoing export compliance problems that may not be evident on paper.

(iii) Addressing the Target Company's Failure to Turn Over Relevant Documents, and Compliance Problems Identified During Due Diligence

Even if the acquiring company is diligent about requesting the relevant documents for its export and sanctions compliance review, the acquiring company must ultimately rely on the target company to comply with its requests for production. To the extent that the target company is unwilling to produce the relevant documents, or in acquisition contexts where complete due diligence is impossible for other reasons, the acquiring company will have to determine the degree of risk it is willing to undertake in order to complete the transaction.

In the event that full due diligence is not possible, the acquiring company has a number of options. The acquiring company could insist on an adjustment to the purchase price to try to account for unknown future liability, but arriving at an appropriate valuation of such potential future liability may prove difficult. The acquiring company could require that the target company provide warranty or indemnity language in the contract to help protect the acquirer from the risk of monetary penalties in the event that export or sanctions compliance violations are discovered after the deal is finalized, but requiring such language has the potential to complicate negotiations. If the nature of the target company's business makes it unlikely that significant export controls or sanctions violations have occurred in the past, the acquiring company may determine that it feels comfortable taking the risk of proceeding with the transaction even with incomplete information. Alternatively, the acquiring company may decide to walk away from the deal altogether if the risks seem too high.

In addition to determining how it will deal with incomplete information, the acquiring company will also need to be prepared to address export controls and sanctions violations that are in fact uncovered during the course of its due diligence review. If the acquiring company discovers ongoing export controls or sanctions violations, the problematic activity should be stopped as quickly as possible, and an internal investigation should be undertaken in order to understand the nature and extent of the violations. The acquiring company, together with the target, must then make a decision regarding whether to disclose the violation to the relevant government agency, and, if so, which party makes the disclosure and at what time.

While in most cases disclosure of past violations of export control and sanctions laws is not mandatory, it frequently will be in the best interest of the acquiring company to disclose any significant violations that are uncovered. First, it may be that taking the necessary corrective measures is likely to alert the government to the violation anyway (e.g., obtaining new licenses, correcting false statements, etc.) thus essentially necessitating a disclosure, even if one is not technically mandatory. But more importantly, as discussed herein, a voluntary disclosure will generally be viewed as a mitigating factor when an agency is determining whether to assess penalties, as well as the nature of those penalties. However, the benefits of a voluntary disclosure are available only if the company comes forward before the relevant government agency becomes aware of the problem through other means.

Furthermore, in the event that export controls or sanctions violations are discovered during the due diligence review, the acquiring company may decide that it wants to make closing the transaction contingent on the resolution of those violations. Disclosing a violation to the relevant government agency allows the parties to resolve the issue of liability and understand the exact nature of any penalties that may be assessed. Accordingly, the parties will have the necessary information to determine whether the purchase price needs to be renegotiated, whether an escrow arrangement should be established to handle any penalties, and whether the transaction should proceed at all. However, it can take time – often a long time – for the relevant enforcement agencies to determine how to adjudicate a violation, so the parties to the transaction must be prepared to wait. Alternatively parties may craft another solution that is mutually acceptable while resolution of the enforcement action is pending.

One question frequently asked is who should make the voluntary disclosure. It is common for the acquirer to insist that the target company file an initial notice of voluntary disclosure *prior to* the close, noting that the violations were discovered during the due diligence process, and that the acquiring company will complete the investigation and submit the final voluntary disclosure report. This underscores to the relevant agencies that these errors were made by the target company, and not the acquiring company, and that the acquiring company was careful in its due diligence efforts and that it is serious about addressing any compliance shortcomings. It is also acceptable for the acquiring company to file the initial notice as soon as possible post-close. In both contexts, however, the acquiring company should take steps to ensure that any investigation was conducted thoroughly and in good faith, and that any voluntary disclosure report fully and accurately reflects the information uncovered in the investigation. It is helpful if the acquirer can obtain access to the documents and personnel relevant to the investigation and disclosure.

(c) Conclusions on Due Diligence

Adequate export controls and sanctions compliance due diligence is a crucial part of a merger or acquisition, particularly where the relevant government agencies have made it clear that they will not hesitate to hold an acquiring company liable for past violations committed by a target company without the acquiring company's knowledge. In addition to ensuring that it is aware of a target company's international regulatory compliance posture, an acquiring company must also work with the target company to ensure that the parties comply with any notification obligations that may arise from the merger or acquisition, as discussed in the following section.

10.4 NOTIFICATION REQUIREMENTS

(a) Department of State

Pursuant to §122.4 of the International Traffic in Arms Regulations (ITAR), a registrant must notify the Office of Defense Trade Controls Compliance if there is a material change in the information contained in its Registration Statement, including "a change in the senior officers; the establishment, acquisition or divestment of a subsidiary or foreign affiliate; a merger; a change of location; or the dealing in an additional category of defense articles or defense services."[25] In preparation for a merger or acquisition, the parties should confer about the licenses and agreements that will need to be transferred to the buyer after closing, recognizing that not all existing authorizations may be needed after the deal is finalized.

Section 122.4(b) of the ITAR requires that the parties to a transaction provide DDTC with at least 60-days advance notice of any sale or transfer that will result in a foreign person acquiring ownership or control of a U.S. registrant.[26] Upon receipt of a 60-day notification, DDTC will assign a transaction number and will provide that number to the parties.

In all transactions, including those subject to the 60-day advance notification requirement and those involving only U.S. persons, companies must provide DDTC with certain information within five days of the closing of a deal which results in a material change to the Registration Statement.[27] While much of the information is basic, such as the new company name and the registration number that will survive, some of the necessary information will require some advance notice to gather, including all license numbers with unshipped balances, and a list of DDTC-approved agreements.[28] The parties should also provide the effective date of the closing of the transaction, and a point of contact at each of the U.S. subsidiaries. Pursuant to §122.4(c), any licenses not identified in the notification, and any amendments not properly executed within 60 days of the notification, will be considered invalid.[29]

In addition to the 5-day notification, a revised DS-2032 Statement of Registration should simultaneously be provided to DDTC for the surviving registration number.[30] The updated information – including changes to the name and location of the company, ITAR categories for defense articles/services produced or provided, changes in senior officers, etc. – should be highlighted in the form.[31] Upon receipt of the 5-day notification letter and the updated DS-2032 form, DDTC will notify the company of any deficiencies in the application, or authorize it to proceed with amending the licenses and agreements listed in the 5-day notification letter. If a transaction number was not previously provided (because a 60-day advance notification was not required), it will be included in this letter from DDTC. A General Correspondence letter can now be used to accomplish the change if the amendment is required only

---

25.   22 C.F.R. § 122.4(a)(2).

26.   22 C.F.R. § 122.4(b).

27.   22 C.F.R. §122.4(a) and (c).

28.   22 C.F.R. § 122.4(c).

29.   *Id.*

30.   *See* Notification of Changes in Registration Information, *available at* http://www.pmddtc.state.gov/registration/notification_chreg.html.

31.   *Id.*

due to a change in name, address, or registration code, though DSP amendments and major agreement amendments are still required for other types of changes.[32]

According to DDTC's guidance on amending existing ITAR authorizations due to a U.S. company name/address or registration code change, a GC request should be submitted within 60 days after DDTC has authorized the changes.[33] DDTC requires that the GC request have a subject line stating that the GC request is to amend export licenses and agreements due to a merger or acquisition.[34] The GC request should include a cover letter identifying the requested changes, as well as a certification letter, a copy of DDTC's letter acknowledging the requested changes, and a spreadsheet listing all authorizations to be transferred.[35] If the U.S. entity's name changes, an executed amendment itself must be submitted to DDTC under separate cover, in accordance with §124.1(d), though the agreement should be listed in the spreadsheet/matrix included in the GC request. The DDTC response to the GC will include an annotated spreadsheet/matrix, identifying any authorizations not amended. If there are no such annotations, then all requested changes have been made.[36]

(b) Department of Commerce
The Bureau of Industry and Security also requires that a Commerce licensee seek written approval from BIS in order to transfer any export licenses or other export authorizations to another party as the result of a merger or acquisition. Pursuant to section 750.10 of the EAR, such approval must be requested via a letter to BIS from the licensee, and that letter must describe the reason for the requested transfer, indicate which license numbers are to be transferred, list all pending license applications that are to be transferred, and state the entity to which they will be transferred. The letter should also describe why the transfer is necessary (including transaction details) and whether any consideration has been or will be paid for the transfer.[37] The transferee must submit a similar letter, accompanied by various certifications.[38] Unlike the ITAR, the EAR do not provide specific deadlines for the submission of such a letter to BIS. Also unlike the ITAR, the EAR do not require a notification process where the licenses will continue to be owned by the same legal entity, and it is only the legal entity's parent company that has changed.

---

32. *See* General Correspondence for Amendment of Existing ITAR Authorizations Due to U.S. Entity Name/Address and/or Registration Code Changes, updated June 21, 2011, *available at* http://www.pmddtc.state.gov/licensing/documents/gl_GCsUSu.pdf.
33. *Id.*
34. *Id.*
35. *Id.*
36. *Id.*
37. 15 C.F.R. § 750.10(b).
38. *Id.*

10.5 POSSIBLE CFIUS REVIEW

If the acquiring company is foreign owned or controlled, and depending on the nature of the target company's activities and the degree of control that will be exercised by the acquiring company after the merger or acquisition, the parties may elect to file for review with the Committee on Foreign Investment in the United States (CFIUS). CFIUS focuses on mergers and acquisitions that could pose potential threats to U.S. national security, broadly defined. CFIUS is chaired by the Department of Treasury, and includes representatives from fifteen other U.S. government departments, agencies and offices. CFIUS has jurisdiction over "any merger, acquisition, or takeover by or with any foreign person which could result in foreign control of any person engaged in interstate commerce in the United States."[39] This does not mean, however, that CFIUS review is necessary in all cases where a merger or acquisition will result in foreign control of a U.S. business, as the CFIUS process is voluntary. However, if there are national security issues of any kind potentially implicated by a transaction the parties should very seriously consider making a CFIUS filing to avoid a potentially painful review and mitigation process (or even forced unwinding of the deal) at a later date.

While many CFIUS cases involve mergers and acquisitions within the defense industry, CFIUS commonly reviews transactions in the aerospace, telecommunications, engineering, energy, pharmaceutical, and transportation industries, among others. CFIUS can initiate a review of a transaction on its own initiative at any time, and can recommend that the President force the parties to "unwind" a deal after the fact.[40] Thus, filing for CFIUS review prior to closing is the wiser course of action if there may be potential U.S. national security concerns associated with the merger or acquisition.

If the parties intend to file for CFIUS review, CFIUS encourages them to engage in informal consultations with the Committee prior to filing a voluntary notice in order to ensure that the process is efficient once it is actually underway.[41] The official review process begins when the voluntary notice is filed with the Department of Treasury.[42] If the filing is complete, it is then circulated to the other CFIUS members, and a lead agency is assigned to the case.[43] After 30 days, all CFIUS agencies must approve the transaction, or determine that a further 45-day investigation is warranted.[44] If national security concerns remain at the end of that 45-day period, CFIUS may elect to enter into an agreement with the parties in which it imposes conditions on the transaction

---

39. The Foreign Investment and National Security Act of 2007 (FINSA), H.R. 556, 110th Cong., §2(a), (2007).
40. 31 C.F.R. §800.401(b).
41. 31 C.F.R. §800.401(f).
42. 31 C.F.R. §800.401(a).
43. 31 C.F.R. §800.502.
44. 31 C.F.R. §800.502 – 800.506.

in order to mitigate perceived risks.[45] Alternatively, CFIUS may send a report to the President, who then has 15 days in which he must decide whether to permit or block the transaction.[46]

One cautionary note for parties that elect to undergo CFIUS review is that CFIUS filings are circulated to BIS, DDTC, and OFAC. In other words, if any information in the CFIUS filings describes activities that are regulated under the export controls or sanctions laws, these agencies will be put on notice of such activities. For example, if the CFIUS filing describes business activities which require a license from DDTC, and DDTC knows that the company is not licensed for such activities, or not even registered under the ITAR, the information could trigger DDTC to initiate a separate investigation or enforcement action. In fact, DDTC has been known to contact counsel where merely the nature of the products themselves suggest they might be subject to the ITAR. Therefore, parties that elect to undergo CFIUS review should strongly consider filing a voluntary disclosure with the relevant agency prior to, or concurrent with, their CFIUS filing if they are aware of any past unauthorized activity relating to export controls or sanctions.

10.6 APPLYING EXPORT CONTROLS AND ECONOMIC SANCTIONS POLICIES TO NEWLY ACQUIRED COMPANIES

The risk of international regulatory compliance violations does not cease after a deal has closed. In addition to any risk for pre-acquisition infractions that the acquirer may face as a successor in interest, the acquiring company also becomes responsible for any ongoing and future violations of export controls and economic sanctions laws committed by the acquired company. Therefore, the acquiring company should carefully consider how best to integrate the newly formed or acquired entity into its compliance framework. Steps that can be undertaken to accomplish this objective are outlined below.

(a) Identifying and/or Appointing Transition Point Persons.

An effort to integrate a newly-acquired company into an acquiring company's existing export and sanctions compliance framework, or to integrate the export and sanctions compliance policies and procedures of two companies that have merged, will not succeed unless appropriate personnel are identified to spearhead the transition, provide feedback, and implement the procedures that are chosen. Often both the acquiring and the acquired company are large enough to have one or more personnel dedicated to supporting export controls and sanctions compliance full time. Any such people should be made part of the transition team, as they are likely to be highly familiar not

---

45.   FINSA, *supra* n.620, §5.
46.   31 C.F.R. §800.506. Only the President has the authority to actually suspend or prohibit a transaction.

only with the compliance policy and procedures, but may also have valuble insight into how they evolved, and why they are written as they are.

Of course, in some cases one of the companies involved in the M&A activity may not have dedicated compliance personnel in place. In this case, it is critical to promptly identify one or more people who can spearhead the integration process within that company. Every effort should be made to utilize existing employees if at all possible, as this role requires knowledge of previously existing company personnel and procedures. However, if the person(s) selected are not highly knowledgeable about export controls and sanctions compliance, they will need either outside or in house training early in the process, and also will need support from international regulatory compliance personnel within the compliance structure of the other party to the merger or acquisition.

Employees other than export and sanctions compliance personnel also should be heavily involved in the transition. For example, it is very helpful – some would say essential – to have somebody in upper management on the business side of the company (rather than legal or compliance) involved. The right business person can help both to legitimize the process and drive employees to participate in providing feedback and implement the new procedures. Also, if the compliance function is not housed in the legal department, it can be helpful to involve an attorney with knowledge of export controls and sanctions compliance. Finally, it is critical to engage the employees who actually implement the policies and procedures on a daily basis. They are the ones who are the most likely to spot omissions or incongruities that can prevent newly-implemented procedures from being fully effective, and their cooperation and dedication is essential to ensuring that the newly implemented procedures are followed.

(b) Identify Policies and Procedures That Will Be Applied to the Acquired Company.

Once a transition team is in place (or at least after the primary stakeholders have been selected), the parties must identify which compliance policies and procedures will be applied to the acquired or newly merged company. While it is certainly possible for different members of a corporate family to maintain different compliance policies and procedures, especially during a transitional period, it is generally viewed as good corporate practice to have a single policy that applies to all parts of the corporation, even if it is tweaked or supplemented by some members of the corporate family to address their specific risk profile. By contrast, specific procedures may need to be tailored to the target's risk profile, particularly when the target is in a different line of business that its acquirer.

Whether to adopt one company's policy and procedures outright, or to pick and choose amongst the previously-existing policies and procedures of two companies, very much depends on the companies, their similarities, their lines of business, how they will be functioning as part of the corporate family, etc. Normally large corporations that acquire a small company allow for a transition period to implement the corporation's policy within the newly-acquired company, but the corporation's policy and procedures are often implemented in their entirety. However, in other situations the decision is often made based on a variety of factors, including which company has a stronger compliance program, whose Enterprise Resource Planning software will be adopted, etc. In short, there is no "right" answer, and each merger or acquisition will present unique facts and circumstances that should be evaluated in arriving at a determination.

We note that sometimes conflicts of laws issues will present themselves in international merger and acquisition situations. For example, a U.S. company's policy to ensure compliance with deemed export restrictions potentially could run afoul of EU privacy and data protection laws. Similarly, certain aspects of a U.S. sanctions compliance policy could conflict with so-called "blocking" statutes in Canada, the EU, and elsewhere. Companies facing such conflicts would be wise to seek local counsel in the relevant jurisdictions to assess their risks and understand their options for implementing effective and lawful compliance programs.

Once policies and procedures are selected, many companies provide drafts for employee review and comment prior to finalizing. As noted above, employee review can help to identify and inadvertent shortcomings or oversights, and ultimately will lead to a stronger compliance program.

(c) Providing Compliance Training

Providing thorough export controls and sanctions compliance training is critical to ensuring that the policies and procedures that have been selected are fully understood and implemented by the key stakeholders. Conducting a basic export and sanctions compliance training for all employees is generally a good place to start, though whether this is the best approach can depend in the size and nature of the company. There is almost always a need for additional training beyond a basic overview training. Those responsible for implementing procedures on a daily basis should receive targeted training. For example, logistics personnel should be trained in the procedures for ensuring that an export has the appropriate authorization, completion of AES entries, recordkeeping, etc. Human resources personnel should be trained in procedures relating to hiring and identification of foreign national employees. Business development personnel should be trained in limitations on the release of controlled technical data to prospective customers, foreign national visitor policies, etc. Depending on the topic, training can be either formal or hands-on, or both. Training provided by U.S. Government agencies or outside vendors also can be informative.

Conducting such training has numerous benefits. It increases understanding of relevant policies and procedures and therefore reduces the risk of future violations. Training can lead to the uncovering – and termination – of prior shortcomings. And training can create a link between export compliance personnel and employees, which often makes it more likely that the employees will reach out to the compliance personnel should they have questions or concerns, thus minimizing the likelihood of future violations.

(d) Performing Benchmark and Periodic Compliance Audits

Acquiring companies should strongly consider conducting a benchmark audit within a certain period of time (usually a few months) after an acquisition closes. Even if the acquiring company conducted thorough export controls and sanctions due diligence on the target company prior to acquisition, there is almost always greater access to documents and personnel after a deal closes. Conducting an audit with full access to relevant information can yield additional insights beyond those gleaned in the due diligence process. The sooner a benchmark audit can be undertaken, the better, as it is advantageous to identify and stop problematic activity (or inaction) that could lead to a violation early on. If problematic activity and infractions are uncovered soon after the acquisition, the acquiring company can explain to the Government that it affirmatively performed an audit intended to identify and discontinue problematic activity, which can be viewed as a mitigating factor (though, as discussed above, will not necessarily preclude the imposition of penalties). Conversely, if problematic activity remains undiscovered for many months or even years, the likelihood that the acquiring company would be granted mitigating credit for violations that took place after the acquisition is slim (though it may receive mitigating credit based on other factors).

10.7 CONCLUSION

Merger and acquisition activity presents unique export controls and sanctions compliance risks. Those risks can be mitigated with thorough due diligence, careful integration into the export controls and sanctions compliance framework, identification of appropriate personnel to assist with the transition process, and implementation of a tailored training and audit program. With proper planning, export and sanctions compliance issues need not diminish the value of the underlying merger and acquisition activity, and in fact can serve as a vehicle for building an even stronger compliance program.

Sample Preliminary Due Diligence Information Request List: Export Controls and Sanctions[47]

Please answer the following question and provide documentation where requested for target company and any entities owned or controlled by target company

I. **Structure of the Company's Business:**

   A. Does the company export any product, technology or service? NO/YES

   B. Does the company's business involve products/technologies that are controlled under U.S. export regulations? NO/YES

   C. Does the company have any foreign subsidiaries, greater than 50% ownership, or a controlling interest in, a foreign corporation, partnership, joint venture, or other business entity? NO/YES (List any applicable entities and the countries in which they are located)

   D. Are there foreign entities that form part of the company's supply chain? NO/YES (List any applicable entities and the countries in which they are located)

   E. Does the company employ any foreign persons within the U.S.? NO/YES (if yes, please answer the questions below)

   1. Are there any Technology Control Plans (TCPs) in place for any foreign person employees? NO/YES (Provide copy)

   2. Does any foreign person employed in the U.S. have access to any information subject to ITAR or EAR controls? NO/YES (Explain)

   a. If yes, has authorization been received from the relevant agency to permit such access? NO/YES (Provide copy)

   F. Please provide an organizational chart for the company, identifying those areas and personnel associated with export compliance.

II. **Compliance Policy:**

   A. Does the company have a written export controls or sanctions compliance program, policy, or procedures? NO/YES (Provide copy)

   B. Does the company have a training program for export controls or sanctions compliance? NO/YES (Provide copy of training manuals/procedures and any relevant certifications)

   C. Does the company screen for denied and restricted parties? NO/YES (if yes, please answer the questions below)

   1. Which lists does the company screen against?

   2. Who is responsible for the screening?

   3. How is screening documented?

---

47. The type of information that should be sought during a merger & acquisition due diligence review will necessarily vary depending on the nature of the transaction. Therefore, this sample list should be tailored to each particular situation.

4. What is the procedure when there is a potential match to one of the relevant lists?

D. Does the company have an export controls or sanctions audit/assessment program? NO/YES (Provide copy of the written procedures and reports from the last five years)

III. Export Documentation

For the questions in A-E, below, please respond for the last five years, and please provide copies of any correspondence with the agencies listed below.

A. Department of Commerce

1. Does the company have export licenses issued by BIS? NO/YES (Provide copies)

2. Does the company export or re-export dual-use items listed on the Commerce Control List? NO /YES (Provide a list of CCL items and classifications, showing to whom these items were exported)

B. Department of State

1. Does the company manufacture or export defense articles, or furnish defense services? NO/YES (Provide a list defense articles and/or services, showing to whom these articles/services are/were provided)

2. Does the company have any export licenses or other authorization issued by DTCC? NO/YES (Provide copies)

3. Is the company registered under 22 CFR Part 122 as a manufacturer or exporter? NO/YES (expiration date)

4. Is the company registered as a broker under 22 CFR Part 129? NO/YES (expiration date)

5. Who is the company's ITAR senior Empowered Official? (Provide contact information)

a. If there is no Empowered Official, please provide contact information for the senior person responsible for the company's export compliance.

6. Has the company made any ITAR-reportable political contributions, fees, or commissions within the last 5 years? NO /YES (List and explain)

7. Has any senior official (CEO, president, vice-president, comptroller, treasurer, or general counsel) ever been indicted for or convicted of violating any of the criminal statutes in 22 CFR 120.27? NO/YES (Explain)

C. Department of Treasury

1. Does the company (or any entity controlled by the company) export to or engage in other business transactions with the Balkans, Belarus, Burma, Cote D'Ivoire, Cuba, Democratic Republic of Congo, Iran, Iraq, Lebanon, Liberia, North Korea, Somalia, Sudan, Syria, Zimbabwe, or any other U.S. sanctioned country? NO/YES (List countries and explain business relationships)

      2. Does the company have any licenses issued by Treasury/OFAC? NO/YES (Provide copies)

  D. Other U.S. Government Agency Jurisdiction:

      1. Has the company received export licenses or authorizations from other U.S. Government agencies? No /Yes (List)

  E. Foreign Government Agency Jurisdiction:

      1. Does the company have export licenses issued by foreign governments? No/Yes (Provide copies)

  F. Does the company have a procedure for classifying products, technology, or services under the USML and the CCL? No/Yes (Provide copy)

  G. Who is responsible for classifying products, technology, or services under the USML and the CCL? (Provide contact information)

  H. Please provide sample documentation for five transactions with foreign entities during the past five years (for both commercial and defense end-users, if applicable), from the expression of interest through the fulfillment of the order.

IV. Export Controls and Sanctions Compliance and Violations

  A. Is the company aware of any potential noncompliance with export controls laws or regulations that has occurred within the past five years and that has not been disclosed to the regulating government agency? No/Yes (Explain)

  B. Has the company filed any disclosures (voluntary or directed) of suspected noncompliance with the export controls or sanctions laws or regulations?

  C. Has the company been subject to any fines, penalties, suspensions of export privileges, or any other enforcement activity or corrective action by any government agency, U.S. or foreign, for suspected noncompliance with government export controls or sanctions laws or regulations? NO/YES (List)

  D. Has the company received any inquiries, including but not limited to subpoenas, from a government agency regarding export controls or sanctions laws or regulations? No/Yes (Explain)

  E. Does the company have a process for investigating and reporting instances of possible non-compliance with export controls and sanctions laws or regulations? No/Yes (Explain)

  F. What changes has the company made to ensure that past violations of export controls or sanctions laws or regulations do not recur?

V. Recordkeeping

  A. What are the company's procedures for recordkeeping and reporting of export transactions? (Explain and provide copies of written procedures)

$$\textbf{11}$$

Nuclear Export Controls

William E. Fork and Elina Teplinsky (United States)
and Martha Harrison and Katrina Reyes (Canada)

11.1 INTRODUCTION

Although there are important peaceful uses for nuclear and nuclear-related goods and technologies, including for nuclear energy production, some technologies used in these activities are also capable of being diverted for the production of nuclear weapons. The potential for states to acquire the materials and technologies to develop nuclear weapons capabilities has generated strong support for national and international nuclear nonproliferation mechanisms. Many states have implemented comprehensive regulatory controls on the import and export of nuclear and nuclear-related goods and technologies to ensure these items are used only for nonexplosive and peaceful means. This chapter provides an overview of the international nuclear export control regime and the licensing requirements, policies, and international obligations that frame the export and import controls of nuclear and nuclear-related materials in the United States and Canada.

11.2 INTERNATIONAL NUCLEAR EXPORT CONTROL REGIME

The Treaty on the Non-proliferation of Nuclear Weapons (NPT) provides the legal basis for the key aspects of the international nuclear export control regime. The NPT, which entered into force in 1970, granted nonnuclear weapon states (NNWS)[1] access to nuclear material, equipment, and technology for peaceful purposes so long as these states committed not to develop nuclear weapons.

Article IV of the NPT underscores the "inalienable right of all the Parties to the Treaty to develop research, production and use of nuclear energy for peaceful purposes without discrimination . . ." This inalienable right, however, is subject to a state's conformity to other provisions of the NPT. Under Article III.1, NNWS undertake to conclude safeguard agreements with the International Atomic Energy Agency (IAEA). Additionally, under Article III.2, all parties to the treaty pledge not to provide "(a) source or special fissionable material, or (b) equipment or material

---

1. Five states are recognized by the NPT as nuclear weapon states (NWS): China, France, Russia, the United Kingdom, and the United States. All other states are NNWS.

especially designed or prepared for the processing, use or production of special fissionable material, to any non-nuclear-weapon State for peaceful purposes, unless the source or special fissionable material shall be subject to [IAEA safeguards established under Article III.1]."

Recognizing that materials and technologies used in peaceful nuclear programs could be used to develop weapons, several NPT nuclear supplier states sought to determine what specific equipment and materials could be shared with NNWS under the NPT, and under what conditions. These nuclear supplier states formed the Zangger Committee in 1971 with a view of harmonizing the interpretation of nuclear export control policies under Article III.2 for NPT nuclear supplier states. In 1974, the Zangger Committee published a "trigger list" of nuclear-related goods (i.e., equipment that will trigger safeguards as a condition of supply) to assist NPT nuclear supplier states in identifying equipment and materials that should be subject to export controls.

India's explosion of a nuclear device in 1974 led nuclear supplier states to establish the Nuclear Suppliers Group (NSG) to further regulate nuclear-related exports beyond those provided for in the NPT. The NSG added technologies to the original Zangger Committee trigger list and agreed on a set of guidelines incorporating the trigger list. The NSG guidelines were first published in 1978 as IAEA Document INFCIRC/254. In 1992, in response to concerns that export control provisions then in force had not effectively prevented Iraq, a party to the NPT, from pursuing a clandestine nuclear weapons program through acquiring dual-use items not covered by the NSG guidelines, the NSG established a second set of guidelines for transfers of nuclear-related dual-use material, equipment, and technology. The dual-use guidelines were published as part 2 of INFCIRC/254, and the original guidelines published in 1978 became part 1 of INFCIRC/254 (collectively, the NSG Guidelines).

The NSG is a voluntary regime, and the NSG Guidelines are implemented by each NSG member in accordance with its national laws and practices. Decisions on export applications are taken at the national level in accordance with national export licensing requirements. Some states, such as the United States, have export control regimes that predate the establishment of the NSG Guidelines. Other states have adopted regimes that mirror the NSG Guidelines in many ways. States can also choose to adhere to the guidelines even if they are not members of the NSG.

NSG members review the guidelines periodically to ensure that they are up to date and continue to meet evolving nuclear proliferation challenges. Because the NSG Guidelines are incorporated into the export control regimes of most NSG member states, familiarity with the NSG Guidelines is important in understanding export controls on nuclear and nuclear-related items.

11.3 UNITED STATES: EXPORT CONTROLS

(a) Overview

The United States, one of the first countries to develop the use of nuclear energy for peaceful purposes, first catalyzed international civil nuclear cooperation through its "Atoms for Peace" program. The United States was also one of the first countries to control nuclear trade and nuclear-related assistance. U.S. controls over the exports and reexports of nuclear materials, equipment, and technologies predate the establishment of an international nuclear export controls regime. Today, the United States has a complex and comprehensive system of controls over nuclear civilian, dual-use, and military items and related technologies and software.

What Is Regulated? United States – The primary laws governing exports of nuclear material and equipment are promulgated under the U.S. Atomic Energy Act of 1954 (AEA),[2] as amended by the Nuclear Nonproliferation Act of 1978[3] and interpreted by several sets of regulations issued by U.S. federal agencies.

Where to Find the Regulations: United States – The U.S. Nuclear Regulatory Commission (NRC) controls the exports of certain nuclear material and equipment under the AEA, as specified in the NRC's regulations at 10 C.F.R. part 110. The U.S. Department of Energy (DOE) controls the export of certain nuclear technologies and specific nuclear reactor and nuclear weapons technologies under the AEA and various nonproliferation mandates. The DOE regulations are set out at 10 C.F.R. part 810.

Who Is the Regulator? United States – The export and reexport of nuclear and nuclear-related commodities and technologies are regulated by the NRC, the DOE, the U.S. Department of Commerce (DOC), and the U.S. Department of State (DOS).

(b) Federal Statutes and Authorities

The import and export of nuclear and nuclear-related items, technology, and software in the United States is primarily controlled in accordance with the requirements of the AEA, as amended. Four U.S. agencies have jurisdiction over nuclear and nuclear-related exports. The two key nuclear export control agencies are the NRC and the DOE. Each agency's jurisdiction is designed to be exclusive of the other and is divided as follows:

- The NRC controls the exports of certain nuclear material and equipment (e.g., equipment within or attached directly to a reactor vessel) under the AEA, as specified in the NRC's regulations at 10 C.F.R. part 110.

---

2.   42 U.S.C. §§ 2011 *et seq.*
3.   22 U.S.C. §§ 3201 *et seq.*

- The DOE controls the export of certain nuclear technologies and specific nuclear reactor and nuclear weapons technologies (e.g., nuclear-related information, technology, and software) under the AEA and various nonproliferation mandates. The DOE regulations are set out at 10 C.F.R. part 810.

Further, the DOC and the DOS have jurisdiction over the exports and reexports of certain nuclear-related items, technologies, and software:

- The DOC, through its Bureau of Industry and Security (BIS), is responsible for implementing and enforcing the Export Administration Regulations (EAR). The EAR regulate the export and reexport of commercial items that are viewed as having "dual-use" (i.e., both commercial and military or proliferation applications). Furthermore, the EAR regulate exports of nuclear balance of plant (BOP) items and related technology.
- The DOS controls the export of defense articles and services under the International Traffic in Arms Regulations (ITAR).[4] These are items and services that, at the time of export, are considered inherently intended for military use. ITAR-controlled defense articles, services, and technology are listed in the U.S. Munitions List.

(c) NRC Export Controls

The NRC controls the export and reexport of nuclear reactors, nuclear reactor equipment and components, and source, special nuclear, and by-product materials in accordance with the requirements of the AEA. The NRC may only issue an export license if the recipient country provides assurances that meet the export criteria set forth in AEA sections 127 and 128 and if the NRC determines that the export will not be inimical to national security. These assurances include a pledge of peaceful use of supplied items, IAEA safeguards over supplied items, maintenance of adequate physical protection measures, and agreement to seek consent of the United States prior to retransfer of supplied items. Some of the AEA export criteria can only be satisfied through pledges made in bilateral peaceful nuclear cooperation agreements entered into pursuant to section 123 of the AEA (123 Agreement). For this reason, the NRC can only authorize certain exports of nuclear equipment and materials if a 123 Agreement is in force between the United States and the recipient country.

With respect to nuclear reactors, the NRC exercises export control authority over any equipment especially designed or made for use in a nuclear reactor. For illustrative purposes, the NRC states that a nuclear reactor includes the items within or attached directly to the reactor vessel, the equipment that controls the level of power

---

4. For a detailed review of the ITAR, see chapter 2, above, at page 31.

in the core, and the components that normally contain or come in direct contact with or control the primary coolant of the reactor core.[5] Examples include reactor pressure vessels, complete reactor control rod systems, reactor primary coolant pumps, and reactor control rod drive mechanisms. This illustrative list is similar to the portion of the NSG Guidelines' "trigger list" that concerns nuclear power reactors, equipment, and components.[6] The NRC also exercises export control authority over radioactive materials, which include source, special, and by-product materials. The NRC recently amended portions of its part 110 regulations related to imports and exports of radioactive materials listed in 10 C.F.R. part 110, Appendix P to take into account provisions in the IAEA Code of Conduct on the Safety and Security of Radioactive Sources (IAEA Code)[7] concerning the import and export of radioactive sources and the supplemental IAEA Guidance on the Import and Export of Radioactive Sources adopting internationally harmonized guidance for the import and export of radioactive sources.[8]

Certain exports — depending on the commodity exported and its destination — may be exported under an NRC general license (i.e., no license application required). In particular, certain minor nuclear reactor components can be exported to destinations listed at 10 C.F.R. § 110.26(b). Such countries include, for example, Canada, France, Japan, the Republic of Korea, Taiwan, and the UK. Other items require the exporter to obtain an NRC-specific export license. This is conducted by submitting NRC form 7, Application for NRC Export or Import License, Amendment, Renewal or Consent Request(s), and a fee in accordance with 10 C.F.R. §§ 110.31 and 110.32 and by meeting the applicable criteria provided in 10 C.F.R. § 110.42.

(d) DOE's Part 810 Regulations

The U.S.'s DOE regulations concerning "assistance to foreign atomic energy activities," codified at 10 C.F.R. part 810, implement the broadly stated requirements of section 57b of the AEA. Section 57b forbids "any person to directly or indirectly engage in the production of any special nuclear material outside the United States," except when provided for in an agreement for cooperation or when authorized by the DOE.[9] The DOE's regulations at part 810 provide the DOE's interpretation of this prohibition, indicate activities that require authorization by the Secretary of Energy,

---

5. *See* 10 C.F.R. pt. 110, app. A.
6. *See* INFCIRC/254 pt. 1, Annex A.
7. International Atomic Energy Agency (IAEA), Code of Conduct on the Safety and Security of Radioactive Sources (IAEA/CODEOC/2004), Vienna, 2004, *available at* http://www.ns.iaea.org/tech-areas/radiation-safety/code-of-conduct.asp.
8. 70 Fed. Reg. 37,993 (July 1, 2005); 71 Fed. Reg. 20,340 (Apr. 20, 2006).
9. DOE's rules define "special nuclear material" as "(1) plutonium, (2) uranium-233, or (3) uranium enriched above 0.711 percent-by-weight in the isotope uranium-235." 10 C.F.R. § 810.3.

and set out reporting requirements for controlled activities. In accordance with 10 C.F.R. § 810.2(c), the DOE's regulations apply, but are not limited to:

> activities involving nuclear reactors and other nuclear fuel cycle facilities for the following: fluoride or nitrate conversion; isotope separation (enrichment); the chemical, physical or metallurgical processing, fabricating, or alloying of special nuclear material; production of heavy water, zirconium (hafnium-free or low-hafnium), nuclear-grade graphite, or reactor-grade beryllium; production of reactor-grade uranium dioxide from yellowcake; and certain uranium milling activities.

The regulations do not provide any specific criteria or guidance as to the scope of controls over each broadly stated activity listed in § 810.2(c). As interpreted by DOE and its predecessor agencies, part 810 applies to virtually all activities by a U.S. citizen or company involving the transfer of key nuclear technologies to other countries.

With respect to technologies involved in the commercial nuclear industry, there are two primary activities controlled by part 810 regulations: nuclear fuel cycle activities and commercial nuclear power activities. Part 810 applies to nuclear fuel cycle activities because such activities result in the production of plutonium or enriched uranium and are thus considered to be directly "engaging" in the "production of special nuclear material." In addition, because commercial nuclear power reactors produce "special nuclear material," the provision of any technical assistance or products that relate to the nuclear power plant's key systems may be considered to be "directly or indirectly engag[ing] in the production of any special nuclear material outside the United States" and thus within the scope of the regulations. It is important to note that part 810 regulations primarily apply to activities that involve the transfers of nuclear-related information, technology, and software, but not to activities that involve the transfers of nuclear equipment and material that are regulated by the NRC. Part 810 regulations also do not apply to exports of information and technology related to components located strictly in the balance of plant (BOP). Those exports are controlled by the DOC EAR.[10]

Part 810 regulations apply to activities conducted by U.S. companies and persons within the United States and abroad and extend to the activities of subsidiaries or contractors under their direction, supervision, responsibility, or control.[11] The DOE's regulations at part 810 provide for two types of authorizations: general and specific. A general authorization allows for a company to engage in certain activities without the

---

10.   There are instances where DOE and DOC appear to have overlapping jurisdiction. For example, DOE has issued part 810 authorizations for exports of reactor control room simulators, although certain export classification control numbers (ECCNs) of the EAR also identify such simulators as items subject to the EAR.

11.   *See* 10 C.F.R. § 810.2(b).

need to secure prior authorization from the DOE. Generally authorized activities are listed in 10 C.F.R. § 810.7 and include the provision of public information, participation in open meetings, and activities related to nuclear power reactors in countries not listed at 10 C.F.R. § 810.8(a). All other activities subject to part 810 controls require specific authorization (essentially a license) from the secretary of energy. Such activities include assistance involving nuclear power reactor technology to countries listed at 10 C.F.R. § 810.8(a), such as Russia, China, and India.[12] Exporters seeking a specific authorization from the DOE must submit a request in accordance with the parameters set out in 10 C.F.R. § 810.10 and 10 C.F.R. § 810.12. The DOE does not provide a form for part 810 applications; therefore, all applications are submitted in free form. In accordance with the requirements of the AEA, the secretary of energy must personally sign each specific authorization issued to an exporter. The secretary of energy will approve an application for specific authorization based on a determination—with concurrence of the DOS and after consultation with the NRC, the DOC, and the U.S. Department of Defense—that the activity will not be inimical to the interest of the United States. In making this determination, the secretary takes into account several factors, including whether the United States has an agreement for nuclear cooperation with the recipient country, whether the recipient country is a party to the NPT, whether the recipient country has entered into an agreement with the IAEA for the application of safeguards on all its peaceful nuclear activities, and other nonproliferation conditions.

(e) Retransfer Controls in 123 Agreements

The United States has entered into agreements on civilian nuclear cooperation, commonly known as 123 Agreements, with over twenty-five states and groups of states, including Japan, the Republic of Korea, China, India, Russia, and the member states of the European Atomic Energy Community. 123 Agreements provide for two types of U.S. consent rights over U.S.-supplied nuclear commodities transferred under these agreements: (1) retransfer consent rights, a requirement that the recipient state obtain prior approval from the United States before retransferring items supplied under the agreement to a third country, and (2) reprocessing consent rights, a requirement that

---

12. Countries currently listed in 10 C.F.R. § 810.8(a), with nonnuclear-weapon states that do not have full-scope IAEA safeguards agreements in force marked with an asterisk, are Afghanistan, Albania, Algeria, Andorra,* Angola,* Armenia, Azerbaijan,* Bahrain,* Belarus, Benin,* Botswana,* Burkina Faso,* Burma (Myanmar), Burundi,* Cambodia,* Cameroon,* Cape Verde,* Central African Republic,* Chad,* China, People's Republic of, Comoros,* Congo* (Zaire), Cuba,* Djibouti,* Equatorial Guinea,* Eritrea,* Gabon,* Georgia,* Guinea,* Guinea-Bissau,* Haiti,* India,* Iran, Iraq,* Israel,* Kazakhstan, Kenya,* Korea, People's Democratic Republic of,* Kuwait,* Kyrgyzstan,* Laos,* Liberia,* Libya, Macedonia, Mali,* Marshall Islands,* Mauritania,* Micronesia,* Moldova,* Mongolia, Mozambique,* Niger,* Oman,* Pakistan,* Palau,* Qatar,* Russia, Rwanda,* Sao Tome and Principe,* Saudi Arabia,* Seychelles,* Sierra Leone,* Somalia,* Sudan, Syria, Tajikistan,* Tanzania,* Togo,* Turkmenistan,* Uganda,* Ukraine, United Arab Emirates,* Uzbekistan, Vanuatu,* Vietnam, Yemen,* and Yugoslavia.

nuclear material transferred pursuant to these agreements and special nuclear material produced through the use of transferred nuclear material and certain equipment (e.g., plutonium that is produced through the irradiation of fuel in reactors) may only be reprocessed upon agreement of the parties.

As an example, on October 11, 2008, the United States and India signed a landmark 123 Agreement that lifted a three-decade-long U.S. moratorium on nuclear-related trade with India that was imposed when India conducted a nuclear test in 1974. The agreement laid the foundation for U.S. companies to supply nuclear components and technology to construct new reactors in the expanding Indian market, as well as provide nuclear fuel to the Indian reactor fleet. The 2006 Hyde Act,[13] which allowed for the implementation of the 123 Agreement under U.S. law, placed additional conditions on nuclear exports to India. These conditions include additional approval requirements, limitations on the scope of licenses, intellectual property protection requirements, and enhanced reporting. For example, the act requires that India provide assurances that U.S. technology transferred to India will not be retransferred without prior U.S. consent, even in the case of domestic transactions within India.

(f) Penalties and Enforcement

Violations of U.S. nuclear export control laws and regulations are subject to civil and criminal penalties. Permanent and temporary injunctions and restraining orders to prevent violations of part 110 and part 810 are possible. Violations of part 810 are subject to fines up to $10,000 or up to ten years in prison; if offenses are committed with intent to injure the United States or to aid any foreign nations, the penalty rises to up to life imprisonment and a $20,000 fine.[14] Violations of part 110 are subject to civil fines of up to $140,000 per violation[15] and criminal penalties are in the form of a fine of up to $5,000 or imprisonment for up to two years, or both; offenses committed with intent to injure the United States or with intent to secure an advantage to any foreign nation can be punished by a fine of up to $20,000 or by imprisonment for up to twenty years, or both.[16]

The NRC will normally take enforcement action for violations of requirements related to import and export of NRC-regulated radioactive material. Specifically, the import and export of the radioactive material (1) within the scope of an NRC license and (2) with implementation of any security programs that may be required are two

---

13. 22 U.S.C. §§ 8001 *et. seq*; Pub. L. No. 109–401.
14. AEA sec. 222 and 10 C.F.R. § 810.15.
15. For continuing violations, each day is a separate violation. AEA sec. 234.
16. AEA sec. 223.

examples of matters of importance where violations of corresponding requirements warrant consideration of escalated enforcement action.[17]

11.4 CANADA: NUCLEAR EXPORT CONTROL POLICY

Although Canada renounced interest in nuclear weapons development shortly after World War II, Canada remains an active participant in the nuclear economy and is a major exporter of uranium and radioisotopes for medical and industrial purposes.[18] Through Atomic Energy of Canada, Ltd., a Canadian Crown Corporation, Canada has also been involved in the construction of CANDU nuclear power plants in several countries, including Romania and China.[19]

Though Canada has strong business interests in the commercial market for nuclear technologies and goods, it also imposes strict regulatory controls on the export of these items to ensure compliance with its nuclear nonproliferation policies and international commitments. Canada is a signatory to the NPT.[20] Before it will consider nuclear cooperation with a nonnuclear-weapon state, Canada requires the state to become a party to the NPT or commit to an equivalent international legally binding agreement and accept the application of IAEA safeguards.[21] Canada is also a founding member of the Zangger Committee of the IAEA and the NSG.[22]

In 2010, Canada ended a decades-long restriction on trade in nuclear-related goods with India when the two countries signed a nuclear cooperation agreement.[23] Like the United States, Canada had prohibited nuclear trade with India as a result of India's diversion of plutonium for use in a nuclear explosive device in 1974. The plutonium was produced in a reactor that had been provided by Canada for peaceful nuclear purposes.[24] The NSG ban on nuclear trade with India that was imposed as a result of

---

17.   NRC Enforcement Policy (June 7, 2012), available in the NRC's Agencywide Document Access and Management System (ADAMS) at ML12132A394.

18.   The Canadian Nuclear Association (CNA), *Does Canada Contribute to Nuclear Weapons Proliferation?* (2010), http://www.cna.ca/english/nuclear_facts/safety/nuclear_proliferation.html; World Nuclear Association, *Uranium in Canada* (Feb. 15, 2012), http://www.world-nuclear.org/info/inf49.html.

19.   *See* CNA, *supra* note 18.

20.   729 U.N.T.S. 161. The Treaty was signed on July 1, 1968, and came into force in 1970.

21.   Foreign Affairs and International Trade Canada, *Nuclear Cooperation Agreements* (Jan. 27, 2012), http://www.international.gc.ca/arms-armes/nuclear-nucleaire/nca-acn.aspx?lang=eng&view=d.

22.   Canadian Nuclear Safety Commission, *Regulatory Impact Analysis Statement to the Regulations Amending the Nuclear Non-proliferation Import and Export Control Regulations* (May 13, 2010), http://www.gazette.gc.ca/rp-pr/p2/2010/2010-05-26/html/sor-dors106-eng.html.

23.   *Canada and India Sign Nuclear Co-Operation Deal*, BBC News (June 28, 2010), http://www.bbc.co.uk/news/10430904.

24.   Ian Anthony, Christer Ahlström & Vitaly Fedchenko, *Reforming Nuclear Export Controls — The Future of the Nuclear Suppliers Group*, 22 SIPRI Research Report, 6 (2007), *available at* http://books.sipri.org/files/RR/SIPRIRR22.pdf.

this activity was lifted in 2008.[25] Canada's cooperation agreement with India provides assurances that nuclear material, equipment, and technology originating in Canada will be used only for civilian, peaceful, and nonexplosive purposes.[26]

What Is Regulated? Canada – The import and export of nuclear and nuclear-related goods and technologies is primarily regulated under the Nuclear Safety and Control Act[27] (NSCA) and the Nuclear Non-proliferation Import and Export Control Regulations[28] (NNIECR).

Where to Find the Regulations: Canada – The statutory authority of the NNIECR is the NSCA. The NNIECR set out the import and export licensing application requirements for a prescribed list of controlled nuclear and nuclear-related substances, equipment, and technologies detailed in its schedule. The Export and Import Permits Act[29] (EIPA) sets out import and export permit requirements.

Who Is the Regulator? Canada – The Canadian Nuclear Safety Commission (CNSC) is the federal authority that implements regulatory controls for the production, use, storage, and movement of nuclear material in Canada. The Department of Foreign Affairs and International Trade Canada (DFAIT) oversees permit requirements under the EIPA.

(a)   Statutes and Federal Authorities

The import and export of nuclear and nuclear-related goods and technologies in Canada is primarily controlled through the NSCA, which came into force on May 31, 2000, and the NNIECR.

The CNSC, established under the NSCA, is the federal authority that implements regulatory controls for the production, use, storage, and movement of nuclear material in Canada.[30] The import and export of nuclear substances, prescribed equipment, information, and technology is subject to regulatory control through the CNSC

---

25.   Somini Sengupta & Mark Mazzetti, *Backed by U.S., India Is Approved for Nuclear Trade*, N.Y. Times, Sept. 7, 2008, *available at* http://www.nytimes.com/2008/09/07/world/asia/07iht-india.1.15946952.html?_r=1. The NSG waiver permits NSG country members to engage in nuclear trade for civilian nuclear power purposes with India, despite India not being a member of the NSG group or a signatory to the NPT. India agreed to IAEA safeguards.

26.   As of March 20, 2013, the cooperation agreement had yet to be ratified. However, as per Article 18 of the Vienna Convention on the Law of Treaties, Canada must maintain the object and purpose of the agreement until it is ratified. Vienna Convention on the Law of Treaties art. 18, May 23, 1969. It is also noted that on November 6, 2012, Prime Minister Stephen Harper, together with Indian Prime Minister Manmohan Singh, announced the conclusion of negotiations for the Administrative Arrangement between Canada and India that will allow the implementation of the cooperation agreement signed between the two countries in 2010.

27.   S.C. 1997, c. 9. The predecessor statute of the NSCA was the Atomic Energy Control Act.

28.   SOR/2000-210.

29.   R.S.C. 1985, c. E-19.

30.   *Supra* note 27 at s. 8. Prior to the establishment of the CNSC under the NSCA, the regulation of the Canadian nuclear industry was conducted by the Atomic Energy Control Board.

licensing regime, as well as through permit requirements under the EIPA administered by the DFAIT.

The CNSC licensing and compliance process is structured to ensure that nuclear imports and exports meet Canada's regulatory requirements, nuclear nonproliferation policy, and international obligations and commitments. The principle underlying these measures is that controlled nuclear substances, material, equipment, and technology transferred between Canada and other countries should only be used for peaceful and nonexplosive purposes.[31]

(b) Import and Export Licensing of Nuclear and Nuclear-Related Items

Importers and exporters of nuclear and nuclear-related goods and technologies in Canada must obtain and comply with CNSC licenses controlling the international transfer of these goods. The NNIECR set out the import and export licensing application requirements for a prescribed list of controlled nuclear and nuclear-related substances, equipment, and technologies described in detail in its schedule.[32] It is particularly important for exporters to review whether an export, despite having nonnuclear-related commercial application, is nevertheless controlled by the NNIECR as a dual-use nuclear substance, equipment, or information or technology.[33]

The categories in the schedule to the NNIECR are:

A.1.   Nuclear substances (including special fissionable material such as plutonium and uranium, as well as nuclear-grade graphite)

A.2.   Nuclear equipment (including nuclear reactors and specially designed components)

A.3.   Parts for nuclear equipment identified in A.2

A.4.   Nuclear information and technology (including technical data such as drawings and operating manuals)

B.1.   Dual-use nuclear substances

B.2.   Dual-use nuclear equipment

B.3.   Dual-use nuclear information and technology

The basic license application requirements include a detailed description of the substance, equipment, or information and its classification in the schedule, as well as

---

31.   Canadian Nuclear Safety Commission, *Import and Export Controls* (Feb. 28, 2012), http://nuclear safety.gc.ca/eng/licenseesapplicants/importexport.

32.   *Supra* note 28. The list of substances described in the schedule to the NNIECR is reproduced, with some modifications, from International Atomic Energy Agency Information Circulars INFCIRC/254/Rev.9/Part 1, INFCIRC/254/Rev.7/Part 2, and INFCIRC/209/Rev.2.

33.   Lawrence Herman, Export Controls and Economic Sanctions: A Guide to Canadian Trade Restrictions 3 (2011). *See also generally* our discussion of *R. v. Yadegari* (July 6, 2010), Toronto, Mocha J (Ont. C J), aff'd 2011 ONCA 287, below, for analysis on how a dual-use item may fall within certain technical parameters and therefore be subject to export restrictions.

the intended end use and end-use location.[34] Where the application relates to a controlled substance included in Category 1, 2, or 3 of the Nuclear Security Regulations,[35] the application must also outline the measures that will be taken to facilitate Canada's compliance with the Convention on the Physical Protection of Nuclear Material.[36] In addition to the enumerated license application requirements, the CNSC also has broad authority under the NNIECR to request any additional information necessary to satisfy the CNSC that the licensee is qualified to carry on the activity, the activity makes adequate provisions for the protection of the environment, health, and safety, and takes all measures required to implement international obligations.[37] Application forms for a license to import nuclear items, and a license to export nuclear and nuclear-related dual-use items, are available for download on the CNSC website.[38] Once completed, application forms must be returned to the CNSC, addressed to the Licensing Administrator, Safeguards Accounting and Technology Division, Directorate of Security and Safeguards.

In 2010, the NNIECR were amended to reflect changes to the NSG Guidelines that had taken place since the NNIECR came into force in 2000. The changes reflect advances in nuclear and nuclear-related technologies and changing proliferation risks.[39] Select amendments include new notes that aim to clarify obligations and reduce regulatory burden on exporters, as well as a requirement for new end-use control for nuclear-related dual-use items to make regulations consistent with international controls.[40]

(c) Import and Export Licenses for Risk-Significant Radioactive Sources
(i) Export of Risk-Significant Radioactive Sources

Transaction-specific export licenses from the CNSC are required to export risk-significant radioactive sources listed in Category 1 and 2 of Table I of the IAEA Code.[41] Substances such as curium 244 and plutonium 238 above certain threshold

---

34. *Supra* note 28, at s.3.
35. SOR/2000-209.
36. *Supra* note 28, at s.3(1)(h); INFCIRC/274/Rev.1.
37. *Id.* at s.3(2).
38. *Supra* note 31.
39. The revision and implementation of the amended regulations involve, among other activities, a pre-consultation with existing licensees and stakeholders, consultation with the Export Control Division of DFAIT, as well as the collection of feedback from licensees and stakeholders. Canadian Nuclear Safety Commission, Amendments to the Non-Proliferation Import and Export Control Regulations: Pre-Consultation Disposition Report, 1 http://nuclearsafety.gc.ca/eng/lawsregs/actsregulations/proposedamendments/nniecr/NNIECR_amendments.cfm.
40. *See supra* note 22.
41. Canadian Nuclear Safety Commission, *Control of the Export and Import of Risk-Significant Radioactive Sources INFO-0791*, April 2010 at pg. 2, available at http://www.nuclearsafety.gc.ca//pubs_catalogue/uploads/Info_0791_e.pdf.

activity levels are included in these categories. These licensing requirements reflect the Canadian government's commitment to working to meet the standards of the code and IAEA Guidance on the Import and Export of Radioactive Source.[42]

Export licenses can contain any term or condition and are issued at the discretion of a designated officer of the CNSC. The CNSC advises that exporters should provide sufficient details in their application for the CNSC to effectively evaluate compliance with its standards. Assessment by the CNSC includes consideration of the risk that a risk-significant radioactive source may be diverted for other purposes, as well as a review of whether the regulatory controls of the importing state provide sufficient safeguards for the source to be managed safely and securely. Where an application relates to the export of risk-significant substances in Category 1 of Table I of the IAEA Code,[43] such as certain radionuclide typically used in radiothermal generators, irradiators, and radiation teletherapy, the CNSC will consult with the importing government authority as part of its assessment of the application.[44]

Generally speaking, a license to export a risk-significant radioactive source is required for each export transaction or specific set of transactions that are expected to occur within a specified period of time. The CNSC service standards for review of these license applications is typically within three weeks following receipt of a completed application. That said, the CNSC suggests submitting these license applications at the earliest opportunity, as processing periods can vary depending on factors such as whether the substance falls within Category 1 or Category 2, the required international communications and consultations, and the availability of information on the importer, among other factors.[45]

(ii) Import of Risk-Significant Radioactive Sources

Unlike export license requirements for risk-significant radioactive sources, importers of these substances are not required to obtain a transaction-specific license. Licensees authorized to possess risk-significant radioactive sources may import these sources without a specific import license from the CNSC, provided the activity complies with the general import authorization in their possession license.[46] The CNSC requires prior shipment notifications from the exporting facility or exporting state authority for the import of all Category 1 and 2 radioactive sources. Additionally, the import of Category 1 radioactive sources into Canada is subject to prior import consent from the CNSC. [47]

---

42. IAEA/CODEOC/IMPEXP/2005, IAEA, Vienna, 2005.
43. *Supra* note 7, at 15–16.
44. *Supra* note 41, at 2–3.
45. *Id.* at 3–4.
46. *Id.* at 3.
47. *Supra* note 31.

(d) Export and Import Permits Act

In addition to CNSC licensing requirements, the international transfer of nuclear and nuclear-related goods and technologies may also be subject to export controls under the EIPA where the item appears on the Export Control List (ECL).[48] Nuclear and nuclear-related items are principally outlined in Group 3 (Nuclear Non-proliferation) and Group 4 (Nuclear-Related Dual Use).[49] Where an item is regulated under the NSCA and EIPA, both an export permit and an export license are required.

The export permit process is administered by DFAIT. Applicants may apply for an export permit through Export Controls On-Line (EXCOL). EXCOL is an Internet-based system that allows applicants to apply for export control documents electronically. Alternatively, applicants may submit paper applications for export permits; however, some processing delay may result.[50]

Where applications are filed with each agency, both agencies consult with each other to coordinate licensing and permit decisions. Where the CNSC refuses to issue a license, DFAIT will typically defer to this decision and consequently deny the issuance of an export permit.[51] Exporters of Group 3 items may submit their export permit application to the Export Controls Division of DFAIT, which will forward all relevant information to the CNSC. Group 4 items require separate applications to the two federal authorities.[52] In 2010, DFAIT issued 267 permits of Group 3 items and 112 export permits for Group 4 items. The median processing performance times for nuclear items was fourteen days, and for nuclear dual-use items it was six days.[53]

---

48. SOR/89-202. A detailed description of controlled items is included in the Foreign Affairs and International Trade Canada, A Guide to Canada's Export Controls (June 2010), http://www.international.gc.ca/controls-controles/about-a_propos/expor/guide.aspx?view=d. Exporters should note that some nuclear and nuclear-related items not listed on the Export Control List are controlled under the NSCA and regulations, and require licenses from the CNSC prior to export. *See* Foreign Affairs and International Trade Canada, Export Controls Handbook (Feb. 2012) at F.8, *available at* http://www.international.gc.ca/controls-controles/export-exportation/TOC-exp_ctr_handbook-manuel_ctr_exp.aspx?lang=eng&view=d.

49. Nuclear-related goods and technologies may also appear in other sections of the List, including the catch-all provisions of Item 5505, which imposes permit requirements on an item if it is determined that the end use could be related to the development or production of certain weapons, including nuclear weapons. *See* generally, Foreign Affairs and International Trade Canada, *Export Controls over Goods and Technology for Certain Uses-Notice to Exports* (Mar. 2011) http://www.international.gc.ca/controls-controles/systems-systemes/excol-ceed/notices-avis/176.aspx?lang=eng&view=d.

50. Export Controls Handbook, *supra* note 48, at E.2.

51. Herman, *supra* note 33.

52. Export Controls Handbook, *supra* note 48.

53. Foreign Affairs and International Trade Canada, Update: Canadian Export Controls Policy and Practices (Feb. 3, 2011), http://www.international.gc.ca/controls-controles/about-a_propos/expor/policy-export_ctrl-politique.aspx?lang=eng&view=d.

(e) Judicial Consideration: *R. v. Yadegari*

The 2010 conviction of Mahmoud Yadegari in *R. v. Yadegari*[54] on offenses related to the attempted exportation of pressure transducers to an individual in Iran provided a rare opportunity for the judiciary to consider Canadian export controls that apply to nuclear and nuclear-related goods and technologies. *R. v. Yadegari* is the first conviction under the NSCA and marks the first charge against a Canadian under the United Nations Act[55] (U.N. Act).[56] In addition to these charges, Mr. Yadegari was convicted for various offenses under the EIPA, Criminal Code,[57] and the Customs Act.[58] The Trial and Ontario Court of Appeal decisions set out a useful illustration of the interaction of various export controls that apply to nuclear-related goods and the judicial approach to enforcing these controls.

In 2009, Mahmoud Yadegari procured a number of pressure transducers from a foreign supplier and then attempted to export a number of these items from Canada to Iran. While pressure transducers have commercial applications in medical sterilization and food freeze-drying, they are also capable of being used in the enrichment of uranium through gas centrifugation.[59] Mr. Yadegari did not obtain any export licenses or permits and removed labels identifying the items as pressure transducers. The shipment was intercepted by authorities before the transducers crossed Canadian borders.

Though Mr. Yadegari argued that the transducers did not meet threshold content and accuracy requirements and were therefore not subject to export restrictions, the trial judge found and the Court of Appeal affirmed that the technical specifications of the pressure transducers met the technical parameters in the specifications set out in the IAEA Information Circular 254 and were therefore restricted under the Regula-

---

54. *R. v. Yadegari* (July 6, 2010), Toronto, Mocha J (Ont. C J) (Yadegari Trial Decision), aff'd 2011 ONCA 287 (Yadegari Appeal Decision).
55. R.S.C. 1985, c. U-2.
56. Canadian Nuclear Safety Commission, Information Update: Mahmoud Yadegari Sentenced in Ontario Court of Justice for Offences under the NSCA (July 30, 2010), http://nuclearsafety.gc.ca/eng/mediacentre/updates/2010/July_30_2010_Yadegari_sentence.cfm.
57. R.S.C. 1985, c. C-46.
58. R.S.C. 1985, c. 1 (2nd Supp.). Mr. Yadegari failed to obtain a Certificate of Exemption pursuant to s.20 of the Iran Regulations, an export permit pursuant to s.7 of the EIPA, and a license pursuant to s.26 of the NCSA. The pressure transducers are also considered "restricted goods" under the Customs Act, and Mr. Yadegari failed to report the export of these goods to the Canada Border Services Agency, as required by law, and also failed to report the export of goods with a value over $2,000 and also made a false declaration of their value.
59. Yadegari Appeal Decision, *supra* note 54, at para. 2.

tions Implementing the United Nations Resolutions on Iran.[60] They also determined that the technical characteristics of the pressure transducers described in the specifications were essentially the same as those described under the NNIECR[61] and the ECL[62] and therefore required the appropriate regulatory approvals for export outlined in those authorities.

The judicial discussion of sentencing principles underscores the serious nature and international ramifications of activities involving the transfer of nuclear-related goods. The trial judge and the Court of Appeal agreed that breaches of the U.N. Act, the NSCA, and the EIPA were of "paramount significance" given the potential harm involved in the actions of the appellants and that sentencing "should promote responsibility in the offender given the potential harm to the global community."[63]

To date, the Yadegari case is the only case in which the Canadian nuclear export control regime has been given any substantive judicial consideration.

---

60. SOR/2007-44. These regulations were enacted under the UN Act to uphold Canada's obligation under the UN Security Council Resolution 1737m UNSCOR, 2006, UN DOC. S/RES/1737, which imposed sanctions on Iran for its failure to adhere to its obligations under the NPT. The regulations prescribe it an offense to "knowingly sell, supply or transfer, directly or indirectly," certain products to any person in Iran or for the benefit of Iran (s.3). The list of proscribed goods and technology are set out in IAEA Information Circular *Communications Received from Certain Member States Regarding Guidelines for Transfers of Nuclear-related Dual-use Equipment, Materials, Software and Related Technology*, UNI-AEA OR, 2006, UN Doc. INFCIRC/254/Rev. 7/Part 2, and include pressure transducers that meet certain technical parameters.
61. *Supra* note 28, at Schedule, Part B, B.2.2.8.
62. *Supra* note 48.
63. Yadegari Appeal Decision, *supra* note 54, at para. 95.

Appendixes

Appendix A to Chapter 1

Individual Summaries of U.S. Country-Based Economic Sanctions Programs

Jeanine P. McGuinness

Currently, the United States maintains broad, country-based economic sanctions with respect to Cuba, Iran, Sudan, and Syria. It also maintains less extensive economic sanctions programs that target specific activities occurring in or related to Burma (Myanmar) and North Korea and their governments. The following discussion of these programs also includes, as appropriate, references to their associated list-based aspects. However, changes to these programs are frequent, and these summaries should only be used in tandem with an analysis of the revisions to their respective regulations and other sources of legal authority that may have occurred since the date that this chapter was written.

BURMA (MYANMAR)

The Burmese Sanctions Regulations (BSR)[1] prohibit the U.S. importation of articles of Burmese origin (although the BSR do not prohibit trade in Burmese articles with third countries), the exportation of financial services to Burma (Myanmar), and the making of certain forms of new investment in Burma (Myanmar). However, these economic sanctions generally allow the U.S. exportation of goods, technology, and services to Burma (Myanmar), other than financial services (unless the financial services are incident to otherwise permitted exports) and prohibited forms of new investment.[2]

U.S. financial services that are barred from exportation or reexportation include funds transfers and most banking, insurance, and securities brokerage activities. This financial services prohibition includes, without limitation, lending, trade financing, and providing services related to travelers checks, money orders, credit cards, and prepaid access cards.

The U.S. economic sanctions for Burma (Myanmar) also prohibit U.S. persons from facilitating any financial transaction by a non-U.S. person if the BSR would pro-

---

1. 31 C.F.R. pt. 537.
2. The U.S. economic sanctions against the Burmese government have been greatly relaxed by general licenses posted on OFAC's website, but not yet made permanent. *See* discussion below and OFAC'S posted Frequently Asked Questions Related to Burmese Sanctions.

hibit U.S. persons from directly participating in that transaction. However, OFAC guidance remains unclear regarding whether financial services received outside Burma (Myanmar) for persons resident in Burma (Myanmar), such as payments into the Thai account of a Burmese national, create a violation by providing a benefit that is received in Burma (Myanmar).

Additionally, the BSR generally prohibit U.S. persons from engaging in or facilitating transactions that meet the complex definition of "new investment" (occurring after May 20, 1997) for the development of resources in Burma (Myanmar) (with certain exceptions for subcontracting arrangements).[3]

The BSR block all property within U.S. jurisdiction (including property within the possession or control of U.S. persons, wherever located) in which an interest is held or controlled by the Burmese State Peace and Development Council or its successors, by designated banks controlled by the Burmese government, or by other designated persons in the Burmese government or providing material support to it. On July 11, 2012, in conjunction with the issuance of broad general licenses described below, the President issued Executive Order 13,619,[4] authorizing the Secretary of the Treasury, in consultation with or at the suggestion of the Secretary of State, to designate and block the assets of persons (a) whose acts threaten Burma's peace, security, or stability; (b) involved in the commission of human rights abuses in Burma; or (c) involved in strategic trade with North Korea, including persons who are senior officials of entities engaging in the foregoing actions, or who have materially supported such actions or persons whose assets are blocked under the order.

The BSR include a wide range of exceptions to their prohibitions. For example, the regulations either exempt or provide a general license for continued performance of contracts agreed to prior to May 21, 1997, with Burma (Myanmar) or Burmese entities (other than contracts for the exportation to the United States of Burmese origin articles, which are prohibited). IEEPA exempts in-kind donations to relieve human suffering, and the application of the Berman Amendment exempts trade in permitted information and informational materials and transactions related to travel. In addition, the BSR include, and OFAC has separately issued, a number of broad general licenses permitting transactions in or with Burma (Myanmar).

Of particular note, on May 17, 2012, in response to the democratic reforms and election that took place in Burma (Myanmar) in spring 2012, Secretary of State Clinton issued a press statement in connection with the visit by the foreign minister of Burma (Myanmar). She stated that "The United States will issue a general license that will enable American businesses to invest across the economy, allow citizens access to international credit markets and dollar-based transactions."[5]

---

3. *See* 31 C.F.R. §§ 537.204, 537.311, and 537.410–537.413.
4. 77 Fed. Reg. 41,243–41,245 (July 13, 2012).
5. *See* http://www.state.gov/secretary/rm/2012/05/190260.htm.

On July 11, 2012, OFAC issued General Licenses 16 and 17 authorizing most exports and reexports of financial services to Burma (Myanmar) from the United States or by U.S. persons, and most new investment in Burma (Myanmar) by U.S. persons, with certain limitations. First, General License 16 prohibits financial service exports or reexports in connection with the provision of security services to the Burmese Ministry of Defense, to a state or non-state armed group, or to an entity owned 50 percent or more by the foregoing. Second, General License 16 bars the export or reexport of financial services to SDNs of Burma (Myanmar) (except transfers involving accounts at blocked Burmese financial institutions not on the books of a U.S. person). Third, no debits to blocked accounts are authorized for exports or reexports of financial services to Burma (Myanmar).

The restrictions on new investments under General License 17 are, first, that they not be undertaken under an agreement with the Burmese Ministry of Defense or a state or non-state armed group, or an entity 50 percent or more owned by the foregoing; second, that the transactions not be with SDNs of Burma; and third, that all new investment be in compliance with State Department reporting requirements contained in "Reporting Requirements on Responsible Investment in Burma."[6]

On November 16, 2012, OFAC issued General License 18, authorizing the importation of any article that is a product of Burma with the exception of jadeite and rubies mined or extracted in Burma and jewelry containing such jadeite or rubies. The license does not authorize transactions with persons whose property is blocked pursuant to the Burma sanctions.[7]

On February 22, 2013, OFAC issued General License 19, authorizing all transactions with four major Burmese banks: Asia Green Development Bank, Ayeyarwady Bank, Myanma Economic Bank and Myanma Investment and Commercial Bank, including the opening of correspondent accounts with U.S. financial institutions for these banks. The license does not unblock any funds previously blocked. The lifting of the special anti-money laundering measures previously imposed under section 311 of the USA PATRIOT Act applies to all transactions through the four banks' correspondent accounts that are authorized pursuant to the BSR.[8]

Note that General Licenses 16 through 19 have not been codified in the BSR. Because sanctions programs seek changes in behavior in their target governments, the general licenses serve as incentives for the government of Burma (Myanmar) to continue its progress toward political reform. Thus, the broad prohibitions of the BSR are merely suspended, not dropped.

---

6. *See* reporting requirements at http://www.HumanRights.gov/BurmaResponsibleInvestment. *See* 78 Fed. Reg. 12, 132-12, 134 (Feb. 21, 2013), which remained pending at March 15, 2013.
7. Available online at http://www.treasury.gov/resource-center/sanctions/Programs/Documents/burma gl18.pdf.
8. Available online at http://www.treasury.gov/resource-center/sanctions/Programs/Documents/burma gl19.pdf.

CUBA

The Cuban Assets Control Regulations (CACR)[9] are built on the wartime blocking model, and they are the most sweeping economic sanctions currently imposed by the United States. Without a license, the CACR prohibit "persons subject to the jurisdiction of the United States" (i.e., U.S. persons and non-U.S. entities owned or controlled by U.S. persons) from engaging, directly or indirectly, in transactions with respect to property in which the Cuban government, Cuban nationals (defined below), or, with minor exceptions, anyone located in Cuba has an interest or has had an interest at any time since the July 8, 1963, effective date of the CACR. This prohibition applies to interests held or controlled, directly or indirectly, by the government of Cuba or by Cuban nationals regardless of the location of those interests. The CACR require that any person subject to U.S. jurisdiction block any such property and interests in property within that person's possession or control or otherwise within U.S. jurisdiction. These sweeping economic sanctions also prohibit persons subject to U.S. jurisdiction from exporting goods, services, or technology to Cuba, importing Cuban property into the United States, or dealing in Cuban goods anywhere in the world. In addition, these regulations prohibit persons subject to U.S. jurisdiction from exporting services to, or otherwise facilitating a transaction that will provide a benefit to, the government of Cuba or any Cuban national.

Section 515.302 of the CACR defines a "Cuban national" as any person who or which has met any of the following tests on or since the July 8, 1963, effective date of the Cuban sanctions program: (1) any individual who is a Cuban citizen, has been domiciled in Cuba, or has been a permanent resident of Cuba; (2) any entity that is organized in Cuba, has had its principal place of business in Cuba, or has been, directly or indirectly, controlled by—or a "substantial part of the . . . securities or obligations of which was or has been controlled by"—the Cuban government or a Cuban national; (3) any office or other location within Cuba of a foreign organization; (4) any person who has acted, or purported to act, directly or indirectly, for the benefit or on behalf of any of the foregoing; and (5) any other person "who there is reasonable cause to believe is a 'national' as defined in this section."

This definition of "national" is the broadest of any OFAC-administered economic sanctions program. OFAC's blocking jurisdiction is asserted over all Cuban nationals, wherever located. For that reason, OFAC has issued a general license unblocking the assets of Cuban nationals lawfully resident in the United States. To obtain unrestricted services from persons subject to the jurisdiction of the United States, Cuban refugees in third countries must first come to OFAC to request and obtain unblocking of their property. Otherwise, persons subject to the jurisdiction of the United

---

9. 31 C.F.R. pt. 515.

States (such as non-U.S. subsidiaries of U.S. financial institutions) must either obtain two pieces of identification issued by the government of the new country of permanent residence of the Cuban national, or they must refuse service. Non-U.S. governments have protested this extraterritorial assertion of jurisdiction by the United States in their jurisdictions by prohibiting compliance in their territories with the U.S. economic sanctions against Cuba.

TWEA's Berman Amendment exempts trade in permitted informational materials (but not for transactions related to travel) from regulation. Under a process similar to TSRA, licensing for trade in agricultural commodities, medical devices, and medicines is administered by the U.S. Department of Commerce, whereas OFAC has jurisdiction over incidental travel transactions and the associated payment process by Cuba. Sales to Cuba under these agricultural and medical licenses require advance payment in cash or third-country bank financing.

IRAN

U.S. economic sanctions against Iran have evolved in their targets and mechanisms in response to worsening relations with the United States from the time of the 1979 revolution. This program originated with a 1986 ban on U.S. importation of Iranian-origin goods and services and then was expanded in 1995 into to create a general trade embargo against Iran and a requirement to reject transactions with its government. The current economic sanctions target, expressly or through a blocking regime, most transactions with Iran and its government worldwide, whether conducted or facilitated by U.S. persons, their non-U.S. subsidiaries or, to an increasing extent, by non-U.S. persons acting wholly outside U.S. jurisdiction.

The following discussion of the economic sanctions against Iran reflects a program that continues to evolve rapidly and, like all OFAC programs, is subject to change without prior notice.[10] As of [March 15, 2013], certain recent legislation mandating new economic sanctions on Iran had not yet been implemented through executive order delegations or OFAC regulations, and legislation to further tighten those economic sanctions was pending in Congress, reflecting the continued worsening of U.S. relations with Iran over issues of terrorism, human rights and nuclear nonproliferation.

Blocking, transactional, and trade restrictions with respect to Iran are contained in two country-based sets of OFAC regulations: the Iranian Transactions and Sanctions

---

10.   Between 2010 and 2013, the statutory, executive order, and regulatory measures imposing primary and secondary economic sanctions against Iran demonstrated how rapidly U.S. economic sanctions programs implemented by OFAC can change. Therefore, persons seeking to understand or provide advice regarding any economic sanctions program, and particularly regarding the program against Iran, are strongly advised to check both the OFAC website and the updated versions of OFAC and other agency regulations implementing economic sanctions found on the Electronic Code of Federal Regulations website of the U.S. Government Printing Office.

Regulations (ITSR)[11] and the Iranian Financial Sanctions Regulations (IFSR).[12,13] In general, the ITSR implement the trade and transaction sanctions and prohibitions concerning Iran and its government, and the IFSR impose restrictions on certain activities by U.S. financial institutions' non-U.S. subsidiaries and implement secondary economic sanctions against non-U.S. financial institutions. The following summary of the economic sanctions against Iran discusses the ITSR, recent Iran-related statutes and executive orders, and the IFSR.

The ITSR. The ITSR block the property and property interests within U.S. jurisdiction of (1) the government of Iran (including its political subdivisions, agencies and instrumentalities, such as Bank Markazi, which is the central bank of Iran); (2) all financial institutions located or organized in Iran or owned or controlled by the government of Iran, including their non-Iranian branches (Iranian financial institutions); (3) any person found by the Secretary of the Treasury, in consultation with the Secretary of State, to be owned by, controlled by or acting for or on behalf of the government of Iran or any Iranian financial institution; and (4) any person found by the Secretary of the Treasury, in consultation with the Secretary of State, to have materially assisted, sponsored or provided material support for (a) the National Iranian Oil Company (NIOC); the Naftiran Intertrade Company (NICO); any entity owned or controlled by, or operating for or on behalf of, NIOC or NICO; the Central Bank of Iran; or (b) the purchase or acquisition of U.S. bank notes or precious metals by the government of Iran.

The blocking measures in the ITSR generally bar U.S. persons from engaging in any transaction in Iran, with its government (including entities owned or controlled by it) or with persons acting on the government's behalf.

The ITSR further prohibit U.S. persons from importing Iranian-origin goods or services and from exporting goods, technology or services if such exports' benefit will be received in Iran or by its government. They also contain a prohibition on facilitation, which prohibits U.S. persons from facilitating any transaction by a non-U.S. person if these regulations would prohibit a U.S. person from directly engaging in that transaction.

With regard to the effect of licensing, the ITSR's interpretation contained in section 560.405 of the ITSR that all transactions "ordinarily incident" to a licensed transaction are also authorized states that payments and funds transfers incident to a licensed transaction involving Iran are not authorized.[14] This differs from OFAC's

---

11.   31 C.F.R. pt. 560. From 1986 through October 22, 2012, this part was known as the Iranian Transactions Regulations (ITR).

12.   31 C.F.R. pt. 561, originally issued in August 2010.

13.   OFAC also administers a list-based blocking program targeting persons designated for Iranian human rights abuses, the Iranian Human Rights Abuses Sanctions Regulations, 31 C.F.R. pt. 562, which is not discussed here.

14.   31 C.F.R § 560.405.

"ordinarily incident" interpretation in most programs.[15] Instead, in the ITSR, such payments and transfers must be explicitly authorized in the text of separate general or specific licenses, such as the general license authorizing U.S. depository institutions and registered securities brokers and dealers to undertake such transactions.[16] Among other effects, this narrow interpretation limits the ability of hawalas and money service businesses to initiate such transfers. The ITSR include a limited license authorizing personal remittances through U.S. banks to non-blocked individuals ordinarily resident in Iran.[17] Certain transactions related to inheritance and other family-related transactions are also generally licensed.[18]

Exemptions for trade in permitted information and informational materials, transactions related to travel and the making of in-kind donations to relieve human suffering apply to the ITSR. Pursuant to the Trade Sanctions Reform and Export Enhancement Act (TSRA),[19] OFAC issues specific licenses, which are valid for one year, for U.S. exports of agricultural commodities, medical devices, medicines and incidental transactions. As a part of this licensing program, the ITSR contain general licenses authorizing exports and reexports of certain food, medicine and basic medical devices to Iran and incidental financial transactions under stated conditions.[20]

Recent Iran-Related Statutes and Executive Orders. The United States has recently strengthened sanctions against Iran through a number of statutes and executive orders. These include the Comprehensive Iran Sanctions, Accountability, and Divestment Act of 2010 (CISADA),[21] Executive Order 13,622 of July 30, 2013,[22] section 1245 of the National Defense Authorization Act for Fiscal Year 2012 (NDAA),[23] the Iran Threat Reduction and Syria Human Rights Act of 2012 (TRA),[24] and the Iran Freedom and Counter-Proliferation Act of 2012 (IFCA), which is part of the National Defense Authorization Act for Fiscal Year 2013.[25] An important impact of these statutes and executive orders is the expanded assertion of U.S. jurisdiction over non-U.S. persons, including non-U.S. subsidiaries of U.S. companies. For example, the TRA prohibits non-U.S.-organized entities owned or controlled by U.S. persons from knowingly engaging in any transaction directly or indirectly with the government of Iran or any person subject to the jurisdiction of the government of Iran that would be prohibited by the ITSR or any other executive order or regulation if engaged in by a

---

15. *See*, for example, 31 C.F.R. § 510.404 (North Korea).
16. 31 C.F.R. § 560.516.
17. *See* 31 C.F.R. § 560.550
18. *See*, for example, 31 C.F.R. §§ 560.542 and 560.543.
19. Title IX of Pub. L. No. 106-387 (October 28, 2000).
20. *See* 31 C.F.R. §§ 560.530 and 560.532.
21. 22 U.S.C. §§ 8501 et seq., Pub. L. No. 111-195 (Jul. 1, 2010).
22. 77 Fed. Reg. 45,897–45,902 (Aug. 2, 2013).
23. Pub. L. No. 112-81 (Dec. 31, 2011).
24. Pub. L. No. 112-158 (Aug. 10, 2012).
25. Title XII, subtitle D of the National Defense Authorization Act for Fiscal Year 2013, Pub. L. No. 112-239 (Jan. 1, 2013).

U.S. person or in the United States, and it provides that the U.S. persons owning or controlling those non-U.S. persons are liable for civil penalties for such transactions. In addition, these statutes and executive orders impose secondary economic sanctions on non-U.S. persons engaging in certain transactions that are not consistent with U.S. policy toward Iran, even where such transactions are lawful in the jurisdictions where they occur and involve no transactions within the United States (e.g., non-U.S. trade not involving U.S. dollar transactions).

CISADA. The Iran Sanctions Act of 1996 (ISA)[26] generally remained a marginal component of U.S. efforts to apply pressure on the Iranian government until it was amended by CISADA on July 1, 2010. CISADA added significant new secondary economic sanctions against persons doing business with Iran. CISADA amended the ISA by, among other things, targeting new Iran-related activities for sanctions and adding to the menu of sanctions the President can choose to impose on persons that knowingly engage in such activities. The ISA was further amended by the TRA, as discussed below. CISADA also includes provisions that prohibit domestic financial institutions from opening or maintaining correspondent accounts or payable-through accounts in the United States for "foreign financial institutions"[27] that have been found by the Secretary of the Treasury to engage in specified activities related to Iran. These provisions of CISADA have been implemented by the IFSR, as discussed below.

The NDAA. Among other things, Section 1245 of the NDAA expanded the financial institution sanctions in CISADA. Subject to certain exceptions and possible waivers, the NDAA requires the President to prohibit the opening, and to prohibit or impose strict conditions on the maintenance, in the United States, of correspondent or payable-through accounts for certain non-U.S. financial institutions. The requirement applies when the President determines that such non-U.S. financial institutions have knowingly conducted or facilitated any "significant financial transaction" with the Central Bank of Iran or certain blocked Iranian financial institutions designated for sanctions under the International Emergency Economic Powers Act, as amended (IEEPA). The President may grant a renewable 180-day exception for the imposition of sanctions under the NDAA to all foreign financial institutions in a country if the President determines that the country has "significantly" reduced its volume of crude oil purchases from Iran within a specified reporting period. This exception was tightened effective February 6, 2013, as discussed below.

Executive Order 13,599. Executive Order 13,599 of February 8, 2012 blocks all property within U.S. jurisdiction of the government of Iran, any person owned or controlled by or acting for or on behalf of the government of Iran, and all Iranian financial institutions.

Executive Order 13,606. In Executive Order 13,606 of April 22, 2012, the President directed the blocking of the property of named persons operating or directing

---

26.   50 U.S.C. § 1701 note.
27.   Defined at 31 C.F.R. § 561.308.

the operation of information and communications technology to facilitate computer or network disruption, monitoring or tracking that could assist in or enable serious human rights abuses by or for the government of Iran or Syria; directly or indirectly selling, leasing or otherwise providing any good, service or technology to either government if it could be used for those purposes; materially assisting or supporting such governmental activities; or being owned or controlled by or acting for any person designated for engaging in such activities. The authority to make these designations has been delegated to the Secretary of the Treasury, in consultation with the Secretary of State.

Executive Order 13,608. In Executive Order 13,608 of May 1, 2012, the President authorized the Secretary of the Treasury, in consultation with the Secretary of State, to impose economic sanctions on "foreign sanctions evaders" if they have been found to have violated, to have attempted or conspired to violate, or to have caused a violation of U.S. economic sanctions against Iran or Syria. The order authorizes the Secretary of the Treasury to prohibit all direct or indirect transactions or dealings involving identified sanctions evaders. While such identification under this executive order will not result in the blocking of any assets of such parties, the Treasury Department explained that "[u]pon Treasury's identification and listing of a foreign sanctions evader, U.S. persons will generally be prohibited from providing to, or procuring from, the sanctioned party goods, services, or technology, effectively cutting the evader off from the U.S. marketplace."[28]

Executive Order 13,622. Executive Order 13,622 of July 30, 2012 authorized additional sanctions regarding Iran's energy and petrochemical sectors. It specifically authorized the Secretary of the Treasury, in consultation with the Secretary of State, to impose sanctions on foreign financial institutions found to have knowingly conducted or facilitated any significant financial transaction with NIOC or NICO, and to impose sanctions on foreign financial institutions found to have knowingly conducted or facilitated (or any persons who engage in) significant transactions for the purchase or acquisition of petroleum, petroleum products or petrochemical products from Iran, with certain exceptions. The NDAA exception discussed above, when in effect with respect to a particular country, applies with respect to the purchase of petroleum or petroleum products from Iran.

The TRA. The TRA strengthens existing economic sanctions on Iran, especially those aimed at third-country nationals engaging in business with Iran. It also includes measures relating to human rights abuses in Iran and Syria. The TRA further expanded the list of Iran-related activities that expose a person to economic sanctions.[29]

---

28. See http://www.treasury.gov/resource-center/faqs/Sanctions/Pages/answer.aspx#216 (July 31, 2012).
29. In addition to provisions discussed here, the TRA requires issuers to include in their annual and quarterly reports to the U.S. Securities and Exchange Commission disclosure with respect to certain Iran-related transactions, and transactions involving persons designated by the U.S. for terrorism or weapons of mass destruction reasons, conducted by the issuer and/or its affiliates.

Accordingly, the ISA, as amended by CISADA and the TRA, authorizes the President to impose foreign exchange, banking, trade, investment, travel and asset blocking sanctions against non-U.S. firms and their principal executive officers if those firms knowingly make certain investments in the development of Iranian petroleum resources; export certain levels of refined petroleum products to Iran; provide goods, services, technology or support for the development of Iranian petroleum refining capabilities, the importation of refined petroleum products into Iran, or the domestic production of refined petroleum products or petrochemical products in Iran; participate in certain petroleum-related joint ventures outside of Iran; transport crude oil from Iran; or conceal the Iranian origin of crude oil and refined petroleum products transported on vessels. The ISA also targets transactions related to Iran's acquisition or development of weapons of mass destruction (WMD) or other military capabilities, and participation in joint ventures with the government of Iran relating to uranium.

The U.S. Department of State has overseen the implementation of the ISA since its inception. Under delegated authority from the President, the State Department determines which sanctions to impose on persons who engage in activities targeted by the ISA,[30] whereas OFAC is delegated responsibility for the blocking of designated persons' assets and for enforcing ISA sanctions that restrict private U.S. loans, U.S. banking services, investments by U.S. persons in targeted entities, and U.S. foreign exchange transactions.

The unilateral, secondary boycott provisions of ISA and CISADA, as expanded by the TRA, have the potential to affect many non-U.S. entities engaged in business with Iran that may be lawful under U.N. Security Council sanctions and their respective national laws.

The TRA also provides for the blocking of property within U.S. jurisdiction, and suspending the entry into the United States, of persons who knowingly provide to Iran, the government of Iran, or for use in Iran, goods or technologies likely to be used by the government of Iran to commit serious human rights abuses or to provide services related to such goods or technology after they are transferred to Iran. Executive Order 13,628 of October 9, 2012,[31] implements many of the additional blocking requirements of the TRA, and delegates to the Secretary of State or the Secretary of the Treasury, as appropriate, the administration of the new sanctions that the TRA added to the ISA. Executive Order 13,628 also imposes the TRA requirement that non-U.S. entities owned or controlled by U.S. persons comply with U.S. Iran sanctions, and provides for enforcement against the U.S. persons that own or control such non-U.S. entities in the event those entities fail to comply.

---

30.   State Department guidance on the ISA and other Iran economic sanctions is available online at http://www.state.gov/e/eb/tfs/spi/iran/index.htm.
31.   77 Fed. Reg. 62,139–62,145 (Oct. 12, 2012).

On February 6, 2013, section 504 of the TRA became effective, amending provisions of section 1245 of the NDAA targeting the Central Bank of Iran, designated Iranian financial institutions and Iran's energy sector. Section 504, among other things, tightened the conditions for eligibility under a provision that excepts from certain secondary economic sanctions transactions related to Iran by financial institutions in a country that has "significantly reduced" its purchases of Iranian crude oil. As of February 6, 2013, the exception applies only to financial transactions that facilitate bilateral trade between the country granted the exception and Iran. Further, for the exception to apply to a specific financial transaction, funds owed to Iran as a result of such bilateral trade must be credited to an account located in the country granted the exception and may not be repatriated to Iran. Provisions implementing section 504 of the TRA were included in the IFSR amendments published on March 15, 2013, referenced below.

The IFCA. On January 2, 2013, the President signed the IFCA into law. This act imposes prospective economic sanctions with respect to (i) the energy, shipping and shipbuilding sectors of Iran; (ii) the sale, supply or transfer to or from Iran of certain precious and other metals and materials; (iii) the provision of underwriting services, insurance or reinsurance with respect to certain activities relating to Iran; (iv) non-U.S. financial institutions that facilitate significant transactions involving (i) or (ii) or Iranian persons identified on the SDN list (except for Iranian financial institutions not designated for WMD proliferation, terrorism or human rights abuses); (v) transactions with respect to the Islamic Republic of Iran Broadcasting and its President; and (vi) the diversion of goods intended for the Iranian people. The IFCA further expands the scope of secondary boycotts requiring third country persons to terminate their dealings with Iran in order to maintain economic ties with the United States. The new economic sanctions are effective July 1, 2013, unless individually waived by the President for maximum successive periods of 180 days.

The IFSR. In August 2010, OFAC promulgated the IFSR to implement the CISADA requirement that the Secretary of the Treasury restrict or prohibit the opening or maintenance of U.S. correspondent or payable-through accounts for a "foreign financial institution"[32] found to engage in activities that facilitate Iranian efforts to acquire or develop WMD, their delivery systems or to support terrorist organizations. On October 11, 2011, the U.S. Treasury Department's Financial Crimes Enforcement Network (FinCEN) issued a final rule under CISADA that requires U.S. banks to conduct due diligence and, upon request, report certain information to FinCEN about any non-U.S. bank for which they maintain a correspondent account regarding that non-U.S. bank's contacts with certain entities linked to Iran.[33] The IFSR prohibit

---

32. Defined at 31 C.F.R. § 561.308.
33. *Adding* Provisions Relating to the Comprehensive Iran Sanctions, Accountability, and Divestment Act of 2010, 31 C.F.R. pt. 1060, 76 Fed. Reg. 62,607–62,630 (Oct. 11, 2011).

non-U.S. entities owned or controlled by U.S. financial institutions from engaging in transactions for or benefiting Iran's Revolutionary Guard Corps (IRGC) or its affiliates or agents blocked pursuant to IEEPA. They further restrict or deny access to U.S. correspondent and payable-through accounts for foreign financial institutions found generally to have engaged in or facilitated a "significant" transaction with any listed Iranian or non-Iranian person, including but not limited to the IRGC, the Central Bank of Iran or a designated Iranian financial institution, entities designated under U.N. Security Council economic sanctions on Iran, the NIOC and NICO. The transactions targeted generally are those related to Iran's WMD program, support for terrorism or for the purchase or acquisition of petroleum, petroleum products or petrochemicals from Iran. On February 27, 2012, November 8, 2012, and March 15, 2013, OFAC amended the IFSR to implement section 1245(d) of the NDAA, Executive Orders 13,622 and 13,628, and certain sections of the TRA that amended the financial institutions provisions of CISADA.

U.S. State Sanctions. CISADA specifically authorizes U.S. state governments, local governments and public universities to enact certain legislation or investment policies that target companies that make investments, or provide financing, above certain threshold levels in support of Iran's energy sector. CISADA further purports to shield such measures from federal preemption, despite the vague distinction between congressional commerce powers and presidential foreign affairs powers under the Constitution with regard to economic sanctions programs. A number of state and local laws and university endowment investment policies now prohibit investment in, or the procurement of goods or services by state governments from, companies that engage in certain activities related to Iran.

NORTH KOREA

On June 26, 2008, the United States terminated its existing economic sanctions program against North Korea, which had been implemented under TWEA in 1950. However, on that same day, Executive Order 13,466 implemented a new economic sanctions program under IEEPA. Whereas the previous economic sanctions regime for North Korea was most comparable to the current Cuban economic sanctions program, the reinstituted economic sanctions against North Korea impose a narrower scope of prohibitions. Initially implemented solely under a series of IEEPA-based and UNPA-based executive orders, OFAC more formally implemented this new regime through the North Korea Sanctions Regulations (NKSR).[34] OFAC initially issued these regulations in November 2010 and amended them in June 2011. However, under the new program, the property of the North Korean government and nationals within U.S. jurisdiction or within the possession or control of a U.S. person remains blocked

---

34.   31 C.F.R. pt. 510.

if it had been blocked under the TWEA-based economic sanctions as of June 16, 2000, and remained blocked immediately prior to June 26, 2008.

The current economic sanctions against North Korea prohibit U.S. persons from owning, leasing, operating, or insuring any vessel flagged by North Korea; registering vessels in North Korea; or otherwise obtaining authorization for a vessel to fly the flag of North Korea. U.S. persons also may not directly or indirectly import goods, services, or technology from North Korea into the United States. In addition to implementing U.N. Security Council Resolutions 1718 and 1874, the NKSR block the property of designated persons involved in activities related to North Korean arms sales, luxury goods procurement, money laundering, the counterfeiting of currency, and other illicit financial activities.[35]

As discussed in other chapters, the U.S. Departments of Commerce and State separately maintain very tight restrictions prohibiting the export, reexport, and transfer of nearly all products, software, and technology, except for certain foods and medicine.

SUDAN

In a manner similar to the Iranian Transactions and Sanctions Regulations (ITSR), the Sudanese Sanctions Regulations (SSR)[36] are country-based economic sanctions that prohibit most trade in goods, technology, and services with Sudan. They also block the property and interests in property of the government of Sudan and its agencies, instrumentalities, and controlled entities (whether or not designated on the SDN List). The IEEPA Berman Amendment's exemptions for trade in permitted information and informational materials and transactions related to travel, and IEEPA's exemption for in-kind donations to relieve human suffering apply to this program. OFAC issues specific licenses under TSRA for exports to Sudan of agricultural goods, medical devices, medicines, and incidental transactions. OFAC also issued a TSRA-based general license authorizing exports and reexports of food to Sudan and incidental transactions on October 13, 2011.[37]

On April 12, 2011, OFAC published guidance regarding the July 9, 2011 independence of the Republic of South Sudan. Pursuant to that guidance, the U.S. economic sanctions on Sudan and the government of Sudan do not apply to South Sudan and its government. However, some sectors of the economy and infrastructure of South Sudan and those of Sudan are highly interdependent. Therefore, as a general matter, activities by U.S. persons relating to South Sudan remain subject to OFAC's jurisdiction if they also involve interdependent interests of the government of Sudan. However, OFAC issued general licenses, effective December 8, 2011, that authorize

---

35. U.N. Security Council Resolution 2094 of March 7, 2013, mandates new economic sanctions against North Korea. OFAC has implemented the blocking requirements of the resolution through designations to the SDN List.

36. 31 C.F.R. pt. 538.

37. *See* 31 C.F.R. § 538.523(a)(3).

many activities in South Sudan relating to the petroleum and petrochemical industries affecting the government of Sudan as well as South Sudanese imports and exports that transit Sudan.

In addition, the Sudan Accountability and Divestment Act (SADA)[38] authorizes U.S. state and local governments to adopt divestment laws targeting Sudan that seek to prohibit investment by state and local governments and their instrumentalities in companies engaging in certain activities related to Sudan. A number of U.S. state and local governments have adopted such legislation.

SYRIA

As discussed in other chapters, the U.S. Departments of Commerce and State administer certain U.S. export and reexport controls against Syria that were adopted in 2004. These export and reexport controls generally prohibit all U.S. exports and reexports of goods to Syria, except for food and medicine. OFAC administers a list-based blocking program in conjunction with these 2004 export and reexport controls. Additionally, U.S. economic sanctions adopted in Executive Order 13,582 of August 17, 2011, generally prohibit:

- the engagement in or facilitation by U.S. persons of new investment in Syria;
- the U.S. exportation or reexportation of any services to Syria; and
- the importation of Syrian petroleum or petroleum products into the United States.
- They also target transactions related to Syrian-origin petroleum by non-U.S. persons.
- In addition, these economic sanctions block the property of the government of Syria, its agencies, its instrumentalities, its controlled entities, and any other persons—as designated by the Secretary of the Treasury, in consultation with the Secretary of State—who or that have provided material support for, or who or that are owned or controlled by, other persons whose property is blocked under this program.

As of March 15, 2013, OFAC had not issued implementing regulations for Executive Order 13,582. However, a number of general licenses under the executive order have been issued and are posted on OFAC's website. On March 14, 2013, OFAC issued General License 16, authorizing U.S. persons to provide certain service, including funds transfers, to the National Coalition of Syrian Revolutionary and Opposition Forces. As previously discussed regarding Iran, Executive Orders 13,606 and 13,608 (issued in April and May 2012, respectively) also target and apply to Syria.

---

38.   Pub. L. No. 110-174 (2007).

Appendix B to Chapter 1

Important Court Decisions Affecting U.S. Economic Sanctions

Susan Klavens Hutner

FEDERAL PREEMPTION

Crosby v. National Foreign Trade Council, 530 U.S. 363 (2000). The Court found that a Massachusetts law restricting state agencies from buying goods or services from designated persons doing business with Burma (Myanmar) was preempted under the supremacy clause of the U.S. Constitution by federal legislation imposing economic sanctions on Burma (Myanmar), implemented in part by executive order. (*Note:* CIS-ADA and the Sudan Accountability and Divestment Act of 2007 purport to remove federal preemption and to permit state and local governments to adopt legislation, and university endowments to adopt policies, prohibiting those governments and endowments from investing in companies or corporate groups that engage in certain activities in Iran and Sudan.)

EXECUTIVE AUTHORITY

United States v. Curtiss-Wright Export Corp., 299 U.S. 304 (1936). The Court held that the delegation by Congress to the President of the authority to prohibit arms sales to foreign countries was not an invalid delegation of legislative power to the executive branch. The authority to conduct foreign affairs vests in the federal government independently of the authority granted in the Constitution and constitutes "the very delicate, plenary and exclusive power of the President as the sole organ of the federal government in the field of international relations—a power which does not require as a basis for its exercise an act of Congress" 299 U.S. at 320.

Regan v. Wald, 468 U.S. 222 (1984). The President's grandfathered authority under section 5(b) of TWEA provides the basis for executive action restricting transactions related to travel to Cuba. The Court also concluded, in part because "[m]atters relating 'to the conduct of foreign relations . . . are so exclusively entrusted to the political branches of government,'" that the travel restrictions do not violate the freedom to travel protected by the due process clause of the Fifth Amendment.

LEGALITY OF TWEA AND IEEPA

Dames & Moore v. Regan, 453 U.S. 654 (1981). The Court upheld the President's broad exercise of authority under IEEPA, including the authority to impose and modify blocking actions and the authority to nullify judicial attachments and judgments involving blocked property in connection with the implementation of an agreement between the governments of Iran and the United States.

Sardino v. Federal Reserve Bank of New York, 361 F.2d 106 (2d Cir. 1965). The President's exercise of authority under TWEA to declare a national emergency and to delegate authority to the Secretary of the Treasury to issue regulations blocking the assets of Cuban nationals does not violate the Constitution.

Blocked Property and Property Interests – Cases Illustrating a Narrow Interpretation of "Property Interest"

Centrifugal Casting Machine Co. v. American Bank & Trust Co., 966 F.2d 1348 (10th Cir. 1992). The Court rejected OFAC's interpretation of property interest because it was inconsistent with the law governing the letters of credit at issue.

Consarc Corp. v. Iraqi Ministry, 27 F.3d 695 (D.C. Cir. 1994). The Court followed the reasoning of *Centrifugal* in affirming OFAC's interpretation of "property" and "property interest" where "OFAC's determination was fully in accord with the general law governing letters of credit and thus survive[d]" judicial review. 27 F.3d at 702.

Consarc Corp. v. U.S. Department of the Treasury, Office of Foreign Assets Control, 71 F.3d 909 (D.C. Cir. 1995). This case illustrates the broad authority granted to OFAC to interpret its regulations and notes "the general interpretive principle that exceptions to a broad regulatory scheme are to be read narrowly." 71 F.3d at 915.

Blocked Property and Property Interests – Cases Illustrating a Broad Interpretation of "Property Interest"

Milena Ship Management v. Newcomb, 995 F.2d 620 (5th Cir. 1993). OFAC acted reasonably in finding a blocked property interest of the government of Yugoslavia in vessels based on its interpretation of Yugoslav law and resulting presumption of state ownership of the vessels. *See also Behring Int'l, Inc. v. Miller*, 504 F. Supp. 552 (D. N.J. 1980); *United States v. Broverman*, 180 F. Supp. 631 (S.D.N.Y. 1959).

Terrorism / Material Support

Holder v. Humanitarian Law Project, 561 U.S., 130 S. Ct. 2705 (2010). It is not a violation of the First Amendment to the Constitution for the federal government to prohibit nonviolent "material support" (including legal services, advice, and advocacy) to a foreign terrorist organization—even if that support is limited to humanitarian activities—provided that the material support is coordinated with, directed by, or controlled by the foreign terrorist organization.

Blocking versus Takings under the Fifth Amendment

Nielsen v. Secretary of the Treasury, 424 F.2d 833 (D.C. Cir. 1970). The blocking of Cuban assets pursuant to TWEA is not subject to the "takings clause" of the Fifth Amendment to the Constitution, although the Court states that the question of whether blocking constitutes a taking subject to due process becomes more difficult if the blocking continues indefinitely.

Tran Qui Than v. Regan, 658 F.2d 1296 (9th Cir. 1981). Neither blocking of the assets of a Vietnamese bank under TWEA nor prohibiting a Vietnamese shareholder of the bank from obtaining the bank's blocked assets constitute a taking without just compensation in violation of the Fifth Amendment to the Constitution.

Chas. T. Main International, Inc., v. Khuzestan Water & Power Authority, 651 F.2d 800 (1st Cir. 1981). Neither the nullification of judicial attachments nor the transfer of Iranian blocked property pursuant to IEEPA constitutes a taking without just compensation in violation of the Fifth Amendment to the Constitution.

Appendix A to Chapter 5
Commerce Department Antiboycott Compliance Summary

PROHIBITIONS

The prohibitions outlined below apply to all U.S. persons and companies and controlled-in-fact subsidiaries of U.S. companies. A controlled-in-fact subsidiary includes a foreign company more than 50 percent owned by a U.S. company or that is otherwise "managed" or controlled by the U.S. company. Accordingly, all foreign affiliates "controlled" by a U.S. company should be treated as a "U.S. person."

Refusals to do Business

- No United States person (including foreign affiliates) may refuse, knowingly agree to refuse, require any other person to refuse, or knowingly agree to require any other person to refuse to do business with or in a boycotted country, with any business organized under the laws of a boycotted country, or with any national or resident of a boycotted country when such refusal is pursuant to an agreement with the boycotting country, a requirement of the boycotting country, or a request from the boycotting country.
- This includes not only specific express refusals, but also refusals implied by a pattern of conduct.
- Use of either a boycott-based "blacklist" or "whitelist" constitutes a refusal to do business.
- An agreement to comply generally with the laws of the boycotting country with which it is doing business or an agreement that local laws of the boycotting country shall apply is not, in and of itself, a refusal to do business.
- An agreement is not a prerequisite to a violation because the prohibitions extend to actions taken pursuant not only to agreements but also to requirements of and requests on behalf of a boycotting country.

Discriminatory Actions

No U.S. person (including foreign affiliates) may:

1. refuse to employ or otherwise discriminate against any other U.S. person on the basis of race, religion, sex, or national origin.

2. discriminate against any corporation or organization that is a U.S. person on the basis of race, religion, sex, or national origin of any owner, director, or employee.

3. knowingly agree to take any of the actions described in 1 or 2 above or require another to take such action.

   The prohibition applies whether the action is taken by a U.S. person on its own or in response to a request from or requirement of a boycotting country.

Furnishing Information about Race, Religion, Sex, or National Origin

1. No U.S. person (including foreign affiliates) may furnish or agree to furnish information about the race, religion, sex, or national origin of any U.S. person or any owner, director, or employee of any corporation or organization that is a U.S. person.

2. The prohibition shall apply whether the information is specifically requested or is offered voluntarily and whether it is stated in the affirmative or negative.

3. Information in the form of code words or symbols that could identify a U.S. person's race, religion, sex, or national origin comes within the prohibition.

Furnishing Information about Business Relationships

1. No U.S. person may furnish or knowingly agree to furnish information concerning past, present, or proposed business relationships:
   a. with or in a boycotted country;
   b. with any business concern organized under the laws of a boycotted country;
   c. with any national or resident of a boycotted country; or
   d. with any other person believed to be restricted from having any business relationship with or in a boycotted country.

2. The prohibition applies whether the information pertains to a sale, purchase, or supply transaction, a legal or commercial representation, shipping or other transportation transaction, insurance, investment, or any other type of business transaction/relationship.

   It also applies whether the information is directly or indirectly requested or is furnished on the initiative of the U.S. person.

3. It does not apply to the furnishing of normal business information in a commercial context such as would normally be found in documents available to the public (annual reports, catalogs, etc.).

4. If the information is of a type that is generally sought for a legitimate business purpose, it may be furnished even if the information could be used or, without the knowledge of the person supplying it, is intended to be used for boycott purposes.

   However, no information may be furnished in response to a boycott request, even if the information is otherwise publicly available.

Information Concerning Association with Charitable and Fraternal Organizations

No U.S. person (including foreign affiliates) may furnish or knowingly agree to furnish information whether any person is a member of, has contributed to, or is otherwise associated with any charitable or fraternal organization that supports a boycotted country.

Letters of Credit

1. No U.S. person (including foreign affiliates) may implement a letter of credit that contains a condition or requirement regarding compliance with boycott laws or terms that are prohibited, nor shall any U.S. person be obligated to pay such a letter of credit.
2. "Implementing" a letter of credit includes:
   a. issuing or opening a letter of credit at the request of a customer;
   b. honoring it by accepting it as being a valid instrument of credit;
   c. paying, under a letter of credit, a draft or other demand for payment by the beneficiary;
   d. confirming it; or
   e. negotiating it by voluntarily purchasing a draft from a beneficiary and presenting such draft for reimbursement to the issuer.
3. The prohibition applies only when the transaction to which the letter of credit applies is in U.S. commerce and the beneficiary is a U.S. person.
4. A letter of credit implemented in the United States by a U.S. person located in the United States will be presumed to apply to a transaction in U.S. commerce and to be in favor of a U.S. beneficiary where it specifies a U.S. address for the beneficiary.
5. Letters of credit implemented outside the United States will be presumed to apply to a transaction in U.S. commerce and to be in favor of a U.S. beneficiary where the letter of credit:
   a. specifies a U.S. address for the beneficiary and
   b. calls for documents indicating shipment from the United States or otherwise indicating that the goods are of U.S. origin.

Exceptions to the Prohibitions

Import Requirements of a Boycotting Country

In supplying goods or services to a boycotting country, a U.S. person may comply or agree to comply with requirements of the boycotting country that prohibit the import of:

1. goods or services from the boycotted country or
2. goods produced or services provided by any business concern organized under the laws of the boycotted country or by any of its nationals or residents.

Shipment of Goods to a Boycotting Country

1. In shipping goods to a boycotting country, a U.S. person may comply with the requirements of that country that prohibit the shipment of goods:
   a. on a carrier of the boycotted country or
   b. by a route other than that prescribed by the boycotting country.
2. The exception applies whether the purchaser:
   a. explicitly states the shipment should not pass through a port of the boycotted country or
   b. affirmatively describes a route of shipment that does not include a port in the boycotted country.

Import and Shipping Document Requirements of a Boycotting Country

1. In shipping goods to a boycotting country, a U.S. person may comply with that country's shipping document requirements with respect to:
   a. country of origin of goods;
   b. name of carrier;
   c. route of shipment;
   d. name of the supplier of the shipment; or
   e. name of the provider of other services.
2. All such information must be stated in positive terms except for information with respect to the names of carriers or routes of shipment (e.g., the goods are 100 percent U.S. origin).

Compliance with Unilateral and Specific Selection

1. A U.S. person may comply in the normal course of business with the unilateral and specific selection by a boycotting country (national or resident) of carriers, insurers, suppliers of services to be performed in a boycotting country, or specific goods provided that:
   a. with respect to services, it is necessary and customary that a not insignificant part of the services be performed within the boycotting country, and
   b. with respect to goods, the items are identifiable as to their source or origin at the time they enter the boycotting country by
      (1) uniqueness of design or appearance or
      (2) trademark or other identification normally on the items themselves, including their packaging.
2. The exception pertains to what is permissible for a U.S. person who is the recipient of a unilateral and specific selection of goods or services to be furnished by a third person.
   a. It does not pertain to whether the act of making such a selection is permitted.

b. It does not pertain to the U.S. person who is to supply his or her own goods or services. A U.S. person may fill an order him- or herself even if he or she is selected by the buyer on a boycott basis.

3. A "specific" selection is one that is stated in the affirmative and that specifies a particular supplier of goods or services.

4. A "unilateral" selection is one in which the discretion in making the selection is exercised by the boycotting country buyer without the assistance of the U.S. person. However, provision of preselection/preaward services such as providing lists of qualified suppliers, subcontractors, or bidders does not alone destroy the unilateral character of a selection, provided such services are not boycott based. Furthermore, provision of such services must be customary practice in nonboycotting countries.

5. A U.S. person may be considered a bona fide resident of a boycotting country depending on the following factors:
   a. physical presence in the country;
   b. whether residence is needed for legitimate business reasons;
   c. continuity and intent to maintain residency;
   d. whether the person is registered to do business or is incorporated in the country or whether he or she has a valid work visa.

6. If a U.S. person receives from another person located in the United States what may be a unilateral selection by a customer in a boycotting country, and has reason to know that the selection is made for boycott reasons, he or she has a duty to inquire of the transmitting person to determine who actually made the selection.

7. No U.S. person may comply with any unilateral selection if he or she has reason to know that the purpose of the selection is to effect discrimination against any U.S. person on the basis of race, religion, sex, or national origin.

Compliance with a Boycotting Country's Requirements Regarding Shipment of Exports

1. A U.S. person may comply with the export requirements of a boycotting country with respect to shipments or transshipments of exports to:
   a. a boycotted country;
   b. any business concern organized under the laws of a boycotted country; or
   c. any national or resident of a boycotted country.

2. This exception applies to restrictions a boycotting country may place on direct exports to a boycotted country, on indirect exports, or on exports to residents, nationals, or business concerns of a boycotted country, including those located in third countries.

3. Exception also applies to any restriction on the route of export shipments when reasonably related to preventing them from coming into contact with or under the jurisdiction of the boycotted country.

Compliance with Employment Requirements of a Boycotting Country

1. A U.S. person may comply with immigration, passport, visa, or employment requirements of a boycotting country and with requests for information to ascertain whether such individual meets requirements for employment *provided* he or she furnish information only about him- or herself and not about any other U.S. person.

2. A U.S. person may not furnish information about its employees or executives but may allow any individual to respond on his or her own.

3. A U.S. person may proceed with a project in a boycotting country even if other employees or prospective participants are denied entry for boycott reasons; however, no employees/participants may be selected in advance in a manner designed to comply with a boycott.

Compliance with Local Law

1. A U.S. person who is a bona fide resident of a foreign country may comply with local law with respect to his or her activities exclusively within the foreign country as well as with local import laws.

2. Local laws may derive from statutes, regulations, directives, or other official sources having the effect of law in the host country; exception is not available for presumed policies or understandings unless reflected in official sources.

3. Activities exclusively within the host country include:
   a. entering into contracts that provide that local law governs;
   b. employing residents of the host country;
   c. retaining local contractors to perform work within the host country; and
   d. furnishing information within the host country.

4. A U.S. person may comply with local import laws provided that:
   a. the items are for his or her own use or for use in performing contractual services within that country, and
   b. in the normal course of business, the items are identifiable as to their source or origin at the time of entry into the foreign country by uniqueness of design/appearance or by trademark/trade name.

5. The bona fide residence of a U.S. company's employee in a foreign country does not confer such residence on the entire company. However, a bona fide resident may take action through an agent outside the country so long as the agent acts at the direction of the resident and not of his or her own discretion.

6. Goods are for the U.S. person's own use if:
   a. they are to be consumed by him or her;
   b. they are to remain in his or her possession to be used by him or her;

c. they are to be used by him or her in performing contractual services for another; or

d. they are to be further manufactured or incorporated into another product for the use of another.

7. However, goods acquired to fill the order of another are not for the U.S. person's own use. Nor does the exception apply to the import of services.

Reporting Requirements

Scope

1. A U.S. person (including a foreign affiliate) who receives a request to take any action that effectively furthers or supports a restrictive trade practice or boycott imposed by a foreign country against a country friendly to the United States or against any U.S. person must report the request to the DOC, to the Office of Antiboycott Compliance, and to the IRS. The request may be either written or oral and may include a request to furnish information or enter into or implement an agreement.

2. A request received by a U.S. person is reportable if the U.S. person knows or has reason to know that the request is to enforce, implement, or otherwise further an unsanctioned foreign boycott.

   a. A request such as a boycott questionnaire unrelated to a particular transaction is reportable when the U.S. person has or anticipates a business relationship with or in a boycotting country involving the sale, purchase, or transfer of goods or services in interstate or foreign commerce of the United States.

   b. However, an unsolicited invitation to bid containing a boycott request is not a reportable request where the U.S. person does not respond to the invitation or other proposal.

3. The following specific requests are *not* reportable:

   a. To refrain from shipping goods on a carrier flying the flag of a particular country or that is owned or chartered by a particular country.

   b. To supply a positive certification as to country of origin of goods.

   c. To supply a positive certification as to name of supplier or manufacturer of goods or provider of services.

   d. To comply with laws of another country except where the request expressly requires compliance with boycott laws.

   e. To supply information about oneself or family member for immigration, visa, or employment purposes.

   f. To supply certification indicating destination of exports.

   g. To supply certificate by the owner that a vessel, aircraft, truck, or other vehicle is eligible to enter a particular port or country pursuant to the laws of that port or country.

   h. To supply a certificate from an insurance company stating that it has a duly authorized agent or representative within a boycotting country.

Manner of Reporting

1. Each reportable request must be reported; however, if more than one document containing the same request is received as part of the same transaction, only the first request need be reported.
2. According to the regulations, each U.S. person receiving a reportable request must report it; however, he or she may designate another to report on his or her behalf.

Examples of Prohibited and Reportable Requests or Requirements

In connection with the sale of goods or services covered by the antiboycott regulations, U.S. persons and their controlled-in-fact foreign affiliates may not:

- give or agree to give any information about the company's business relationships with a boycotted country or with blacklisted persons (e.g., "we have no business relations with Israel" or "the company does not maintain an office or a branch in Israel");
- state that the company is not the mother company, sister company, subsidiary, or branch of a blacklisted company;
- certify that "the company is not a company boycotted by the Ministry of Customs and Imports, Israel Boycott Office, or State of (boycotting country) and that it is not in any way affiliated to such company";
- refuse to do business with a boycotted country or with a blacklisted person because of his or its relationship with the boycotted country, if done by agreement, requirement, or request from a boycotting country—e.g., "the vessel (or insurance carrier) is not blacklisted";
- agree to do business only with a person who is approved or "whitelisted" by a boycotting country;
- give information as to the blacklist status of another person;
- state the origin of goods in negative terms—e.g., "the goods covered by this invoice are not of Israeli origin, they contain no Israeli components, materials, or capital";
- agree to comply with a provision of another country's law that expressly requires compliance with that country's boycott laws;
- respond to a boycott questionnaire from a central boycott office with regard to a specific transaction or if you do business with a boycotting country or anticipate doing business with that country;
- submit the company's annual report if it is submitted in response to a boycott-related request;
- certify that goods will not be shipped on a vessel that is ineligible to enter boycotting country's waters;

- certify that "the company is permitted to trade with Arab countries"; or
- certify that "the goods nor the packing bear a sixpointed star emblem."

The above list of examples is not exhaustive; it is prudent to report any potential boycott-related requests to qualified export compliance personnel or legal counsel for review.

Examples of Permitted and Nonreportable Requests or Requirements

The following specific requests are not reportable. However, any requests not falling squarely within one of these areas should be submitted to export compliance personnel or legal counsel for review.

The company and its affiliates may:

- refrain from shipping goods on a carrier flying the flag of a boycotted country or that is registered or owned by a boycotted country;
- supply positive certification as to country of origin of goods;
- supply positive certification as to the name of the supplier or manufacturer of goods or provider of services;
- comply with the laws of another country except where the request expressly requires compliance with boycott laws;
- supply information about oneself or a family member for immigration, visa, or employment purposes;
- supply certification indicating destination of exports;
- supply a certificate by the owner that a vessel is eligible to enter a particular port or country pursuant to the laws of the port or country; and
- supply a certificate from an insurance company stating that it has a duly authorized agent or representative within a boycotting country.

However, all the above requests must be stated in the positive, for example:

Reportable: (prohibited)	Request for certification that the exported goods are not of (boycotted country) manufacture.
Not Reportable: (not prohibited)	Request for certification that the exported goods are of U.S. manufacture.

Additionally, an "unsolicited" invitation to bid containing a boycott request is not reportable if the U.S. person does not respond to it. "Unsolicited" is a defined term in part 760 of the EAR, and this exception is more narrowly construed than common usage of the term might suggest.

Application to Foreign Affiliates of U.S. Companies

The antiboycott rules apply to all "U.S. persons" who engage in "activities in U.S. Commerce." A U.S. person includes individuals, U.S. corporations, and "controlled-in-fact"[39] foreign branch offices, subsidiaries, and affiliates. Thus, application of the boycott regulations depends on whether the transaction constitutes an activity in U.S. Commerce.

Activities in U.S. Commerce

The law applies only to the interstate or foreign commerce of the United States. This has been defined very broadly and can include activities of controlled-in-fact branch offices, affiliates, or subsidiaries, no matter where located, of U.S. companies that deal with third parties located outside the United States.

Activities of the company's foreign affiliates that are U.S. persons are deemed to be "activities in U.S. Commerce" if a transaction is between such subsidiary and a person or entity outside the United States involving goods (or services) acquired by the U.S. person subsidiary from a person or entity in the United States, under any of the following circumstances:

1. if the goods (or services) were acquired for the purpose of filling an order from a person outside the United States;
2. if the goods (or services) were acquired for incorporation into, refining into, reprocessing into, or manufacture of another product for the purpose of filling an order from a person outside the United States; or
3. if the goods were acquired and ultimately used, without substantial alteration or modification, in filling an order from a person outside the United States (whether or not the goods were originally acquired for that purpose).

Goods and services are considered to be acquired for the purpose of filling an order with a person outside the United States when:

1. goods are purchased from a U.S. source by the foreign subsidiary upon receipt of an order from the customer outside the United States, with the intention that those goods go to the customer;
2. goods are purchased by the foreign subsidiary from a U.S. source in order to meet the needs of specified customers outside the United States pursuant to understandings—even though not for immediate delivery; or
3. goods are purchased from a U.S. source by the foreign subsidiary based on anticipated needs of specified customers.

---

39. The definition of a controlled-in-fact subsidiary or affiliate is slightly different under DOC and IRS regulations. Under DOC regulations, U.S. companies include, but are not limited to, foreign affiliates where the U.S. company owns 50% or more of the foreign affiliate's voting stock. Under IRS regulations, the ownership interest threshold is only 10%.

Activities Outside U.S. Commerce

1. A transaction between a company's foreign affiliate and a person outside the United States, not involving the purchase or sale of goods or services to or from a person in the United States, is not an activity in the U.S. Commerce.

2. It should be noted that even if goods are acquired by the affiliate from the United States, such goods will not be considered "activities in U.S. Commerce" *if* the following two conditions are met:

    a. such goods were acquired by the subsidiary without reference to a specific order from or transaction with a person outside the United States and

    b. such goods were further substantially manufactured, incorporated into, refined into, or reprocessed into another product.

Final determination of whether the goods involved in a particular transaction are connected with "activities in U.S. Commerce" should be made only after consultation with legal counsel and review of the regulations.

Appendix B to Chapter 5
Treasury Department Antiboycott Summary

Section 999 of the Internal Revenue Code requires U.S. taxpayers to report their operations in boycotting countries and penalizes taxpayers who *agree* to "participate in or cooperate with" an unsanctioned foreign boycott by denying them certain tax benefits. Reports are filed in conjunction with the filing of the taxpayer's annual return.

I. REPORTING REQUIREMENTS

  A. Must report operations in or with boycotting countries included on the list published by Treasury.
  1. "Operations" include any type of business transaction, regardless of whether it generates revenue.
  2. Treasury has identified the following as "boycotting" countries for purposes of section 999: Iraq, Kuwait, Lebanon, Libya, Qatar, Saudi Arabia, Syria, Yemen, and the United Arab Emirates.
  3. In addition to these countries, boycott requests in connection with business in other countries may be reportable as well.
  B. Must report any request to enter into any impermissible boycott-related agreement, as defined below in section II.
  C. Must report receipt of requests to participate in or cooperate with the boycott, even if agreement not reached.

II. IMPERMISSIBLE AGREEMENTS

The following are impermissible agreements to "participate in or cooperate with" a boycott:
  A. agreements to refuse to do business in Israel, or with Israel, Israeli companies, or Israelis;
  B. agreements to refuse to do business with U.S. persons who do business in Israel, or with Israel, Israeli companies, or Israelis;
  C. agreements to refuse to do business with companies owned or managed by individuals of a particular race, religion, or nationality;
  D. agreements to select or retain corporate directors of a particular race, nationality, or religion;

E. agreements to refrain from employing persons of a particular race, religion, or nationality;

F. agreements to refuse to ship or insure products on carriers owned or operated by persons who do not participate in or cooperate with the boycott, but *may* agree that goods will not be shipped on an Israeli vessel; and

G. agreements that local laws, including boycott laws, that "apply" to a transaction are *not* penalized, but agreements to "comply" with local laws (with some exceptions) *are* penalized.

III. EXCEPTIONS

The following types of agreements are permissible under section 999:

A. agreements to comply with prohibitions on the importation of Israeli goods into a boycotting country and

B. agreements to comply with prohibitions on the export of boycotting country goods to Israel.

IV. PENALTIES

A. For participating in or cooperating with the boycott: denial of certain tax privileges, including denial of foreign tax credits, denial of foreign tax deferral, and denial of the benefits of DISC, FSC, and ETI with respect to boycott-related income.

B. For failure to make required reports: fines up to $25,000 or imprisonment up to one year, or both.

Appendix C to Chapter 5
U.S. Antiboycott Law Issue Spotting Summary

U.S. companies, taxpayers, and their foreign affiliates may be subject to U.S. anti-boycott laws, which prohibit the company from engaging in, or agreeing to engage in, certain activities relating to unsanctioned non-U.S. boycotts, primarily the Arab League boycott of Israel.

You should review transactions for terms that could raise antiboycott compliance issues. While it is permissible to comply with a limited subset of boycott-related contract terms and requests, *all such terms and requests (written or oral) should be reviewed by qualified legal counsel as soon as they are identified and before agreeing to the request.*

— **Common Prohibitions.** Actions prohibited under U.S. antiboycott laws include the following:
  - refusing to do business with Israel, Israeli companies, or Israelis; in Israel; or with "blacklisted" companies;
  - furnishing boycott-related information, including information about one's business relationships with Israel, Israeli companies, Israelis, or "blacklisted" companies;
  - providing negative certificates of origin (e.g., product not from Israel) or vessel eligibility certificates (e.g., vessel not blacklisted);
  - discriminating against any U.S. person on the basis of race, religion, sex, or national origin (furnishing such information also may be prohibited);
  - agreeing, orally or in writing, to do any of the above; and
  - failing to report a reportable boycott-related request within the established legal timetables.

— **Common Boycott Terms.** Terms often used in boycott-related requests include the following:
  - "Jewish," "Hebrew," "Israel," "Israeli," or "goods originating in a country boycotted by" a boycotting country.
  - "Boycott," "boycotted," "blacklist," "black list," "boycott list," or "Israel Boycott Office."
  - Certification that a vessel is "eligible to enter the ports" of a boycotting country.

- Certification that an insurer is "permitted to do business" in a boycotting country.
- Prohibition on the use of "six-pointed stars" on packaging.
- Agreement to "comply with" or "abide by" the laws of a boycotting country, regardless of whether laws concerning the boycott of Israel are expressly mentioned. (In contrast, an acknowledgment that the laws of a boycotting country shall "apply" is permissible.)

— **Key Business Functions.** Those business functions most likely to encounter boycott-related requests in international business transactions include the following:
  - sales & marketing/trading (e.g., tenders, RFQs, offers, contracts, oral requests);
  - contracts administration (e.g., contract documents or general terms and conditions);
  - shipping/logistics/scheduling related to vessels (e.g., shipping documents, charter party agreements, and vessel eligibility certificates);
  - credit/treasury (e.g., letters of credit or other financing documents); and
  - legal (e.g., any of the above, agreements, or other legal documents).

Appendix D to Chapter 5

Countries That May Require Compliance with, Furthering of, or Support of an Unsanctioned Foreign Boycott

The following chart lists a number of countries that support the boycott of Israel or other unsanctioned foreign boycotts and sometimes issue boycott-related requests. For this reason, you should be particularly alert to antiboycott compliance issues when transacting business involving the following countries.

Algeria
Bahrain (removed from 999 list)
Bangladesh
People's Republic of China (boycotts Taiwan)
India (boycotts Pakistan)
Indonesia
Iran
Iraq*
Kuwait*
Lebanon*
Libya*
Malaysia
Mauritania
Nigeria
Oman (removed from 999 list)
Pakistan (boycotts India and Israel)
Qatar*
Saudi Arabia*
Somalia
Sudan
Syria*
United Arab Emirates (including Dubai and Abu Dhabi)*
Yemen, Republic of *

*The U.S. Treasury Department has determined that these countries have official policies supporting an unsanctioned foreign boycott, which takes the form of a secondary or tertiary boycott (i.e., a boycott that prohibits trading with persons and entities that choose to do business with Israel as opposed to prohibitions against direct trading with Israel).

Countries other than those listed above might impose a boycott that the United States does not support, in which case, any requests made or actions sought may be subject to the U.S. antiboycott laws.

Appendix E to Chapter 5
Antiboycott "Savings Clause"

The use of a general antiboycott "savings clause" along the lines set forth below can help prevent companies from inadvertently agreeing to a boycott-related request. The request may nonetheless be reportable.

> *"Notwithstanding any other provision of this Agreement, no Party shall take or be required to take any action inconsistent with or penalized under the laws of the United States or any applicable foreign jurisdiction[, including without limitation the anti-boycott laws administered by the U.S. Commerce and Treasury Departments]."*

Appendix F to Chapter 5
U.S. Antiboycott Law Jurisdictional Summary

Directly covered by U.S. antiboycott laws	Companies incorporated or based in the U.S.	Foreign branches/ offices of U.S. companies	Foreign entities wholly or majority- owned by a U.S. person	Foreign entities minority- owned but effectively controlled by a U.S. person	Foreign entities not owned or controlled by a U.S. person; foreign nationals	U.S. persons (U.S. citizens and permanent residents)	Foreign national employees or agents of covered person or company
Commerce	Yes	Yes	Yes, if transaction is in the "interstate or foreign commerce of the United States"	Yes, if transaction is in the "interstate or foreign commerce of the United States"	No	Yes, with limited exceptions for U.S. persons who are bona fide residents of a boycotting country	Actions can be imputed to the U.S. company
Treasury	Yes	Yes	Yes, if a member of taxpayer's "controlled group"	Yes, if a member of taxpayer's "controlled group"	Yes, if a member of taxpayer's "controlled group"	Yes, if a member of taxpayer's "controlled group"	Actions can be imputed to the U.S. taxpayer

Appendix G to Chapter 5

Comparison of Commerce and Treasury Antiboycott Laws & Regulations/Guidelines

(Note: This table is an illustrative summary and is not a substitute for statutory and regulatory provisions. Specific questions should be referred to the experts at the Departments of Commerce and Treasury.)

1. Authorities	Commerce	Treasury
Statutory provisions	Section 8 of the Export Administration Act of 1979, as amended, 50 U.S.C. app. §§ 2401 – 2420 (2000), International Emergency Economic Powers Act, 50 U.S.C. §§ 1701–1707 (2000)	"Ribicoff Amendment" to the Tax Reform Act of 1976, adding § 999 to the Internal Revenue Code
Regulatory provisions	Part 760 "Restrictive Trade Practices and Boycotts" of the Export Administration Regulations (15 C.F.R. part 760) (2008)	Treasury Guidelines (TG)
2. Principal Features		
To whom applicable?	U.S. persons, including individuals who are U.S. residents and nationals, businesses, and "controlled-in-fact" foreign subsidiaries, with respect to activities in the interstate or foreign commerce of the U.S.	Any U.S. taxpayer or member of a controlled group that includes such taxpayer. Also includes U.S. shareholders of foreign companies. Not limited to activities in U.S. commerce.
Intent required?	Yes, for prohibitions. ("intent to comply with, further, or support an unsanctioned foreign boycott")	No.
Form of implementation?	The Export Administration Regulations contain prohibitions, with certain limited exceptions.	Denial of certain tax benefits for boycott agreements.
Sanctions?	Criminal and civil penalties and/or denial of export privileges.	Denial of tax benefits such as foreign tax credit and foreign subsidiary deferral benefits. If the U.S. taxpayer has no such tax benefits, there is no sanction—but still has to report.

Reporting requests?	Required to report receipt of boycott-related requests on a quarterly basis on BIS form 621-P.	On IRS form 5713, required to report annually operations in, with, or related to boycotting countries and any boycott-related requests and agreements. Plus operations and requests of entire controlled group in, with, or related to boycotting countries.
	Reporting of requests on multiple transaction basis permitted on BIS form 6051-P.	Reporting of operations required on a country-by-country basis. Boycott requests and agreements must also be reported.
	Reports publicly available.	Reports kept confidential as part of tax return.
	Failure to report can lead to imposition of sanctions (even if there is no violation of law's prohibitions).	Failure to report can subject taxpayer to fines and criminal proceedings.
3. Principal Differences in Treatment of Conduct		
a. **"Vessel Eligibility" Certificates**	Permitted if furnished [only] by owner, master, or charterer of the vessel [not an agent]; exporter may request and pass on such a certificate. No restrictions on such certificates for shipments to Saudi Arabia since the Saudi government does not consider the requirement to be boycott-related under its laws. Not reportable.	Can constitute boycott agreement that results in denial of certain tax benefits unless certificate is requested by Saudi Arabia, which has explained that it applies only to maritime matters such as the condition and safety standards of the vessel.
b. **Local Law Clauses in Contractual Documents:**		
• Agreement to comply generally with laws and regulations of a boycotting country –	Permitted	Penalized
• Agreement that laws of a boycotting country shall apply –	Permitted	Not penalized
• Agreement to comply with boycott laws of a boycotting country –	Prohibited	Penalized
• Agreement that boycott laws of a boycotting country shall apply –	Prohibited	Not penalized
c. **Furnishing Information**	Furnishing and/or agreeing to furnish certain boycott-related information prohibited.	Not penalized, as § 999 penalizes agreements to refrain from doing business, not furnishing information. However, an agreement to furnish boycott-related information at a later date will be penalized.

Above table reproduced from: http://www.bis.doc.gov/complianceandenforcement/comparison-antiboycott-laws.pdf. Please note that this table highlights certain key distinctions between the two sets of antiboycott laws but should not be relied on as a substitute for reviewing part 760 of the EAR and the Treasury Department's section 999 guidelines.

INDEX